FLAMMABLE AND COMBUSTIBLE LIQUIDS CODE HANDBOOK

FLAMMABLE AND COMBUSTIBLE LIQUIDS CODE HANDBOOK

Based on the 1987 Edition of NFPA 30, *Flammable and Combustible Liquids Code*, and NFPA 30A, *Automotive and Marine Service Station Code*

ROBERT P. BENEDETTI, Editor
Flammable Liquids Field Service Specialist

Third Edition

National Fire Protection Association
Quincy, Massachusetts

This *Handbook* has not been processed in accordance with NFPA Regulations Governing Committee Projects. Therefore, the commentary in it shall not be considered the official position of NFPA or any of its committees and shall not be considered to be, nor relied upon as, a Formal Interpretation of the meaning or intent of any specific provision or provisions of NFPA 30, *Flammable and Combustible Liquids Code,* or NFPA 30A, *Automotive and Marine Service Station Code.*

Copyright © 1987
National Fire Protection Association
All rights reserved

NFPA No. 30HB-87
ISBN No. 0-87765-333-X
Library of Congress No. 86-61653
Printed in the United States of America

First Printing, November 1987

Dedication

This third edition of the *Flammable and Combustible Liquids Code Handbook* is dedicated to Miles E. Woodworth and Richard E. Stevens.

Miles Woodworth served as NFPA's Flammable Liquids Field Service Specialist for twenty-six years, until his retirement in 1978. Richard Stevens served as Vice President and Chief Engineer until his retirement in 1984.

During the years that I worked with these two gentlemen, I had the benefit of their experience, knowledge, wisdom, and humor. More importantly, I have the benefit of their friendship. I am deeply indebted to both.

Contents

Flammable and Combustible Liquids Code, NFPA 30

Foreword XIX

Chapter 1 General Provisions 1
  1-1 Scope and Application 1
  1-2 Definitions 7
  1-3 Storage 26
  1-4 Pressure Vessel 26
  1-5 Exits 27

Chapter 2 Tank Storage 29
  2-1 Design and Construction of Tanks 29
  2-2 Installation of Outside Aboveground Tanks 35
  2-3 Installation of Underground Tanks 85
  2-4 Installation of Tanks Inside of Buildings 95
  2-5 Supports, Foundations, and Anchorage for All Tank Locations 98
  2-6 Sources of Ignition 102
  2-7 Testing 102
  2-8 Fire Protection and Identification 104
  2-9 Prevention of Overfilling of Tanks 105
  2-10 Leakage Detection and Inventory Records for Underground Tanks 107

Chapter 3 Piping, Valves, and Fittings 109
  3-1 General 109
  3-2 Materials for Piping, Valves, and Fittings 110
  3-3 Pipe Joints 112
  3-4 Supports 113
  3-5 Protection Against Corrosion 113
  3-6 Valves 113
  3-7 Testing 114
  3-8 Identification 115

Chapter 4 Container and Portable Tank Storage 117
  4-1 Scope 117
  4-2 Design, Construction, and Capacity of Containers 119
  4-3 Design, Construction, and Capacity of Storage Cabinets 123
  4-4 Design, Construction, and Operation of Separate Inside Storage Areas .. 128
  4-5 Indoor Storage 139
  4-6 Protection Requirements for Protected Storage of Liquids .. 153
  4-7 Fire Control 156
  4-8 Outdoor Storage 158

Chapter 5 Operations 163
  5-1 Scope 164
  5-2 General 164
  5-3 Facility Design 165
  5-4 Liquid Handling, Transfer, and Use 177
  5-5 Fire Prevention and Control 189

Chapter 6 Referenced Publications 195

Appendix A Additional Explanatory Material........................ 199

Appendix B Emergency Relief Venting for Fire Exposure for Aboveground Tanks 201

Appendix C Abandonment or Removal of Underground Tanks 209

Appendix D. 213

Appendix E. 223

Appendix F Chapter 5 Source Tables............................... 231

Appendix G Referenced Publications................................ 239

Index. 241

Supplement Case Investigations of Recent Incidents 245
    Fuel Oil Storage Tank Fire Boil-over 245
    Gasoline Storage Tank Overfill and Fire 257
    General-Purpose Warehouse Fire 266

Contents

Automotive and Marine Service Station Code, NFPA 30A

Foreword 275

Chapter 1 General Provisions 277
  1-1 Scope and Application 277
  1-2 Definitions 277

Chapter 2 Storage 283
  2-1 General Provisions 283
  2-2 Special Enclosures 285
  2-3 Inside Buildings 286

Chapter 3 Piping, Valves, and Fittings 289

Chapter 4 Fuel Dispensing System 291
  4-1 Location of Dispensing Devices and Emergency Power Cutoff 291
  4-2 Fuel Dispensing Device 292
  4-3 Remote Pumping Systems 295
  4-4 Vapor Recovery Systems 297
  4-5 Vapor Processing Systems 298

Chapter 5 Service Stations Located Inside Buildings 301
  5-1 General 301
  5-2 Dispensing Area 301
  5-3 Ventilation 302
  5-4 Piping 302
  5-5 Drainage Systems 302

Chapter 6 Electrical Equipment 305

Chapter 7 Heating Equipment 311

Chapter 8 Operational Requirements 313
  8-1 Fuel Delivery Nozzles 313
  8-2 Dispensing into Portable Containers 314
  8-3 Attendance or Supervision of Dispensing 315
  8-4 Attended Self-Service Stations 318
  8-5 Unattended Self-Service Stations 319
  8-6 Drainage and Waste Disposal 321
  8-7 Sources of Ignition 321
  8-8 Fire Control 322
  8-9 Signs 322

Chapter 9 Referenced Publications 323

Appendix A 325

Index 327

Foreword

For almost 80 years, there has been an NFPA Technical Committee at work developing what is now known as the *Flammable and Combustible Liquids Code*. Members of that Committee have given generously of their time and expertise in order to assure that provisions of the *Code* are reasonable, effective, and enforceable. Total committee membership, counting alternates and nonvoting participants, exceeds 50 people. Most members of the group are engineers by training and education, and about half of the principals belong to the Society of Fire Protection Engineers. All members, without exception, bring a sincere dedication to protection of life and property from the ravages of fire no matter what the cause. In effect, their mission and NFPA's mission are parallel.

However, the Committee's participation does not constitute the totality of the code making process. You, the user of NFPA 30 and 30A, are equally important, regardless of the interest you represent. Since the NFPA code making process is totally open to public input and scrutiny, the user of these documents plays a vital role in their development. Where there are perceived inconsistencies, ambiguities, or shortcomings in these *Codes*, and this *Code Handbook*, your advisements will help to bring about change. You need not be an NFPA member in order to participate in this process. Simply write to NFPA, pointing out the specific changes that you feel are needed, and your thoughts will be brought to the attention of the Technical Committee. These *Codes* will become more effective and enforceable by virtue of your participation.

Martin F. Henry
Editor of Second Edition

Preface to the Third Edition

This *Handbook* strives to provide the user with background information for the many provisions of NFPA 30, *Flammable and Combustible Liquids Code*, and NFPA 30A, *Automotive and Marine Service Station Code*. For the experienced user, it provides the rationale for the many technical changes that occur from edition to edition. For the user with less experience or who is just undertaking on responsibilities that involve use of either *Code*, the *Handbook* attempts to provide basic information on the chemical, physical, and fire hazard properties of flammable and combustible liquids.

The *Handbook* is not complete, however; a work such as this never is. It evolves, changing gradually as the *Code* to which it is a companion changes. Users who feel that specific topics are not adequately addressed, or perhaps not addressed at all, are urged to write to the Editor. All suggestions for improvement will be most seriously considered.

Robert P. Benedetti
Staff Liaison and Secretary,
Technical Committee on General Storage
of Flammable Liquids

Acknowledgements

A work such as the *Flammable and Combustible Liquids Code Handbook* is rarely the result of one individual's efforts. It is first, and probably foremost, a collection of the knowledge and opinions of many individuals involved in fire protection of flammable liquids and in the development of NFPA 30, *Flammable and Combustible Liquids Code.* The list of these individuals extends well beyond the members of NFPA's Committee on Flammable and Combustible Liquids and includes the two gentlemen to whom this third edition is dedicated: Miles E. Woodworth and Richard E. Stevens.

Two individuals deserve special recognition: Donald M. Johnson and Orville M. (Bud) Slye, who contributed greatly to this *Handbook* by thoroughly reviewing the commentary. I sincerely appreciate the time and effort they devoted to their reviews. This *Handbook* is more valuable because of their assistance.

The following NFPA staff members deserve special recognition for their efforts in the production of this *Handbook*. The care and attention they devoted to this project is commendable.

> Louise Grant, Keying and Typesetting
> Patricia Donegan, Handbook Project Editor
> Sharon Summers, Composition
> Jennifer Evans, Project Manager
> Elizabeth Carmichael, Production Coordinator
> Donald McGonagle, Printing Purchasing Agent

Artwork for the commentary was done by George Nichols. The cover design is by George Lucas.

I would also like to acknowledge my wife, Diana, for her support and patience during the time devoted to this project.

About the Editor

Robert P. Benedetti is NFPA's Flammable Liquids Field Service Engineer. He is technical secretary to the NFPA Committees on Flammable and Combustible Liquids and Automotive and Marine Service Stations, as well as several other NFPA Committees that deal with the properties, handling, and use of flammable and combustible liquids. He serves as liaison between NFPA and the Safety and Fire Protection Committee of the American Petroleum Institute, the Fire and Accident Prevention Committee of the National Petroleum Refiners Association, the Coordinating Committee on Flash Point Methodology, and Committee E27 on Hazard Potential of Chemicals of the American Society for Testing and Materials.

Mr. Benedetti graduated from Northeastern University with a Bachelor of Science Degree in Chemical Engineering. He was employed by the Factory Insurance Association (now Industrial Risk Insurers) from 1972 until 1974 as a Field Engineer. In June, 1974, he accepted a position with the National Fire Protection Association's Engineering Division as Staff Chemical Specialist and was appointed to his current position in April, 1986.

Mr. Benedetti is a member of NFPA, ASTM, the Society of Fire Protection Engineers, and the American Institute of Chemical Engineers. He is Secretary of the New England Chapter of SFPE and is a Director of the AIChE Safety and Health Division.

Note:

The text, illustrations, and captions to photographs that make up the commentary on the various sections of the *Flammable and Combustible Liquids Code Handbook* are printed in color. The photographs, all of which are part of the commentary, are printed in black for better clarity. The text of the *Codes* is printed in black.

Flammable and Combustible Liquids Code

NFPA 30—1987

Information on referenced publications can be found in Chapter 6 and Appendix G.

Foreword

This standard, known as the *Flammable and Combustible Liquids Code*, is recommended for use as the basis of legal regulations. Its provisions are intended to reduce the hazard to a degree consistent with reasonable public safety, without undue interference with public convenience and necessity which require the use of flammable and combustible liquids. Thus, compliance with this standard does not eliminate all hazard in the use of flammable and combustible liquids.

1 General Provisions

The serious student is encouraged to study NFPA 321, *Standard on Basic Classification of Flammable and Combustible Liquids*; NFPA 325M, *Fire Hazard Properties of Flammable Liquids, Gases, and Volatile Solids*; and NFPA 49, *Hazardous Chemicals Data*. These publications contain characteristics and fire hazard properties of many flammable and combustible liquids, as well as other chemicals. Also, the student is referred to the following sections and chapters of the NFPA *Fire Protection Handbook*: Chapters 1, 2, and 4 of Section 4; Chapters 4 and 11 of Section 5; Chapters 7, 8, 10, 14, and 21 of Section 10; and Chapter 4 of Section 11.

1-1 Scope and Application.

1-1.1 This code applies to all flammable and combustible liquids except those that are solid at 100°F (37.8°C) or above.

A complete understanding of the scope and limitations of the *Code* is desirable when using it as a guide, and essential where it is referenced in laws or ordinances.

The words "flammable" and "combustible" have essentially the meanings of common usage, subject to the limitations given in Section 1-2 of the *Code* and in the NFPA *Fire Protection Handbook*, Chapter 4 of Section 5.

The term "liquid" excludes materials having a vapor pressure exceeding 40 psia (276 kPa) at 100°F (37.8°C). An example of such a material is liquefied petroleum gas, which is covered in NFPA 58, *Standard for the Storage and Handling of Liquefied Petroleum Gases*. Other liquefied gases are covered in NFPA 59A, *Standard for the Production, Storage, and Handling of Liquefied Natural Gas (LNG)*, and NFPA 50B, *Standard for Liquefied Hydrogen Systems at Consumer Sites*.

Solids having a melting point below 100°F (37.8°C) are covered because they may be liquid at some ambient temperatures, are easily ignited, and may spread or flow to reach ignition sources.

Solids having a melting point of 100°F (37.8°C) or above, however, are excluded from the provisions of the *Code*. Although tables of physical properties of liquids and volatile solids may list them as having flash points and they behave like Class III liquids when melted, they may be shipped as solids in metal or other containers, or even in paper bags (subject to U.S. Department of Transportation regulations). Therefore, rules designed for materials that are normally liquid are not appropriate.

Finally, some materials (asphalt, for example) do not have a sharp dividing line between the liquid and solid states. This *Code* defines a liquid as any material more fluid than 300 penetration asphalt. (*See Section 1-2, Liquid.*)

1-1.2 Requirements for the safe storage and use of the great variety of flammable and combustible liquids commonly available depend primarily on their fire characteristics, particularly the flash point, which is the basis for the several classifications of liquids as defined in Section 1-2. It should be noted that the classification of a liquid can be changed by contamination. For example, filling a Class II liquid into a tank which last contained a Class I liquid can alter its classification, as can exposing a Class II liquid to the vapors of a Class I liquid via an interconnecting vapor line (*see 2-2.6.4 and 2-3.5.6*). Care shall be exercised in such cases to apply the requirements appropriate to the actual classification.

Flash point was selected as the basis for classification because it is directly related to a liquid's ability to generate vapor, i.e., its volatility. Since it is the vapor of the liquid, not the liquid itself, that burns, vapor generation becomes the primary factor in determining the fire hazard. The expression "low flash-high hazard" applies. Liquids having flash points below ambient storage temperatures generally display a rapid rate of flame spread over the surface of the liquid, since it is not necessary for the heat of the fire to expend its energy in heating the liquid to generate more vapor. Within a closed container, a liquid held at a temperature slightly above its flash point will produce a mixture that can be ignited to burn with explosive violence. Any vapors released from the container can spread to an ignition source some distance away. At higher temperatures, assuming confinement, vapor is generated at a rate such that the mixture becomes "too rich" to burn. (*See Section 1-2, Flash Point, for more detailed information.*)

Also keep in mind that *controlling the vapors* of a flammable or combustible liquid is the primary means of controlling the fire risk.

1-1.3 The volatility of liquids is increased by heating. When Class II or Class III liquids are exposed to storage conditions, use conditions or process operations where they are naturally or artificially heated to or above their flash points, additional requirements may be necessary. These requirements include consideration for such items as ventilation, exposure to ignition sources, diking, and electrical area classification.

Increasing the ambient temperature in the space where combustible liquids are stored or heating a combustible liquid above its flash point may create a hazardous atmosphere. This hazardous condition normally occurs in the space where the temperature of the vapors remains above the flash point of the liquid, although condensation of a mixture that is within or above the flammable range may result in a flammable mist. The mist droplets eventually settle, resulting in a thin film of liquid on surrounding surfaces. Fuel Oil No. 6, for example, normally has a flash point above 140°F (60°C). When heated above its flash point, its volatility increases and it assumes some characteristics of lower flash point liquids.

Precautions will have to be taken to avoid ignition. These precautions should include preventive measures, such as ventilating the vapor space to prevent vapor accumulation and controlling sources of ignition. Fire control and suppression measures that are normally provided for flammable liquids should also be considered.

It is important to remember that any Class II or Class III liquid that is heated above its flash point will present the same degree of fire and explosion risk, at least in the immediate vicinity of the liquid, as a flammable liquid. Further precautions will be needed when liquids are heated above their autoignition temperatures. Leaks of any liquid heated above its autoignition temperature will usually result in almost immediate ignition of the vapors without any ignition source being present. Also, a mist of a Class II or Class III liquid will present a deflagration hazard somewhat similar to a dust explosion, although not as violent. These characteristics of combustible liquids are often not fully appreciated and are sometimes ignored.

1-1.4 Additional requirements may be necessary for the safe storage and use of liquids that have unusual burning characteristics, that are subject to self-ignition when exposed to the air, that are highly reactive with other substances, that are subject to explosive decomposition, or have other special properties that dictate safeguards over and above those specified for a normal liquid of similar flash point classification.

NFPA 49, *Hazardous Chemicals Data*, gives the fire hazard properties of many chemicals, including a number of reactive, water-reactive, or otherwise unstable flammable and combustible liquids. This publication should be studied when a material having these properties is encountered. Special protective measures, such as increased spacing between tanks, are outlined in Chapters 2 and 5. Other protective measures, such as tank insulation, water spray systems, or inhibitor injection systems, may be appropriate. Only a few flammable liquids are violently water-reactive. Where such liquids are stored, it will be prudent to follow precautions given in NFPA 49, *Hazardous Chemicals Data.*

Another convenient source of information is NFPA 491M, *Manual of Hazardous Chemical Reactions.* This manual contains information on chemical reactions that have the potential for dangerous release of energy.

1-1.5   In certain installations the provisions of this code may be altered at the discretion of the authority having jurisdiction after consideration of the special features such as topographical conditions, barricades, walls, adequacy of building exits, nature of occupancies, proximity to buildings or adjoining property and character of construction of such buildings, capacity and construction of proposed tanks and character of liquids to be stored, nature of process, degree of private fire protection to be provided, and the adequacy of facilities of the fire department to cope with flammable or combustible liquid fires.

When evaluating specific situations, other physical characteristics and chemical properties of liquids, such as boiling point, vapor pressure, vapor density, specific gravity, water solubility, and toxicity, may have to be considered, along with the topography, building construction features, and exposure conditions. Conditions that may allow spillage or percolation into water supplies, or vapor travel that might prevent the escape of persons from the area in the event of an accident must be considered by the engineer who designs the facility to comply with NFPA 30, *Flammable and Combustible Liquids Code*, and by the authority that enforces NFPA 30. Greater protection, or even prohibition of an installation, may be necessary in densely populated neighborhoods or in areas where the public fire suppression capabilities are not sufficient to provide reasonable protection for the public.

The authority having jurisdiction may also apply the provisions of this *Code* less restrictively, if convinced that safety has not been compromised and an equivalent degree of protection has been achieved.

1-1.6   Existing plants, equipment, buildings, structures, and installations for the storage, handling, or use of flammable or combustible liquids that are not

NFPA 30—GENERAL PROVISIONS

in strict compliance with the terms of this code may be continued in use at the discretion of the authority having jurisdiction provided they do not constitute a recognized hazard to life or adjoining property. The existence of a situation that might result in an explosion or sudden escalation of a fire, such as inadequate ventilation of confined spaces, lack of adequate emergency venting of a tank, failure to fireproof the supports of elevated tanks, or lack of drainage or dikes to control spills may constitute such a hazard.

Codes are designed to protect life and property. If exposure were limited to property alone, noncomplying conditions in existence prior to adoption of the *Code* might be allowed to continue via a "grandfather clause."* This approach is reasonable since code provisions are often developed or evolve as a result of fire loss experience. Requiring current compliance with laws that did not exist at the time of construction would be unreasonable, unless subsequent experience clearly shows a high degree of risk to life or to exposed property. The "recognized hazards" enumerated in 1-1.6 serve as a guide to the authority having jurisdiction and are not all-inclusive. Where such recognized hazards exist, a "grandfather clause" exclusion may not have application and the recognized hazard may constitute grounds for applying the *Code* retroactively.

1-1.7 This code shall not apply to:

1-1.7.1 Transportation of flammable and combustible liquids. These requirements are contained in the U.S. Department of Transportation regulations or in NFPA 385, *Standard for Tank Vehicles for Flammable and Combustible Liquids*.

"Transportation" is intended to include movement of flammable and combustible liquids by air, rail, truck, ship, and pipeline. The U.S. Department of Transportation (DOT) regulations are normally applied only to interstate shipments, with intrastate shipment being regulated by state or local laws. These regulations are contained in Title 49 of the *Code of Federal Regulations*, Parts 172 through 179. NFPA 385, *Standard for Tank Vehicles for Flammable and Combustible Liquids*, is often used as the basis for local and state legislation that regulates intrastate truck shipments, although the DOT regulations are sometimes adopted by reference for the same purpose.

A recent NFPA Formal Interpretation (84-4) addressed the question of applicability of NFPA 30, *Flammable and Combustible Liquids Code*, to storage in tank vehicles:

---

* A clause that creates an exemption from current regulations for circumstances that existed prior to such regulations.

Background: Tank trailers and semi-trailers are loaded with flammable or combustible liquid and moved to a storage yard. There, the tankers may be kept for days, weeks, or months before being shipped to another location or being moved to another part of the same plant site. Some of the tankers are not roadworthy.

Question: Do such tank vehicles, used for the temporary storage of flammable and combustible liquids, need to meet the requirements of NFPA 30, *Flammable and Combustible Liquids Code*, for drainage, impoundment, separation distances, etc.?

Answer: Yes.

In some situations, applicability of NFPA 30 may depend on one's definition of "temporary." A tank vehicle that is routinely used to store a liquid for periods of time exceeding several days is being used as a portable storage tank and should be treated according to the requirements of the *Code*. However, a tank vehicle holding a liquid awaiting shipment to a consignee may be considered to be in transport and not subject to the *Code*, even though there may be a delay of several days between loading and actual shipment.

1-1.7.2 Storage, handling, and use of fuel oil tanks and containers connected with oil burning equipment. These requirements are covered separately in NFPA 31, *Standard for the Installation of Oil Burning Equipment*.

1-1.7.3 Storage of flammable and combustible liquids on farms and isolated construction projects. These requirements are covered separately in NFPA 395, *Standard for the Storage of Flammable and Combustible Liquids on Farms and Isolated Construction Projects*.

1-1.7.4 Liquids without flash points that can be flammable under some conditions, such as certain halogenated hydrocarbons and mixtures containing halogenated hydrocarbons. (*See NFPA 321, Standard on Basic Classification of Flammable and Combustible Liquids*.)

Examples of liquids without flash points that may be flammable under certain conditions (such as being heated in a closed vessel) are: methyl bromide, dichloromethane, trichloroethane, and trichloroethylene. NFPA 49, *Hazardous Chemicals Data*; and NFPA 491M, *Manual of Hazardous Chemical Reactions*, may be useful in identifying such materials.

1-1.7.5 Mists, sprays, or foams. (*Except flammable aerosols in containers, which are included in Chapter 4.*)

Details on some operations that produce mists, sprays, or foams are given in NFPA 33, *Standard for Spray Application Using*

Flammable and Combustible Materials. (See also the discussion following 1-1.4.)

1-1.8 Installations made in accordance with the applicable requirements of standards of the National Fire Protection Association: NFPA 32, *Standard for Drycleaning Plants;* NFPA 33, *Standard for Spray Application Using Flammable and Combustible Materials;* NFPA 34, *Standard for Dipping and Coating Processes Using Flammable or Combustible Liquids;* NFPA 35, *Standard for the Manufacture of Organic Coatings;* NFPA 36, *Standard for Solvent Extraction Plants;* NFPA 37, *Standard for the Installation and Use of Stationary Combustion Engines and Gas Turbines;* NFPA 45, *Standard for Fire Protection for Laboratories Using Chemicals;* and Chapter 10 of NFPA 99, *Standard for Health Care Facilities,* shall be deemed to be in compliance with this code.

NFPA publishes many standards that apply to specific hazards or processes and compliance with a more specifically oriented standard takes the place of the less specific requirements of NFPA 30, *Flammable and Combustible Liquids Code.*

1-1.9 Metrication. If a value for measurement as given in this standard is followed by an equivalent value in other units, the first stated is regarded as the requirement. The given equivalent value may be approximate.

1-2 Definitions.

Aerosol. A material that is dispensed from its container as a mist, spray, or foam by a propellant under pressure.

This definition applies to the contained product, not the container or the propellant. (*See definition of "Flammable Aerosol."*)

Apartment House. A building or that portion of a building containing more than two dwelling units.

This definition is intended to include triplexes, quadruplexes, townhouses, and condominiums, provided there are more than two dwelling units under the roof of the building and each dwelling unit has independent cooking and bathroom facilities.

Approved. Acceptable to the "authority having jurisdiction."

NOTE: The National Fire Protection Association does not approve, inspect or certify any installations, procedures, equipment, or material nor does it approve or evaluate testing laboratories. In determining the acceptability of installations or procedures, equipment or materials, the authority having jurisdiction may base acceptance on compliance with NFPA or other appropriate standards. In the absence of such standards, said authority may require evidence of proper installation, procedure or use. The authority having jurisdiction may also refer to the listings or labeling practices of an organization concerned with product evaluations which is in a position to determine compliance with appropriate standards for the current production of listed items.

Acceptable performance is usually proven by fire tests, actual fire experience, or both.

Assembly Occupancy. All buildings or portions of buildings used for gathering 50 or more persons for such purposes as deliberation, worship, entertainment, dining, amusement, or awaiting transportation.

Atmospheric Tank. A storage tank that has been designed to operate at pressures from atmospheric through 0.5 psig (760 mm Hg through 786 mm Hg) measured at the top of the tank.

The expression 0.5 psig means one half pound per square inch above prevailing atmospheric pressure. An ordinary pressure gage indicates the difference in pressure between a container to which it is connected and the pressure of the surrounding atmosphere. This is in contrast to the expression "psia"—pounds per square inch absolute—in which the reference point is zero pounds absolute pressure, or full vacuum (0.0 psig = 14.7 psia). Except for the reference to psia in the definitions of flammable liquids, boiling point, and vapor pressure, all pressures in the *Code* are gage pressures, psig. The addition of the phrase "measured at the top of the tank" is an editorial clarification, but serves to ensure that the gage is measuring only the pressure in the vapor space of the tank and is not also measuring the static pressure head of the liquid in the tank.

Authority Having Jurisdiction. The "authority having jurisdiction" is the organization, office or individual responsible for "approving" equipment, an installation or a procedure.

NOTE: The phrase "authority having jurisdiction" is used in NFPA documents in a broad manner since jurisdictions and "approval" agencies vary as do their responsibilities. Where public safety is primary, the "authority having jurisdiction" may be a federal, state, local or other regional department or individual such as a fire chief, fire marshal, chief of a fire prevention bureau, labor department, health department, building official, electrical inspector, or others having statutory authority. For insurance purposes, an insurance inspection department, rating bureau, or other insurance company representative may be the "authority having jurisdiction." In many circumstances the property owner or his designated agent assumes the role of the "authority having jurisdiction"; at government installations, the commanding officer or departmental official may be the "authority having jurisdiction."

Barrel. A volume of 42 U.S. gal (158.9 L).

The 42-gallon designation for a barrel is a petroleum industry measurement standard. A common mistake is to consider the drum and the barrel as equivalents; however, the drum is normally a volume of 55 U.S. gallons (208 L).

NFPA 30—GENERAL PROVISIONS

Basement. A story of a building or structure having ½ or more of its height below ground level and to which access for fire fighting purposes is unduly restricted.

In any particular case, an interpretation of this definition is best left to the authority having jurisdiction, who should know to what extent access for fire fighting will be required. Openings for the injection of gaseous extinguishing agents, water spray, or high-expansion foam may, in some cases, be considered sufficient. (*See Figure 1-1.*)

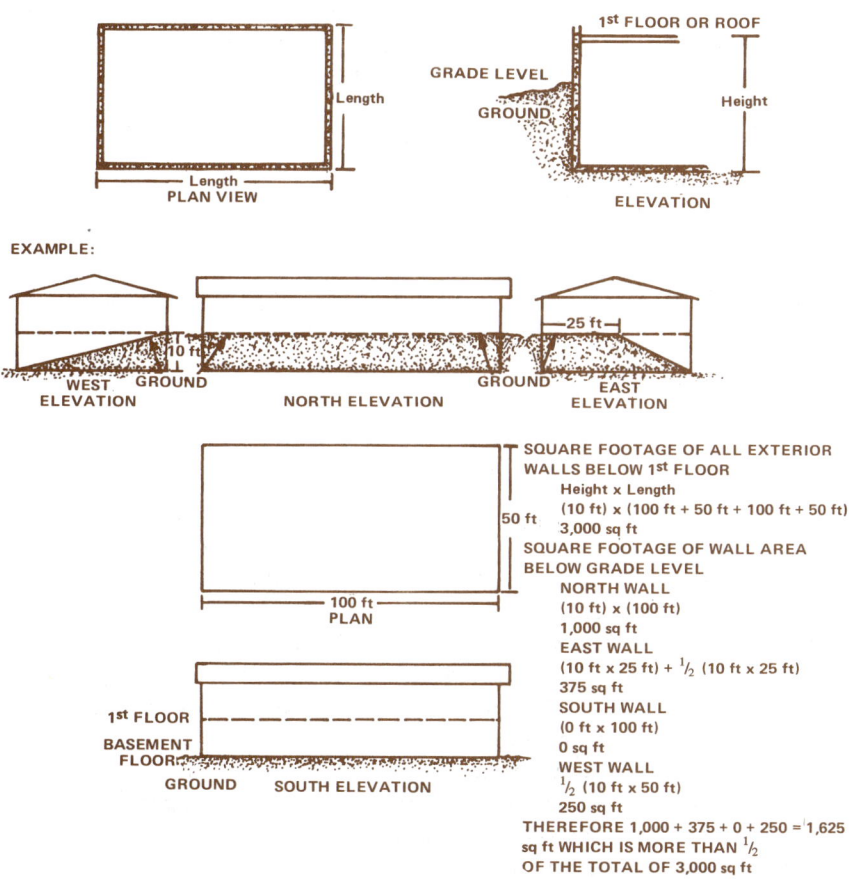

SI Units: 1 ft = 0.30 m; 1 sq ft = 0.09 m².

Figure 1-1 This example is not considered a basement by this *Code* in spite of the square footage computation *if* there are adequate windows or doors on one or more sides so that fire fighting access can be made into *all* areas of this lower floor (basement) from the exterior. The definition of basement for this *Code* may differ from that of other NFPA codes and standards and adopted building codes. For purposes of this *Code*, access from the exterior for fire fighting purposes is the more critical factor.

Boiling Point. The temperature at which a liquid exerts a vapor pressure of 14.7 psia (760 mm Hg). Where an accurate boiling point is unavailable for the material in question, or for mixtures that do not have a constant boiling point, for purposes of this code the 10 percent point of a distillation performed in accordance with ASTM D 86-82, *Standard Method of Test for Distillation of Petroleum Products*, may be used as the boiling point of the liquid.

The boiling point of a liquid is the temperature at which its vapor pressure equals the atmospheric pressure. Above this temperature the pressure of the atmosphere can no longer hold the liquid in the liquid state and bubbles begin to form. The lower the boiling point, the greater the vapor pressure at normal ambient temperatures, and consequently the greater the fire risk. For any given liquid, the boiling point decreases with elevation above sea level, since the pressure of the atmosphere decreases with increasing elevation. Conversely, the boiling point rises with an increase in pressure. For purposes of comparison, water boils at 212°F (100°C) at sea level, and at 208°F (97.8°C) at 2,200 ft (671 m) elevation.

Some liquids are mixtures of components having both high and low boiling points. These liquids will boil over a wide temperature range, called the distillation range. Gasoline is a good example; its distillation range is about 100°F to 400°F (37.8°C to 204.4°C). The temperature at which 10 percent will have boiled off will be about 150°F (65.6°C).

Boil-Over. An event in the burning of certain oils in an open top tank when, after a long period of quiescent burning, there is a sudden increase in fire intensity associated with expulsion of burning oil from the tank. Boil-over occurs when the residues from surface burning become more dense than the unburned oil and sink below the surface to form a hot layer, which progresses downward much faster than the regression of the liquid surface. When this hot layer, called a "heat wave," reaches water or water-in-oil emulsion in the bottom of the tank, the water is first superheated, and subsequently boils almost explosively, overflowing the tank. Oils subject to boil-over consist of components having a wide range of boiling points, including both light ends and viscous residues. These characteristics are present in most crude oils, and can be produced in synthetic mixtures.

NOTE: A boil-over is an entirely different phenomenon from a slop-over or froth-over. Slop-over involves a minor frothing, which occurs when water is sprayed onto the hot surface of a burning oil. Froth-over is not associated with a fire but results when water is present or enters a tank containing hot viscous oil. Upon mixing, the sudden conversion of water to steam causes a portion of the tank contents to overflow.

For a discussion of the mechanism of boil-over, refer to the comments following 2-2.1.1 and to the description of the Tacoa, Venezuela tank fire in the Supplement on page 245 of this *Handbook*.

Formal Interpretation 81-1 is pertinent here:

Question: Is it the intent of NFPA 30 that Fuel Oil #6 [viz., crude oil (or certain other liquids)] be considered a boil-over liquid, as per the definition of boil-over and as per the applicability of Table 2-3 of NFPA 30 governing boil-over liquids?

Answer: No.

It is important to note that this Formal Interpretation was processed prior to the incident in Tacoa, Venezuela (*see Supplement*). Definitive findings on that incident were not available until after publication of the 1984 edition of the *Code*, but it has since been learned that the fuel involved had the *characteristics* of Fuel Oil #6. The fuel had been formulated by diluting an oil heavier than Fuel Oil #6 with lighter, more volatile oils, possibly even with Class I or Class II liquids.

Bulk Plant or Terminal. That portion of a property where liquids are received by tank vessel, pipelines, tank car, or tank vehicle, and are stored or blended in bulk for the purpose of distributing such liquids by tank vessel, pipeline, tank car, tank vehicle, portable tank, or container.

Chemical Plant. A large integrated plant or that portion of such a plant other than a refinery or distillery where liquids are produced by chemical reactions or used in chemical reactions.

At times chemical plants are not easily distinguished from processing plants. However, chemical plants are generally "large" and "integrated." Like refineries, they usually handle liquids in large quantities, often in continuous processes and usually in unhoused equipment and vessels supported by process structures (process "racks"), sometimes elevated above grade. However, some operations may be contained in buildings or protective structures. Process plants, on the other hand, generally handle liquids in much smaller quantities and at lower flow rates. Usually, process plants produce an end product, as opposed to another plant's raw material.

Closed Container. A container as herein defined, so sealed by means of a lid or other device that neither liquid nor vapor will escape from it at ordinary temperatures.

The container is not allowed to have any vents, either automatic, fixed, or pressure operated.

Combustible Liquids. See Liquids.

Container. Any vessel of 60 U.S. gal (227 L) or less capacity used for transporting or storing liquids.

> This includes small cans, such as a 2-oz can of lighter fluid, and also the typical 55-gal drum.

Crude Petroleum. Hydrocarbon mixtures that have a flash point below 150°F (65.6°C) and that have not been processed in a refinery.

> Technically, hydrocarbons are chemical compounds consisting of only the elements hydrogen and carbon; e.g., heptane {$CH_3(CH_2)_5CH_3$} and hexane {$CH_3(CH_2)_4CH_3$}.

Distillery. A plant or that portion of a plant where liquids produced by fermentation are concentrated, and where the concentrated products may also be mixed, stored, or packaged.

> The process of distilling is used to remove impurities from a product or to separate products with different boiling points and to concentrate desired components. It involves the vaporization of a liquid, followed by condensation of its vapors. Fermentation, on the other hand, is the process of chemically changing animal or vegetable matter by rearranging its elements or molecules through the use of bacteria, enzymes, yeasts, or molds.

Dwelling. A building occupied exclusively for residence purposes and having not more than two dwelling units or as a boarding or rooming house serving not more than 15 persons with meals or sleeping accommodations or both.

> The 15 persons may or may not be related.

Dwelling Unit. One or more rooms arranged for the use of one or more individuals living together as a single housekeeping unit, with cooking, living, sanitary, and sleeping facilities.

Educational Occupancy. The occupancy or use of a building or structure or any portion thereof by persons assembled for the purpose of learning or of receiving educational instruction.

Fire Area. An area of a building separated from the remainder of the building by construction having a fire resistance of at least 1 hr and having all communicating openings properly protected by an assembly having a fire resistance rating of at least 1 hr.

> Such fire resistive construction must completely separate the area from all other portions of the building, from the floor through the

roof or ceiling, in such a manner as to *completely enclose* the fire area (top, bottom, and sides). The fire resistive separation must extend into any attic, basement, crawl space, or joist spaces. Thus, in a single-story building, the fire wall must cut off the crawl space and attic area from the rest of the building, including the joist spaces. If not, then the ceiling and floor must be of rated construction, in addition to the walls. Fire walls cannot be penetrated by joists, beams, etc.

The reader is reminded that this definition applies to this *Code* only and may differ from those in other codes and standards. For further information, see NFPA 220, *Standard on Types of Building Construction*, and NFPA 251, *Standard Methods of Fire Tests of Building Construction and Materials.*

Flammable Aerosol. An aerosol that is required to be labeled "Flammable" under the U.S. Federal Hazardous Substances Labeling Act.

See 4-1.3 for further treatment of flammable aerosols.

Flash Point. The minimum temperature at which a liquid gives off vapor in sufficient concentration to form an ignitible mixture with air near the surface of the liquid within the vessel as specified by appropriate test procedure and apparatus as follows:

(a) The flash point of a liquid having a viscosity less than 45 SUS at 100°F (37.8°C) and a flash point below 200°F (93°C) shall be determined in accordance with ASTM D 56-82, *Standard Method of Test for Flash Point by the Tag Closed Tester.*

(b) The flash point of a liquid having a viscosity of 45 SUS or more at 100°F (37.8°C) or a flash point of 200°F (93°C) or higher shall be determined in accordance with ASTM D 93-80, *Standard Method of Test for Flash Point by the Pensky Martens Closed Tester.*

(c) As an alternate, ASTM D 3828-81, *Standard Methods of Tests for Flash Point of Petroleum and Petroleum Products by Setaflash Closed Tester*, may be used for testing aviation turbine fuels within the scope of this procedure.

(d) As an alternate, ASTM D 3278-82, *Standard Method of Tests for Flash Point of Liquids by Setaflash Closed Tester*, may be used for paints, enamels, lacquers, varnishes, and related products and their components having flash points between 32°F (0°C) and 230°F (110°C), and having a viscosity lower than 150 stokes at 77°F (25°C).

(e) As an alternate, ASTM D 3828-79, *Standard Test Methods for Flash Point of Liquids by Setaflash Closed Tester*, may be used for materials other than those for which specific Setaflash Methods exist (cf., ASTM D 3243-77 for aviation turbine fuels and ASTM D 3278-78 for paints, enamels, lacquers, varnishes, related products, and their components).

14   FLAMMABLE AND COMBUSTIBLE LIQUIDS CODE HANDBOOK

As stated in the comment following 1-1.2, flash point was chosen as the basis for classification because of its direct relationship to volatility. A liquid that has a flash point in the range of normal ambient temperatures (or below) will, without any external heating, evolve vapors at concentrations that can be ignited by a small source of ignition, such as a pilot flame or spark. A liquid with a higher flash point will require some heating before ignition is possible, thus presenting a lesser degree of hazard. At the flash point, the vapor concentration is just great enough to be ignited by an external ignition source, but generally not enough for burning to continue. Sustained burning occurs at a slightly higher (by only a few degrees) temperature, the "fire point."

The temperatures for flash point and boiling point are lowered as altitude increases due to corresponding increase in liquid volatility as atmospheric pressure is reduced. This increased volatility and the consequent drop in flash point and boiling point must be emphasized to users of Class II liquids at high altitudes. A recent incident at a mine facility situated at a high altitude vividly illustrates this point: A worker was seriously burned while loading diesel fuel through the open dome of a tank truck using a hose and a gasoline-driven portable pump when the diesel fuel vapors ignited at the dome. The ignition source was not definitely determined, but could have been a discharge of static electricity or a leaky fitting at the portable pump. This incident illustrates the effect of an increase in altitude on the flash point of a customarily safe combustible liquid.

Several hundred degrees above the flash point is the autoignition temperature. At this temperature, self-sustained combustion is initiated without an external ignition source. Autoignition temperature is significant when handling very hot liquids or when a liquid is exposed to a hot surface.

Studies have shown that vapors require varied durations of exposure to hot surfaces before ignition can actually occur. A general rule is that hot surfaces need to be about 400°F (204°C) above the autoignition temperature of the vapor for ignition to occur. For further information, see API Petroleum Safety Data Sheet 2216, *Ignition Risk of Hot Surfaces in Open Air.*

Flash point measurements have been made using a variety of test methods. Originally, flash point was determined by heating the liquid in a small container open to the ambient air, the flash point being the lowest temperature at which a small flame was observed to pass across the liquid surface when a small test flame was applied to it. This is the "open-cup flash test." Subsequently, when more emphasis was placed on the ignition of vapors within closed containers (such as in tank explosions), the belief developed that "closed-cup" testing would more accurately reflect the hazard of handling the liquid. Closed cup test methods had been used, but were not widely accepted until 1970. Currently, the NFPA recognizes only the five closed-cup methods listed above. The most widely used is the Tag Closed Tester, ASTM D 56-82. The other four test methods are used for special purposes, such as high-viscosity fluids and fluids that form a film on the surface. Experience has shown that the Tag Closed Tester has difficulties with these liquids.

There are some advantages to using a closed-cup test versus an open cup: closed-cup methods are more easily used; the results are more reproducible (meaning that different laboratories will produce the same test results); and closed-cup testers will indicate the presence of small amounts of a low flash point liquid in an otherwise high flash point liquid.

Details of construction of the testers and the prescribed procedures for performing the tests are contained in the ASTM publications. (*See Figures 1-2 and 1-3 on the following pages.*)

Hazardous Material or Hazardous Chemical. Material presenting dangers beyond the fire problems relating to flash point and boiling point. These dangers may arise from but are not limited to toxicity, reactivity, instability, or corrosivity.

Hazardous Reaction or Hazardous Chemical Reaction. Reactions that result in dangers beyond the fire problems relating to flash point and boiling point of either the reactants or of the products. These dangers may include but are not limited to toxic effects, reaction speed (including detonation), exothermic reaction, or production of unstable or reactive materials.

The preceding two definitions have been added to the *Code* as a result of the consolidation of the four occupancy-specific chapters of previous editions into a single chapter on operations. The terms appear in the scope of Chapter 5 and serve to identify materials and situations that are outside the scope of NFPA 30, *Flammable and Combustible Liquids Code*, and which will likely involve protection measures beyond those required by this *Code*. Examples of flammable liquids that can present hazardous reactions are monomers, such as styrene and methyl methacrylate.

Hotel. Buildings or groups of buildings under the same management in which there are sleeping accommodations for hire, primarily used by transients

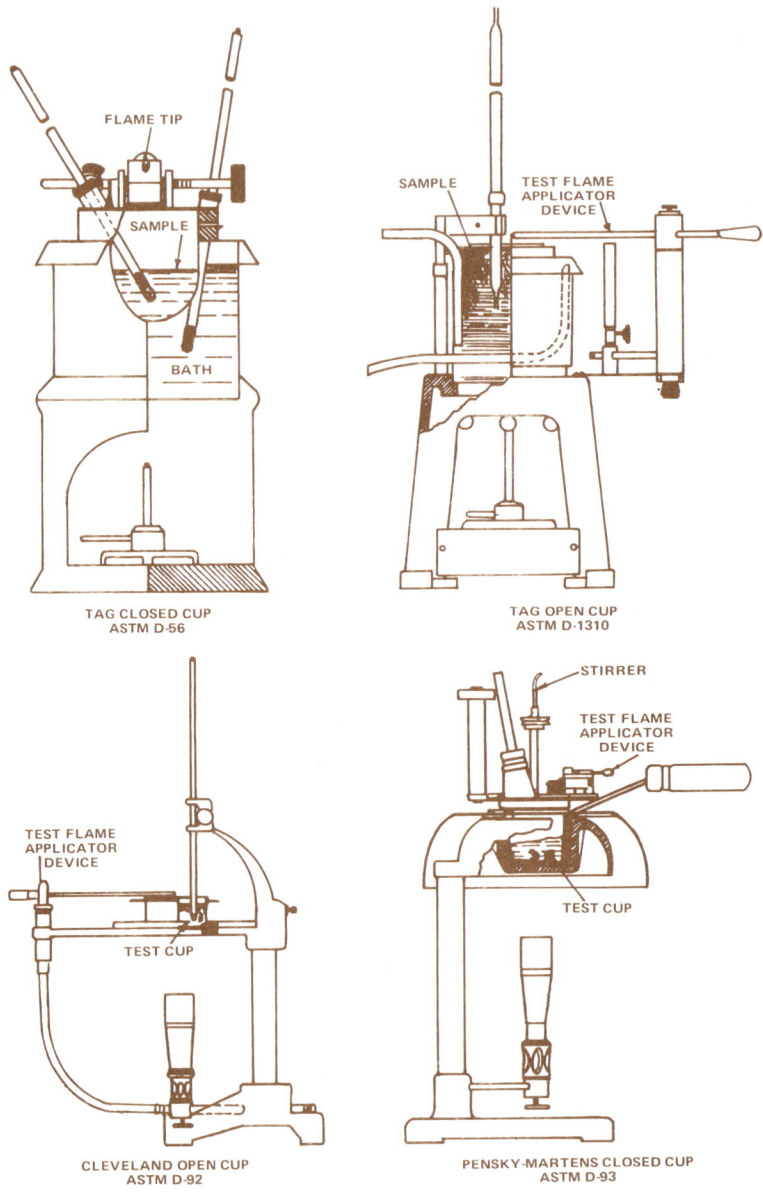

Figure 1-2 Four commonly used testers for determining flash points of flammable or combustible liquids. The material to be tested is slowly heated, and at periodic intervals a test flame is applied to the vapor space. Flash point is the temperature at which a flash of fire is seen when the test flame is applied. More detailed descriptions for conducting tests for each type of testing apparatus are given in the applicable standard of the American Society for Testing and Materials or by the manufacturer.

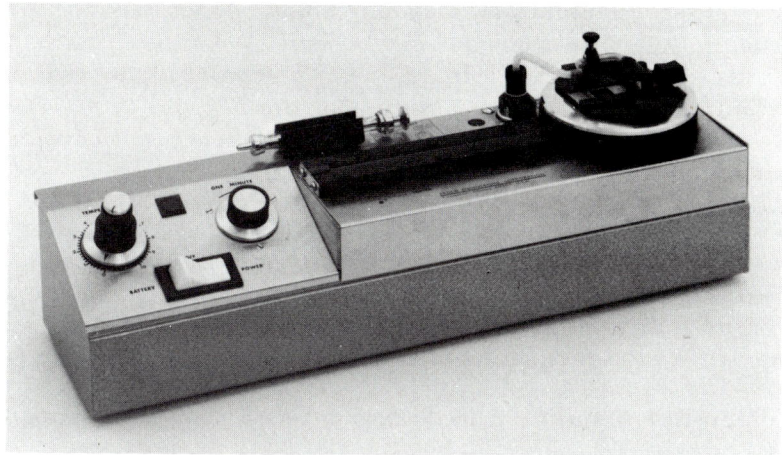

Figure 1-3 Setaflash low temperature, closed-cup tester. (Erdco Engineering Corp., Evanston, IL)

who are lodged with or without meals, including but not limited to inns, clubs, motels, and apartment hotels.

Incidental Liquid Use or Storage. Use or storage as a subordinate activity to that which established the occupancy or area classification.

> This definition originated in the former chapter on industrial plants.

Institutional Occupancy. The occupancy or use of a building or structure or any portion thereof by persons harbored or detained to receive medical, charitable, or other care or treatment, or by persons involuntarily detained.

Labeled. Equipment or materials to which has been attached a label, symbol or other identifying mark of an organization acceptable to the "authority having jurisdiction" and concerned with product evaluation, that maintains periodic inspection of production of labeled equipment or materials and by whose labeling the manufacturer indicates compliance with appropriate standards or performance in a specified manner.

Liquid. For the purpose of this code, any material that has a fluidity greater than that of 300 penetration asphalt when tested in accordance with ASTM D 5-78, *Test for Penetration for Bituminous Materials*. **When not otherwise identified, the term** *liquid* **shall mean both flammable and combustible liquids.**

> As previously mentioned, the scope of the *Code* excludes materials that are solid at 100°F (37.8°C) or above, thus creating a need to distinguish liquids from solids. It was decided that any material

that could spread or flow on a hot day should be considered a liquid. A material having the flow characteristics of 300 penetration asphalt was arbitrarily selected as being the most viscous material warranting classification as a liquid for the purpose of this *Code*; anything more viscous would be a solid and, hence, not covered.

Three hundred penetration asphalt is the most fluid grade of paving asphalt recognized by ASTM D 946-82. Penetration is measured by recording the distance that a weighted, pointed rod penetrates into a sample in 5 seconds at controlled temperature (*see ASTM D 5-86 for detailed procedure*). This definition first appeared in the 1972 revision of the *Code*.

Combustible Liquid. A liquid having a flash point at or above 100°F (37.8°C).

Combustible Liquids shall be subdivided as follows:
Class II liquids shall include those having flash points at or above 100°F (37.8°C) and below 140°F (60°C).
Class IIIA liquids shall include those having flash points at or above 140°F (60°C) and below 200°F (93°C).
Class IIIB liquids shall include those having flash points at or above 200°F (93°C).

The U.S. Department of Transportation (DOT) requires "Flammable Liquid" labels on containers of any liquid that has a flash point below 100°F (37.8°C), closed cup. Many areas reach ambient temperatures of 100°F (37.8°C). Under such circumstances, only moderate heating or ambient conditions are required to raise a liquid's temperature to 100°F (37.8°C).

The word "combustible" first appeared in the title of the 1963 revision of the *Code*. The term "Class III" was applied to liquids having a flash point at or above 140°F (60°C) and below 200°F (93°C). At that time, liquids having flash points above Class III were excluded from the scope of the *Code*.

In the 1966 revision, Class III was subdivided into Class IIIA and IIIB, the former being the same as the previous Class III and the latter including liquids of higher flash points. In spite of being defined, Class IIIB liquids were still excluded from the scope of the *Code*.

In the 1972 revision, the scope was broadened to *include* Class IIIB liquids. The results of this change were minor, affecting principally some aspects of tank location and container storage.

The term "Class II" was applied to liquids having flash points at or above 100°F (37.8°C) and below 140°F (60°C). This corresponded to the solvent permitted in a Class II drycleaning plant (*see NFPA 32, Standard for Drycleaning Plants*). This definition has remained unchanged in both *Codes*. Prior to the 1973 edition of the *Code*, Class II liquids were included under the definition of flammable liquid. When the U.S. Occupational Safety and Health Administration (OSHA) was established in 1972, the *Code* was adopted as legally binding under the OSHA regulations. An immediate conflict arose between OSHA and DOT regulations because each used a different breakpoint between flammable and combustible: 140°F versus 100°F, respectively. The conflict was eliminated when the *Code* redefined Class II liquids as combustible liquids in the 1973 edition.

Flammable Liquid. A liquid having a flash point below 100°F (37.8°C) and having a vapor pressure not exceeding 40 lbs per sq in. (absolute) (2,068 mm Hg) at 100°F (37.8°C) shall be known as a Class I liquid.

Gases that are normally stored and shipped as liquids under pressure or refrigeration, e.g., liquefied petroleum gas, liquefied natural gas, etc., are not covered by this *Code*, since it is the stored pressure or refrigeration that causes the gases to liquefy.

A vapor pressure of 40 psia (absolute), or 25.3 psig, at 100°F (37.8°C) is the accepted dividing line between liquids and gases, except that DOT's Office of Pipeline Safety uses a different definition for liquefied petroleum gases, liquefied natural gas, and liquefied ammonia, defining them as "highly volatile liquids."

Class I liquids shall be subdivided as follows:

Class IA shall include those having flash points below 73°F (22.8°C) and having a boiling point below 100°F (37.8°C).

Class IB shall include those having flash points below 73°F (22.8°C) and having a boiling point at or above 100°F (37.8°C).

Class IC shall include those having flash points at or above 73°F (22.8°C) and below 100°F (37.8°C).

Vapors from flammable and combustible liquids, in the pure state, are heavier than air. However, vapors in the pure state can exist only at or above the boiling point of the liquid. For all other conditions, the vapor is mixed with some air and the density is proportionately reduced. At the flash point temperature, the vapor-air mixture will be less than about five percent vapor. The rest is air, and this mixture is only slightly heavier than uncontaminated air. Thus, dispersion of the mixture can easily result from wind or convection currents.

On the other hand, this means that a mixture within the flammable range can be expected to flow along at grade level, often for some distance, until dispersed. Such mixtures can and have been known to be ignited by sources of ignition remote from the source of the vapors and above grade level.

The 73°F (22.8°C) dividing line for flash point temperature between Classes IA and IB and Class IC is based on an old U.S. Interstate Commerce Commission regulation that required a red label with the word "Flammable" on all liquids offered for interstate shipment that exhibited a flash point below 80°F (26.6°C), open cup. (Note that the U.S. Consumer Product Safety Commission still uses the 80°F open-cup criterion.) It was eventually agreed that 73°F (22.8°C), closed cup, was the approximate equivalent of 80°F (26.6°C), open cup. The addition of the boiling point characteristic for distinguishing between Class IA and Class IB is included because the low boiling point liquids have a high vapor pressure that may approach the dividing line between liquids and gases {40 psia (25.3 psig)} and may require storage in other than atmospheric tanks. NFPA 30, *Flammable and Combustible Liquids Code*, thus specifies greater requirements for those more hazardous materials. Under normal ambient temperatures, both Class IA and Class IB liquids generate sufficient vapors to create vapor concentrations within the flammable range at all times. Pressure vessels or other strongly constructed containers capable of withstanding an internal pressure of as much as 5 psig must be used to store Class IA flammable liquids. Otherwise, the product will evaporate from the container, creating a hazardous atmosphere as well as causing a loss of product. The differentiation between Class IA and Class IB becomes important in selecting the type of tank and in placing limits on quantities stored in buildings. (*See Chapter 4, "Container and Portable Tank Storage."*)

Listed. Equipment or materials included in a list published by an organization acceptable to the "authority having jurisdiction" and concerned with product evaluation, that maintains periodic inspection of production of listed equipment or materials and whose listing states either that the equipment or material meets appropriate standards or has been tested and found suitable for use in a specified manner.

NOTE: The means for identifying listed equipment may vary for each organization concerned with product evaluation, some of which do not recognize equipment as listed unless it is also labeled. The "authority having jurisdiction" should utilize the system employed by the listing organization to identify a listed product.

NFPA 30—GENERAL PROVISIONS

Low-Pressure Tank. A storage tank designed to withstand an internal pressure above 0.5 psig (3.5 kPa) but not more than 15 psig (103.4 kPa) measured at the top of the tank.

Mercantile Occupancy. The occupancy or use of a building or structure or any portion thereof for the displaying, selling, or buying of goods, wares, or merchandise.

Occupancy Classification. The system of defining the predominant operating characteristic of a portion of a building or plant for purposes of applying relevant sections of this Code. This may include but is not limited to distillation, oxidation, cracking, and polymerization.

Office Occupancy. The occupancy or use of a building or structure or any portion thereof for the transaction of business, or the rendering or receiving of professional services.

Operating Unit (Vessel) or Process Unit (Vessel). The equipment in which a unit operation or unit process is conducted.

Operations. A general term that includes but is not limited to the use, transfer, storage, and processing of liquids.

Outdoor Occupancy Classification. Similar to occupancy classification except that it applies to outdoor operations not enclosed in a building or shelter.

> The preceding three definitions and the definitions for "Occupancy Classification," "Process or Processing," and "Unit Operation or Unit Processing" have been added to the *Code* as a result of the consolidation of the four occupancy-specific chapters of previous editions into a single chapter on operations. These terms are critical to the proper application of Chapter 5.

Portable Tank. Any closed vessel having a liquid capacity over 60 U.S. gallons (227 L) and not intended for fixed installation.

> Note that portable tanks not exceeding 660 gal are covered by Chapter 4, while portable tanks exceeding 660 gal are covered by Chapter 2.

Pressure Vessel. Any fired or unfired vessel within the scope of the applicable section of the ASME *Boiler and Pressure Vessel Code*.

Process or Processing. An integrated sequence of operations. The sequence may be inclusive of both physical and chemical operations, unless the term is modified to restrict it to one or the other. The sequence may involve, but is not limited to preparation; separation; purification; or change in state, energy content, or composition.

Protection for Exposures. Fire protection for structures on property adjacent to liquid storage. Fire protection for such structures shall be acceptable when located either within the jurisdiction of any public fire department, or adjacent to plants having private fire brigades capable of providing cooling water streams on structures on property adjacent to liquid storage.

> Adequate exposure protection depends on a fire protection system or fire protection agency that can provide a barrier to the transmission of heat or a method for absorbing the heat generated by a fire. A public fire department will normally have sufficient hose stream capability to provide a thermal barrier in the form of a water curtain, and the *Code* recognizes this capability. The larger plant fire brigades will normally have this capability also, but an extensive private water supply and hose system or a fire apparatus pumping engine will be required in addition to personnel.
>
> It is important to note that the "protection for exposure" concept, as applied in the *Code*, refers to the adjacent property, not to the property on which the liquid is stored. Thus, for example, a bulk plant can position its storage tanks closer to a neighboring facility if the latter has protection for exposures, such as a fire brigade. The bulk plant may or may not have a fire brigade of its own.

Refinery. A plant in which flammable or combustible liquids are produced on a commercial scale from crude petroleum, natural gasoline, or other hydrocarbon sources.

Safety Can. An approved container, of not more than 5 gal (18.9 L) capacity, having a spring-closing lid and spout cover and so designed that it will safely relieve internal pressure when subjected to fire exposure.

> The safety can is not designed or intended for use in areas where the periodic release of flammable vapors may create a hazardous atmosphere (such as in the trunk of an automobile). The main purpose of the safety can is preventing explosion of the overheated container while still providing the utility of a closed container. To accomplish this, a spring-operated cap is provided on the pouring spout, eliminating the need for a flame arrestor in the spout. Even if the vapors coming past the spring-loaded cover are in the flammable range, their velocity would be at least an order of magnitude greater than the intrinsic velocity of a flame through the vapors, so a flashback into the safety can would be unlikely should

Figure 1-4 Metal safety can with flame arrestor (Justrite).

the vapors be ignited by an external source. (*See Figure 1-4.*) In spite of this, it is customary to find safety cans fitted with flame arrestors in order to meet specific listing requirements.

Separate Inside Storage Area. A room or building used for the storage of liquids in containers or portable tanks, separated from other types of occupancies. Such areas may include:

Inside Room. A room totally enclosed within a building and having no exterior walls.

Cut-Off Room. A room within a building and having at least one exterior wall.

Attached Building. A building having only one common wall with a building having other type occupancies.

Exterior walls of cutoff rooms or attached buildings must provide some form of access for fire fighting purposes and, under certain circumstances, provisions to vent the overpressure developed by an explosion (deflagration venting). (*See 4-4.2.1.*) Other details and construction requirements are set forth in Section 4-4. (*See Figure 1-5.*)

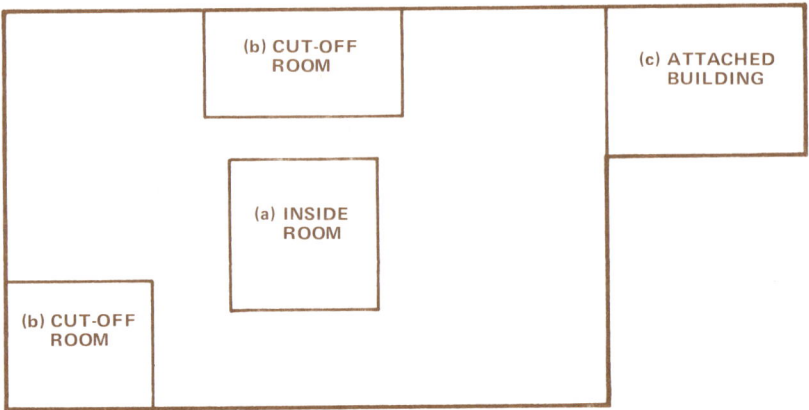

Figure 1-5 Diagram of: (a) inside room, (b) cutoff rooms, and (c) attached buildings.

Service Stations.

Automotive Service Station. That portion of property where liquids used as motor fuels are stored and dispensed from fixed equipment into the fuel tanks of motor vehicles and shall include any facilities available for the sale and service of tires, batteries, and accessories, and for minor automotive maintenance work. Major automotive repairs, painting, body and fender work are excluded.

Marine Service Station. That portion of a property where liquids used as fuels are stored and dispensed from fixed equipment on shore, piers, wharves, or floating docks into the fuel tanks of self-propelled craft, and shall include all facilities used in connection therewith.

Service Station Located Inside Buildings. That portion of an automotive service station located within the perimeter of a building or building structure that also contains other occupancies. The service station may be enclosed or partially enclosed by the building walls, floors, ceilings, or partitions, or may be open to the outside. The service station dispensing area shall mean that area of the service station required for dispensing of fuels to motor vehicles. Dispensing of fuel at manufacturing, assembly, and testing operations is not included within this definition.

> Although the preceding three definitions appear in this *Code*, requirements for service stations are no longer included as a chapter in the *Code*. Service stations are now covered by NFPA 30A, *Automotive and Marine Service Station Code*, which is also a part of this Handbook.

Stable Liquid. Any liquid not defined as unstable.

Unit Operation or Unit Process. A segment of a physical or chemical process that may or may not be integrated with other segments to constitute the manufacturing sequence.

Unstable Liquid. A liquid which, in the pure state or as commercially produced or transported, will vigorously polymerize, decompose, undergo condensation reaction, or will become self-reactive under conditions of shock, pressure, or temperature.

Vapor Pressure. The pressure, measured in lb per sq in. (absolute), exerted by a volatile liquid as determined by ASTM D 323-82, *Standard Method of Test for Vapor Pressure of Petroleum Products (Reid Method).*

Vapor pressure is a measure of a liquid's propensity to evaporate. The higher the vapor pressure, the more volatile the liquid and, thus, the more readily the liquid gives off vapors. Vapor pressure is significant in determining whether a product is a liquid or a gas. Vapor pressure varies with temperature, increasing as the temperature of the liquid increases, until it equals the pressure of the surrounding atmosphere and the liquid begins to boil.

Vapor Processing Equipment. Those components of a vapor processing system designed to process vapors or liquids captured during filling operations at service stations, bulk plants, or terminals.

Vapor Processing System. A system designed to capture and process vapors displaced during filling operations at service stations, bulk plants, or terminals by use of mechanical and/or chemical means. Examples are systems using blower-assist for capturing vapors, and refrigeration, absorption, and combustion systems for processing vapors.

The processing of vapors may include combustion of the vapors or the condensation of vapors to the liquid state.

Vapor Recovery System. A system designed to capture and retain, without processing, vapors displaced during filling operations at service stations, bulk plants, or terminals. Examples are balanced-pressure vapor displacement systems and vacuum-assist systems without vapor processing.

The basic function of a vapor recovery system is to prevent vapors from being released into the atmosphere either by returning the vapors to the container from which the liquid is being withdrawn or by otherwise confining the vapors to prevent their release into the atmosphere.

Ventilation. As specified in this code, ventilation is for the prevention of fire and explosion. It is considered adequate if it is sufficient to prevent accumulation of significant quantities of vapor-air mixtures in concentration over one-fourth of the lower flammable limit.

Ventilation is vital to the prevention of flammable liquid fires and explosions. Ventilation is used to remove vapor to a safe location and also to dilute the vapor concentration. This can be accomplished through natural or forced air movement.

The lower flammable limit is the minimum concentration of vapor in air below which propagation of a flame will not occur in the presence of an ignition source. The upper flammable limit is the maximum concentration of vapor in air above which propagation of flame will not occur. If the vapor concentration is below the lower flammable limit, it is "too lean" to propagate flame; if it is above the upper flammable limit, it is "too rich."

When the vapor concentration is between the lower and upper flammable limits, ignition can occur and explosions may result.

When the *Code* describes ventilation as being adequate when vapor-air mixtures are not over one-fourth of the lower flammable limit, a safety factor of four-to-one is established.

Warehouses.

General-Purpose Warehouse. A separate, detached building or portion of a building used only for warehousing-type operations.

NOTE: Warehousing operations referred to above are those operations not accessible to the public and include general purpose, merchandise, distribution, and industrial warehouse-type operations.

Liquid Warehouse. A separate, detached building or attached building used for warehousing-type operations for liquids.

One of the key distinctions between a general-purpose warehouse and a liquid warehouse is that the former handles a variety of combustible commodities, a regulated portion of which may be liquids, and the latter handles liquids exclusively, with some minimal exceptions. Regulations governing each type can vary significantly. (See 4-5.6 and 4-5.7.)

Wharf. Any dock, pier, bulkhead, or other structure over or contiguous to navigable water with direct physical access from land, the primary function of which is the transfer of liquid cargo in bulk between shore installations and any tank vessel, such as ship, barge, lighter boat, or other mobile floating craft.

1-3 Storage. Liquids shall be stored in tanks or in containers in accordance with Chapter 2 or Chapter 4.

Portable tanks exceeding 660 gal capacity are covered by Chapter 2.

1-4 Pressure Vessel. All new pressure vessels containing liquids shall comply with 1-4.1, 1-4.2, or 1-4.3, as applicable.

1-4.1 Fired pressure vessels shall be designed and constructed in accordance with Section I (Power Boilers), or Section VIII, Division 1 or Division 2 (Pressure Vessels), as applicable, of the 1983 ASME *Boiler and Pressure Vessel Code*.

1-4.2 Unfired pressure vessels shall be designed and constructed in accordance with Section VIII, Division 1 or Division 2, of the 1983 ASME *Boiler and Pressure Vessel Code*.

> A fired pressure vessel is a vessel to which heat is applied by direct flame contact. Fired pressure vessels are mostly used to contain endothermic (heat-absorbing) chemical reactions, such as cracking of heavy oil to get lighter products, such as gasoline. A pressure vessel is necessary because of the high vapor pressures created by applied heat.
>
> An unfired pressure vessel is a vessel that is either unheated or is heated by steam or other means not involving direct flame contact. Unfired pressure vessels are most often used to contain liquefied gases, to contain reacting systems that may require some heat to initiate reaction or, as in the case of nickel carbonyl, to contain highly toxic vapors.
>
> Both fired and unfired pressure vessels may be used for flammable and combustible liquid storage, if desired or if required by process conditions or characteristics of the liquid.

1-4.3 Fired and unfired pressure vessels that do not conform to 1-4.1 or 1-4.2 may be used provided approval has been obtained from the state or other governmental jurisdiction in which they are to be used. Such pressure vessels are generally referred to as "State Special."

1-5 Exits. Egress from buildings and areas covered by this code shall be in accordance with NFPA *101*®, *Life Safety Code*®.

References Cited in Commentary

NFPA 30A, *Automotive and Marine Service Station Code*, NFPA, Quincy, MA, 1987.

NFPA 32, *Standard for Drycleaning Plants*, NFPA, Quincy, MA, 1985.

NFPA 33, *Standard for Spray Application Using Flammable and Combustible Materials*, NFPA, Quincy, MA, 1985.

NFPA 49, *Hazardous Chemicals Data*, NFPA, Quincy, MA, 1975.

NFPA 50B, *Standard for Liquefied Hydrogen Systems at Consumer Sites*, NFPA, Quincy, MA, 1985.

NFPA 58, *Standard for the Storage and Handling of Liquefied Petroleum Gases*, NFPA, Quincy, MA, 1986.

NFPA 59A, *Standard for the Production, Storage and Handling of Liquefied Natural Gas (LNG)*, NFPA, Quincy, MA, 1985.

NFPA 220, *Standard Types of Building Construction*, NFPA, Quincy, MA, 1985.

NFPA 251, *Standard Methods of Fire Tests of Building Construction and Materials*, NFPA, Quincy, MA, 1985.

NFPA 321, *Standard on Basic Classification of Flammable and Combustible Liquids*, NFPA, Quincy, MA, 1987.

NFPA 325M, *Fire Hazard Properties of Flammable Liquids, Gases, and Volatile Solids*, NFPA, Quincy, MA, 1984.

NFPA 385, *Standard for Tank Vehicles for Flammable and Combustible Liquids*, NFPA, Quincy, MA, 1985.

NFPA 491M, *Manual of Hazardous Chemical Reactions*, NFPA, Quincy, MA, 1986.

NFPA *Fire Protection Handbook*, 16th ed., NFPA, Quincy, MA, 1986.

API Petroleum Safety Data Sheet 2216, *Ignition Risk of Hot Surfaces in Open Air*, American Petroleum Institute, Washington, DC, 1980.

ASTM D 5-86, *Standard Test Method for Penetration of Bituminous Materials*, American Society for Testing and Materials, Philadelphia, 1986.

ASTM D 56-82, *Standard Method of Test for Flash Point by the Tag Closed Tester*, American Society for Testing and Materials, Philadelphia, 1982.

ASTM D 86-82, *Standard Method of Test for Distillation of Petroleum Products*, American Society for Testing and Materials, Philadelphia, 1982.

ASTM D 946-82, *Specification for Asphalt Cement for Use in Pavement Construction*, American Society for Testing and Materials, Philadelphia, 1982.

ASTM E 502-84, *Standard Method of Test for Flash Point of Chemicals by Closed-Cup Methods*, American Society for Testing and Materials, Philadelphia, 1984.

Title 49, Transportation, *U.S. Code of Federal Regulations*, U.S. Government Printing Office, Washington, DC, 1986.

2 Tank Storage

2-1 Design and Construction of Tanks.

2-1.1 Materials. Tanks shall be designed and built in accordance with recognized good engineering standards for the material of construction being used, and shall be of steel or approved noncombustible material, with the following limitations and exceptions:

> "Recognized good engineering standards" for the design and erection of tanks for the storage of flammable liquids have evolved from over one hundred years of experience. No single standard is universally applicable because of the wide variety of liquids and their properties, and latitude in the choice of materials is permitted where circumstances warrant. The standards listed in 2-1.3, 2-1.4, and 2-1.5 cover designs that embody a suitable factor of safety to ensure that tanks will safely contain their contents under normal operating conditions. Emergency conditions, such as exposure to fire, require special details of construction or special protection. Such requirements are dealt with later.
>
> The phrase "or approved noncombustible material" was added to the 1984 edition of the *Code* to allow other construction materials where desirable or where need dictates. Use of the word "approved" empowers the authority having jurisdiction to exercise discretion regarding what is acceptable.

(a) The material of tank construction shall be compatible with the liquid to be stored. In case of doubt about the properties of the liquid to be stored, the supplier, producer of the liquid, or other competent authority shall be consulted.

(b) Tanks constructed of combustible materials shall be subject to the approval of the authority having jurisdiction and limited to:

    1. Installation underground, or

    2. Use where required by the properties of the liquid stored, or

    3. Storage of Class IIIB liquids aboveground in areas not exposed to a spill or leak of Class I or Class II liquid, or

4. Storage of Class IIIB liquids inside a building protected by an approved automatic fire extinguishing system.

(c) Unlined concrete tanks may be used for storing liquids having a gravity of 40 degrees API or heavier. Concrete tanks with special linings may be used for other services provided the design is in accordance with sound engineering practice.

The expression "40 degrees API" is a measure of the specific gravity of the liquid. Through long custom, the specific gravity of petroleum products has been designated in terms of degrees API, as measured with a hygrometer calibrated according to the following formula:

$$\text{Degrees API} = \frac{141.5}{\text{sp.gr.}} - 131.5$$

The API gravities for petroleum products range from about 10° (for heavy lubricating oils) up to 80° or more (for casinghead gasoline). A low number indicates a more dense, more viscous, less volatile fluid. Normal motor grade gasoline has an API gravity in the range of 55° to 65°. The 40° gravity material mentioned in this paragraph corresponds roughly to kerosene or light stove distillate oil. Such materials have flash points of about 130°F (54.4°C). Thus, a minor leak of a 40° API liquid from an unlined tank would not create an ignition hazard, and such tanks are permitted.

(d) Tanks may have combustible or noncombustible linings.

Tanks are occasionally lined with plastic material, such as spray-on epoxy resins, to provide corrosion protection or to provide protection against minor leaks. It does not matter whether the lining material is combustible or noncombustible because the quantity is small and will not contribute to fire loss. Such a lining, even though electrically insulating, will not increase the risk of ignition from static electricity. (*See NFPA 77, Recommended Practice on Static Electricity.*)

This paragraph is the basis for allowing the repair of tanks that have developed minor leaks by spray-on application of an epoxy resin liner to the inside wall of the tank. The decision to allow such a repair has historically been left to the authority having jurisdiction. However, pending U.S. Environmental Protection Agency regulations for underground storage systems may disallow such repairs on underground tanks in many cases or may exert more stringent control. At the least, it is expected that such a repair will be allowed only once in the lifetime of a tank.

(e) Special engineering consideration may be required if the specific gravity of the liquid to be stored exceeds that of water or if the tank is designed to contain liquids at a liquid temperature below 0°F (-17.8°C).

These considerations are addressed in API 650, *Welded Steel Tanks for Oil Storage*, [see 2-1.3.1(b)]. The word "may" (line 1 above) is an indication that special engineering consideration is not always required.

2-1.2 Fabrication.

2-1.2.1 Tanks may be of any shape or type consistent with sound engineering design.

Sound engineering design can provide a structurally acceptable tank of any shape. However, as a practical matter, economy in fabrication, the material used, and the operating pressure limit the shape of a tank to one of the following:

1. Vertical cylindrical tanks with flat or nearly flat bottoms and flat, coned, or domed fixed roofs, or open tops with floating roofs.

2. Horizontal cylindrical tanks with flat or domed ends.

3. Spherical or toroidal tanks.

In all cases, the foundation and supporting structure must be considered as an integral part of the design. (*See Section 2-5.*)

2-1.2.2 Metal tanks shall be welded, riveted, and caulked, or bolted, or constructed by use of a combination of these methods.

Tanks must be constructed to be liquidtight up to the maximum fill level.

2-1.3 Atmospheric Tanks.

The term "atmospheric tank" is defined in Section 1-2 as a tank operating at pressures from atmospheric up to and including 0.5 psig (3.5 kPa). API 650, *Welded Steel Tanks for Oil Storage*, uses the expression "internal pressures approximating atmospheric." For most large atmospheric tanks, the maximum permissible operating pressure will be somewhat less than 0.5 psig because it is considered undesirable that the roof plate welds be continuously stressed by pressure. A maximum operating pressure of about 1 in. (2.5 cm) of water or 0.6 oz/sq in. (0.25 kPa) is considered acceptable for large tanks.

2-1.3.1 Atmospheric tanks, including those incorporating secondary containment, shall be built in accordance with recognized standards of design *or* approved equivalents. Atmospheric tanks shall be built, installed, and used within the scopes of their approvals or any of the following:

(a) Underwriters Laboratories Inc., *Standard for Steel Aboveground Tanks for Flammable and Combustible Liquids*, UL142—1981; *Standard for Steel Underground Tanks for Flammable and Combustible Liquids*, UL58—1976; or *Standard for Steel Inside Tanks for Oil Burner Fuel*, UL80—1980.

(b) American Petroleum Institute Standard No. 650, *Welded Steel Tanks for Oil Storage*, Sixth Edition, 1980.

(c) American Petroleum Institute Specifications 12B, *Bolted Tanks for Storage of Production Liquids*, Twelfth Edition, January 1977; 12D, *Field Welded Tanks for Storage of Production Liquids*, Eighth Edition, January 1982; or 12F, *Shop Welded Tanks for Storage of Production Liquids*, Seventh Edition, January 1982.

(d) American Society for Testing and Materials, *Standard Specification for Glass-Fiber Reinforced Polyester Underground Petroleum Storage Tanks*, ASTM D 4021-81.

(e) Underwriters Laboratories Inc., *Standard for Glass-Fiber Reinforced Plastic Underground Storage Tanks for Petroleum Products*, UL 1316-83.

> The wording of this paragraph is broad enough to allow flexibility in tank design and installation methods. The authority having jurisdiction may now allow departures from recognized standards (e.g., for double-walled tanks) in cases where special needs or unusual situations warrant, so long as equivalent performance is ensured. This enhanced flexibility will prove beneficial to users of the *Code* as environmental protection receives more attention, especially for underground storage systems.
>
> The allowance for bolted tanks storing crude oil in producing areas, 2-1.3.1(c), recognizes the fact that the tanks are usually small. An oil well may have a short useful life so, consequently, the need for tanks may be temporary. A bolted tank is easily dismantled and moved to a new location. Although such tanks are vulnerable to fire damage from a ground fire because of possible damage to the gaskets, the advantages outweigh the shortcomings. At main gathering stations and pipeline terminals, more substantial tanks would be required.

2-1.3.2 Low-pressure tanks and pressure vessels may be used as atmospheric tanks.

> This simply means that a tank designed for pressure will be acceptable for a less demanding service. However, the more stringent spacing requirements for pressure tanks specified in 2-2.1 are

not to be waived unless the emergency venting system has the required capacity at atmospheric pressure.

2-1.3.3 Atmospheric tanks shall not be used for the storage of a liquid at a temperature at or above its boiling point.

A liquid having a boiling point below the prevailing atmospheric temperature would be expected to boil continuously if stored in an atmospheric tank, involving considerable product loss and a greatly increased risk of ignition. (The boiling rate would depend on the rate at which the tank received heat from the surrounding atmosphere and from solar radiation.) In interpreting this paragraph, the liquid's atmospheric boiling point should be taken as that at the location of the tank, not at sea level. The boiling point of a liquid at an altitude of 10,000 ft (3,050 m) may be as much as 20°F (11°C) lower than it would be at sea level. As a practical matter, this usually dictates that liquids at temperatures close to their boiling points be stored in pressure tanks, simply to avoid product loss.

2-1.4 Low-Pressure Tanks.

2-1.4.1 The normal operating pressure of the tank shall not exceed the design pressure of the tank.

2-1.4.2 Low-pressure tanks shall be built in accordance with recognized standards of design. Low-pressure tanks may be built in accordance with:

(a) American Petroleum Institute Standard No. 620, *Recommended Rules for the Design and Construction of Large, Welded, Low-Pressure Storage Tanks*, Fifth Edition, 1982.

(b) The principles of the *Code for Unfired Pressure Vessels*, Section VIII, Division I of the ASME *Boiler and Pressure Vessel Code*, 1983 Edition.

2-1.4.3 Tanks built according to Underwriters Laboratories Inc. requirements in 2-1.3.1 may be used for operating pressures not exceeding 1 psig (6.9 kPa) and shall be limited to 2.5 psig (17.2 kPa) under emergency venting conditions.

Tanks constructed to UL 142 specifications are shop-built and leak-tested prior to shipment as completely assembled units. Although horizontal tanks are pressure-tested to 5 to 7 psig (34.4 to 48.2 kPa), they are limited to service at a 1 psig (6.9 kPa) maximum internal operating pressure and to 2.5 psig (17.2 kPa) under emergency venting conditions. These restrictions recognize that failure of a horizontal tank is invariably accompanied by release of the tank contents. Vertical tanks are only required to be tested to a pressure that exceeds 1.5 psig (10.3 kPa); however, they are also subject to liquid release upon failure, so the same service restrictions apply. There is an exception: vertical tanks built to UL 142 specifications and labeled "Built to Weak Shell-to-Roof Joint Design" are not expected to fail in such a manner as to release the contents. It is assumed that the weak seams will fail upon overpressure and only vapors will be released.

The term "emergency venting conditions" is not defined in Section 1-2. It is meant to describe a situation where a tank is fully exposed to flame, resulting in heating and boiling of the tank contents. Normal venting is based solely on liquid addition or withdrawal and atmospheric temperature and pressure changes. (*See also 2-2.4 and 2-2.5.*)

Since consequences of fire exposure can have a substantial effect on the permissible spacing and location of tanks as set forth in Section 2-2 and Tables 2-1 and 2-4, it is necessary to deal with this subject before commenting on specific requirements.

Flames contacting aboveground tanks can heat the contained liquid, causing it to boil, and may also damage tank supports and the unwet portion of the tank shell. Boiling effects can be mitigated by design (2-2.5.3) or by additional relief valves (2-2.5.4 through 2-2.5.9). Supports for elevated tanks can be insulated to delay failure or constructed of fire-resistive materials, as covered in Section 2-5.

Flame contact on the unwet portion of the shell of a steel tank can heat that portion of the shell to the point that it loses much of its structural strength. For a vertical tank, this heating may result in distortion at the top of the shell, but tank collapse and spill of contents is not likely. Heating the top of the shell of a horizontal tank, however, is likely to result in structural failure, with release of contents.

For a pressure tank, the result of heating the unwet portion of the shell can be serious. Such tanks usually store liquids having boiling points below atmospheric temperature and therefore, their relief valves are set to maintain the resulting higher pressure. When heated sufficiently, the shell will lose strength and the resulting tear is likely to spread below the liquid level. This tear may extend completely around a horizontal tank so as to sever the head, release the contents, and cause the pieces to rocket. The possibility of this type of failure is recognized in Table 2-2. This phenomenon is known as a "BLEVE" (Boiling Liquid-Expanding Vapor Explosion), defined as a catastrophic failure of a container into two or more major pieces at a moment in time when the contained liquid is at a temperature well above its boiling point at normal atmospheric pressure. The classic cases of BLEVEs have involved tank cars of liquefied petroleum gases, but the phenomenon is applicable to liquids as well.

2-1.4.4 Pressure vessels may be used as low-pressure tanks.

2-1.5 Pressure Vessels.

2-1.5.1 The normal operating pressure of the vessel shall not exceed the design pressure of the vessel.

2-1.5.2 Storage tanks designed to withstand pressures above 15 psig (103.4 kPa) shall meet the requirements of Section 1-4.

> The 15 psig (103.4 kPa) criterion corresponds to the definition of a pressure vessel by the ASME *Boiler and Pressure Vessel Code*. [*See 2-1.4.2(b).*]

2-1.6 Provisions for Internal Corrosion.

2-1.6.1 When tanks are not designed in accordance with the American Petroleum Institute, American Society of Mechanical Engineers, or the Underwriters Laboratories Inc. Standards, or if corrosion is anticipated beyond that provided for in the design formulas used, additional metal thickness or suitable protective coatings or linings shall be provided to compensate for the corrosion loss expected during the design life of the tank.

> The choice of a suitable protective lining will depend on the nature of the liquid stored.

2-2 Installation of Outside Aboveground Tanks.

> The requirements of this section are intended to ensure that tanks are located so they will not jeopardize structures on the property of others. In the early days when tanks had wood-supported combustible roofs, it was not uncommon for fire to spread from one tank to another. Thus, regulations provided that tanks be widely spaced from each other and from all other facilities. With the advent of the steel roof, this risk greatly decreased. Experience indicated that, given no ground-spill fire, one tank could burn without damaging neighboring tanks or adjoining property. However, distance between adjacent tanks and between tanks and property lines or adjacent structures remain principal planning criteria. Instead of basing spacing on an arbitrarily selected distance, it is now considered more practical and realistic to base it on a fraction of tank diameter. Tables 2-1 through 2-4

employ this concept, while Tables 2-5 and 2-6 determine spacing by tank capacity.

2-2.1 Location with Respect to Property Lines, Public Ways, and Important Buildings on the Same Property.

2-2.1.1 Every aboveground tank for the storage of Class I, Class II, or Class IIIA liquids, (except as provided in 2-2.1.2) and those liquids with boil-over characteristics and unstable liquids, operating at pressures not in excess of 2.5 psig (17.2 kPa) and designed with a weak roof-to-shell seam (*see 2-2.5.3*), or equipped with emergency venting devices that will not permit pressures to exceed 2.5 psig (17.2 kPa), shall be located in accordance with Table 2-1. Where tank spacing is contingent on a weak roof-to-shell seam design, the user shall present evidence certifying such construction to the authority having jurisdiction, upon request.

This paragraph introduces Table 2-1, states its scope, and, by inference, serves also to introduce Tables 2-2 through 2-7. In effect, it states that the spacings in Table 2-1 apply to all tanks storing Class I, Class II, and Class IIIA liquids, with the important exceptions discussed in paragraphs 2-2.1.2 through 2-2.1.5.

Tables 2-1 through 2-4 base their spacing requirements on the characteristics of the liquid, type of tank, protection provided for the tank, and protection provided for exposures. "Protection for exposures" is defined in Section 1-2. The tables recognize that it may be difficult or impossible to extinguish a tank fire. Therefore, efforts are directed at protecting adjacent buildings and adjoining properties. Fire protection for exposures should not be confused with fire suppression systems and equipment used to fight a tank fire. The tables also recognize that there is little possibility of extingushing a fire in a tank that exceeds 150 ft (45 m) in diameter. Even with fixed fire suppression equipment installed, set-up time is often required, during which exposed tanks or structures will need to be protected from radiant heat to prevent fire spread.

This paragraph contains several terms having somewhat special meanings. (They are used repeatedly in the tables as well.) Understanding these terms will help the user understand the provisions of this chapter. These terms are: "liquids with boil-over characteristics," "unstable liquids," "operating at pressures not in excess of 2.5 psig," "weak roof-to-shell seam," and "emergency venting devices." They are discussed in a slightly different order in the following paragraphs.

Boil-over. Tanks storing liquids having boil-over characteristics are subject to the stricter spacing requirements of Table 2-3.

Although the term "boil-over" is defined in Section 1-2, an adequate understanding of the concept requires more detailed explanation.

Any liquid will boil if sufficiently heated. In open-pool burning, the liquid surface receives radiant energy from the flames and this energy supports the boiling. For most liquids, a steady state condition develops and burning proceeds until the liquid is consumed. (In fact, once steady state is reached, the burning rate is predictable.) In a tank, boiling can result in a rise in the liquid level due to the entrained bubbles. Thus, a full tank may overflow. This, however, is *not* a boil-over.

To have boil-over characteristics, a liquid must have a wide range of boiling points, including a substantial proportion of volatile components and a highly viscous residue. It must also have at least a small amount of water-in-oil emulsion. This combination is present in most crude oils, but seldom in other petroleum products. When an open-top tank of crude oil is involved in a fire, the following sequence of events occurs. As the fire burns, the surface layer is depleted of its volatile components, becomes hotter and denser than the original mixture, and sinks below the surface to be replaced by fresh, unburned oil. A gradually deepening layer of very hot oil {200°F (93°C) or more} migrates downward through the tank contents. When this layer reaches a previously-settled layer of emulsion near the bottom of the tank, the water droplets in the emulsion are superheated to a temperature well above the boiling point at the prevailing pressure (atmospheric pressure plus liquid head). Boiling proceeds with explosive violence, resulting in the expulsion of as much as half of the tank contents, a sudden spread of burning oil over a wide area, and an overhead fireball. This is a boil-over and is the reason for the restrictions given in 2-2.1.4 and Table 2-3. Figure 2-1 illustrates what leads to a boil-over. (See also Appendix B of API 2021, *Guide for Fighting Fires In and Around Petroleum Storage Tanks*.)

Emergency Venting Devices. Emergency venting is covered in 2-2.5, but is nowhere defined in the *Code*. The word "emergency" means something unusual or beyond the conditions of normal operation, such as the exposure of a tank to surrounding fire. All of the tanks subject to the requirements of this *Code* contain a liquid that can burn. Fires seldom originate in tanks, and when they do, the fire normally burns itself out without serious consequences. The emergency arises when liquid spilled from a tank or its supporting pipeline is ignited, producing what is commonly known as a "ground fire" or "spill fire." Tank contents exposed to such a fire are subject to boiling and evolution of vapor far in excess of what

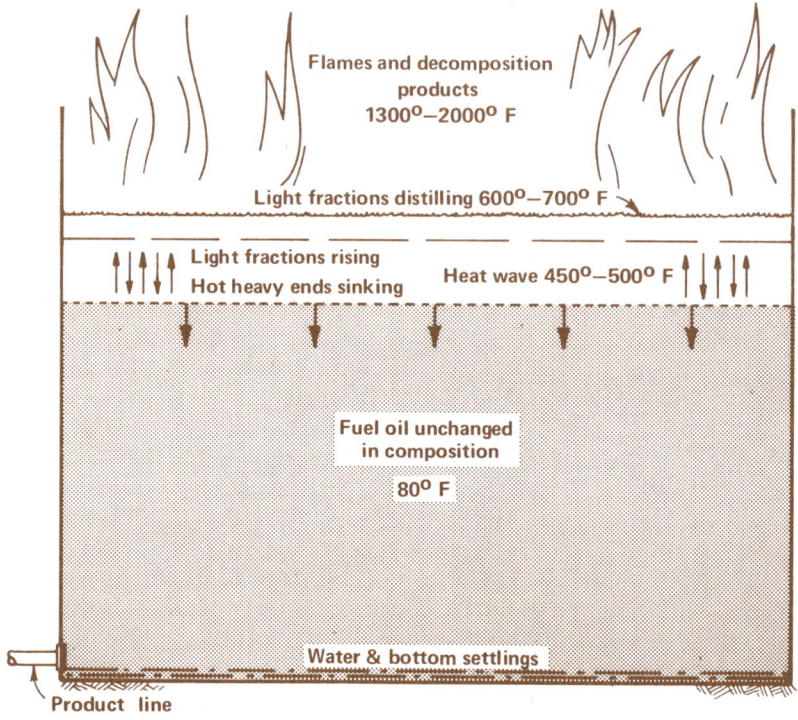

Figure 2-1   Boil-over process in a fuel oil tank fire.

might be produced by normal operation. (*See 2-2.4.*) Emergency relief venting as described in 2-2.5 is required to accommodate this excess vapor development. A weak roof-to-shell seam is one acceptable mechanism. This is also discussed following 2-1.4.3, in the comment concerning tanks built to UL requirements. The objective of this type of construction is to ensure that a vertical tank will fail in such a way that no liquid will escape. (*See also 2-2.5.3 and its following commentary.*)

Unstable Liquids. Unstable liquids are defined in Section 1-2 (under "Liquid") and examples are given in the commentary that follows the definition. Their unpredictable characteristics require special spacing (*see 2-2.1.5 and Table 2-4*).

Operating Pressures. The wording of 2-2.1.1 provides that Table 2-1 will apply to tanks with operating pressures up to 2.5 psig (17.2 kPa), provided they are equipped with emergency venting of sufficient capacity to prevent pressures rising above this point. Tanks with operating pressures in excess of 2.5 psig (17.2 kPa) are covered by Table 2-2. The reason for the substantially increased spacing requirements of Table 2-2 is that a tank at higher pressure

NFPA 30—TANK STORAGE

is more likely to fail violently. A further restriction in the placement of these tanks is given in 2-2.1.8.

(a) For the purpose of Section 2-2, a floating roof tank is defined as one that incorporates either:

1. A pontoon or double-deck metal floating roof in an open-top tank in accordance with API Standard 650, or

2. A fixed metal roof with ventilation at the top and roof eaves in accordance with API Standard 650, and containing a metal floating roof or cover meeting any one of the following requirements:

   a. A pontoon or double-deck metal floating roof meeting the requirements of API Standard 650.

   b. A metal floating cover supported by liquidtight metal floating devices that provide sufficient buoyancy to prevent the liquid surface from being exposed when half of the flotation is lost.

Experience has shown that tanks having floating roofs, as described in 2-2.1.1(a), are not likely to be involved in serious fires. Most fires in such tanks have burned only at the seal and are usually easily extinguished. If the tank is of the open-top type, hand-held extinguishing equipment may prove adequate. In cases where a floating roof has sunk, resulting in an open-top tank fire, boil-over has apparently only occurred once, at the Trieste, Italy, Pipeline Terminal in the early 1970s. In this incident, two 500-ft (153-m) diameter crude oil tanks were set afire by explosive charges set by a terrorist group. The floating roofs sunk and boil-over occurred about 12 hours later. In most such cases, it is thought that the sunken roof will present a barrier to the downward progress of the hot oil layer, thus preventing a boil-over. It is for these reasons that floating roof tanks are given preferred treatment in Table 2-3. For a further discussion of floating roofs, see Table 2-1.

With this edition of the *Code*, this subparagraph now recognizes flotation devices other than pontoons or floats—honeycomb panels, for example. Also, the requirement is somewhat stricter in that the cover may not tip in any manner that results in exposure of the liquid surface. The previous edition of the *Code* only required that the pan or cover not sink completely. It is now recognized that a cover that tips and exposes any liquid presents as great a degree of fire risk as one that sinks and exposes the entire surface of the liquid.

(b) An internal metal floating pan, roof, or cover that does not meet the requirements of (a) 2., or one that uses plastic foam (except for seals) for flotation, even if encapsulated in metal or fiberglass, shall be considered a fixed roof tank.

Such construction is considered to be equivalent to a fixed roof tank because metal pan roofs are prone to sinking and because foamed plastic and similar floation devices will not withstand the conditions imposed by a fire.

2-2.1.2 Vertical tanks having a weak roof-to-shell seam (*see 2-2.5.3*) and storing Class IIIA liquids may be located at one-half the distances specified in Table 2-1, provided the tanks are not within a diked area or drainage path for a tank storing a Class I or Class II liquid.

The relaxation of the spacing requirements in Table 2-1 recognizes that Class IIIA liquids cannot produce a flammable mixture in the vapor space at ordinary temperatures, coupled with the fact that a well-maintained tank with a weak roof-to-shell seam, in the absence of mechanical damage or an extremely violent earthquake, will not fail in such a way as to spill its contents.

2-2.1.3 Every aboveground tank for the storage of Class I, Class II, or Class IIIA liquids, except those liquids with boil-over characteristics and unstable liquids, operating at pressures exceeding 2.5 psig (17.2 kPa) or equipped with emergency venting that will permit pressures to exceed 2.5 psig (17.2 kPa), shall be located in accordance with Table 2-2.

2-2.1.4 Every aboveground tank for storage of liquids with boil-over characteristics shall be located in accordance with Table 2-3. Liquids with boil-over characteristics shall not be stored in fixed roof tanks larger than 150 ft (45.7 m) in diameter, unless an approved inerting system is provided on the tank.

Liquids having boil-over characteristics are permitted in fixed roof tanks larger than 150 ft (45 m) in diameter only if provided with an approved inerting system. The inerting system will not prevent a boil-over, but will greatly reduce the likelihood of ignition by preventing an ignitible mixture from being formed in the vapor space of the tank during all phases of its operation. NFPA 69, *Standard on Explosion Prevention Systems*, defines inerting as "the technique by which a combustible mixture is rendered nonignitible by addition of an inert gas."

The process of inerting an enclosed or nearly enclosed vessel requires that the oxygen concentration in the vapor space be kept low enough (usually below 11 or 12 percent) that combustion cannot be initiated. This requires addition of inert gas at specific flow rates that depend on the maximum oxygen concentration allowed for the tank contents and the size of the tank. (Maximum oxygen concentrations may be found in NFPA 69, *Standard on Explosion Prevention Systems*.) A suitable inert gas does not have to be truly chemically inert, only incapable of supporting combustion, nonreactive with the tank contents, and compatible with tank construction materials. Nitrogen, carbon dioxide, and flue or stack gas containing less than 10% oxygen are commonly used. Helium and argon are quite effective, but usually too expensive, except for special applications. Steam is seldom used because it requires that the protected system be continuously heated above 160°F (71°C), and this is usually not practical. An inerting system requires a continuously dependable source of inert gas and a complex control system. Such systems must meet all applicable requirements of **NFPA 69**, *Standard on Explosion Prevention Systems*, and should be designed, installed, tested, and maintained only by qualified personnel.

It should be noted that in producing fields and in some refinery operations, fuel gas is sometimes used to inert tanks that contain liquids that do not have boil-over characteristics.

2-2.1.5 Every aboveground tank for the storage of unstable liquids shall be located in accordance with Table 2-4.

An "unstable liquid," as defined in Section 1-2, is one that can undergo violent decomposition or reaction. Because these tanks are unable to contain the violent reaction caused by heating under fire conditions, greater spacing for these tanks than for tanks storing stable liquids is mandated. Tanks storing unstable liquids have the most stringent spacing requirements from property that can be built upon. (*See Figure 2-2.*)

2-2.1.6 Every aboveground tank for the storage of Class IIIB liquids, excluding unstable liquids, shall be located in accordance with Table 2-5, except when located within a diked area or drainage path for a tank(s) storing a Class I or Class II liquid. When a Class IIIB liquid storage tank is within the diked area or drainage path for a Class I or Class II liquid, 2-2.1.1 or 2-2.1.2 shall apply.

Class IIIB liquids are considered to be almost immune from accidental fire because of their high flash points and extremely low vapor pressures. Thus, required distances from tanks to property lines are minimal. However, if a tank containing a Class IIIB liquid is situated in the drainage path of a Class I or II liquid (e.g., in the same diked area), then this tank will be exposed by a spill fire.

Table 2-1 is based on the location restrictions given in the preceding paragraphs. It is more readily understood by first considering the headings of the four vertical columns, noting that as one progresses downward in the table, the required spacing becomes progressively greater.

Table 2-1 Stable Liquids (Operating Pressure 2.5 psig or Less) (17.2 kPa)

Type of Tank	Protection	Minimum Distance in Feet from Property Line Which Is or Can Be Built Upon, Including the Opposite Side of a Public Way and Shall Be Not Less Than 5 Feet	Minimum Distance in Feet from Nearest Side of Any Public Way or from Nearest Important Building on the Same Property and Shall Be Not Less Than 5 Feet
Floating Roof [See 2-2.1.1(a)]	Protection for Exposures*	½ times diameter of tank	⅙ times diameter of tank
	None	Diameter of tank but need not exceed 175 feet	⅙ times diameter of tank
Vertical with Weak Roof-to-Shell Seam (See 2-2.5.3)	Approved foam or inerting system** on tanks not exceeding 150 feet in diameter***	½ times diameter of tank	⅙ times diameter of tank
	Protection for Exposures*	Diameter of tank	⅓ times diameter of tank
	None	2 times diameter of tank but need not exceed 350 feet	⅓ times diameter of tank
Horizontal and Vertical with Emergency Relief Venting to Limit Pressures to 2.5 psig	Approved inerting system** on the tank or approved foam system on vertical tanks	½ times Table 2-6	½ times Table 2-6
	Protection for Exposures*	Table 2-6	Table 2-6
	None	2 times Table 2-6	Table 2-6

*See definition for "Protection for Exposures."
**See NFPA 69, *Standard for Explosion Prevention Systems*.
***For tanks over 150 ft in diameter, use "Protection for Exposures" or "None," as applicable.
SI Units: 1 ft = 0.30 m.

Figure 2-2 Not all property can be built upon—for example, waterways, steep bluffs, railroad right-of-ways, and public streets and highways. This may have an effect on the location of tanks. It is possible that they could be located closer to property lines that cannot be built upon, as long as necessary precautions are taken to protect the public in areas beyond the property line.

Type of Tank

Floating Roof. The first category consists of tanks having floating roofs. Experience has shown that open-top tanks with floating roofs are not likely to have the total liquid surface involved in fire because the only place where an ignitible mixture exists is in the narrow space above the liquid surface, within the seal space between the floating roof and the tank shell.

Such tanks are unlikely to be ignited by flaming brands because such brands rarely fall close to the seal space. A floating roof tank is unlikely to be ignited by a direct lightning strike unless the roof is almost at the top of the tank. As first designed, floating roof tanks were occasionally ignited by an electrical charge on the roof surface that was released coincident with a lightning strike. This charge could escape from the roof to the shell, producing a spark in the seal space and igniting a small fire around the rim of the roof. Corrective measures involved placing metallic conductors (shunts) between the rim of the floating roof and the metallic parts of the seal that bear against the tank shell. Such measures have been largely effective. In any event, a fire in the seal space of a floating roof tank can often be extinguished by hand extinguishers or small hose lines. Of importance is the fact that if a floating roof sinks, it will probably interfere with the thermal circulation of the oil and obstruct development of a boil-over.

For all of the preceding reasons, a vertical steel tank with a floating roof is given preferred treatment from the standpoint of exposing surrounding property to fire. This applies even if the floating roof is covered with a fixed roof having adequate ventilation.

Note that a floating roof having a metal pan or combustible flotation components {2-2.1.1(b)}, which are subject to destruction from a seal fire, is considered no better than a fixed roof tank and is treated as such.

Fixed Roof. The next two categories involve fixed roof tanks, defined here as any tank with a metallic roof other than a covered floating roof tank. The difference between the two categories lies in their manner of handling emergency venting requirements.

The second category listed in column 1 of Table 2-1 covers vertical tanks with fixed roofs having weak roof-to-shell seams. These are assigned a slightly greater spacing requirement. Many large vertical tanks have an inherently weak roof attachment. Other tanks have this feature incorporated in them by design. (*See Figure 2-3.*)

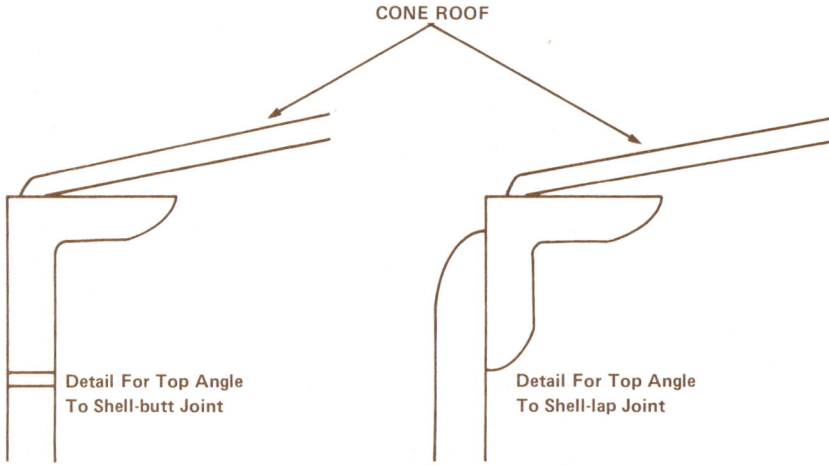

Figure 2-3 In a fire emergency, the design of a weak roof-to-shell seam allows the roof to tear free from the shell prior to the failure of any other seam. This type of construction is acceptable for relieving excessive internal pressure caused by exposure fires.

NFPA 30—TANK STORAGE

The third category includes both horizontal and vertical tanks with emergency relief devices (other than a weak roof-to-shell attachment) capable of limiting the tank pressure to 2.5 psig (17.2 kPa) under fire exposure conditions. In spite of adequate pressure relief, these tanks are not immune to failure if unwet portions of the shell are weakened by flame contact. Therefore, greater spacing requirements are assigned. Tanks that can be subjected to pressures greater than 2.5 psig (17.2 kPa) under fire exposure conditions are covered by Table 2-2.

Tanks without any form of roof are not recognized in the *Code*.

Protection

In all three tank categories, distinction is made between presence or absence of exposure protection.

Protection for exposures is defined in Section 1-2. The intent is that, if fire should occur in the tank, there will be some fire fighting capability available to prevent the ignition of adjacent property. It is assumed that the fire in the tank can safely burn out and that no attempt will be made to extinguish it.

For the second tank category, additional credit is given for tanks equipped with an inerting system or a foam extinguishing system. However, for tanks exceeding 150 ft (45 m) in diameter, provision of a foam system is not given any credit because of the problem of pumping foam onto the fuel surface at a rate fast enough to be effective.

The third category is identical, except that the 150 ft (45 m) diameter limitation for foam systems no longer applies.

Minimum Distance to Property Lines

These two columns deal with slightly different situations. In the first, permanent structures can be built adjacent to a property line. In the second, intervening space is assured because of a public right-of-way, easement, railroad right-of-way, etc. In no case can a tank be placed less than 5 ft (1.5 m) from a property line. Spacing is prescribed as a function of tank diameter and tank construction and assumes that the effects of a fire may spread beyond the limits of the owner's property. The recognition of the type of liquid stored is covered in Sections 2-2, 2-3, and 2-4.

All of the preceding spacings have been carefully developed through fire experience over the seventy or more years since the

Code was first conceived. Spacing distances to adjoining property, and also between tanks (Table 2-7), have occasionally been decreased over the years as the mechanism of fire spread has become better understood through experiment and experience.

The increased spacing in Table 2-2 for all types of tanks and all conditions is required because a tank operating at a pressure greater than 2.5 psig can create a more sudden and violent incident upon release of vapor than one operating at a lower pressure. Such an incident might include the failure of a tank by sudden tearing of the roof or shell, as a result of heating and softening of the metal from direct flame contact.

Table 2-3 considers the phenomenon of a "boil-over," which was discussed following paragraph 2-2.1.1.

Boiling results when heat is transmitted to the contents of a tank by the flame-exposed shell. The tank is usually intact and may not be involved in fire, other than vapor burning at the vent. If the tank has a weak roof-to-shell connection or is adequately vented, no liquid spill is likely. The fire can burn out without serious incident.

By contrast, a *boil-over* results from fire in an open-top tank, not from surrounding fire on the ground. A tank having a fixed roof will not burn over the total surface area of the liquid unless the roof has been removed, as by explosion. However, a fixed roof tank with an internal floating roof may experience partial burning of the contents as evidenced by burning at the vents. If the roof has been removed and the tank contains an oil having boil-over characteristics, one or more boil-overs will likely occur. The increased spacing required by Table 2-3 reflects the need for safeguarding adjoining structures against this situation.

Table 2-4 applies to tanks containing unstable liquids (as defined in Section 1-2) that perform unpredictably during fire exposure. For this reason, greater spacings are required.

In Table 2-5, spacing requirements for tanks storing Class IIIB liquids are minimal because such tanks are rarely involved in fire.

2-2.1.7 Where two tank properties of diverse ownership have a common boundary, the authority having jurisdiction may, with the written consent of the owners of the two properties, substitute the distances provided in 2-2.2.1 through 2-2.2.6 for the minimum distances set forth in 2-2.1.

This simply says that, where owners agree, each may accept the risk from any of the tanks on the others' property to the same extent that he accepts the risks from his own.

Table 2-2 Stable Liquids (Operating Pressure Greater Than 2.5 psig) (17.2 kPa)

Type of Tank	Protection	Minimum Distance in Feet from Property Line Which Is or Can Be Built Upon, Including the Opposite Side of a Public Way	Minimum Distance in Feet from Nearest Side of Any Public Way or from Nearest Important Building on the Same Property
Any Type	Protection for Exposures*	1½ times Table 2-6 but shall not be less than 25 feet	1½ times Table 2-6 but shall not be less than 25 feet
	None	3 times Table 2-6 but shall not be less than 50 feet	1½ times Table 2-6 but shall not be less than 25 feet

*See definition for "Protection for Exposures."
SI Units: 1 ft = 0.30 m.

Table 2-3 Boil-over Liquids

Type of Tank	Protection	Minimum Distance in Feet from Property Line Which Is or Can Be Built Upon, Including the Opposite Side of a Public Way and Shall Be Not Less Than 5 Feet	Minimum Distance in Feet from Nearest Side of Any Public Way or from Nearest Important Building on the Same Property and Shall Be Not Less Than 5 Feet
Floating Roof [See 2-2.1.1(a)]	Protection for Exposures*	½ times diameter of tank	⅙ times diameter of tank
	Approved foam or inerting system**	Diameter of tank	⅙ times diameter of tank
Fixed Roof [See 2-2.1.4(a)]	Protection for Exposures*	Diameter of tank	⅓ times diameter of tank
	None	4 times diameter of tank but need not exceed 350 feet	⅔ times diameter of tank
		2 times diameter of tank	⅔ times diameter of tank

*See definition for "Protection for Exposures."
**See NFPA 69, *Standard for Explosion Prevention Systems.*
SI Units: 1 ft = 0.30 m.

Table 2-4 Unstable Liquids

Type of Tank	Protection	Minimum Distance in Feet from Property Line Which Is or Can Be Built Upon, Including the Opposite Side of a Public Way	Minimum Distance in Feet from Nearest Side of Any Public Way or from Nearest Important Building on the Same Property
Horizontal and Vertical Tanks with Emergency Relief Venting to Permit Pressure Not in Excess of 2.5 psig	Tank protected with any one of the following: Approved water spray, Approved inerting,* Approved insulation and refrigeration, Approved barricade	Table 2-6 but not less than 25 feet	Not less than 25 feet
	Protection for Exposures**	2½ times Table 2-6 but not less than 50 feet	Not less than 50 feet
	None	5 times Table 2-6 but not less than 100 feet	Not less than 100 feet
Horizontal and Vertical Tanks with Emergency Relief Venting to Permit Pressure Over 2.5 psig	Tank protected with any one of the following: Approved water spray, Approved inerting,* Approved insulation and refrigeration, Approved barricade	2 times Table 2-6 but not less than 50 feet	Not less than 50 feet
	Protection for Exposures**	4 times Table 2-6 but not less than 100 feet	Not less than 100 feet
	None	8 times Table 2-6 but not less than 150 feet	Not less than 150 feet

* See NFPA 69, *Standard for Explosion Prevention Systems*.
** See definition for "Protection for Exposures."
SI Units: 1 ft = 0.30 m.

Table 2-5 Class IIIB Liquids

Capacity Gallons	Minimum Distance in Feet from Property Line Which Is or Can Be Built Upon, Including the Opposite Side of a Public Way	Minimum Distance in Feet from Nearest Side of Any Public Way or from Nearest Important Building on the Same Property
12,000 or less	5	5
12,001 to 30,000	10	5
30,001 to 50,000	10	10
50,001 to 100,000	15	10
100,001 or more	15	15

SI Units: 1 ft = 0.30 m; 1 gal = 3.8 L.

2-2.1.8 Where end failure of horizontal pressure tanks and vessels can expose property, the tank shall be placed with the longitudinal axis parallel to the nearest important exposure.

This requirement is based on the fact that a horizontal pressure tank exposed to fire is likely to travel (rocket) axially upon failure. Application of this rule involves the difficult decision as to which structure constitutes the nearest important risk. An office building on the same property or any occupied buildings on adjoining property would be considered "important exposures." A tank containing flammable liquids might also be so considered. A normally unoccupied storage shed would likely not.

Table 2-6
Reference Table for Use in Tables 2-1 to 2-4

Capacity Tank Gallons	Minimum Distance in Feet from Property Line Which Is or Can Be Built Upon, Including the Opposite Side of a Public Way	Minimum Distance in Feet from Nearest Side of Any Public Way or from Nearest Important Building on the Same Property
275 or less	5	5
276 to 750	10	5
751 to 12,000	15	5
12,001 to 30,000	20	5
30,001 to 50,000	30	10
50,001 to 100,000	50	15
100,001 to 500,000	80	25
500,001 to 1,000,000	100	35
1,000,001 to 2,000,000	135	45
2,000,001 to 3,000,000	165	55
3,000,001 or more	175	60

SI Units: 1 ft = 0.30 m; 1 gal = 3.8 L.

50 FLAMMABLE AND COMBUSTIBLE LIQUIDS CODE HANDBOOK

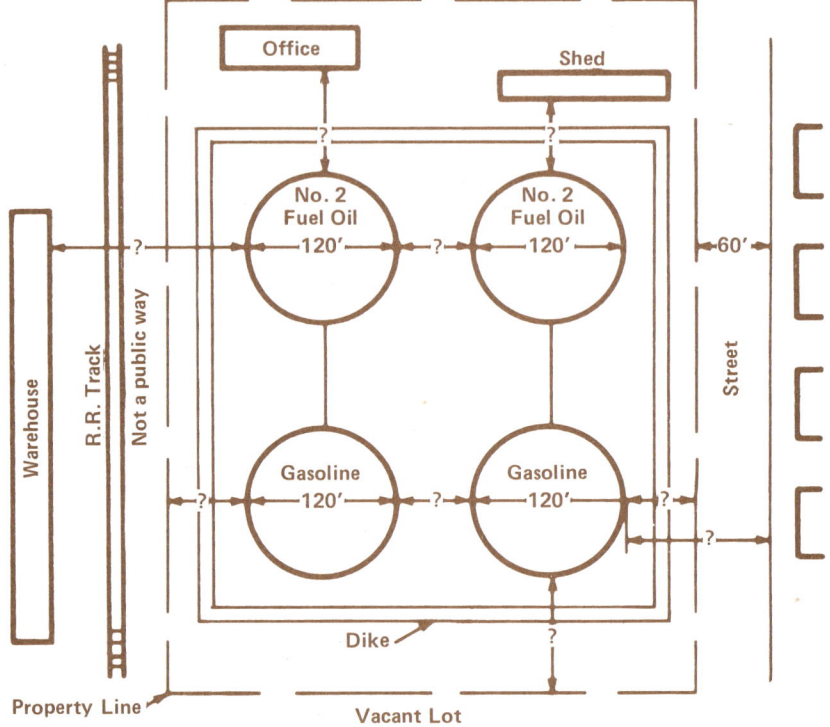

PROTECTION FOR EXPOSURES

SI Units: 1 ft = 0.30 m.

Figure 2-4 Example No. 1: DETERMINING REQUIRED DISTANCES. Assume that you have the responsibility for approving plans to place four additional tanks in a bulk plant. Two tanks will store No. 2 fuel oil and two will store gasoline. Your job is to ensure that the spacing requirements of NFPA 30, *Flammable and Combustible Liquids Code*, are followed. Assume that there is protection for exposures. All four tanks will be vertical tanks built to API 650 specifications, 120 ft (36 m) in diameter, and will have weak roof-to-shell seams. You must determine the required distance from:

1. The gasoline tanks to the vacant lot.
2. The tanks to the near side of the street.
3. The tanks to the opposite side of the street. How does this affect the distance from the tank to the near side of the street in the preceding item? What options do you have to remedy the situation?
4. The fuel oil tank to the shed.
5. The fuel oil tank to the office building.
6. The tanks to the warehouse on the opposite side of the railroad tracks.
7. The tanks to the property line abutting the railroad right-of-way.
8. One tank to another; i.e., shell-to-shell spacing.

Solutions:

1. Table 2-1 indicates that, for a vertical tank with protection for exposures and with weak roof-to-shell seams, the distance to a property line that is or can be built upon should be the diameter of the tank. The distance, then, should be 120 ft (36 m).

2. Table 2-1 indicates a distance of ⅓ the diameter of the tank from the near side of the street. In this case, that would mean 40 ft (12 m).
3. The distance to the opposite side of the street should be the diameter of the tank, or 120 ft (36 m). However, since the street is 60 ft (18 m) wide and the distance to the near side (in item 2) is just 40 ft (12 m), the plans must be altered in some way. There are a few options. If land availability is favorable, the tanks could be moved; the tanks could be decreased in diameter, to 90 ft (27 m), for example; an approved foam system could be installed that would then lessen the distance requirement to ½ of the diameter, or 60 ft (18 m); finally, one might change the design of the tank to incorporate a floating roof, which would decrease the distance requirement to ½ of the tank diameter.
4. Given no additional pertinent information, one can assume that the shed constitutes an unimportant building on the company's premises. Therefore, there is no specified distance requirement. Naturally, the shed cannot be located within the diked area, so some minimum distance is actually provided, depending on the site layout.
5. The office building must be considered an important structure on the same property, since it is an occupied building. Table 2-1 advises ⅓ of the tank diameter as a reasonable safe distance, therefore 40 ft (12 m) is the answer.
6. The warehouse constitutes a property line. Table 2-1 requires the separating distance to be the tank diameter, in this case 120 ft (36 m).
7. A railroad is not considered a public way. Therefore, Table 2-1 does not recommend any specific distance. In other words, there is no requirement for separation in the case of railroads.
8. Table 2-7 must be consulted to determine shell-to-shell spacing requirements. Since these tanks are less than 150 ft (45 m) in diameter, have fixed roofs, and are storing Class I and Class II liquids, the requirement calls for ⅙ of the sum of adjacent tank diameters. One-sixth of 240 (120 + 120) indicates a 40-ft (12-m) separation between adjacent tanks. Note that the adjacent tank distances are determined on a "one-to-one" basis. The word "adjacent" as used in the *Code* does not mean all four tanks in the diagram, but rather a single tank adjacent to its nearest neighbor.

2-2.2 Spacing (Shell-to-Shell) between Any Two Adjacent Aboveground Tanks.

2-2.2.1 Tanks storing Class I, II, or IIIA stable liquids shall be separated in accordance with Table 2-7, except as provided in 2-2.2.2.

A minimum spacing between tanks storing stable liquids is given in Table 2-7. The 3 ft (0.90 m) minimum is based on the need for access for maintenance and painting and for application of cooling streams. Spacing for larger tanks is an arbitrary fraction of tank diameter, adequate to permit an orderly and safe arrangement for pipelines and to prevent spread of fire from one tank to another. Spacing alone is not a safeguard against fire spread from spilled liquid, control of which is covered in 2-2.3. Exceptions to the preceding follow. (For problem-solving situations concerning spacing requirements, see Figures 2-4, 2-5, and 2-6.)

52 FLAMMABLE AND COMBUSTIBLE LIQUIDS CODE HANDBOOK

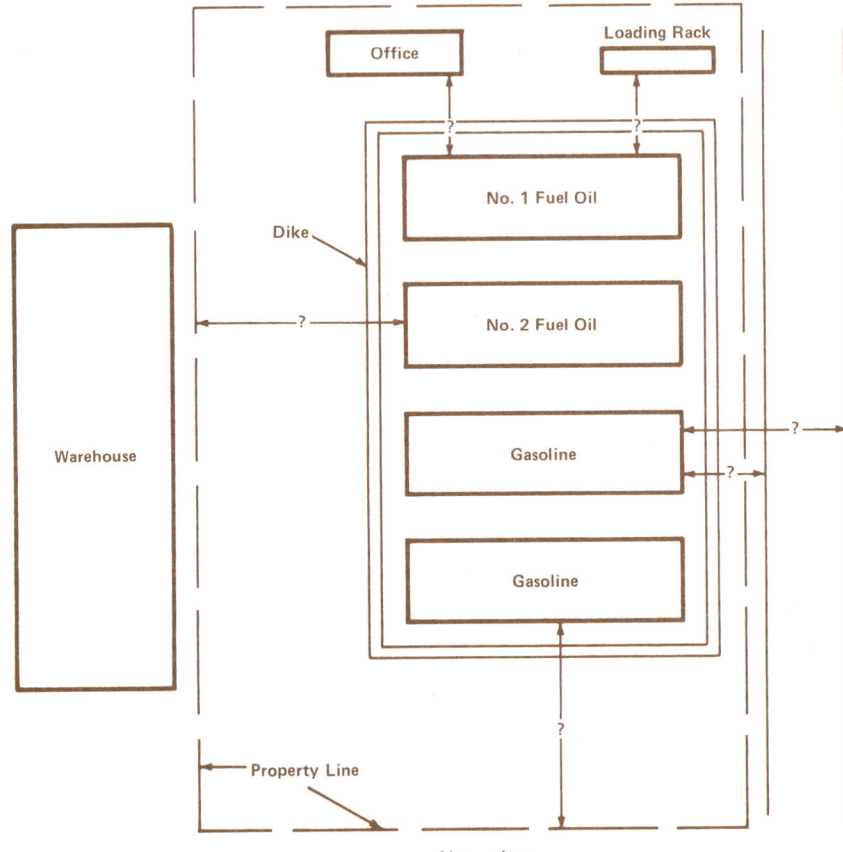

ALL TANKS — 20,000 GALLONS CAPACITY
PROTECTION FOR EXPOSURES

SI Units: 1 gal = 3.8 L.

Figure 2-5 Example No. 2: DETERMINING REQUIRED DISTANCES. Assume you are a County Fire Inspector responsible for inspecting the small bulk plant illustrated in this figure. All four tanks are horizontal, equipped with emergency relief venting to limit pressures to 2.5 psig (17.2 kPa). There is protection for exposures. Each of the tanks has a capacity of 20,000 gal (75 700 L). In order to verify compliance with NFPA 30, *Flammable and Combustible Liquids Code*, you must determine the minimum distances required from:

1. The gasoline tank to the property line adjoining the vacant lot.
2. The gasoline tanks to the near side and opposite side of the street.
3. The tank storing No. 1 fuel oil to the loading rack.
4. The tank storing No. 1 fuel oil to the office building.
5. The tank storing No. 2 fuel oil to the property line on which the warehouse is built.

Solutions:
1. Table 2-1 refers the *Code* user to Table 2-6 for this situation. Table 2-6 indicates that the distance to the property line must be 20 ft (6 m).

2. Table 2-6 indicates 5 ft (1.5 m) from the nearest side of any public way and 20 ft (6 m) from the opposite side of the public way.

3. The loading rack is certainly an important structure on the same property and the distance indicated by Table 2-6 prescribes a minimum of 5 ft (1.5 m). However, another paragraph of the *Code*, 5-4.4.1.1, gives specific distances for loading racks, namely 15 ft (4.6 m) for Class II and III liquids and 25 ft (7.6 m) for Class I liquids. Since the loading rack handles Class I and Class II liquids, it should be a distance of 25 ft (7.6 m) from aboveground tanks, warehouses, other plant buildings, or nearest line of adjoining property that can be built upon.

4. Table 2-6 indicates that a 5-ft (1.5-m) distance is required between the tank and the office building.

5. Table 2-6 requires tanks of the indicated capacity to be spaced 20 ft (6 m) from the nearest property line.

NOTE 1: If the preceding set of problems involved tanks on which the emergency venting permitted pressure to exceed 2.5 psig (17.2 kPa), Table 2-2 would have been used. Table 2-2 refers the reader to Table 2-6 and indicates that the distances should be 1½ times those in Table 2-6, but not less than 25 ft (7.6 m).

NOTE 2: If the examples involved an unstable liquid with venting that limited pressures to 2.5 psig (17.2 kPa), Table 2-4 would have required distances 2½ times those in Table 2-6, but not less than 50 ft (15 m).

Application of Table 2-7 to horizontal tanks was initiated in the 1984 edition of the *Code* to address questions raised about required distances between adjacent horizontal tanks. For spacing purposes, it was determined that horizontal tanks should be treated the same as fixed roof tanks.

2-2.2.2 Crude petroleum tanks having individual capacities not exceeding 126,000 gal (3,000 barrels), when located at production facilities in isolated locations, need not be separated by more than 3 ft (0.90 m).

This exception is made because, in a location that does not expose neighboring property, it would be illogical to require large spaces between several tanks where one single tank storing the same quantity of oil would be permissible. Thus, tanks may be placed closer together, resulting in economic piping installation and supervision, without increasing the risk to others.

2-2.2.3 Tanks used only for storing Class IIIB liquids may be spaced no less than 3 ft (0.90 m) apart unless within a diked area or drainage path for a tank storing a Class I or II liquid, in which case the provisions of Table 2-7 apply.

2-2.2.4 For unstable liquids, the distance between such tanks shall not be less than one-half the sum of their diameters.

2-2.2.5 When tanks are in a diked area containing Class I or Class II liquids, or in the drainage path of Class I or Class II liquids, and are compacted in three or more rows or in an irregular pattern, greater spacing or other means may be

54 FLAMMABLE AND COMBUSTIBLE LIQUIDS CODE HANDBOOK

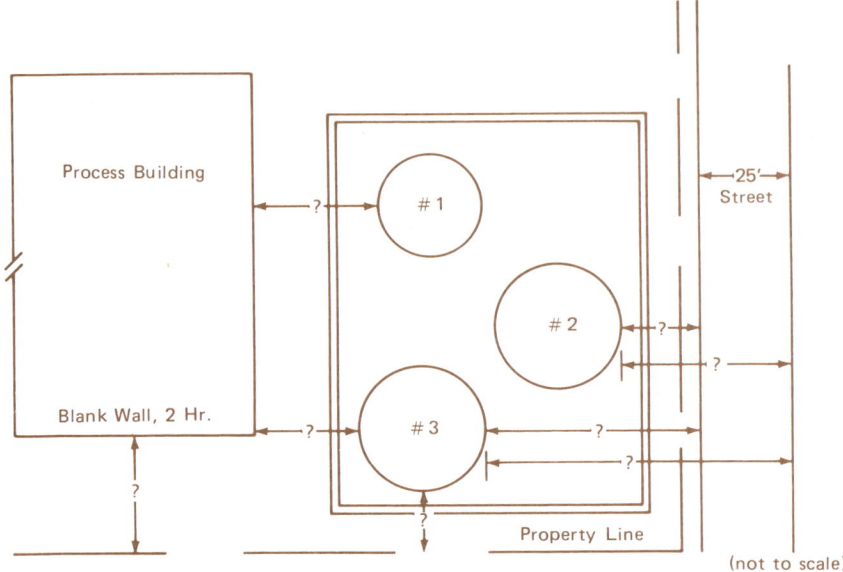

Figure 2-6   Example No. 3: DETERMINING REQUIRED DISTANCES WHERE AN UNSTABLE LIQUID IS INVOLVED. As County Fire Inspector, you must evaluate site plans for the process plant shown in Figure 2-6. You must verify compliance with NFPA 30, *Flammable and Combustible Liquids Code*. Tanks #1 and #2 are vertical fixed roof tanks with weak roof-to-shell seams and are 25 ft in diameter and 30 ft high. They contain, respectively, 100,000 gallons each of toluene and xylene, both stable Class I liquids. Tank #3 is a vertical fixed roof tank with emergency relief venting to permit internal pressure to rise no higher than 2.5 psig (17.2 kPa). This tank is 20 ft in diameter and 30 ft high and contains 70,000 gallons of styrene. Styrene is considered an unstable liquid by this *Code*, so the tank is insulated and is protected with a water spray system. The process building houses process vessels. The wall of this building that faces the adjacent property is a blank, two-hour firewall. You must determine the distances required from:

1. The process building to the property line.
2. Tank #3 to the property line and to the process building.
3. The tanks to the near side of the street.
4. The tanks to the far side of the street.
5. Tank #1 to the process building.
6. One tank to another; i.e., shell-to-shell spacing.

Solutions:

1. Chapter 2 does not provide required separation distances for process vessels. This information must be taken from Chapter 5, "Operations." Minimum separation distances are given in Table 5-3.1.1, but paragraph 5-3.1.2 states that, if the process vessels are housed in a building whose exposing wall is a blank, 2 hr. firewall, then the separation distance need only exceed 25 ft (7.6 m). Any greater distance called for by Table 5-3.1.1 is waived.

Thus, the separation distance from process building to property line is "greater than 25 ft (7.6 m)".

2. The separation distances for unstable liquids are found in Table 2-4, which bases itself, in part, on Table 2-6. For separation distance from the property line, the tables require a 50-ft (15-m) separation. For the required distance from the process building, Table 2-4 sets a 25 ft (7.5 m) minimum.

3 and 4. To determine the required distances between the tanks and the near and far sides of the street, only tanks #2 and #3 need be considered. (Tank #1 is set back farther than tank #2 and contains the same class of liquid.) Referring again to Table 2-4, the required distances between Tank #3 and the near and far sides of the street are 25 ft (7.5 m) and 50 ft (15 m), respectively. Note that if the tank itself is not protected, the required distances increase dramatically—by a factor of 2½, if only exposure protection is provided, and by a factor of 5 if no protection at all.

For Tank #2, Table 2-1 provides the required separation distances. Assuming protection for exposures, this tank must be located one-third the tank diameter from the near side of the street, or 8 ft 4 in. (2.5 m), and one tank diameter from the far side of the street, i.e., 25 ft (7.5 m). Since the street itself is 25 ft (7.5 m) wide and the set-back from the near side is 8 ft 4 in. (2.5 m), an extra margin of safety exists for any property on the opposite side of the street.

5. The distance between Tank #1 and the process building is given in the last column of Table 2-1. This distance is one-third the diameter of the tank, or 8 ft 4 in. (2.5 m).

6. Shell-to-shell spacing is found in Table 2-7. The minimum spacing between Tanks #1 and #2 is one-sixth the sum of the tank diameters: ⅙ (25 + 25) = 8 ft 4 in. (2.5 m). The minimum spacing between Tanks #2 and #3, according to Table 2-7, is slightly less: ⅙ (25 + 20) = 7 ft 6 in. (2.25 m). However, paragraph 2-2.2.4 sets a minimum spacing of one half the sum of the tank diameters where unstable liquids are involved: ½ (45) = 22.5 ft (6.75 m).

required by the authority having jurisdiction to make tanks in the interior of the pattern accessible for fire fighting purposes.

2-2.2.6 The minimum horizontal separation between an LP-Gas container and a Class I, Class II, or Class IIIA liquid storage tank shall be 20 ft (6 m), except in the case of Class I, Class II, or Class IIIA liquid tanks operating at pressures exceeding 2.5 psig (17.2 kPa) or equipped with emergency venting which will permit pressures to exceed 2.5 psig (17.2 kPa), in which case the provisions of 2-2.2.1 and 2-2.2.2 shall apply. Suitable measures shall be taken to prevent the accumulation of Class I, Class II, or Class IIIA liquids under adjacent LP-Gas containers such as by dikes, diversion curbs, or grading. When flammable or combustible liquid storage tanks are within a diked area, the LP-Gas containers shall be outside the diked area and at least 10 ft (3 m) away from the centerline of the wall of the diked area. The foregoing provisions shall not apply when LP-Gas containers of 125 gal (475 L) or less capacity are installed adjacent to fuel oil supply tanks of 660 gal (2498 L) or less capacity. No horizontal separation is required between aboveground LP-Gas containers and underground flammable and combustible liquid tanks installed in accordance with Section 2-3.

Table 2-7 Minimum Tank Spacing (Shell-to-Shell)

		Fixed or Horizontal Tanks	
	Floating Roof Tanks	Class I or II Liquids	Class IIIA Liquids
All tanks not over 150 feet in diameter	1/6 sum of adjacent tank diameters but not less than 3 feet	1/6 sum of adjacent tank diameters but not less than 3 feet	1/6 sum of adjacent tank diameters but not less than 3 feet
Tanks larger than 150 feet in diameter			
If remote impounding is in accordance with 2-2.3.2	1/6 sum of adjacent tank diameters	1/4 sum of adjacent tank diameters	1/6 sum of adjacent tank diameters
If impounding is around tanks in accordance with 2-2.3.3	1/4 sum of adjacent tank diameters	1/3 sum of adjacent tank diameters	1/4 sum of adjacent tank diameters

SI Units: 1 ft = 0.30 m.

2-2.3 Control of Spillage from Aboveground Tanks.

2-2.3.1 Facilities shall be provided so that any accidental discharge of any Class I, II, or IIIA liquids will be prevented from endangering important facilities, and adjoining property, or reaching waterways, as provided for in 2-2.3.2 or 2-2.3.3. Tanks storing Class IIIB liquids do not require special drainage or diking provisions for fire protection purposes.

> The requirements of this paragraph are based on the rationale that release of product from a tank, however caused, must not be permitted to endanger important facilities and adjoining property or to reach any waterways. The principal fear is that such a spill might be ignited and cause extensive spread of fire. Another major concern is environmental pollution that may be more difficult to control. Tanks storing Class IIIB liquids do not require spill control for fire protection purposes alone because of the small chance that ignition could occur, although environmental contamination will likely result whether or not a fire occurs.

2-2.3.2 Remote Impounding. Where protection of adjoining property or waterways is by means of drainage to a remote impounding area, so that impounded liquid will not be held against tanks, such systems shall comply with the following:

(a) A slope of not less than 1 percent away from the tank shall be provided for at least 50 ft (15 m) toward the impounding area.

(b) The impounding area shall have a capacity not less than that of the largest tank that can drain into it.

> A 1 percent slope means a 1 ft (0.3 m) change in elevation per 100 ft (30 m) of horizontal distance. For a 50-ft run, this means a 6-in. (15-cm) drop.

(c) The route of the drainage system shall be so located that, if the liquids in the drainage system are ignited, the fire will not seriously expose tanks or adjoining property.

(d) The confines of the impounding area shall be located so that, when filled to capacity, the liquid level will not be closer than 50 ft (15 m) from any property line that is or can be built upon, or from any tank.

> The concept here is that any spilled liquid will be led, by ditches or other channels, to an impounding area large enough to contain all of the liquid in the largest tank that can drain into it. The impounding area must be so located that, if the spill ignites, the fire will not seriously damage other tanks or adjoining property. A reasonable slope away from the tank is required so that liquid will not come to rest closer than 50 ft (15 m) from the tank or 50 ft

58 FLAMMABLE AND COMBUSTIBLE LIQUIDS CODE HANDBOOK

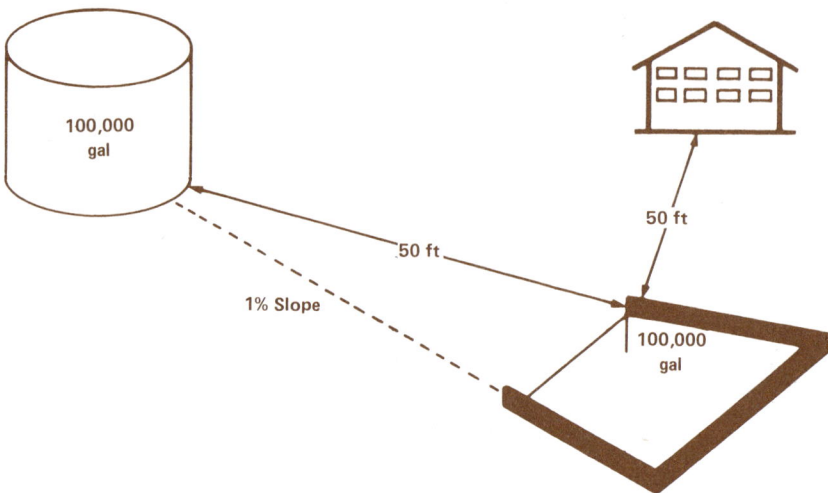

Figure 2-7 The remote impounding area must be large enough to contain all of the liquid from the largest tank that can drain into it. A one percent slope away from the tank generally ensures adequate drainage control.

(15 m) from any property line that can be built upon. In early tank installations (where tanks were often placed on hills to achieve gravity flow), this objective was easily attained. Installations on relatively flat terrain present a much more difficult problem. It is, nonetheless, possible to achieve significant drainage control with a minimum of grading. This is much preferred to the short-cut practice of placing each tank in the center of a flat diked area, where even a minor spill will make it likely that piping and control valves will be inaccessible and subject to fire damage. (*See Figure 2-7.*)

2-2.3.3 Impounding Around Tanks by Diking. When protection of adjoining property or waterways is by means of impounding by diking around the tanks, such system shall comply with the following:

> Diking is less desirable than remote impounding because it may expose the leaking tank or adjacent tanks to a ground spill fire. (*See Figure 2-8.*)

(a) A slope of not less than 1 percent away from the tank shall be provided for at least 50 ft (15 m) or to the dike base, whichever is less.

(b) The volumetric capacity of the diked area shall not be less than the greatest amount of liquid that can be released from the largest tank within the diked area, assuming a full tank. To allow for volume occupied by tanks, the capacity of the diked area enclosing more than one tank shall be calculated after deducting the volume of the tanks, other than the largest tank, below the height of the dike.

NFPA 30—TANK STORAGE   59

Figure 2-8   There have been many fires that have involved all of the tanks in a single diked area.

Application of this provision is best illustrated by problem solving:

What is the maximum volumetric dike capacity necessary for a 150-ft (45-m) diameter tank, 40 ft (12 m) high, within a diked enclosure?

1. Paragraph (b) states that the dike enclosure must be capable of holding the greatest amount of liquid that can be released, assuming a full tank. The formula for the volume of a cylinder is

$$V = \frac{\pi d^2 \times h}{4}$$

where

V = volume of the tank in cu ft
π = 3.14
d = diameter of the tank
h = height of the tank

The solution gives the total volumetric capacity of the tank as 706,500 cu ft (19,782 m^3). Therefore, the dike enclosure must be sufficiently large to contain that amount. The height of the dike wall will depend on the square footage available in the diked area. (*See Figure 2-9.*)

2. Paragraph (b) also states that "the capacity of the diked area enclosing more than one tank shall be calculated after deducting

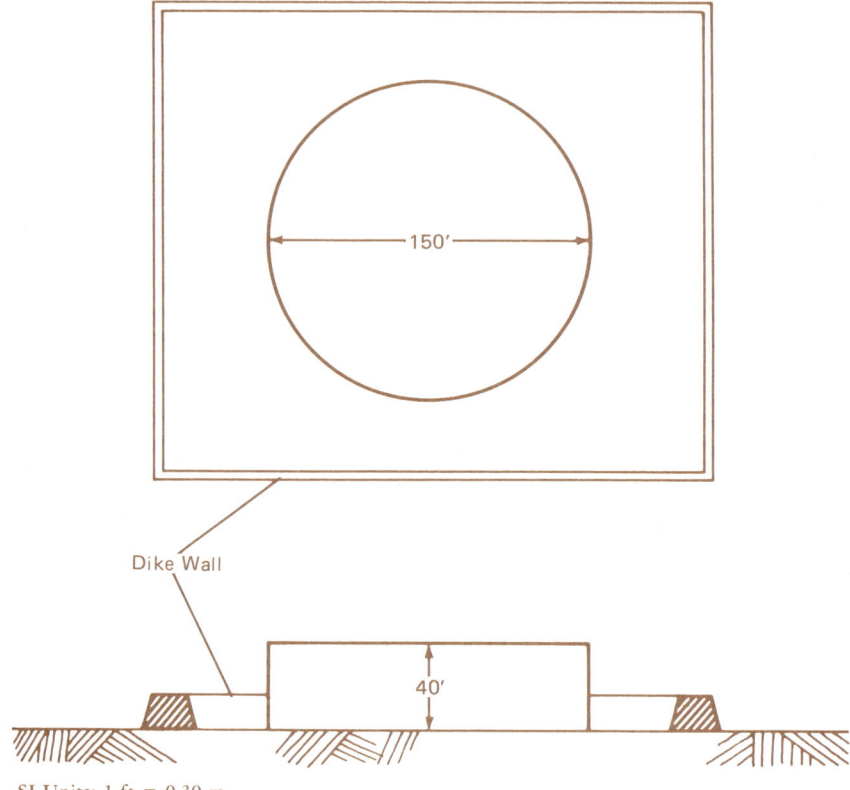

SI Units: 1 ft = 0.30 m.

Figure 2-9 Problem 1.

the volume of the tanks, other than the largest tank, below the height of the dike." The following problem will exemplify the meaning:

There are four tanks in a diked area. The largest is 100 ft (30 m) in diameter and 35 ft (10.5 m) high. Two other tanks are each 50 ft (15 m) in diameter and 20 ft (6 m) high, while the fourth tank is 40 ft (12 m) in diameter and 15 ft (4.5 m) high. The diked area is 70,000 sq ft (6503 m^2) and has a 5 ft (1.5 m) high dike wall. Is the capacity of the dike sufficient for the largest tank?

Begin by determining the total volume of the diked area, which is equal to the area times the height of the dike wall: 70,000 × 5 = 350,000 cu ft (9912 m^3) of capacity. (*See Figure 2-10.*)

We must now deduct the volume occupied by the three smaller tanks from the capacity of the dike enclosure. Keep in mind that they occupy available dike capacity only as high as the dike wall, or

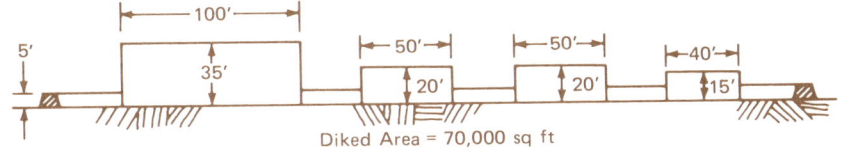

Figure 2-10 Problem 2.

5 ft (1.5 m). The value h in our volume formula, therefore, will be 5 ft (1.5 m).

The total volume of the smaller tanks, up to the 5 ft level, is 25,905 cu ft (734 m³) (9812.5 + 9812.5 + 6280). This volume, subtracted from the overall dike capacity, leaves us 324,095 cu ft (9178 m³) of usable volume within the dike.

We must now determine the volume of the largest tank. Our calculations tell us that the tank has a capacity of 274,750 cu ft (7781 m³). We know, then, that the dike volume is adequate.

(c) To permit access, the outside base of the dike at ground level shall be no closer than 10 ft (3 m) to any property line that is or can be built upon.

This is intended to permit access for fire fighting and to provide additional protection for buildings on adjoining property in the event of a fire in the dike area. (*See Figure 2-11.*)

Figure 2-11 Fire fighters operating within a diked area.

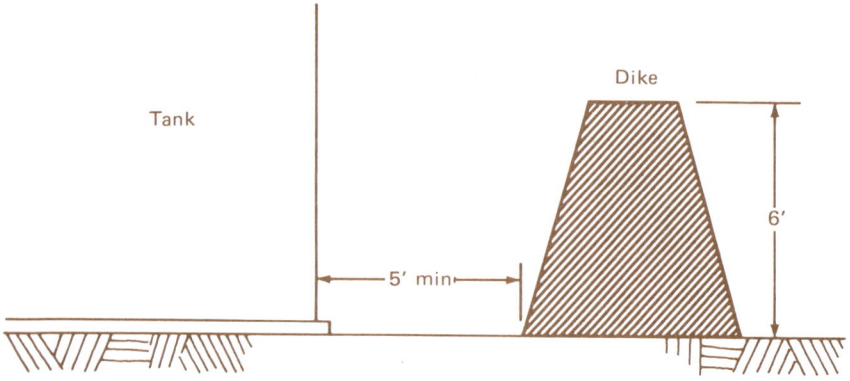

SI Units: 1 ft = 0.30 m.

Figure 2-12 Dike height is generally restricted to 6 ft (1.8 m). Where the dike exceeds this height, the minimum distance between tanks and the toe of the interior of the dike wall must be 5 ft (1.5 m).

(d) Walls of the diked area shall be of earth, steel, concrete, or solid masonry designed to be liquidtight and to withstand a full hydrostatic head. Earthen walls 3 ft (0.90 m) or more in height shall have a flat section at the top not less than 2 ft (0.60 m) wide. The slope of an earthen wall shall be consistent with the angle of repose of the material of which the wall is constructed. Diked areas for tanks containing Class I liquids located in extremely porous soils may require special treatment to prevent seepage of hazardous quantities of liquids to low-lying areas or waterways in case of spills.

Well-compacted clays will resist the permeation of liquid. However, environmental protection regulations may require more substantial treatment, such as an impervious lining.

(e) Except as provided in (f) below, the walls of the diked area shall be restricted to an average interior height of 6 ft (1.8 m) above interior grade.

The reason for limiting the general dike height to 6 ft (1.8 m) is to provide an escape route for fire fighters engaged in combating small fires within the dike. Exceptions to this requirement are allowed, but other precautions are then mandated. (*See Figure 2-12.*)

(f) Dikes may be higher than an average of 6 ft (1.8 m) above interior grade where provisions are made for normal access and necessary emergency access to tanks, valves and other equipment, and safe egress from the diked enclosure.

The reasons for dike heights in excess of 6 ft (1.8 m) involve land costs or land availability in built-up areas and regulations in some jurisdictions requiring individual diking of tanks.

NFPA 30—TANK STORAGE

1. Where the average height of the dike containing Class I liquids is over 12 ft (3.6 m) high, measured from interior grade, or where the distance between any tank and the top inside edge of the dike wall is less than the height of the dike wall, provisions shall be made for normal operation of valves and for access to tank roof(s) without entering below the top of the dike. These provisions may be met through the use of remote-operated valves, elevated walkways, or similar arrangements.

2. Piping passing through dike walls shall be designed to prevent excessive stresses as a result of settlement or fire exposure.

3. The minimum distance between tanks and toe of the interior dike walls shall be 5 ft (1.5 m).

These provisions reflect a concern for Class I vapors reaching unsafe concentrations when confined in the small space between the dike wall and the tank. Remotely operated valves or elevated walkways eliminate the need for personnel to enter the bottom of the diked area to operate a valve.

It should be emphasized that the provisions of 1, 2, and 3 only apply to the high dikes permitted in (f).

(g) Each diked area containing two or more tanks shall be subdivided, preferably by drainage channels or at least by intermediate dikes in order to prevent spills from endangering adjacent tanks within the diked area as follows:

This requirement is designed to control those relatively small spills that, in the past, have resulted in major fire and destruction of all tanks within a dike enclosure. (*See Figure 2-13.*)

1. When storing normally stable liquids in vertical cone roof tanks constructed with weak roof-to-shell seam or floating roof tanks, or when storing crude petroleum in producing areas in any type of tank, one subdivision for each tank in excess of 10,000 bbls. and one subdivision for each group of tanks (no tank exceeding 10,000 bbls. capacity) having an aggregate capacity not exceeding 15,000 bbls.

2. When storing normally stable liquids in tanks not covered in subsection (1), one subdivision for each tank in excess of 2,380 bbls. (378,500 L) and one subdivision for each group of tanks [no tank exceeding 2,380 bbls. (378,500 L) capacity] having an aggregate capacity not exceeding 3,570 bbls. (567,750 L).

3. When storing unstable liquids in any type of tank, one subdivision for each tank except that tanks installed in accordance with the drainage requirements of NFPA 15, *Standard for Water Spray Fixed Systems for Fire Protection*, shall require no additional subdivision. Since unstable liquids will react more rapidly when heated than when at ambient temperatures, subdivision by drainage channels is the preferred method.

64 FLAMMABLE AND COMBUSTIBLE LIQUIDS CODE HANDBOOK

Figure 2-13 These intermediate dikes are required to hold at least 10 percent of the capacity of the tank, not including the volume displaced by the tank, if any tank within the diked area exceeds 150 ft (45 m) in diameter.

4. Whenever two or more tanks storing Class I liquids, any one of which is over 150 ft (45 m) in diameter, are located in a common diked area, intermediate dikes shall be provided between adjacent tanks to hold at least 10 percent of the capacity of the tank so enclosed, not including the volume displaced by the tank.

5. The drainage channels or intermediate dikes shall be located between tanks so as to take full advantage of the available space with due regard for the individual tank capacities. Intermediate dikes, where used, shall be not less than 18 in. (45 cm) in height.

"With due regard for the individual tank capacities" indicates that an intermediate curb should be further removed from the larger of two adjoining different-sized tanks.

(h) Where provision is made for draining water from diked areas, such drains shall be controlled in a manner so as to prevent flammable or combustible liquids from entering natural water courses, public sewers, or public drains, if their presence would constitute a hazard. Control of drainage shall be accessible under fire conditions from outside the dike.

This is because uncontrolled escape from a dike area would defeat the purpose of the dike itself.

(i) Storage of combustible materials, empty or full drums, or barrels, shall not be permitted within the diked area.

NFPA 30—TANK STORAGE 65

2-2.4 Normal Venting for Aboveground Tanks.

This section considers venting only from the fire protection standpoint. Stricter requirements may be imposed by the U.S. Environmental Protection Agency or by local regulations. When such requirements involve the manifolding of vents, reference should be made to 1-1.2. Also, because flame arrestors are not effective in long vent lines, lines may need to be designed to withstand the pressures imposed by compression ignition ("dieseling") and "pressure piling." *Inerting* of the manifolded system or other means may be necessary to avoid hazardous situations. (*See NFPA 69, Standard on Explosion Prevention Systems.*)

2-2.4.1 Atmospheric storage tanks shall be adequately vented to prevent the development of vacuum or pressure sufficient to distort the roof of a cone roof tank or exceeding the design pressure in the case of other atmospheric tanks, as a result of filling or emptying, and atmospheric temperature changes.

The prohibition against distorting the roof of a cone roof tank applies specifically to tanks built in accordance with API Standard 650, *Welded Steel Tanks for Oil Storage*. {*See 2-1.3.1(b)*}. Roof distortion should, by design, cause failure of the weak roof-to-shell type of construction. This should occur only under emergency conditions. (*See Figure 2-14.*)

Figure 2-14 Tanks having inadequate normal venting capacity. Every atmospheric storage tanks must be equipped with normal vents of sufficient size to prevent the development of an internal vacuum or pressure insufficient to distort the roof, or to exceed the design pressure.

The prohibition against exceeding the design pressure applies only to tanks listed in 2-1.4.2(a) and (b) since these are the only tanks built to standards that specify a design pressure and require testing to assure that the specification has been met.

Tanks built according to UL 142, *Standard for Steel Aboveground Tanks for Flammable and Combustible Liquids*, {see 2-1.3.1(a)} are designed for operating pressures between atmospheric and 0.5 psig (3.4 kPa). All UL 142 tanks must pass a leak test using air or water. If the tank is leak-tested using water, the test pressure must be at least 5 psig (34.5 kPa), but not more than 7 psig (48 kPa) for horizontal tanks, and at least 1.5 psig (10 kPa) for vertical tanks. If the tank is leak-tested with water, the tank must first be placed in its installed position. The tank is then filled with water, sealed, and pressurized to 5 psig (34.5 kPa).

In addition to being properly designed to withstand the pressure head produced by the stored liquid, a tank must also be adequately vented to permit filling and emptying.

In order to fill a tank, air and vapor must get out, or the tank will become pressurized. Pushing out this air and vapor requires that the pressure in the tank be slightly above atmospheric pressure. For this reason, tanks are designed to withstand an internal pressure of 8 in. (20 cm) of water gage [⅓ psi (2.3 kPa)].

In order to empty a tank, air must get in or the tank will become underpressurized. To allow air to get in, the pressure in the tank must be slightly below atmospheric pressure. For this reason, tanks are designed to withstand a vacuum of 2.5 in. (6.35 cm) of water gage [¹⁄₁₀ psi (0.689 kPa}.

Consideration of the low pressure for which a tank is designed might lead one to question why more tanks don't fail, even given safety factors of 2 to 1 or higher. Adequate venting is the answer. If the vent is large enough to relieve all of the pressure imposed, and is kept clear at all times, tanks will neither implode nor explode. See Figure 2-15 for a graphic depiction of the above information.

2-2.4.2 Normal vents shall be sized in accordance with either: (1) the American Petroleum Institute Standard No. 2000, *Venting Atmospheric and Low-Pressure Storage Tanks, 1982*, or (2) other accepted standard; or shall be at least as large as the filling or withdrawal connection, whichever is larger, but in no case less than 1¼ in. (3 cm) nominal inside diameter.

Figure 2-16 presents Table I from API 2000-1982, *Thermal Venting Capacity Requirements*. The notes following the table are

NFPA 30—TANK STORAGE　　67

important in explaining the philosophy behind the figures. Consequently, "(2) other accepted standard" is included to cover cases where it is desired to make special calculations to cover special conditions (such as off-gassing when crude oil is delivered from an oil field) or extreme temperature changes (as from night to day) in desert country; the 1¼" diameter minimum is applicable mostly to small tanks that might be filled or emptied rapidly.

2-2.4.3 Low-pressure tanks and pressure vessels shall be adequately vented to prevent development of pressure or vacuum, as a result of filling or emptying and atmospheric temperature changes, from exceeding the design pressure of the tank or vessel. Protection shall also be provided to prevent overpressure from any pump discharging into the tank or vessel when the pump discharge pressure can exceed the design pressure of the tank or vessel.

> For pressures up to of 1 lb (6.89 kPa) or so, pallet-type (weighted check) valves can be used to prevent overpressure. Many of these valves also incorporate vacuum breakers. For tanks built to the specifications of API 620, *Recommended Rules for the Design and Construction of Large, Welded, Low-Pressure Storage Tanks*, a conventional relief valve may be used. In that case, a separate vacuum-breaking device may be needed unless the vapor pressure of the stored product, under all conditions of storage, is high enough to prevent the development of a dangerous vacuum under conditions of maximum possible withdrawal rate. Tanks built to the ASME *Code for Unfired Pressure Vessels* {2-1.4.2(b)}, are often built to withstand full vacuum, so they may not need a vacuum breaker. While an open vent may be adequate to protect the tank from pressure rupture or vacuum collapse, an open vent must not be used if the tank contains a Class I liquid, and should not be used for any liquid heated above its flash point, except as permitted in 2-2.4.6. (*See 1-1.3.*)

2-2.4.4 If any tank or pressure vessel has more than one fill or withdrawal connection and simultaneous filling or withdrawal can be made, the vent size shall be based on the maximum anticipated simultaneous flow.

2-2.4.5 The outlet of all vents and vent drains on tanks equipped with venting to permit pressures exceeding 2.5 psig (17.2 kPa) shall be arranged to discharge in such a way as to prevent localized overheating of, or flame impingement on, any part of the tank, in the event vapors from such vents are ignited.

> This requirement was added many years ago as a result of a fire (one of several similar fires) at the Shamrock Oil Company in the Texas panhandle on July 19, 1956. A spheroid of 15,000 barrel

Figure 2-15 A simple graphic demonstration of atmospheric tank strength.

A STORAGE TANK IS DESIGNED:

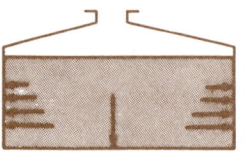

1. TO HOLD LIQUID
Liquid exerts pressure on the sides and base of the tank.
Pressure = head of liquid.

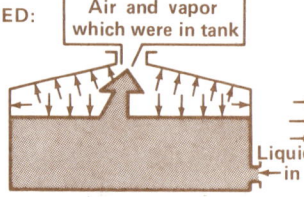

2. TO BE FILLED
For liquid to get in, air and vapor must get out. If they can't, the tank will be pressurized. For air and vapor to be pushed out, the pressure in the tank must be slightly above atmospheric pressure. **The tank is designed for an internal pressure of 8 in. water gage (0.33 psi).**

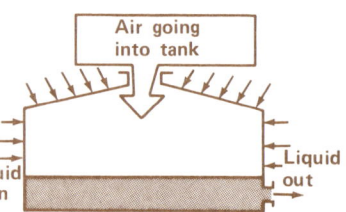

3. TO BE EMPTIED
For liquid to get out, air must get in. If it can't, the tank will be underpressured. For air to be sucked in, the pressure in the tank must be slightly below atmospheric pressure.
The tank is designed for an external pressure (or vacuum in the tank) of 2.5 in. WG. (0.1 psi).

WHAT ARE INCHES WATER GAGE?

2.5 in. WG is the pressure at the bottom of a cup of tea.

8 in. WG is the pressure at the bottom of a pint of beer.

YOU CAN INHALE OR EXHALE ABOUT 24 IN. WATER GAGE.

That means by just using your lungs you could over pressure or underpressure a storage tank. (Because of the volume of air, it would take you a long time).

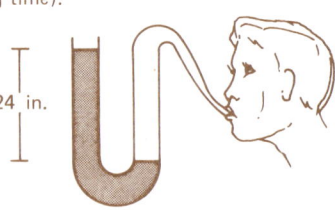

If you don't believe it, because storage tanks always look big and strong, just study the following table.

If a baked bean tin has a strength of 1, then:

	SHELL	ROOF
Baked bean tin (small)	1	1
40 gal drum	$1/2$	$1/3$
50 m^3 tank	$1/3$	$1/8$
100 m^3 tank	$1/4$	$1/11$
500 m^3 tank	$1/6$	$1/33$
1,000 m^3 tank	$1/8$	$1/57$

Next time you eat baked beans, just see how easy it is to push the sides or top in with your fingers — *and then look at the table again.* (Any small tin will do if you don't like baked beans).

Note too: The bigger the tank; the more fragile it is. The roof is weaker than the shell.

Up to 1,000 m^3, the tank shell and roof are only as thick as the line under these words.

NFPA 30—TANK STORAGE 69

IF ALL THAT'S TRUE, IS A STORAGE TANK STRONG ENOUGH?

Yes. A 1,000 m³ tank has factor of safety of 2 against failure (smaller tanks have bigger safety factors) — provided it is operated within the very low pressures allowed.

Most of the pressures we have available are *many times bigger* than the allowable pressures; that is, 8 in. WG inside, 2 ½ in. WG outside.

FOR EXAMPLE:

Full atmospheric pressure outside	= 150 times bigger
Transfer pump head inside	= 120 times bigger
40 psi nitrogen inside	= 120 times bigger
100 psi steam inside	= 300 times bigger

All of these pressures or even a small part of them will cause the tank to

IMPLODE   EXPLODE

   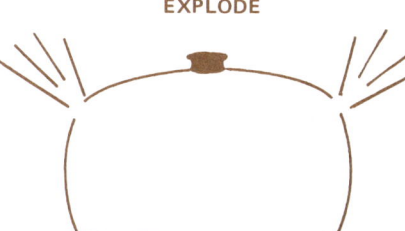

HOW DO WE STOP THIS HAPPENING?

By making sure that:
1. The tank has a vent big enough to relieve all sources of pressure that might be applied to it.
2. The vent is always clear.
3. The vent is never modified without the authorization of the plant or section engineer.

Here are some typical faults in vents which should never happen

Vent blanked off   Vent plugged up   Vent choked by flame arrestor

Adapted with permission from Safety Newsletter No. 115 of the Imperial Chemical Industries, Ltd.

Tank Capacity**		Inbreathing (Vacuum) All Stocks	Outbreathing (Pressure)	
(Barrels)	(Gallons)		Flash Point 100°F (37.8°C) or Above	Flash Point Below 100°F (37.8°C)
1		2	3	4
60	2,500	60	40	60
100	4,200	100	60	100
500	21,000	500	300	500
1,000	42,000	1,000	600	1,000
2,000	84,000	2,000	1,200	2,000
3,000	126,000	3,000	1,800	3,000
4,000	168,000	4,000	2,400	4,000
5,000	210,000	5,000	3,000	5,000
10,000	420,000	10,000	6,000	10,000
15,000	630,000	15,000	9,000	15,000
20,000	840,000	20,000	12,000	20,000
25,000	1,050,000	24,000	15,000	24,000
30,000	---	28,000	17,000	28,000
35,000	---	31,000	19,000	31,000
40,000	---	34,000	21,000	34,000
45,000	---	37,000	23,000	37,000
50,000	---	40,000	24,000	40,000
60,000	---	44,000	27,000	44,000
70,000	---	48,000	29,000	48,000
80,000	---	52,000	31,000	52,000
90,000	---	56,000	34,000	56,000
100,000	---	60,000	36,000	60,000
120,000	---	68,000	41,000	68,000
140,000	---	75,000	45,000	75,000
160,000	---	82,000	50,000	82,000
180,000	---	90,000	54,000	90,000

**Interpolate for intermediate sizes.

NOTES:
1. For tanks with a capacity of more than 20,000 barrels (840,000 gal), the requirements for the vacuum condition are very close to the theoretically computed value of 2 cu ft of air per hr per sq ft of total shell and roof area.
2. For tanks with a capacity of less than 20,000 barrels (840,000 gal), the thermal inbreathing requirements for the vacuum condition has been based on 1 cu ft of free air per hr for each barrel of tank capacity. This is substantially equivalent to a mean rate of vapor space-temperature change of 100°F (37.8°C) per hour.
3. For stocks with a flash point of 100°F (37.8°C) or above, the outbreathing requirement has been assumed at 60 percent of the inbreathing capacity requirement. The tank roof and shell temperatures cannot rise as rapidly under any condition as they can drop, such as during a sudden cold rain.
4. For stocks with a flash point below 100°F (37.8°C), the thermal pressure-venting requirement has been assumed equal to the vacuum requirement in order to allow for vaporization at the liquid surface and for the higher specific gravity of the tank vapors.

*Table I, API Standard 2000, Second Edition, December 1973, "Venting Atmospheric and Low-Pressure Storage Tanks" is reproduced with permission of American Petroleum Institute, 2101 L Street, Northwest, Washington, DC 20037.

Figure 2-16 Table I from API 2000-1982, *Thermal Venting Capacity Requirements* [Expressed in cu ft of free air per hr—14.7 psia at 60°F (15.6°C)].

(630,000 gal) capacity contained about 12,000 barrels of a mixture of pentane [boiling point 97°F (36°C)] and hexane [boiling point 156.2°F (69°C)] having a Reid vapor pressure of 10.2 psia. The spheroid was designed for 15 psig (103.4 kPa), in accordance with API 620, *Recommended Rules for the Design and Construction of Large, Welded, Low-Pressure Storage Tanks*. The spheroid was exposed to a liquid ground fire that was being fought by the plant

Figure 2-17   Shamrock Oil Co., July 19, 1956.

fire brigade with assistance from others. The contents soon reached the boiling point and the vapors coming from the vent caught fire. The vent had a weather hood that directed the flame down onto the top of the tank. Since the tank was not full, the top was not cooled by its contents. The heated tank top lost strength and the tank ruptured. The resulting fireball killed nineteen fire fighters. (*See Figure 2-17.*)

If vents are equipped with outlet pipes that lack weather hoods, rain water or condensate can collect and freeze. Thus, open weep holes are provided to drain off water. Flammable vapors emitted from these holes when the vent operates must be able to burn without heating the top of a tank and pressurizing the tank to more than 2.5 psig (17.2 kPa). Weep holes are often provided with 90° elbows and small lengths of piping so that any vapors emitted can burn safely without impinging on the tank. Failure of a tank top at a pressure less than 2.5 psig (17.2 kPa) will be gradual and will not create a hazardous fireball.

2-2.4.6 Tanks and pressure vessels storing Class IA liquids shall be equipped with venting devices that shall be normally closed except when venting to pressure or vacuum conditions. Tanks and pressure vessels storing Class IB and IC liquids shall be equipped with venting devices that shall be normally closed except when venting under pressure or vacuum conditions, or with listed flame arrestors. Tanks of 3,000 bbls. (476,910 L) capacity or less containing crude petroleum in crude-producing areas, and outside aboveground atmospheric tanks under 23.8 bbls. (3,785 L) capacity containing other than Class IA liquids may have open vents. (*See 2-2.6.2.*)

These requirements are intended to limit the escape of hazardous quantities of flammable vapors in the case of Class IA liquids, which boil below 100°F (37.8°C). In an open tank, such liquids will always be at a temperature below ambient because they are cooled by the loss of heat of vaporization required to produce the vapors needed to fill the vapor space of the tank. When an open vent makes vapor space unlimited, continuous generation of vapors is significant.

In Class IB and Class IC liquids, there is the potential, not present in the Class IA liquids, that the vapor space may be in the flammable range. Therefore, flame arrestors are permitted as an alternate to keeping the vents closed, except when actually venting. Because of their higher boiling points and accompanying lower vapor pressures, the degree of liquid subcooling caused by vaporization, and hence the rate of vaporization, is insignificant from a flammability standpoint.

The exemption for relatively small crude gathering tanks is allowed because such tanks are generally in sparsely populated areas and usually have vapor spaces too rich to burn by reason of release of dissolved gases.

The exemption for tanks under 1,000 gal (3785 L) capacity containing other than Class IA liquids is due to the relatively insignificant rate of vapor release. In addition, the vent location requirement given in 2-2.6.2 makes it highly improbable that a continuous vapor trail in the flammable range will exist between the vapor space of the tank and any exterior source of ignition.

2-2.4.7 Flame arrestors or venting devices required in 2-2.4.6 may be omitted for IB and IC liquids where conditions are such that their use may, in case of obstruction, result in tank damage. Liquid properties justifying the omission of such devices include, but are not limited to, condensation, corrosiveness, crystallization, polymerization, freezing, or plugging. When any of these conditions exist, consideration may be given to heating, use of devices employing special materials of construction, the use of liquid seals, or inerting (*see NFPA 69, Standard on Explosion Prevention Systems*).

An alternate not mentioned here is frequent inspection and periodic removal of the arrestor element for shop cleaning, while replacing the element with a spare. If this procedure is followed, care must be exercised to avoid mechanical damage to the element and to see that it is properly installed.

NFPA 30—TANK STORAGE

Figure 2-18 Failure to provide adequate emergency relief venting can cause tanks to explode violently or rocket great distances.

2-2.5 Emergency Relief Venting for Fire Exposure for Aboveground Tanks.

When exposed to fire, the liquid contents of a tank will be heated and may boil, producing evolution of vapor in excess of that described in 2-2.4.1 for normal operating conditions. (*See Figure 2-18.*) Provisions for safely releasing this vapor are described in the following paragraphs.

2-2.5.1 Except as provided in 2-2.5.2, every aboveground storage tank shall have some form of construction or device that will relieve excessive internal pressure caused by exposure fires.

This section was extensively revised and Appendix A was added to the 1963 edition of the *Code*. The emergency venting section of API 2000, *Venting Atmospheric and Low-Pressure Storage Tanks*, (see 2-2.4.2 where the normal venting requirements are given) was revised in 1966. Now the requirements given here and in API 2000 are identical. Prior to 1963, this *Code* recommended emergency vent sizes based on a heat input of 6,000 Btu/hr/sq ft of tank surface (A) wetted by the contents. Prior to 1966, API Standard 2000 used 21,000 $A^{0.82}$. Experimental work reported from 1942 to 1943 by Duggan, Gilmour, and Fisher suggested use of a figure of 18,000 to 24,000 A, with no exponent. A subcommittee worked to try to find a concensus that would eliminate the conflict. (*See Appendix A.*)

The consensus was reached following a fire in Kansas City, Kansas, on August 18, 1959, during which five fire fighters and one spectator were killed when a 21,000-gal (79,485-L) horizontal tank

Figure 2-19 Five fire fighters and one spectator were killed and 64 fire fighters injured during a bulk plant fire in Kansas City, Kansas, when a horizontal tank failed catastrophically. (*Photo Courtesy of UPI.*)

of gasoline failed and the tank rocketed. (*See Figure 2-19.*) Two brick walls were knocked down by the flying tank which, after traveling 94 ft (28.6 m), landed 15 ft (4.5 m) into the street, where most of the fire fighters were manning hose lines. The tank failed because of internal overpressure and softening of the metal at the end remote from the fire fighters.

2-2.5.2 Tanks larger than 285 bbls. (45,306 L) capacity storing Class IIIB liquids and not within the diked area or the drainage path of Class I or Class II liquids do not require emergency relief venting.

Class IIIB liquids have low vapor pressures and high boiling points. In the time required to start boiling and thus cause excessive internal pressure, tanks of this size will have metal above the internal liquid level so heated and softened that it will fail and the tank will self-vent. However, if the tank is in an area containing a still-burning liquid, it then might add fuel to that fire.

2-2.5.3 In a vertical tank, the construction referred to in 2-2.5.1 may take the form of a floating roof, lifter roof, a weak roof-to-shell seam, or other approved pressure-relieving construction. The weak roof-to-shell seam shall be constructed to fail preferential to any other seam. Design methods which will provide a weak roof-to-shell seam construction are contained in API 650, *Welded Steel Tanks for Oil Storage,* and UL 142, *Standard for Steel Aboveground Tanks for Flammable and Combustible Liquids.*

In a fire emergency, the design of a weak roof-to-shell seam allows the roof to tear free from the shell as the pressure builds up. The tank is then fully vented. Without this or some other emergency relief feature, the tank might rupture randomly, or even rocket, as may happen when the bottom-to-shell seam fails first, as shown in Figure 2-18. (*See also Figure 2-20.*)

2-2.5.4 Where entire dependence for emergency relief is placed upon pressure-relieving devices, the total venting capacity of both normal and emergency vents shall be enough to prevent rupture of the shell or bottom of the tank if vertical, or of the shell or heads if horizontal. If unstable liquids are stored, the effects of heat or gas resulting from polymerization, decomposition, condensation, or self-reactivity shall be taken into account. The total capacity of both normal and emergency venting devices shall be not less than that derived from Table 2-8 except as provided in 2-2.5.6 or 2-2.5.7. Such device may be a self-closing manhole cover, or one using long bolts that permit the cover to lift under internal pressure, or an additional or larger relief valve or valves. The wetted area of the tank shall be calculated on the basis of 55 percent of the total exposed area of a sphere or spheroid, 75 percent of the total exposed area of a horizontal tank, and the first 30 ft (9 m) above grade of the exposed shell area of a vertical tank. (*See Appendix B for the square footage of typical tank sizes.*)

> The reference to unstable liquids (*see definition in Chapter 1*) is intentionally vague. The heat released by a chemical reaction within the tank will often be many times greater than the heat input from a surrounding fire. Styrene and methyl acrylate are examples of such materials. Sizing of emergency vents for tanks containing unstable liquids should be done on a case-by-case basis by someone familiar with the thermodynamics of the specific heat-releasing reaction and chemicals involved, since each reaction will release heat at it own rate. Another implication is that, if the liquid is stable, evolution of vapor that must be vented will take place only at the portions of the container in contact with the liquid. When the liquid is unstable, vapor or gas evolution usually takes place throughout the contents. In this case, the liquid swells because of bubbles of gas or vapor entrained throughout its mass, rather than in the relatively small volume in contact with the heated shell. This usually means that a two-phase mixture of liquid and vapor is discharged from the vent, so the vent size must be large enough to compensate for the drop in capacity because of this mixed flow, as opposed to the flow of all vapor. Vent sizes in the *Code* are calculated for stable liquids and vapor-only venting.
>
> The figures prescribed for determining how much of the total surface of a tank is considered wetted are based on a consensus

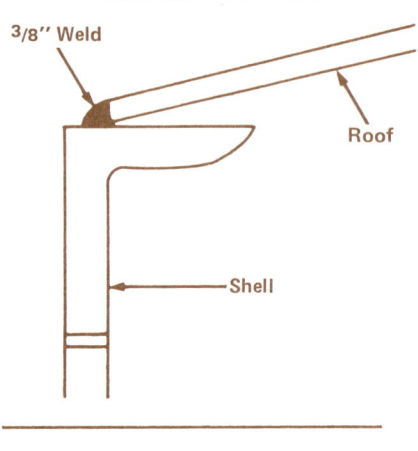

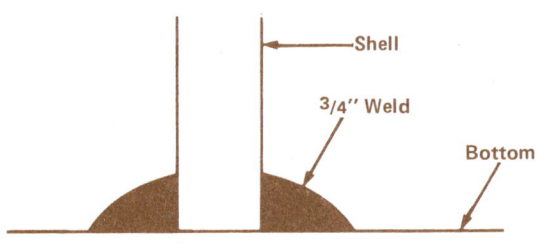

Figure 2-20 Vertical cone roof tanks built to either the specifications of Underwriters Laboratories Inc. or the American Petroleum Institute are allowed to have a weak roof-to-shell seam, if the seam is specifically built with a weak angle iron and the roof has a slope not exceeding 2 in. per ft. The roof is attached to the top angle iron, with only a 3/8-in. (0.95-cm) weld on the top of the angle. On the bottom-to-shell seam, both sides of the joint are secured by a weld of at least 3/4 in. (1.9 cm)—making the bottom-to-shell seam much stronger than the top-to-shell seam. Thus, any pressure that develops within such a tank during fire exposure conditions will be relieved by the roof tearing loose from the shell on part of the tank. In some cases, an internal explosion of the vapor space will completely blow the roof from the tank. (Note: Not all UL 142 or API 650 tanks incorporate a weak roof-to-shell design.)

among Technical Committee members who had witnessed fire tests, accidental fires, and their results. They also consider the "view factor"; i.e., how much energy in the flame is seen by the tanks and the improbability of a tank being completely surrounded by an

Table 2-8 Wetted Area Versus Cubic Feet Free Air per Hour*
(14.7 psia and 60°F) (101.3 kPa and 15.6°C)

Sq Ft	CFH	Sq Ft	CFH	Sq Ft	CFH
20	21,100	200	211,000	1,000	524,000
30	31,600	250	239,000	1,200	557,000
40	42,100	300	265,000	1,400	587,000
50	52,700	350	288,000	1,600	614,000
60	63,200	400	312,000	1,800	639,000
70	73,700	500	354,000	2,000	662,000
80	84,200	600	392,000	2,400	704,000
90	94,800	700	428,000	2,800	742,000
100	105,000	800	462,000	and over	
120	126,000	900	493,000		
140	147,000	1,000	524,000		
160	168,000				
180	190,000				
200	211,000				

SI Units: 10 ft² = 0.93 m²; 36 ft³ = 1.0 m³
*Interpolate for intermediate values.

"optically thick flame." Such a flame is one that is thick enough [about 15 ft (4.5 m)] so that energy radiated into the tank cannot reradiate back through the flame and be dissipated into the environment.

Tables 2-8 and 2-9 are expressed in cubic ft of free air per hour, rather than as size of opening in the tank. This is because any venting device, even a manhole opening, has a specific discharge coefficient. Complicated devices, such as flame arrestors, have coefficients that vary widely according to design. Also, flow through any specific device would be much greater when venting down to atmospheric from a 5-lb (34.5-kPa) tank, than when venting from an atmospheric tank where the permissible pressure drop through the device might be only a few inches of water pressure. The tables are derived from the material given in Appen-

Table 2-9 Wetted Area Over 2,800 sq ft and Pressures Over 1 psig*

Sq Ft	CFH	Sq Ft	CFH
2,800	742,000	9,000	1,930,000
3,000	786,000	10,000	2,110,000
3,500	892,000	15,000	2,940,000
4,000	995,000	20,000	3,720,000
4,500	1,100,000	25,000	4,470,000
5,000	1,250,000	30,000	5,190,000
6,000	1,390,000	35,000	5,900,000
7,000	1,570,000	40,000	6,570,000
8,000	1,760,000		

SI Units: 10 ft² = 0.93 m²; 36 ft³ = 1.0 m³
*Interpolate for intermediate values.

dix A. Appendix A should be consulted for a further discussion of the emergency venting recommendations.

2-2.5.5 For tanks and storage vessels designed for pressures over 1 psig (6.9 kPa), the total rate of venting shall be determined in accordance with Table 2-8, except that when the exposed wetted area of the surface is greater than 2,800 sq ft (260 m²), the total rate of venting shall be in accordance with Table 2-9 or calculated by the following formula:

$$CFH = 1{,}107 \ A^{0.82}$$

Where:
 CFH = venting requirement, in cubic feet of free air per hour
 A = exposed wetted surface, in square feet

The foregoing formula is based on $Q = 21{,}000 \ A^{0.82}$.

As pointed out in Appendix A, pressure vessels or low-pressure tanks will ordinarily be used for the storage of materials with low boiling points. Consequently, some emergency venting is needed to keep the tank from failing at a pressure greatly in excess of the relief valve setting. Following the venting suggestions in Table 2-9 will alleviate this problem. The equation $CFH = 1{,}107 \ A^{0.82}$ is derived by substituting $21{,}000 \ A^{0.82}$ for Q in the formula in Appendix A,

$$CFH = \frac{70.5 Q}{L\sqrt{M}}$$

where $L\sqrt{M}$ is the figure for n-Hexane, 1,337.

2-2.5.6 The total emergency relief venting capacity for any specific stable liquid can be determined by the following formula:

$$\text{Cubic feet of free air per hour} = V \ \frac{1{,}337}{L\sqrt{M}}$$

V = cubic feet of free air per hour from Table 2-8
L = latent heat of vaporization of specific liquid in Btu per pound
M = molecular weight of specific liquids

For many materials, notably alcohols, $L\sqrt{M}$ is larger than 1,337. This paragraph permits smaller emergency vents for tanks storing such materials. However, tanks may later be used for materials other than those for which they were originally intended, so caution should be used when accepting a vent having less capacity than would be required for n-Hexane.

2-2.5.7 For tanks containing stable liquids, the required airflow rate of 2-2.5.4 or 2-2.5.6 may be multiplied by the appropriate factor listed in the following schedule when protection is provided as indicated. Only one factor can be used for any one tank.

NFPA 30—TANK STORAGE

0.5 for drainage in accordance with 2-2.3.2 for tanks over 200 sq ft (18.6 m^2) of wetted area

0.3 for water spray in accordance with NFPA 15, *Standard for Water Spray Fixed Systems for Fire Protection*, and drainage in accordance with 2-2.3.2

0.3 for insulation in accordance with 2-2.5.7(a)

0.15 for water spray with insulation in accordance with 2-2.5.7(a) and drainage in accordance with 2-2.3.2 (*see Appendix B*)

(a) Insulation systems for which credit is taken shall meet the following performance criteria:

1. Remain in place under fire exposure conditions.

2. Withstand dislodgment when subjected to hose stream impingement during fire exposure. This requirement may be waived where use of solid hose streams is not contemplated or would not be practical.

3. Maintain a maximum conductance value of 4.0 Btu per hour per square foot per degree Fahrenheit (Btu/hr/sq ft/°F) when the outer insulation jacket or cover is at a temperature of 1,660°F (904.4°C) and when the mean temperature of the insulation is 1,000°F (537.8°C).

The justification for the factors by which the venting capacity may be reduced is:

1. Paragraph 2-2.3.2 requires that no spill fire can seriously expose a tank. A 50 percent factor is reasonable.

2. Experimental work summarized in A-4-4.3.2 of NFPA 15, *Standard for Water Spray Fixed Systems for Fire Protection*, shows that heat input to protected tanks is reduced to about 6,000 Btu/hr/sq ft of surface exposed to fire and wetted by the contents, and 6,000 divided by 20,000 is 30 percent. However, this factor should not be used unless the water supply to the system is adequate to keep it operating until the emergency is over, keeping in mind other likely demands on the water supply. Some tank farm fires have lasted for days. It must also be considered that water spray systems are subject to internal plugging and damage by explosion.

3. The insulation requirements are not as specific as they seem. Paragraph (a)1. requires that insulation remain in place under fire exposure conditions, although neither this nor the other requirements insist that it be undamaged after the fire and hose stream exposure. It is enough that it remain functional while it is exposed to fire. For example, foam glass and hydrous calcium silicate held on by stainless steel bands can give protection for many hours, particularly if put on in multilayers with the joints broken. They may need replacement after the fire is put out. Only materials such as

mineral wool and refractory materials are likely to survive a severe fire without need for replacement. There is a good discussion of insulation systems in the National Academy of Sciences publication, *Pressure-Relieving Systems for Marine Cargo Bulk Liquid Containers.*

There is some thought that "an emergency is an emergency is an emergency," and that emergency vent sizes should never be reduced, regardless of the permission to do so granted by this *Code*.

2-2.5.8 The outlet of all vents and vent drains on tanks equipped with emergency venting to permit pressures exceeding 2.5 psig (17.2 kPa) shall be arranged to discharge in such a way as to prevent localized overheating of or flame impingement on any part of the tank, in the event vapors from such vents are ignited.

2-2.5.9 Each commercial tank venting device shall have stamped on it the opening pressure, the pressure at which the valve reaches the full open position and the flow capacity at the latter pressure. If the start to open pressure is less than 2.5 psig (17.2 kPa) and the pressure at full open position is greater than 2.5 psig (17.2 kPa), the flow capacity at 2.5 psig (17.2 kPa) shall also be stamped on the venting device. The flow capacity shall be expressed in cubic feet per hour of air at 60°F (15.6°C) and 14.7 psia (760 mm Hg).

(a) The flow capacity of tank venting devices under 8 in. (20 cm) in nominal pipe size shall be determined by actual test of each type and size of vent. These flow tests may be conducted by the manufacturer if certified by a qualified impartial observer, or may be conducted by a qualified, impartial outside agency. The flow capacity of tank venting devices 8 in. (20 cm) nominal pipe size and larger, including manhole covers with long bolts or equivalent, may be calculated provided that the opening pressure is actually measured, the rating pressure and corresponding free orifice area are stated, the word "calculated" appears on the nameplate, and the computation is based on a flow coefficient of 0.5 applied to the rated orifice area.

(b) A suitable formula for this calculation is:

$$\text{CFH} = 1{,}667 \, C_f \, A \, \sqrt{P_t - P_a}$$

where CFH = venting requirement in cubic feet of free air per hour
C_f = 0.5 [the flow coefficient]
A = the orifice area in sq in.
P_t = the absolute pressure inside the tank in inches of water
P_a = the absolute atmospheric pressure outside the tank in inches of water

The requirement that the venting capacity be stamped on the device is to eliminate the need to consult vendors' catalogs. This eases the inspector's job.

The formula given in (b) uses $C_f = 0.5$ as an approximation for the true coefficient that would be made up of a basic orifice factor, a viscosity factor based on the Reynolds number of the vapor, an expansion factor (because the vapor expands as it leaves the orifice), a temperature factor, and a specific gravity factor. The use of 0.5 results in a conservative estimate that will predict a somewhat lower flow than is actually the case, and hence gives a small factor of safety in some cases.

2-2.6 Vent Piping for Aboveground Tanks.

2-2.6.1   Vent piping shall be constructed in accordance with Chapter 3.

There is a slight ambiguity here since Chapter 3 covers piping containing liquids. However, ANSI B31, *American National Standard Code for Pressure Piping*, covers piping for gases under vacuum as well as liquids, so the reference to ANSI B31 in 3-1.1 is pertinent here.

2-2.6.2   Where vent pipe outlets for tanks storing Class I liquids are adjacent to buildings or public ways, they shall be located so that the vapors are released at a safe point outside of buildings and not less than 12 ft (3.6 m) above the adjacent ground level. In order to aid their dispersion, vapors shall be discharged upward or horizontally away from closely adjacent walls. Vent outlets shall be located so that flammable vapors will not be trapped by eaves or other obstructions and shall be at least 5 ft (1.5 m) from building openings.

This *Code* relates only to fire and explosion hazards. The vent termination locations permitted by this paragraph may not be suitable if the vapors are also toxic, irritating, corrosive, or have an objectionable odor.

The 5 ft (1.5 m) separation from building openings and the 12 ft (3.6 m) elevation above ground level are based on an engineering estimate of the distance an ignitable concentration of vapors may exist around the end of a vent pipe. If the hazard extends 5 ft (1.5 m) down, its edge is 12 minus 5, or 7 ft (2 m) above grade, so that ignition by a smoker walking or driving by would not occur. The size of the hazardous volume may be estimated by taking the case of hexane. A sphere of 5 ft (1.5 m) radius has a volume of 523.6 cu ft (14.8 m^3). The lower flammable limit is about 1 percent and would require 5.2 cu ft (0.15 m^3) of hexane vapor. At 60°F (15.6°C), hexane has a vapor pressure of 100 mm of mercury (13.3 kPa), so the vapors coming out of the vent would be 100/760, or 13 percent hexane—

too rich to burn. These vapors would produce 5.236/0.13, or 40 cu ft (1.13 m³) of vapor, more than enough to fill the 5-ft (1.5-m) sphere with a mixture at the lower flammable limit. Assume that the vapor is discharged into air moving at 1 mph, (88 ft/min) (1609 m/sec). This is below 1 on the Beaufort Scale, at which point the leaves on trees do not move and smoke goes straight up. The vapors would be diluted out of the hazardous range long before they filled a 5-ft (1.5-m) radius sphere. The conclusion is that the 5-ft (1.5-m) rule gives ample protection.

When vent piping is modified by the addition of items such as devices to absorb or adsorb unwanted components from the stream being vented, the devices should not unduly restrict the flow of vapors. Also, the piping should not be modified in such a way that liquid collecting in low points could either permit the tank to be overpressured or start a siphoning action that could implode the tank.

2-2.6.3 The manifolding of tank vent piping shall be avoided except where required for special purposes such as vapor recovery, vapor conservation, or air pollution control. When tank vent piping is manifolded, pipe sizes shall be such as to discharge, within the pressure limitations of the system, the vapors they may be required to handle when manifolded tanks are subject to the same fire exposure.

Manifolding of vent piping creates a potential explosion hazard because the entire vent system may, at some time, contain a vapor-air mixture in the flammable range. Listed flame arrestors that are designed to prevent flame propagation through piping must be installed within a specified distance from the open end of the pipe. The listing is based on ignition at the open end, where the pressure is initially atmospheric. In the piping systems considered here, ignition may occur in one of the tanks and may propagate *toward* the open end.

So-called "flame-checks," used in piping that feeds premixed air/gas mixtures to burners, are usually of small diameter and can only prevent propagation in one direction. In a vent system, flame propagation may proceed in *both* directions.

Manifolding of vents from vessels operating under pressure can result in diesel-type ignition of flammable mixtures in "dead ends" of the vent system, due to pressure-piling.

2-2.6.4 Vent piping for tanks storing Class I liquids shall not be manifolded with vent piping for tanks storing Class II or Class III liquids unless positive means are provided to prevent the vapors from Class I liquids from entering tanks storing Class II or Class III liquids, to prevent contamination (*see 1-1.2*) and possible change in classification of the less volatile liquid.

A practical way to prevent such contamination is to introduce a low flow of inert gas into the vent of each tank containing a Class II or Class III liquid. Air should not be used.

2-2.7 Tank Openings Other Than Vents for Aboveground Tanks.

2-2.7.1 Each connection to an aboveground tank through which liquid can normally flow shall be provided with an internal or an external valve located as close as practical to the shell of the tank.

Because repair or maintenance of internal valves usually requires that tanks be emptied, they are seldom used on larger tanks.

2-2.7.2 Each connection below the liquid level through which liquid does not normally flow shall be provided with a liquidtight closure. This may be a valve, plug, or blind, or a combination of these.

Since a valve can be opened by mistake, resulting in a spill of tank contents, it is advisable to plug or blank the outlet of any valve not intended for operating purposes immediately after it is installed.

2-2.7.3 Openings for gaging on tanks storing Class I liquids shall be provided with a vaportight cap or cover. Such covers shall be closed when not gaging.

Gaging openings may also be used for taking samples. Metallic cups, floats, etc., should have electrical continuity with the tank shell to avoid the possibility of ignition by static discharge and a 30-minute static "relaxation" period should be allowed before manual gaging or sampling after a tank is filled unless the tank is fitted with a gaging tube or well. Although the atmosphere in a tank containing a Class I liquid is normally too rich to burn, vapors escaping from the gaging opening may form a hazardous zone in the immediate vicinity. If the tank is being emptied or has recently had liquid withdrawn from it, much of the vapor space in the tank may be in the flammable range, and ignition may propagate into the tank, causing an explosion.

2-2.7.4 For Class IB and Class IC liquids other than crude oils, gasolines, and asphalts, the fill pipe shall be so designed and installed as to minimize the possibility of generating static electricity. A fill pipe entering the top of a tank shall terminate within 6 in. (15 cm) of the bottom of the tank and shall be installed to avoid excessive vibration.

This is the first place in the *Code* that static electricity is specifically mentioned as a possible source of ignition. The excep-

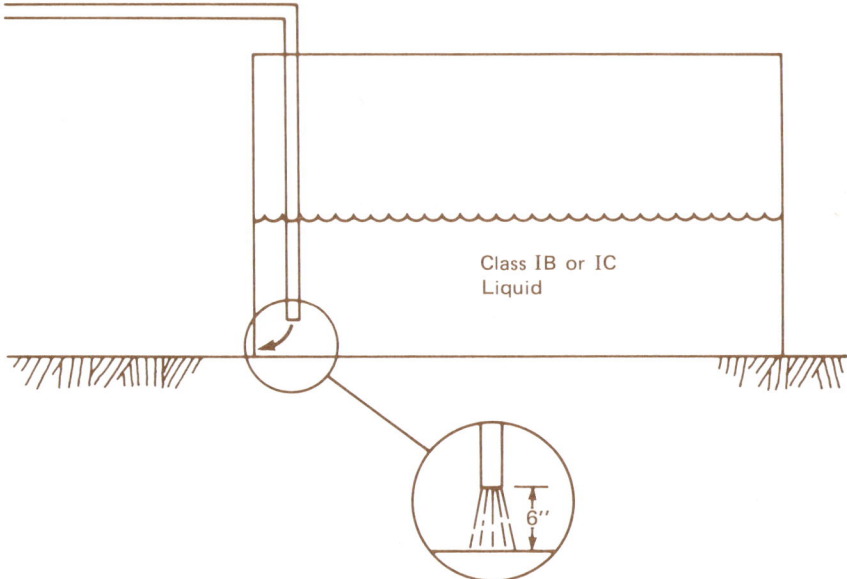

Figure 2-21 A fill pipe entering the top of a tank should terminate within 6 in. (152.4 mm) of the bottom of the tank and should be installed to avoid excessive vibration.

tions in the first sentence recognize that: (1) crude oils and asphalt have such a low electrical resistivity that static generation has not proven to be a problem, and (2) gasoline normally has a vapor-air mixture at its surface too rich to be ignitible, so that static ignition is not possible. The manner in which liquid is admitted to a tank can cause turbulence and splashing, particularly if the inlet pipe terminates above the liquid surface; therefore, it is required that the pipe terminate close to the bottom. (*See Figure 2-21.*) (*See also NFPA 77, Recommended Practice on Static Electricity.*)

There are many ways to accumulate a static charge in a liquid. Charged mists may result when a falling stream of liquid breaks up into fine droplets. Flow of liquid through a pipe generates a charge in the liquid; the effect is more pronounced at high flow velocities and is greatly enhanced if the flow involves two or more phases. In the specific case of filling a tank, the quantity of static charge accumulates as the volume of liquid increases in the tank. In some cases, the charge reaches such high levels that it spontaneously leaks off to grounded objects by nonincendive corona discharge, instead of gradual dissipation. (This will not occur in liquids whose resistivity is less than 10^{10} ohm-centimeters; the charges are able to migrate too easily through the liquid and recombine.) "Nonincendive" means that, although the voltage is high enough to cause discharge, there is insufficient energy to cause ignition.

The risk of producing an incendive (i.e., ignition-capable) spark is dramatically increased when a charged, high-resistivity fluid flows either over or adjacent to an isolated conductor. This conductor will accumulate a static charge. If the isolated conductor is then brought near a grounded conductor, an immediate discharge occurs in the form of a spark of relatively high energy, usually well above that required for ignition of a flammable atmosphere.

No isolated conductors should be introduced into a system that is prone to static generation. These include metal floats on liquid level gages, metal sampling cups on wooden rods or nylon cords, metal parts in plastic dip tubes, and isolated metal parts on intrinsically safe electrical equipment.

For further information, see NFPA 77, *Recommended Practice on Static Electricity*; API Recommended Practice 2003, *Protection Against Ignitions Arising Out of Static, Lightning and Stray Currents*; and *Electrostatic Hazards: Their Evaluation and Control*, by H. Haase.

The reference to vibration in the last sentence of 2-2.7.4 is a warning that a pipe supported only at the top might vibrate and break off, without anyone becoming aware of it. The resulting falling stream would defeat the purpose of having the fill pipe extend to within 6 in. (15 cm) of the bottom.

2-2.7.5 Filling and emptying connections for Class I, Class II, and Class IIIA liquids that are made and broken shall be located outside of buildings at a location free from any source of ignition and not less than 5 ft (1.5 m) away from any building opening. Such connections for any liquid shall be closed and liquidtight when not in use and shall be properly identified.

2-3 Installation of Underground Tanks.

2-3.1 Location. Excavation for underground storage tanks shall be made with due care to avoid undermining of foundations of existing structures. Underground tanks or tanks under buildings shall be so located with respect to existing building foundations and supports that the loads carried by the latter cannot be transmitted to the tank. The distance from any part of a tank storing Class I liquids to the nearest wall of any basement or pit shall be not less than 1 ft (0.30 m), and to any property line that can be built upon, not less than 3 ft (0.90 m). The distance from any part of a tank storing Class II or Class III liquids to the nearest wall of any basement, pit, or property line shall be not less than 1 ft (0.30 m).

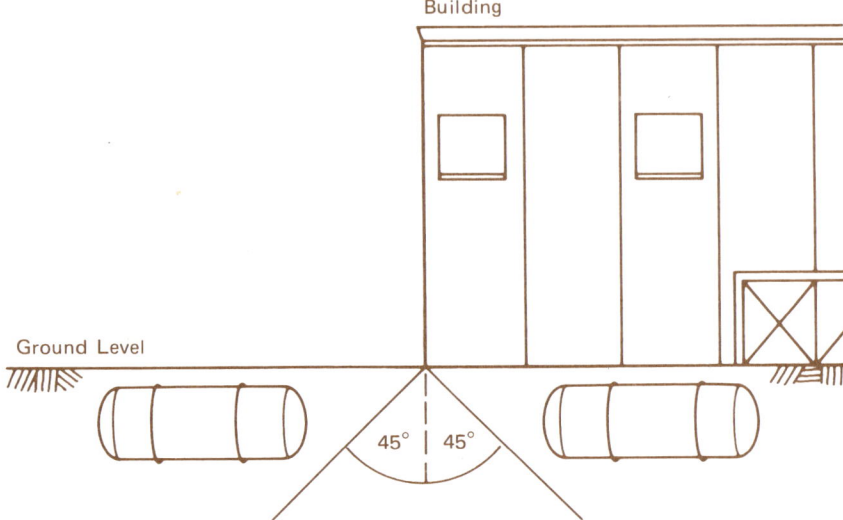

Figure 2-22 A common rule of thumb used by many engineers when locating a tank below the bottom foundation of a building is to place the tank outside of these 45-degree angles, measured from the extension of the foundation. This rule of thumb applies to tanks located under a building or just outside a building.

The first requirement in restricting the location of underground tanks is that the excavation not jeopardize the foundation of any structure or be so placed that settlement of the structure can damage the tank. The minimum spacing of 1 ft (0.30 m) from the tank to the wall of a basement or pit is to provide space for protective measures, such as excavation, well points, etc. If a leak should develop, in the case of Class I liquids, it could result in the presence of flammable vapors in the adjacent underground space.

The distance requirements give the minimum required for installation purposes. With Class I liquids, the 3 ft (0.90 m) distance to a property line that may be built upon is required to minimize the possibility of damage to a gasoline tank or to its protective sand or gravel envelope by construction activities on adjacent property. (*See Figure 2-22.*)

2-3.2 Burial Depth and Cover.

2-3.2.1 All underground tanks shall be installed in accordance with the manufacturer's instructions, where available, and shall be set on firm foundations and surrounded with at least 6 in. (15 cm) of noncorrosive inert material such as clean sand or gravel well tamped in place. The tank shall be placed in the hole with care, since dropping or rolling the tank into the hole can break a weld, puncture or damage the tank, or scrape off the protective coating of coated tanks. (*See Petroleum Equipment Institute (PEI) RP-100-86, Recommended Practice for the Installation of Underground Liquid Storage Systems,* for further information.)

Until the 1987 edition, the *Code* only referred to steel underground tanks. In recent years, other types of tanks, such as fiberglass reinforced plastic and coated steel tanks, have become more common. The *Code* now recognizes any tank suitable for underground installation.

Backfilling with gravel or sand containing large stones can likewise damage a tank's coating or even cause dents or gouges. Gravel should be in accordance with the dictionary definition—i.e., "consist of rounded pebbles." Because it may contain corrosive salt, sea sand should not be used.

2-3.2.2 All underground tanks shall be covered with a minimum of 2 ft (0.60 m) of earth, or shall be covered with not less than 1 ft (0.30 m) of earth, on top of which shall be placed a slab of reinforced concrete not less than 4 in. (10 cm) thick. When they are, or are likely to be, subjected to traffic, they shall be protected against damage from vehicles passing over them by at least 3 ft (0.90 m) of earth cover, or 18 in. (45.7 cm) of well-tamped earth plus either 6 in. (15 cm) of reinforced concrete or 8 in. (20 cm) of asphaltic concrete. When asphaltic or reinforced concrete paving is used as part of the protection, it shall extend at least 1 ft (0.30 m) horizontally beyond the outline of the tank in all directions.

See Figure 2-23.

2-3.2.3 For underground tanks built in accordance with 2-1.3.1, the burial depth shall be such that the static head imposed at the bottom of the tank will not exceed 10 psig (68.9 kPa) if the fill or vent pipe are filled with liquid. If the depth of cover is greater than the tank diameter, the tank manufacturer shall be consulted to determine if reinforcement is required.

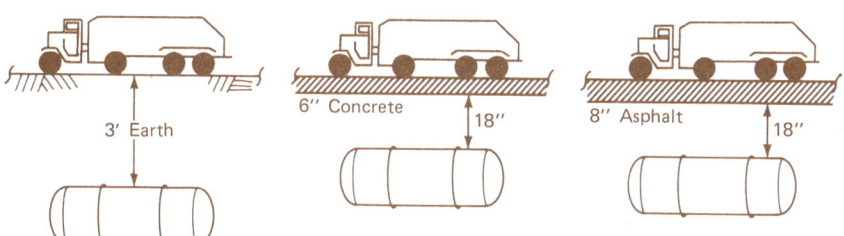

Figure 2-23 The specified methods of covering are intended to be adequate to prevent damage to the tank if a loaded truck is driven over the spot where the tank is buried.

The limit of 10 psig (68.9 kPa) at the bottom of the tank means that if the tank and vent pipe were filled with water, the maximum permissible distance from the bottom of the tank to the top of the vent would be 10/0.434, or 23 ft (7 m). Assuming they were filled with gasoline, the permissible height would be (for 0.7 specific gravity gasoline) 23/0.7, or about 33 ft (10 m). However, the specific gravity of other liquids may be higher than gasoline.

The second sentence alerts the user that excessive external loading due to the weight of the cover may cause partial tank collapse with consequent ejection of part of the contents.

2-3.3 External Corrosion Protection. Tanks and their piping shall be protected by either:

(a) A properly engineered, installed, and maintained cathodic protection system in accordance with recognized standards of design, such as:

1) American Petroleum Institute Publication 1632-1983, *Cathodic Protection of Underground Petroleum Storage Tanks and Piping Systems.*

2) Underwriters Laboratories of Canada ULC-S603.1-M 1982, *Standard for Galvanic Corrosion Protection Systems for Steel Underground Tanks for Flammable and Combustible Liquids.*

3) Steel Tank Institute Standard No. sti-P_3®, *Specifications for sti-P_3® System for External Corrosion Protection of Underground Steel Storage Tanks— 1983.*

4) National Association of Corrosion Engineers Standard RP-01-69 (1983 Rev.), Recommended Practice, *Control of External Corrosion of Underground or Submerged Metallic Piping Systems.*

5) National Association of Corrosion Engineers Standard RP-02-85, Recommended Practice, *Control of External Corrosion on Metallic Buried, Partially Buried, or Submerged Liquid Storage Systems.*

(b) Approved or listed corrosion-resistant materials or systems, which may include special alloys, fiberglass reinforced plastic, or fiberglass reinforced plastic coatings.

It is highly important that buried tanks remain leaktight for the extent of their service life. It is unrealistic to require maximum corrosion protection for tanks in all locations. In favorable soils tanks have lasted leak-free for 20 years and longer. In other locations, tanks have leaked from corrosion within a few years of installation.

The 1981 edition of the *Code* required a soil resistivity test. Its purpose was to determine the potential corrosion rate based on the electrical characteristics of the soil. There were problems associated with this requirement. The resistivity readings obtained at a given tank site would vary considerably from one reading point to another. In addition, soil resistivity is just one of several criteria that might indicate corrosivity. Also, substantial doubt was raised regarding the practicality of requiring cathodic protection on a bare steel tank. Such tanks can be protected adequately by impressed current, given proper design. However, bare steel tanks or those coated with black paint can not be protected satisfactorily with sacrificial anodes, simply because too many anodes are required.

A more practical solution, in the Technical Committee's opinion, was to require either corrosion protection or noncorrosive materials of construction, unless the need for either could be demonstrated to be unnecessary to the satisfaction of the authority having jurisdiction.

The present requirement directs the *Code* user to appropriate standards for guidance in designing corrosion protection for the underground tank installation. Local code officials need assistance in determining what a properly engineered cathodic protection system is, and the above references provide guidance. Paragraph 2-3.3.1 allows the authority having jurisdiction to waive the requirement for corrosion protection, based on previous experience and consultation with an expert. Again, however, impending environmental regulations may mandate corrosion protection in all cases, thus pre-empting local control.

The sti-P_3 standard is referenced here because it is a standard on corrosion protection, not on tank design.

2-3.3.1 Selection of the type of protection to be employed shall be based upon the corrosion history of the area and the judgement of a qualified engineer. The authority having jurisdiction may waive the requirements for corrosion protection where evidence is provided that such protection is not necessary. (*See API Publication 1615-1979, Installation of Underground Petroleum Storage Systems, for further information.*)

2-3.4 Abandonment or Reuse of Underground Tanks.

2-3.4.1 Underground tanks taken out of service shall be safeguarded or disposed of in a safe manner. (*See Appendix C.*)

See Figure 2-24.

2-3.4.2 Only those used tanks that comply with the applicable sections of this Code and are approved by the authority having jurisdiction shall be installed for flammable or combustible liquids service.

Figure 2-24 (Left) Before. (Right) After. Failure to follow the procedures described in Appendix C has resulted in major problems and even fatalities. For example, in the case shown here, an underground tank had been abandoned with gasoline still in it. During the spring, the high water table caused the gasoline from the abandoned tank to enter a crawl space underneath a service station building. Three fire fighters and two service station employees were killed when an explosion occurred in the crawl space.

This provision requires that approval for such reuse be received and further requires that the tank meet all appropriate sections of the *Code*.

2-3.5 Vents for Underground Tanks.

The treatment of vents in this section differs slightly from that in 2-2.4. The differences arise for several reasons: buried tanks never have a cone roof or a floating roof; they are generally of the horizontal cylindrical type; they cannot be seen when being filled or emptied; and the contents are never heated by the sun or severely chilled in cold weather.

2-3.5.1 Location and Arrangement of Vents for Class I Liquids. Vent pipes from underground storage tanks storing Class I liquids shall be so located that the discharge point is outside of buildings, higher than the fill pipe opening, and not less than 12 ft (3.6 m) above the adjacent ground level. Vent pipes shall not be obstructed by devices provided for vapor recovery or other purposes unless the tank and associated piping and equipment are otherwise protected to limit back-pressure development to less than the maximum working pressure of the tank and equipment by the provision of pressure-vacuum vents, rupture discs, or other tank venting devices installed in the tank vent lines. Vent outlets and devices shall be protected to minimize the possibility of blockage from weather, dirt, or insect nests, and shall be so located and directed that flammable vapors will not accumulate or travel to an unsafe location, enter building openings, or be trapped under eaves, and shall be at least 5 feet from building openings. Tanks containing Class IA liquids shall be equipped with pressure and vacuum venting devices that shall be normally closed except when venting under pressure or vacuum conditions. Tanks storing Class IB or Class IC liquids shall be equipped with pressure-vacuum vents or with listed flame arrestors. Tanks storing gasoline are exempt from the requirements for pressure and vacuum venting devices, except as required to prevent excessive back pressure, or flame arrestors, provided the vent does not exceed 3 in. (7.6 cm) nominal inside diameter. (*See also 2-1.1 of NFPA 30A, Automotive and Marine Service Station Code.*)

In some industrial installations where numerous horizontal tanks have been grouped in one area and either buried or mounded over, vents terminating less than 12 ft (3.6 m) above ground level have been accepted if the area is fenced to limit access and the termination is above normal snow level.

Use of the term "maximum working pressure" instead of "design pressure" makes it possible, in the opinion of the Technical Committee, to accept 2½ psig (17.2 kPa) as the maximum working pressure for a tank built to the specifications of UL 58, *Standard for Steel Underground Tanks for Flammable and Combustible Liquids*. This is one half of the minimum pressure required by the tank tightness test that is done before installation. (*See 2-7.3.*) If the tank is built to the specifications of the ASME *Code for Unfired Pressure Vessels*, the design working pressure is given in the papers that accompany the tank. Since leakage from underground tanks is not apparent and usually depends on inventory control for detection (*see 2-10 of this Code*), there is a detailed requirement to prevent overpressure.

The permission to use an open vent pipe of 3 in. (7.6 cm) inside diameter or smaller, provided it terminates 12 ft (3.6 m) aboveground and discharges upward (*see 2-1.1 of NFPA 30A, Automotive and Marine Service Station Code, page 283 of this Handbook*), is based on the properties of gasoline vapor. The properties of gasoline are intentionally varied so that it has a lower initial boiling point in cold weather and so that the Reid vapor pressure is higher in the winter than it is in the summer. On the other hand, the initial boiling point and Reid vapor pressure are naturally lower at high altitudes. The specifications to ensure that it has the proper qualities are given in ASTM D 439, *Standard Specifications for Automotive Gasoline*. Bureau of Mines Bulletin 627, *Flammability Characteristics of Combustible Gases and Vapors*, indicates that at 70°F (21°C), for example, a gasoline-air mixture in equilibrium with liquid gasoline would contain 25 percent gasoline vapor. Since the

Table 2-10 Vent Line Diameters

Maximum Flow GPM	Pipe Length* 50 Ft	100 Ft	200 Ft
100	1¼-inch	1¼-inch	1¼-inch
200	1¼-inch	1¼-inch	1¼-inch
300	1¼-inch	1¼-inch	1½-inch
400	1¼-inch	1½-inch	2-inch
500	1½-inch	1½-inch	2-inch
600	1½-inch	2-inch	2-inch
700	2-inch	2-inch	2-inch
800	2-inch	2-inch	3-inch
900	2-inch	2-inch	3-inch
1,000	2-inch	2-inch	3-inch

SI Units: 1 in. = 2.5 cm; 1 ft = 0.30 m; 1 gal = 3.8 L.
*Vent lines of 50 ft, 100 ft, and 200 ft of pipe plus 7 ells.

flammable range (again, in accordance with Bureau of Mines tests) is 1.4 to 7.6, the vapors in a buried tank would be too rich to burn. The vapors would need to be diluted with more than three times their volume of air to drop into the flammable range. Because of the changes in composition to meet conditions of use, as required by ASTM D439, *Standard Specifications for Automotive Gasoline*, the vapors coming out of a storage tank that is being filled will always be too rich to burn. If a fire were lit at the outlet of the vent pipe while the buried tank was being filled, it could not flash back because the vapor in the vent line would be too rich to burn. If a fire at the vent were burning at the moment of starting to pump gasoline out of the tank, the flame would simply be sucked down into the pipe and be snuffed out because of lack of oxygen.

2-3.5.2 Vent Capacity. Tank venting systems shall be provided with sufficient capacity to prevent blowback of vapor or liquid at the fill opening while the tank is being filled. Vent pipes shall not be less than 1¼ in. (3 cm) nominal inside diameter. The required venting capacity depends upon the filling or withdrawal rate, whichever is greater, and the vent line length. Unrestricted vent piping sized in accordance with Table 2-10 will prevent back-pressure development in tanks from exceeding 2.5 psig (17.2 kPa). Where tank venting devices are installed in vent lines, their flow capacities shall be determined in accordance with 2-2.5.9.

The preceding paragraph recognizes that vent lines may run a considerable distance, usually below ground, before rising up to the termination point. Piping larger than that in Table 2-10 will usually be needed if a flame arrestor or pressure-vacuum vent is installed, as would be the case with many Class IB and IC liquids, because of the reduced flow rate through the vent device.

2-3.5.3 Location and Arrangement of Vents for Class II or Class IIIA Liquids. Vent pipes from tanks storing Class II or Class IIIA liquids shall terminate outside of the building and higher than the fill pipe opening. Vent outlets shall be above normal snow level. They may be fitted with return bends, coarse screens, or other devices to minimize ingress of foreign material.

> By omission from this paragraph, vents for Class IIIB liquids are allowed to terminate indoors. However, doing so is not considered safe for heated Class IIIB liquids. (See 1-1.3.)

2-3.5.4 Vent piping shall be constructed in accordance with Chapter 3. Tank vent pipes and vapor return piping shall be installed without sags or traps in which liquid can collect. Condensate tanks, if utilized, shall be installed and maintained so as to preclude the blocking of the vapor return piping by liquid. The vent pipes and condensate tanks shall be located so that they will not be subjected to physical damage. The tank end of the vent pipe shall enter the tank through the top.

2-3.5.5 When tank vent piping is manifolded, pipe sizes shall be such as to discharge, within the pressure limitations of the system, the vapors they can be required to handle when manifolded tanks are filled simultaneously. Float-type check valves installed in tank openings connected to manifolded vent piping to prevent product contamination may be used provided that the tank pressure will not exceed that permitted by 2-3.2.4 when the valves close.

Exception: For service stations, the capacity of manifolded vent piping shall be sufficient to discharge vapors generated when two manifolded tanks are simultaneously filled.

> The exception for service stations is made because delivery trucks are not currently equipped to fill more than two tanks simultaneously.

2-3.5.6 Vent piping for tanks storing Class I liquids shall not be manifolded with vent piping for tanks storing Class II or Class III liquids unless positive means are provided to prevent the vapors from Class I liquids from entering tanks storing Class II or Class III liquids, to prevent contamination *(see 1-1.2)* and possible change in classification of the less volatile liquid.

2-3.6 Tank Openings Other Than Vents for Underground Tanks.

2-3.6.1 Connections for all tank openings shall be liquidtight.

2-3.6.2 Openings for manual gaging, if independent of the fill pipe, shall be provided with a liquidtight cap or cover. Covers shall be kept closed when not gaging. If inside a building, each such opening shall be protected against liquid overflow and possible vapor release by means of a spring-loaded check valve or other approved device.

Note that 2-3.1 does not prohibit having a tank under a building on the same premises, provided that the restrictions with respect to walls, foundations, and supports are met. However, the only access permitted to the tank within the building is the specially equipped gaging opening.

2-3.6.3 Fill and discharge lines shall enter tanks only through the top. Fill lines shall be sloped toward the tank. Underground tanks for Class I liquids having a capacity of more than 1,000 gal (3785 L) shall be equipped with a tight fill device for connecting the fill hose to the tank.

2-3.6.4 For Class IB and Class IC liquids other than crude oils, gasolines, and asphalts, the fill pipe shall be so designed and installed as to minimize the possibility of generating static electricity by terminating within 6 in. (15 cm) of the bottom of the tank.

This is the same as 2-2.7.4, and the same comments about static electricity apply.

2-3.6.5 Filling and emptying and vapor recovery connections for Class I, Class II, or Class IIIA liquids that are made and broken shall be located outside of buildings at a location free from any source of ignition and not less than 5 ft (1.5 m) away from any building opening. Such connections shall be closed and liquidtight when not in use and shall be properly identified.

Just as vents from tanks containing Class IIIB liquids are permitted to terminate indoors, filling connections are permitted indoors. As with vents, 1-1.3 is pertinent.

2-3.6.6 Tank openings provided for purposes of vapor recovery shall be protected against possible vapor release by means of a spring-loaded check valve or dry-break connection, or other approved device, unless the opening is pipe-connected to a vapor processing system. Openings designed for combined fill and vapor recovery shall also be protected against vapor release unless connection of the liquid delivery line to the fill pipe simultaneously connects the vapor recovery line. All connections shall be vaportight.

This paragraph is intended to regulate two types of systems. In one, vapor displaced when a storage tank is being filled is piped back to the vapor space of the unit from which the liquid is discharged. This is a vapor recovery system. The opening must not permit vapor to escape from the buried tank, except when it is flowing back to the unit from which the tank is being filled. In the second type, the vapor is connected to a special unit where it is incinerated, absorbed in oil or other liquid, or adsorbed on activated carbon or similar material for later recovery or disposal by other environmentally acceptable means.

2-4 Installation of Tanks Inside of Buildings.

2-4.1 Location. Tanks shall not be permitted inside of buildings.

Exception: If the storage of liquids in outside aboveground or underground tanks is not practical because of government regulations, temperature considerations, or production considerations, tanks may be permitted inside of buildings or structures in accordance with the applicable provisions of Chapter 2, Tank Storage. Production considerations that may necessitate storage inside of buildings include but are not limited to high viscosity, purity, sterility, hydroscopicity, sensitivity to temperature change, and need to store temporarily pending completion of sample analysis.

> As used here, "tanks" refers only to storage tanks and not to portable tanks, process vessels, etc. The exception to 2-4.1 recognizes that there may be valid reasons for allowing storage tanks to be located within buildings. Where this can be justified, the authority having jurisdiction can grant such a waiver from the basic requirement. This exception is not new to the *Code*; it was relocated here from the former Chapter 7, "Processing Plants." It is now more generally applicable to any operation covered by this *Code*.

2-4.1.1 Storage tanks inside of buildings shall be permitted only in areas at or above grade have adequate drainage and are separated from other parts of the building by construction having a fire resistance rating of at least 2 hrs. Day tanks, running tanks, and surge tanks are permitted in process areas. Openings to other rooms or buildings shall be provided with noncombustible liquidtight raised sills or ramps at least 4 in. (10 cm) in height, or the floor in the storage area shall be at least 4 in. (10 cm) below the surrounding floor. As a minimum, each opening shall be provided with a listed, self-closing 1½-hr (B) fire door installed in accordance with **NFPA 80**, *Standard for Fire Doors and Windows,* or a listed fire damper installed where required by **NFPA 90A**, *Standard for the Installation of Air Conditioning and Ventilating Systems,* or **NFPA 91**, *Standard for the Installation of Blower and Exhaust Systems for Dust, Stock, and Vapor Removal or Conveying.* The room shall be liquidtight where the walls join the floor.

> Paragraph 2-4.1.1 was likewise relocated here from former Chapter 7, paragraph 7-4.1.3. The intent here is to separate the storage area from the process area so that neither presents a fire exposure to the other. The intent is also to prevent a spill originating in the storage area from flowing into the process area. The two approaches stated here are analogous to the diked area around outdoor tanks. Another approach is to provide a drainage system sized to handle the largest probable spill. A drainage system will have to empty into a safe location, such as a catch tank or basin.

Regardless of the approach taken, the environmental impact of an indoor spill should receive no less consideration than for an outdoor spill.

Permission for the use of day tanks, etc., allows enough storage capacity for a single batch (or for a single shift, where multiple process lines are involved) to be located in the process area. This is often an operational necessity. Many chemical processes depend on reliable, controlled flow of raw materials to the process system and this is most often accomplished by gravity flow. Dependability of a chemical process is directly affected if materials must be pumped from a remote location. The consequences of loss of control of a chemical reaction may be far greater, should a pump fail, than the consequences of a leak or spill in the process area itself.

2-4.2 Vents. Vents for tanks inside of buildings shall be as required in 2-2.4, 2-2.5, 2-2.6.2, and 2-3.5, except that emergency venting by the use of weak roof seams on tanks shall not be permitted. Automatic sprinkler systems designed in accordance with the requirements of NFPA 13, *Standard for the Installation of Sprinkler Systems*, may be accepted by the authority having jurisdiction as equivalent to water spray systems for purposes of calculating the required airflow rates for emergency vents in 2-2.5.7. Except for tanks containing Class IIIB liquids, vents shall terminate outside the buildings.

The prohibition against tanks having weak roof-to-shell seams should, as a matter of good practice, apply also to tanks with floating roofs. The acceptance of sprinklers as equivalent to directional water spray systems is made on the basis that, if the fire is not controlled by sprinklers, structural failure will ruin the tank in any case. Emergency vents are included in the requirement for termination outside the building.

2-4.3 Vent Piping. Vent piping shall be constructed in accordance with Chapter 3.

Here we have the previously mentioned problem (*see comments under 2-2.6.1*) that Chapter 3, except for its reference to ANSI B31, *American National Standard Code for Pressure Piping*, is pertinent only to systems containing liquids.

2-4.4 Tank Openings Other Than Vents for Tanks Inside Buildings.

2-4.4.1 Connections for all tank openings shall be liquidtight.

2-4.4.2 Each connection to a tank inside of buildings through which liquid can normally flow shall be provided with an internal or an external valve located as close as practical to the shell of the tank.

NFPA 30—TANK STORAGE

Since most leaks occur in piping systems, this requirement minimizes the chance of having an uncontrollable leak and facilitates repairs to the piping system.

2-4.4.3 Tanks for storage of Class I or Class II liquids inside buildings shall be provided with either:

(a) a normally closed remotely activated valve,

(b) an automatic-closing heat-activated valve, or

(c) another approved device on each liquid transfer connection below the liquid level, except for connections used for emergency disposal, to provide for quick cutoff of flow in the event of fire in the vicinity of the tank.

This function can be incorporated in the valve required in 2-4.4.2, and if a separate valve, shall be located adjacent to the valve required in 2-4.4.2.

This is to minimize the chance that a fire-related piping failure would cause an uncontrollable spill of liquid to the fire.

2-4.4.4 Openings for manual gaging of Class I or Class II liquids, if independent of the fill pipe, shall be provided with a vaportight cap or cover. Openings shall be kept closed when not gaging. Each such opening for any liquid shall be protected against liquid overflow and possible vapor release by means of a spring-loaded check valve or other approved device. Substitutes for manual gaging include, but are not limited to, heavy-duty flat gage glasses, magnetic, hydraulic, or hydrostatic remote reading devices and sealed float gages.

This expands on the similar requirement for aboveground tanks (*see 2-2.7.3*) by suggesting alternates to openings for gaging. Suitable alternates not mentioned include mounting the tank on a scale or on load cells.

2-4.4.5 For Class IB and Class IC liquids other than crude oils, gasolines, and asphalts, the fill pipe shall be so designed and installed as to minimize the possibility of generating static electricity by terminating within 6 in. (15 cm) of the bottom of the tank.

2-4.4.6 The fill pipe inside of the tank shall be installed to avoid excessive vibration of the pipe.

The above two paragraphs are equivalent to 2-2.7.4, and the same comments apply.

2-4.4.7 The inlet of the fill pipe and the outlet of a vapor recovery line for which connections are made and broken shall be located outside of buildings at a location free from any source of ignition and not less than 5 ft (1.5 m) away from any building opening. Such connections shall be closed and tight when not in use and shall be properly identified.

98   FLAMMABLE AND COMBUSTIBLE LIQUIDS CODE HANDBOOK

The rationale for the 5 ft (1.5 m) spacing was discussed under 2-2.6.2.

2-4.4.8 Tanks storing Class I, Class II, and Class IIIA liquids inside buildings shall be equipped with a device, or other means shall be provided, to prevent overflow into the building. Suitable devices include, but are not limited to, a float valve, a preset meter on the fill line, a valve actuated by the weight of the tank contents, a low head pump incapable of producing overflow, or a liquidtight overflow pipe at least one pipe size larger than the fill pipe discharging by gravity back to the outside source of liquid or to an approved location.

Class IIIB liquids are excluded from this requirement, but only if they are not heated. (See 1-1.3.)

2-4.4.9 Tank openings provided for purposes of vapor recovery shall be protected against possible vapor release by means of a spring-loaded check valve or dry-break connections, or other approved device, unless the opening is pipe-connected to a vapor processing system. Openings designed for combined fill and vapor recovery shall also be protected against vapor release unless connection of the liquid delivery line to the fill pipe simultaneously connects the vapor recovery line. All connections shall be vaportight.

This is identical to 2-3.6.6, and the same comments apply.

2-5 Supports, Foundations, and Anchorage for All Tank Locations.

2-5.1 Tanks shall rest on the ground or on foundations made of concrete, masonry, piling, or steel. Tank foundations shall be designed to minimize the possibility of uneven settling of the tank and to minimize corrosion in any part of the tank resting on the foundation. Appendix E of API Standard 650-1980, *Specification for Welded Steel Tanks for Oil Storage*, and Appendix B of API Standard 620-1982, *Recommended Rules for the Design and Construction of Large, Welded, Low-Pressure Storage Tanks*, provide information on tank foundations.

2-5.2 When tanks are supported above the foundations, tank supports shall be installed on firm foundations. Supports for tanks storing Class I, Class II, or Class IIIA liquids shall be of concrete, masonry, or protected steel. Single wood timber supports (not cribbing) laid horizontally may be used for outside aboveground tanks if not more than 12 in. (0.30 m) high at their lowest point.

Unprotected steel supports are prohibited. Experience has shown that they soften and fail after only a brief exposure to fire, resulting in a rupture of piping and a possible spill of tank contents. (*See Figure 2-25.*) The exception for solid timber supports less than 12 in. (0.30 m) high is based on the "slow burning" characteristic of "heavy timber construction." (*See NFPA Fire Protection Handbook.*)

 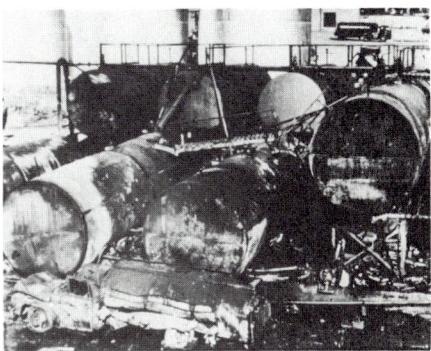

Figure 2-25 (Left) Aboveground tanks on steel supports. (Right) Aftermath of a fire showing collapse of unprotected steel supports. Unfortunately, many tanks are installed on unprotected steel supports even though this practice has been prohibited since the first edition of the *Flammable and Combustible Liquids Code* in 1913. When exposed to fire, unprotected steel supports buckle and fail. The sagging supports allow the tank to tip or fall to the ground, breaking piping connections or even damaging the tank. As a result, spilled tank contents allow the fire to spread beyond control.

It should be noted that this requirement is intended to apply to fixed tanks only. Portable tanks would not be expected to comply, especially if located in areas where loss of the tank contents would not significantly add to consequences of the fire.

2-5.3 Steel supports or exposed piling for tanks storing Class I, Class II, or Class IIIA liquids shall be protected by materials having a fire resistance rating of not less than 2 hrs, except that steel saddles need not be protected if less than 12 in. (0.30 m) high at their lowest point. At the discretion of the authority having jurisdiction, water spray protection in accordance with NFPA 15, *Standard for Water Spray Fixed Systems for Fire Protection*, or NFPA 13, *Standard for the Installation of Sprinkler Systems*, or equivalent may be used.

2-5.4 The design of the supporting structure for tanks such as spheres shall require special engineering consideration. Appendix N of the API Standard 620-1982, *Recommended Rules for the Design and Construction of Large, Welded, Low-Pressure Storage Tanks*, contains information regarding supporting structures.

2-5.5 Every tank shall be so supported as to prevent the excessive concentration of loads on the supporting portion of the shell.

2-5.6 Tanks in Areas Subject to Flooding.

2-5.6.1 Where a tank is located in an area subject to flooding, provisions shall be taken to prevent tanks, either full or empty, from floating during a rise in water level up to the established maximum flood stage.

In several instances, high water level has floated full or partially full tanks from their foundations, resulting in hazardous situations in other areas. The requirements in the paragraphs that follow are intended to prevent such incidents.

2-5.6.2 Aboveground Tanks.

A tank located according to the following requirements will not float if filled with gasoline (specific gravity 0.7). It may float if only partially full. To contend with the possibility that a tank might not be full at the time of a flood, the availability of a water supply to fill the tank in case of a flood emergency is required in 2-5.6.2.4.

2-5.6.2.1 Each vertical tank shall be located so that its top extends above the maximum flood stage by at least 30 percent of its allowable storage capacity.

2-5.6.2.2 Horizontal tanks located so that more than 70 percent of the tank's storage capacity will be submerged at the established flood stage shall be anchored; attached to a foundation of concrete or of steel and concrete of sufficient weight to provide adequate load for the tank when filled with flammable or combustible liquid and submerged by flood water to the established flood stage; or adequately secured from floating by other means. Tank vents or other openings which are not liquidtight shall be extended above maximum flood stage water level.

The strict limitation on location in 2-5.6.2.1 is relaxed in the case of horizontal tanks, because these tanks can be more reliably anchored. However, it is not practical to provide anchoring for an empty tank and provision for water loading is still required.

2-5.6.2.3 A dependable water supply shall be available for filling an empty or partially filled tank, except that where filling the tank with water is impractical or hazardous because of the tank's contents, tanks shall be protected by other means against movement or collapse.

2-5.6.2.4 Spherical or spheroid tanks shall be protected by applicable methods as specified for either vertical or horizontal tanks.

2-5.6.3 Underground Tanks.

Buried tanks have been known to float up out of the ground if exposed to a high water table or flood waters. Means for preventing this are prescribed in the following paragraphs (*see Figure 2-26*).

2-5.6.3.1 At locations where there is an ample and dependable water supply available, underground tanks containing flammable or combustible liquids, so placed that more than 70 percent of their storage capacity will be submerged at the maximum flood stage, shall be so anchored, weighted, or secured as to

NFPA 30—TANK STORAGE 101

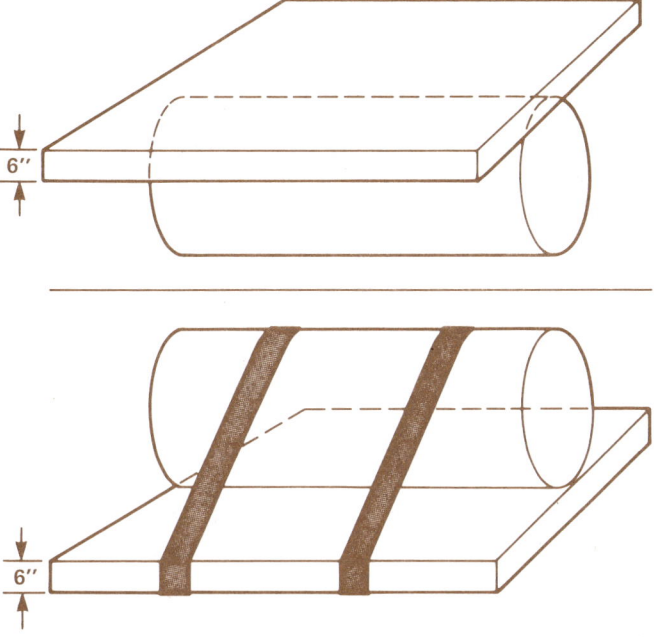

Figure 2-26 One method is to place over the tank 6 in. (15 cm) of reinforced concrete extending 12 in. (30 cm) beyond the tank in all directions. A second method uses a 6-in. (15-cm) reinforced concrete base at the bottom of the hole. Anchoring strips are then placed over the tank and attached to the concrete slab. With both of these methods, the weight of the concrete offsets the buoyancy of the tank.

prevent movement when filled or loaded with water and submerged by flood water to the established flood stage. Tank vents or other openings that are not liquidtight shall be extended above maximum flood stage water level.

2-5.6.3.2 At locations where there is no ample and dependable water supply or where filling of underground tanks with water is impractical because of the contents, each tank shall be safeguarded against movement when empty, and submerged by high ground water or flood water by anchoring or by securing by other means. Each such tank shall be so constructed and installed that it will safely resist external pressures if submerged.

> Reliable means for utilizing water from the flood itself would be considered acceptable.

2-5.6.4 Water Loading. The filling of a tank to be protected by water loading shall be started as soon as flood waters are predicted to reach a dangerous flood stage. Where independently fueled water pumps are relied upon, sufficient fuel shall be available at all times to permit continuing operations until all tanks are filled. Tank valves shall be locked in a closed position when water loading has been completed.

2-5.6.5 Operating Instructions.

2-5.6.5.1 Operating instructions or procedures to be followed in a flood emergency shall be readily available.

2-5.6.5.2 Personnel relied upon to carry out flood emergency procedures shall be informed of the location and operation of valves and other equipment necessary to effect the intent of these requirements.

2-5.7 In areas subject to earthquakes, the tank supports and connections shall be designed to resist damage as a result of such shocks.

2-6 Sources of Ignition. In locations where flammable vapors may be present, precautions shall be taken to prevent ignition by eliminating or controlling sources of ignition. Sources of ignition may include open flames, lightning, smoking, cutting and welding, hot surfaces, frictional heat, sparks (static, electrical, and mechanical), spontaneous ignition, chemical and physical-chemical reactions, and radiant heat. NFPA 77, *Recommended Practice on Static Electricity*, and NFPA 78, *Lightning Protection Code*, provide information on such protection.

> Precautions may include prohibiting smoking and smoking materials from the area, restrictions on entry of unauthorized personnel, a "hot work" permit system to control cutting and welding operations, etc. It must be clearly understood that control of ignition sources are the second line of defense. Preventing the escape of flammable vapors and liquids should be the primary goal.

2-7 Testing.

2-7.1 All tanks, whether shop-built or field-erected, shall be tested before they are placed in service in accordance with the applicable paragraphs of the Code under which they were built. The ASME Code stamp or the Listing Mark of Underwriters Laboratories Inc. on a tank shall be evidence of compliance with this test. Tanks not marked in accordance with the above Codes shall be tested before they are placed in service in accordance with good engineering principles and reference shall be made to the sections on testing in the Codes listed in 2-1.3.1, 2-1.4.2, or 2-1.5.2.

2-7.2 When the vertical length of the fill and vent pipes is such that when filled with liquid the static head imposed on the bottom of the tank exceeds 10 psi (68.9 kPa), the tank and related piping shall be tested hydrostatically to a pressure equal to the static head thus imposed. In special cases where the height of the vent above the top of the tank is excessive, the hydrostatic test pressure shall be determined by using recognized engineering practice.

> The intent is that the tank be tested to the pressure that would be developed if the tank were accidentally overfilled, causing liquid to

NFPA 30—TANK STORAGE

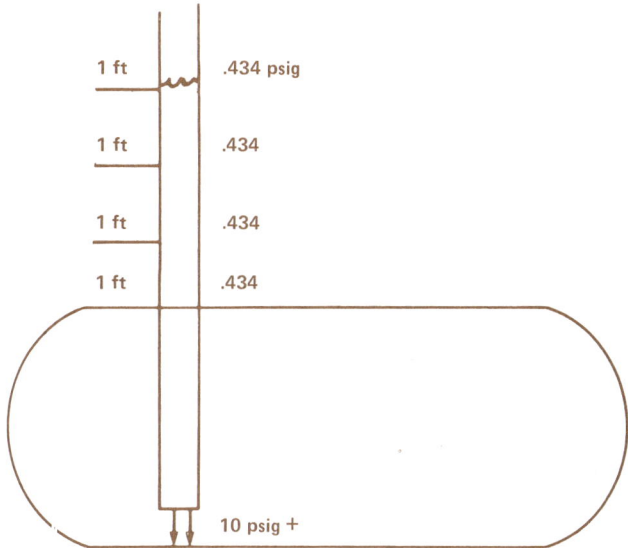

SI Units: 1 ft = 0.30 m.

Figure 2-27 If the vertical length of the fill and vent pipes is such that, when filled with liquid, the static head imposed on the bottom of the tank exceeds 10 psig, then the *Code* requires the tank and related piping to be tested hydrostatically to a pressure equal to the static head thus imposed. When filled with water, for example, such pipes can increase the hydrostatic pressure on the bottom of the tank by 0.434 psig per ft of vertical length above the top of the tank.

rise into the vent pipe. However, under no circumstances should the pressure exceed the design pressure of the tank. (*See Figure 2-27.*)

2-7.3 In addition to the test called for in 2-7.1 and 2-7.2, all tanks and connections shall be tested for tightness. Except for underground tanks, this tightness shall be made at operating pressure with air, inert gas, or water prior to placing the tank in service. In the case of field-erected tanks, the test called for in 2-7.1 or 2-7.2 may be considered to be the test for tank tightness. Underground tanks and piping, before being covered, enclosed, or placed in use, shall be tested for tightness hydrostatically, or with air pressure at not less than 3 psi (20.6 kPa) and not more than 5 psi (34.5 kPa). (*See 3-7.1 for testing pressure piping.*) Air pressure shall not be used to test tanks that contain flammable or combustible liquids or vapors.

> Positive means, such as a relief valve or regulator, should be incorporated in the air supply to ensure that the test pressure does not exceed that specified. Air tests should not be made on top of stored product, which means that the test must be made prior to putting any gasoline or other liquid into the tank, nor should air

tests be made on tanks that have been emptied of liquid, but not purged of vapors. These are safety precautions to prevent formation of an ignitible atmosphere in the tank.

2-7.4 Before the tank is initially placed in service, all leaks or deformations shall be corrected in an acceptable manner. Mechanical caulking is not permitted for correcting leaks in welded tanks except pinhole leaks in the roof.

2-7.5 Tanks to be operated at pressures below their design pressure may be tested by the applicable provisions of 2-7.1 or 2-7.2 based upon the pressure developed under full emergency venting of the tank.

2-7.6 Each underground tank that has been repaired or altered, or is suspected of leaking, shall be tested in a manner approved by the authority having jurisdiction. (See NFPA 329, *Recommended Practice for Handling Underground Leakage of Flammable and Combustible Liquids*, for information on testing methods.)

> Prior to this edition of the *Code*, tanks were only *required* to be tested when first placed in service. In response to increased environmental and firesafety concerns, the *Code* now requires suitable tests *whenever* there is concern for leakage.

2-8 Fire Protection and Identification.

2-8.1 A fire extinguishing system in accordance with an applicable NFPA standard shall be provided or be available for vertical atmospheric fixed roof storage tanks larger than 50,000 gal (189,250 L) capacity, storing Class I liquids, if located in a congested area where there is an unusual exposure hazard to the tank from adjacent property or to adjacent property from the tank. Fixed roof tanks storing Class II or III liquids at temperatures below their flash points and floating roof tanks storing any liquid generally do not require protection when installed in compliance with Section 2-2.

> Fire extinguishing systems are not required for small fixed roof tanks because such tanks are seldom involved in fire. If they should become involved, there is little risk that the fire will spread. Spill fires cannot be extinguished by equipment designed for tank fires, and such fires are usually controlled by public fire departments.

> The spacings in Table 2-2 are based on the considerations contained in 2-8.1.

2-8.2 The application of NFPA 704, *Standard System for the Identification of the Fire Hazards of Materials*, to storage tanks containing liquids shall not be required except when the contents have a health or reactivity degree of hazard of 2 or more or a flammability rating of 4. The marking need not be applied directly to the tank but located where it can readily be seen, such as on the shoulder of an accessway or walkway to the tank or tanks or on the piping outside of the diked area. If more than one tank is involved, the markings shall be so located that each tank can readily be identified.

2-9 Prevention of Overfilling of Tanks.

The requirements of Section 2-9 are partly the result of a tank overfill incident that occurred in Newark, NJ. (The incident is discussed in detail in the Supplement.) This incident, which involved an explosion and fire (but, surprisingly, only one fatality) happened during the revision process for the 1984 edition of the *Code*.

In the 1981 edition of the *Code*, overfill prevention was required only for "tanks . . . located in an area where overfilling may endanger a place of habitation or public assembly." Three options were allowed: manual gaging at frequent intervals; independent high-level alarm located at an attended location; independent high-level alarm with automatic shutdown.

As a result of the Newark incident, a proposal was submitted to the Technical Committee to make all three options mandatory. The Technical Committee discussed this subject at great length, made its decision, and published its report. During the subsequent public review period, a number of comments were submitted on the Technical Committee's actions, suggesting additional or alternate solutions. Again, the Technical Committee met to review and act on the comments. The above Section 2-9 is the culmination of their efforts.

The significant changes from the 1981 edition are:

- Requiring overfill protection *wherever* Class I liquids are transferred from mainline pipelines or marine vessels;
- Including a requirement for formal written procedures.
- Requiring the *continuous* presence of personnel during the transfer operation at those facilities that are manned, and requiring two-way communication with the supply source.
- Requiring that a high-level detection device be independent of any gaging equipment.
- Allowing alternatives to the three options where approved by the authority having jurisdiction.

In addition, a requirement was added that any instrumentation be electrically supervised and that inspection and testing be conducted at least annually.

The Technical Committee did feel, however, that any one of the methods of protection would be adequate to provide an acceptable degree of safety. Thus, a choice among the four alternatives is still allowed. Also, the Technical Committee felt strongly that unmanned, fully automated receiving terminals should still be allowed, because their safety record has been very good. If the original proposal or many of the subsequent comments had been accepted, such unmanned facilities would have been prohibited.

As a further consequence of the Newark incident, the Committee on Safety and Fire Protection of the American Petroleum Institute led an effort to develop an industry guideline for overfill protection. This effort culminated in the development of API Recommended Practice 2350, *Overfill Protection for Petroleum Storage Tanks*. This publication provides comprehensive procedures to be followed in meeting the requirements of Section 2-9 of this *Code*, including procedures for both attended and unattended facilities, and detailed recommendations for written procedures.

2-9.1 Terminals receiving transfer of Class I liquids from mainline pipelines or marine vessels shall follow formal written procedures to prevent overfilling of tanks utilizing one of the following methods of protection:

(a) Tanks gaged at frequent intervals by personnel continuously on the premises during product receipt with frequent acknowledged communication maintained with the supplier so that flow can be promptly shut down or diverted.

(b) Tanks equipped with a high-level detection device that is independent of any tank gaging equipment. Alarms shall be located where personnel who are on duty throughout product transfer can promptly arrange for flow stoppage or diversion.

(c) Tanks equipped with an independent high-level detection system that will automatically shut down or divert flow.

(d) Alternatives to instrumentation described in (b) and (c) where approved by the authority having jurisdiction as affording equivalent protection.

2-9.1.1 Instrumentation systems covered in 2-9.1(b) and (c) shall be electrically supervised or equivalent.

2-9.2 Formal written procedures required in 2-9.1 shall include:

(a) Instructions covering methods to check for proper line up and receipt of initial delivery to tank designated to receive shipment.

(b) Provision for training and monitoring the performance of operating personnel by terminal supervision.

(c) Schedules and procedures for inspection and testing of gaging equipment and high-level instrumentation and related systems. Inspection and testing intervals shall be acceptable to the authority having jurisdiction, but shall not exceed one year.

2-10 Leakage Detection and Inventory Records for Underground Tanks. Accurate inventory records or a leak detection program shall be maintained on all Class I Liquid Storage Tanks for indication of possible leakage from the tanks or associated piping. (*See NFPA 329, Recommended Practice for Handling Underground Leakage of Flammable and Combustible Liquids.*)

Inventory records had been required by the *Code* prior to the 1981 edition, but only in Chapter 7, which governed service stations (now NFPA 30A, *Automotive and Marine Service Station Code*). The Technical Committee felt that this concept should be applied to all underground tanks containing Class I liquids, and so the preceding paragraph was inserted.

References Cited in Commentary

NFPA 15, *Standard for Water Spray Fixed Systems for Fire Protection*, NFPA, Quincy, MA, 1985.

NFPA 30A, *Automotive and Marine Service Station Code*, NFPA, Quincy, MA, 1987.

NFPA 69, *Standard on Explosion Prevention Systems*, NFPA, Quincy, MA, 1986.

NFPA 77, *Recommended Practice on Static Electricity*, NFPA, Quincy, MA, 1983.

NFPA 329, *Recommended Practice for Handling Underground Leakage of Flammable and Combustible Liquids*, NFPA, Quincy, MA, 1987.

Cote, A.E., and Linville, J.L., eds., *Fire Protection Handbook*, 16th ed., NFPA, Quincy, MA, 1986.

American Petroleum Institute, *Recommended Rules for the Design and Construction of Large, Welded, Low-Pressure Storage Tanks*, API 620, Seventh Edition, Washington, D.C., 1982.

American Petroleum Institute, *Welded Steel Tanks for Oil Storage*, API 650, Sixth Edition, Washington, D.C., 1980.

American Petroleum Institute, *Venting Atmospheric and Low-Pressure Storage Tanks*, API 2000, Third Edition, Washington, D.C., 1982.

American Petroleum Institute, *Protection Against Ignitions Arising Out of Static, Lightning, and Stray Currents*, API 2003, Washington, D.C., March 1982.

American Petroleum Institute, *Guides for Fighting Fires In and Around Petroleum Storage Tanks*, API 2021, Washington, D.C., Nov. 1980.

American Petroleum Institute, *Overfill Protection for Petroleum Storage Tanks*, API 2350, Washington, D.C., March 1987.

American Society of Mechanical Engineers, *ASME Boiler and Pressure Vessel Code, Code for Unfired Pressure Vessels*, Section VIII, Division I, New York, 1980.

American National Standards Institute, *American National Standard Code for Pressure Piping*, ANSI B31, New York, 1984.

American Society for Testing and Materials, *Standard Specifications for Automotive Gasoline*, ASTM D439, Philadelphia, 1979.

Bureau of Mines, *Flammability Characteristics of Combustible Gases and Vapors*, Bulletin 627, 1965.

Hasse, H., *Electrostatic Hazards: Their Evaluation and Control*, Verlag Chemie, New York, 1977.

National Academy of Sciences, *Pressure-Relieving Systems for Marine Cargo Bulk Liquid Containers*, Office of Publications, Washington, D.C., 1973.

Underwriters Laboratories Inc., *Standard for Steel Underground Tanks for Flammable and Combustible Liquids*, UL 58, Northbrook, IL, 1986.

Underwriters Laboratories Inc., *Standard for Steel Inside Tanks for Oil Burner Fuel*, UL 80, Northbrook, IL, 1980.

Underwriters Laboratories Inc., *Standard for Steel Aboveground Tanks for Flammable and Combustible Liquids*, UL 142, Northbrook, IL, 1972.

3 Piping, Valves, and Fittings

Any piping system is susceptible to leakage or spill of liquids. Because of the additional fire hazard in piping systems handling flammable and combustible liquids, these systems must be able to withstand the intense heat generated by fire for reasonable periods of time while emergency shutdown procedures are implemented and fire fighting measures begin. Failure of pipes, valves, and fittings during fire conditions can turn a moderate hazard into an extreme emergency.

3-1 General.

3-1.1 The design, fabrication, assembly, test, and inspection of piping systems containing liquids shall be suitable for the expected working pressures and structural stresses. Conformity with the applicable sections of ANSI B31, *American National Standard Code for Pressure Piping*, and the provisions of this chapter shall be considered prima facie evidence of compliance with the foregoing provisions.

It is important to consider the *expected* (or normal) working pressures and structural stresses. This is particularly necessary when high vapor pressure flammable liquids are involved or when tanks and piping systems are subject to heating. Heating may result from exposure to direct sunlight, from heat radiating off a process or piece of equipment, or from the liquid itself at elevated temperature.

3-1.2 This chapter does not apply to any of the following:

(a) Tubing or casing on any oil or gas wells and any piping connected directly thereto.

(b) Motor vehicle, aircraft, boat, or portable or stationary engine.

(c) Piping within the scope of any applicable boiler and pressure vessel code.

3-1.3 Piping systems consist of pipe, tubing, flanges, bolting, gaskets, valves, fittings, flexible connectors, the pressure containing parts of other components such as expansion joints and strainers, and devices that serve such purposes as mixing, separating, snubbing, distributing, metering, or controlling flow.

This paragraph specifies the elements and uses of a piping system.

3-2 Materials for Piping, Valves, and Fittings.

3-2.1 Pipe, valves, faucets, fittings, and other pressure-containing parts as covered in 3-1.3 shall meet the material specifications and pressure and temperature limitations of ANSI B31.3-1980, *Petroleum Refinery Piping*, or ANSI B31.4-1979, *Liquid Petroleum Transportation Piping Systems*, except as provided by 3-2.2, 3-2.3, and 3-2.4. Plastic or similar materials, as permitted by 3-2.4, shall be designed to specifications embodying recognized engineering principles and shall be compatible with the fluid service.

3-2.2 Nodular iron shall conform to ASTM A395-80, *Ferritic Ductile Iron Pressure Retaining Castings for Use at Elevated Temperatures*.

3-2.3 Valves at storage tanks, as required by 2-2.7.1 and 2-4.4.2, and their connections to the tank, shall be of steel or nodular iron except as provided in 3-2.3.1 or 3-2.3.2.

> Valves through which liquid can normally flow, e.g., those on aboveground storage tanks and tanks located inside buildings, should be of steel or nodular iron except when:
>
> (a) the chemical characteristics of the liquid are not compatible with steel (3-2.3.1);
>
> (b) the valves are installed inside the tank (3-2.3.1);
>
> (c) the valves are installed on crude petroleum tanks and they meet the requirements of 2-2.2.2 (3-2.3.2); or
>
> (d) the valves are installed on tanks used to store Class IIIB liquids, and they meet the requirements of 3-2.3.2.

3-2.3.1 Valves at storage tanks may be other than steel or nodular iron when the chemical characteristics of the liquid stored are not compatible with steel or when installed internally to the tank. When installed externally to the tank, the material shall have a ductility and melting point comparable to steel or nodular iron so as to withstand reasonable stresses and temperatures involved in fire exposure, or otherwise be protected such as by materials having a fire-resistance rating of not less than 2 hrs.

> The reason for requiring steel or nodular iron wherever possible is to ensure that the valve or fittings will be able to withstand reasonable stresses and temperatures created by a fire exposure. An

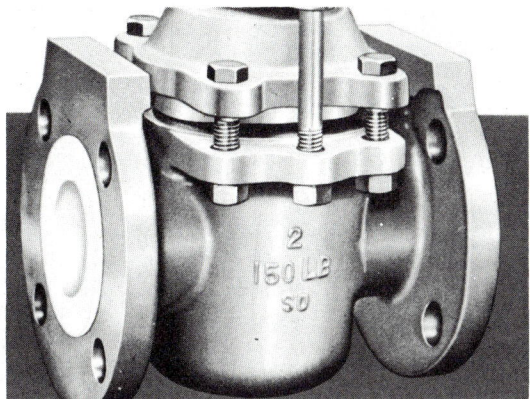

Figure 3-1 Typical installation of an internally mounted valve. Note that the valve mechanism is inside the tank shell and a fusible link is provided for automatic shutoff under fire exposure.

alternative to using steel, nodular iron, or a material of similar properties, is to protect the valve so it will have a fire resistance rating of 2 hrs.

Internal valves can be of other materials because the liquid keeps the piping and valve cool, thus avoiding failure under fire exposure. (*See Figure 3-1.*)

3-2.3.2 Cast iron, brass, copper, aluminum, malleable iron, and similar materials may be used on tanks described in 2-2.2.2 or for tanks storing Class IIIB liquids when the tank is located outdoors and not within a diked area or drainage path of a tank storing a Class I, Class II, or Class IIIA liquid.

3-2.4 Low melting point materials, such as aluminum, copper, and brass; or materials that soften on fire exposure, such as plastics; or nonductile material, such as cast iron, may be used underground for all liquids within the pressure and temperature limits of ANSI B31, *American National Standard Code for Pressure Piping*. If such materials are used outdoors in aboveground piping systems handling Class I, Class II, or Class IIIA liquids or within buildings handling any liquid, they shall be either: (a) suitably protected against fire exposure, or (b) so located that any leakage resulting from the failure would not unduly expose persons, important buildings, or structures, or (c) located where leakage can readily be controlled by operation of an accessible remotely located valve(s).

Questions have been raised involving applicability of this section to small-diameter instrument lines that may be subject to the effects of a flammable or combustible liquid fire. Instrument lines are not within the scope of NFPA 30, *Flammable and Combustible Liquids Code*.

112 FLAMMABLE AND COMBUSTIBLE LIQUIDS CODE HANDBOOK

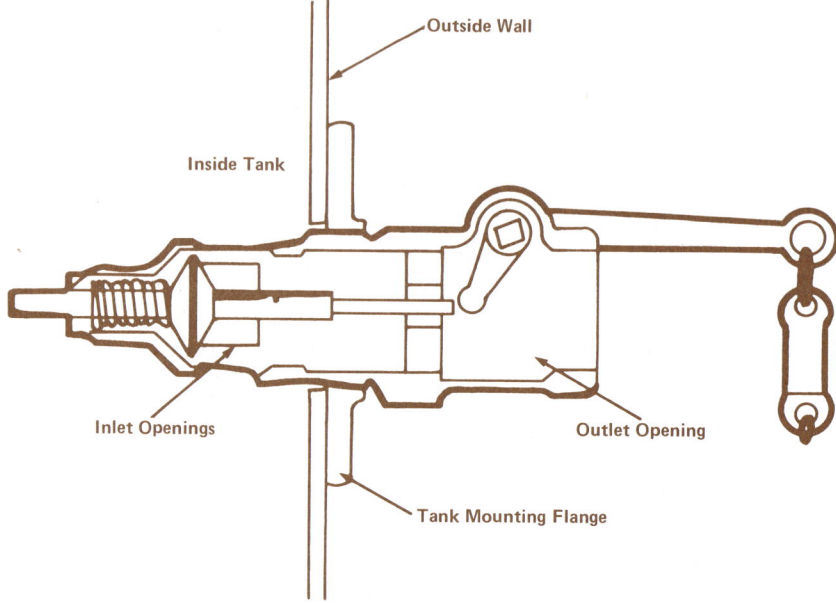

Figure 3-2 The *Code* recognizes both combustible and noncombustible linings for piping, valves, and fittings for corrosion protection and for other process and compatibility requirements.

3-2.5 Piping, valves, and fittings may have combustible or noncombustible linings.

Corrosion is a problem in piping, valves, and fittings. Plastic can be useful in preventing corrosion. The *Code* allows plastic or other such materials to be used internally, as linings in piping, valves, or fittings.

See Figure 3-2.

3-3 Pipe Joints.

3-3.1 Joints shall be made liquidtight and shall be either welded, flanged, or threaded, except that listed flexible connectors may be used when installed in accordance with 3-3.2. Threaded joints shall be made up tight with a suitable thread sealant or lubricant. Joints in piping systems handling Class I liquids shall be welded when located in concealed spaces within buildings.

To prevent the loss of liquid, *all* joints must be liquidtight. This is particularly critical with the more hazardous Class I liquids and explains the requirement for welded joints in concealed areas of a building.

3-3.2 Pipe joints dependent upon the friction characteristics or resiliency of combustible materials for mechanical continuity or liquidtightness of piping

NFPA 30—PIPING, VALVES, AND FITTINGS   113

shall not be used inside buildings. They may be used outside of buildings above or below ground. If used aboveground outside of buildings, the piping shall either be secured to prevent disengagement at the fitting, or the piping system shall be so designed that any spill resulting from disengagement could not unduly expose persons, important buildings, or structures, and could be readily controlled by remote valves.

> The additional restrictions on pipe joints that depend on friction or resiliency to maintain tightness are included because of their susceptibility to softening under fire exposure and because frost heaves may move the piping and thus disengage the joint. This latter problem has been particularly noticeable in the northern areas of the United States, often in service stations. The *Code* does limit use of this type of pipe joint to the outside of buildings. If used aboveground, piping must be secured or specially designed to prevent exposure to humans, important buildings, or structures in the event of failure. In addition, the piping system must be readily controlled by a remote valve(s). Flexible connectors may also be used under the same guidelines. Flexible connectors are often used in underground piping systems to avoid damage should the tank move. Swing joints made up with screwed elbows have been and still are used on some underground tanks, but these can complicate the proper installation of emergency shutoff valves under dispensers.

3-4 Supports. Piping systems shall be substantially supported and protected against physical damage and excessive stresses arising from settlement, vibration, expansion, or contraction. The installation of nonmetallic piping shall be in accordance with the manufacturer's instructions.

> Expansion rods or flexible connectors can be used to prevent undue stresses in piping systems.

3-5 Protection Against Corrosion. All piping for liquids, both aboveground and underground, where subject to external corrosion, shall be painted or otherwise protected. (*See 2-3.3 for protection of piping connected to underground tanks.*)

3-6 Valves. Piping systems shall contain a sufficient number of valves to operate the system properly and to protect the plant. Piping systems in connection with pumps shall contain a sufficient number of valves to control properly the flow of liquid in normal operation and in the event of physical damage. Each connection to piping by which equipment such as tank cars, tank vehicles, or marine vessels discharge liquids into storage tanks shall be provided with a check valve for automatic protection against back-flow if the piping arrangement is such that back-flow from the system is possible. (*See also 2-2.7.1.*)

The *Code* requirements for number of valves are quite broad and nonspecific. This is because of the variety of piping systems and the varying situations dictated by the occupancy and its use. Each piping system must be evaluated on its own merits, based on good engineering practice. If consideration is given to general safety guidelines, and to the potential results of failure, a determination as to the number and placement of valves can be made. Check valves are required only if backflow is possible.

The following Formal Interpretation was processed based on the 1981 edition of the *Code* and is still applicable.

Question: Does the requirement for check valves for automatic protection against backflow in 3-6.1 apply to marine unloading facilities?

Answer: Paragraphs 5-4.4.2.8 through 5-4.4.2.10 are applicable to marine flammable and combustible liquids wharves at bulk plants and provide exceptions and additions to Chapter 3, including 3-6.1. Use of check valves in tanker and barge unloading lines is not mandatory, but 5-4.4.2.8(d) requires the installation of block valves to control flow in the event of physical damage.

3-7 Testing. Unless tested in accordance with the applicable sections of ANSI B31, *American National Standard Code for Pressure Piping*, all piping, before being covered, enclosed, or placed in use, shall be hydrostatically tested to 150 percent of the maximum anticipated pressure of the system, or pneumatically tested to 110 percent of the maximum anticipated pressure of the system, but not less than 5 psi (34.5 kPa) gage at the highest point of the system. This test shall be maintained for a sufficient time to complete visual inspection of all joints and connections, but for at least 10 minutes.

Tests are not a guarantee that the system is perfect or that it will remain in good condition. They are, however, one method to help ensure that the system will perform as desired under normal circumstances and predictable emergency situations. Three methods are acceptable:

(a) meeting the requirements of ANSI B31, or

(b) hydrostatically testing to 150 percent of maximum system design pressure, or

(c) pneumatically testing to 110 percent of the maximum system design pressure. In any case, the test must be conducted for at least ten minutes or until a complete visual inspection is conducted of all joints and connections. The basic reason for the percentage differences between the pneumatic and hydrostatic test limits is safety. In the event of failure, a hydrostatic test will quickly relieve its pressure because of the noncompressibility of most fluids and the escaping water will safely discharge. A pneumatic failure will sometimes involve a violent rupture of the system being tested. As in the testing of tanks, the piping should be cleaned and purged of any flammable vapors and flammable or combustible liquids should not be used for the test fluid.

3-8* Identification. Each loading and unloading riser for liquid storage shall be identified by color code or marking to identify the product for which the tank is used.

A-3-8 Where loading and unloading risers for Class II or Class IIIA liquids are located in the same immediate area as loading and unloading risers for Class I liquids, consideration should be given to providing positive means, such as different pipe sizes, connection devices, special locks, or other methods designed to prevent the erroneous transfer of Class I liquids into or from any container or tank used for Class II or Class IIIA liquids.

Exception No. 1: This provision need not apply to water-miscible liquids when the class is determined by the concentration of liquid in water.

Exception No. 2: This provision need not apply where the equipment is cleaned between transfers.

This new requirement was added to address a continuing problem: that of inadvertent mixing of incompatible materials or of Class I liquids with higher flash point liquids. The appendix item to this section suggests some appropriate methods.

Reference Cited in Commentary

ANSI B31, *American National Standard Code for Pressure Piping*, American National Standards Institute, New York, 1984.

4 Container and Portable Tank Storage

Chapter 4 is based on studies of fire incidents, research, and fire tests that have determined the performance of containers and portable tanks under various fire conditions. Appendixes D and E explain and amplify some of the Chapter 4 requirements and also describe some of the relevant fire incidents and fire tests. Chapter 4 also contains information on the design, construction, and capacity of containers and storage cabinets; the design, construction, and operation of inside storage areas; and fire protection and fire control requirements for both indoor and outdoor storage of flammable and combustible liquids in containers and portable tanks.

4-1 Scope.

4-1.1 This chapter shall apply to the storage of liquids, including flammable aerosols, in drums or other containers not exceeding 60 gal (227 L) individual capacity and portable tanks not exceeding 660 gal (2498 L) individual capacity and limited transfers incidental thereto. For portable tanks exceeding 660 gal (2498 L), Chapter 2 shall apply.

Provisions of Chapter 4 of this *Code* apply to the storage of liquids in vessels with two distinct size limitations: (1) containers up to 60 gal (227 L), and (2) portable tanks of 60 to 660 gal (227 to 2498 L) capacity. This fact should be kept in mind when reading or applying the provisions of this chapter.

The chemical and distillery industries have been using portable tanks with capacities of up to 5,500 gal (20 818 L) for shipping their products. The tanks are built in accordance with U.S. Department of Transportation (DOT) specifications and are considered by the user industries to be portable tanks. Since the tanks do not meet this *Code's* definition of portable tanks because of their capacity, the reader is referred to Chapter 2, "Tank Storage," for guidance.

See also the discussion of Formal Interpretation 84-4 in the commentary following 1-1.7.1.

4-1.2 This chapter shall not apply to the following:

(a) Storage of containers in bulk plants, service stations, refineries, chemical plants, and distilleries.

> The storage of containers in bulk plants, refineries, chemical plants, and distilleries is excluded from the scope of Chapter 4 because each such occupancy has its own storage and handling requirements. (Requirements for the storage of containers in these particular occupancies are further discussed in Chapter 5, "Operations.") Often, these storage requirements are complicated by the fact that the operations inherently involve flammable and combustible liquids. Thus, their handling operations become as important as their safe storage.

(b) Liquids in the fuel tanks of motor vehicles, aircraft, boats, or portable or stationary engines.

> The *Code* is not totally clear on the subject of portable fuel tanks for boating. When these tanks are in the boat and connected to the boat motor, they are clearly exempt from the provisions of Chapter 4, as indicated in this paragraph. When they are removed, however, as for refilling, a question arises: Are they containers, and, if so, do they meet the *Code* requirements and limitations imposed on containers? It has been reported that some service station attendants have refused to fill such tanks because they exceed the maximum allowable size given in Table 4-2.3, and because they do not meet container requirements of NFPA 30A, *Automotive and Marine Service Station Code*. A request from the boating industry for a Formal Interpretation did not result in a clarification of the issue because the request lacked proper terminology and references. The request was withdrawn and has not been resubmitted.

(c) Beverages, when packaged in individual containers not exceeding a capacity of one gallon.

(d) Medicines, foodstuffs, cosmetics, and other consumer products containing not more than 50 percent by volume of water-miscible liquids and with the remainder of the solution not being flammable when packaged in individual containers not exceeding one gallon in size.

(e) The storage of liquids that have no fire point when tested by ASTM D 92-78, the Cleveland Open Cup Test Method, up to the boiling point of the liquid, or up to a temperature at which the sample being tested shows an obvious physical change.

> This may include a physical change (such as the change from a liquid to a gas or a liquid to a solid), a change in color, or an obvious change in viscosity. The reader is again reminded that the fire point is the temperature at which sustained burning will take place upon application of an outside ignition source. The fire point is usually

NFPA 30—CONTAINER AND PORTABLE TANK STORAGE

several degrees higher than the flash point, but still several hundred degrees lower than the autoignition temperature of the liquid. The liquids intended for exclusion by this paragraph of the *Code* are those that show a flash point when tested in accordance with a Tag or other closed-cup test method, but that do not burn. Water-based paints, which are formulated with small amounts of flammable or combustible solvents, are one example. Although these products may exhibit a flash point, the end product will not support combustion until the water boils off and the residue becomes thick and highly viscous.

(f) The storage of distilled spirits and wines in wooden barrels or casks.

When wooden barrels are exposed to fire, they do not fail violently. Rather, the metal hoops on the barrels expand, loosening the staves, and the leaking spirits add fuel to the fire. Sprinkler systems often control the fire before the barrels are affected.

4-1.3 For the purpose of this chapter, unstable liquids and flammable aerosols shall be treated as Class IA liquids.

Even though some of these liquids would not normally be classified as Class IA flammable liquids, additional requirements for their safe storage are recommended. Unstable liquids may decompose or react vigorously during a fire, causing their containers to overpressurize and rupture much more rapidly and violently than would containers of stable liquid. Similarly, flammable aerosols are liquids in pressurized containers that are likely to rupture under fire exposure conditions, spreading fire as they rocket. (*See Section 1-2 for the definition of flammable aerosol.*) When flammable aerosols are stored, the chief risk of ignition and early spread of fire involves their packaging. Any aerosol container will rupture if heated sufficiently, greatly hindering fire fighting efforts.

Concern for the safe storage of flammable aerosols became acute after the disastrous K Mart warehouse fire in June, 1982. In this fire, indiscriminate storage of aerosol containers in a general-purpose warehouse was a major contributor to the spread of the fire throughout this very large building. As a result, insuring organizations began developing their own guidelines for safe storage. For its part, NFPA has just recently authorized a separate Technical Committee project to develop suitable standards for the manufacture and storage of aerosol products.

4-2 Design, Construction, and Capacity of Containers.

4-2.1 Only approved containers and portable tanks shall be used. Metal containers and portable tanks meeting the requirements of, and containing products authorized by, Chapter I, Title 49 of the *Code of Federal Regulations* (DOT Regulations), or NFPA 386, *Standard for Portable Shipping Tanks for Flammable and Combustible Liquids*, shall be acceptable. Polyethylene containers meeting the requirements of, and containing products authorized by, DOT Specification 34, and polyethylene drums authorized by DOT Exemption Procedures, shall be acceptable. Plastic containers meeting the requirements of ANSI/ASTM D 3435-80, *Plastic Containers (Jerry Cans) for Petroleum Products*, used for petroleum products within the scope of that specification shall be acceptable.

> As with the larger storage tanks, the *Code* attempts to reduce fire hazards by setting rigid requirements for the design and construction of containers and portable tanks. Thus, only approved containers and portable tanks are allowed. This *Code* section specifies what *might* be considered an approved container or portable tank. It is important to note and emphasize that NFPA does not approve containers or container designs or specifications.

4-2.2 Each portable tank shall be provided with one or more devices installed in the top with sufficient emergency venting capacity to limit internal pressure under fire exposure conditions to 10 psig (68.9 kPa), or 30 percent of the bursting pressure of the tank, whichever is greater. The total venting capacity shall be not less than that specified in 2-2.5.4 or 2-2.5.6. At least one pressure-actuated vent having a minimum capacity of 6,000 cu ft (170 m^3) of free air per hour [14.7 psia (760 mm Hg) and 60°F (15.6°C)] shall be used. It shall be set to open at not less than 5 psig (34.5 kPa). If fusible vents are used, they shall be actuated by elements that operate at a temperature not exceeding 300°F (148.9°C). When used for paints, drying oils, and similar materials where plugging of the pressure-actuated vent can occur, fusible vents or vents of the type that soften to failure at a maximum of 300°F (148.9°C) under fire exposure may be used for the entire emergency venting requirement.

> The portable tanks described in this paragraph are generally rectangular in shape, of approximately 440 gal (1676 L) capacity, and are used for transporting paints and other finishing products. They may be constructed of steel, aluminum, or alloys containing magnesium.
>
> Vents are installed in the top of the tank to prevent the discharge of liquid under overpressure situations. Normally, the vents expel vapors generated by any increase in temperature. The vent requirements stated here attempt to meet two needs:
>
> (a) minimizing the overpressure due to normal changes in ambient temperature, and
>
> (b) the emergency relief venting required when the tank is subject to extreme temperature increases such as those generated

by a fire situation. The requirements of this paragraph for 6,000 cu ft (170 m³) of free air per hour may not be adequate for unstable liquids. It is assumed that tanks equipped with fusible vents will not exceed 5 psig (34.5 kPa) by the time the container walls are heated to a temperature of 300°F (148.9°C).

4-2.3 Containers and portable tanks for liquids shall conform to Table 4-2.3 except as provided in 4-2.3.1 or 4-2.3.2.

An example of an acceptable high-density polyethylene plastic container is the "Jerry" can that is designed to meet the ANSI/ASTM D 3435-83 requirement and that has been approved by some jurisdictions for storing petroleum products. Plastic containers made of low-density polyethylene, such as found in bleach-bottle-type construction, should not be used for routine, repeated storage of most petroleum products. Although low-density polyethylene containers are allowed for one-time shipment of Classes IC, II, and III liquids, they do not meet the rigid requirements of these special high-density plastic containers.

One minor problem has arisen with the use of the metric equivalents in Table 4-2.3. Strict interpretation of these equivalents would rule out such popular metric container sizes as 0.5, 1.0, and 4.0 liters. (These sizes are becoming more common for containers for laboratory reagents.) Since the difference between these sizes and the metric equivalents of the table values represents only a 5% increase in liquid volume, most authorities would likely overlook the discrepancy. The difference in risk is probably not consequential.

Table 4-2.3 Maximum Allowable Size of Containers and Portable Tanks

Container Type	Flammable Liquids			Combustible Liquids	
	Class IA	Class IB	Class IC	Class II	Class III
Glass	1 pt	1 qt	1 gal	1 gal	5 gal
Metal (other than DOT drums) or approved plastic	1 gal	5 gal	5 gal	5 gal	5 gal
Safety Cans	2 gal	5 gal	5 gal	5 gal	5 gal
Metal Drum (DOT Spec.)	60 gal	60 gal	60 gal	60 gal	60 gal
Approved Portable Tanks	660 gal	660 gal	660 gal	660 gal	660 gal
Polyethylene DOT Spec. 34, or as authorized by DOT Exemption	1 gal	5 gal	5 gal	60 gal	60 gal

SI Units: 1 pt = 0.473 L; 1 qt = 0.95 L; 1 gal = 3.8 L.

4-2.3.1 Medicines, beverages, foodstuffs, cosmetics, and other common consumer products, when packaged according to commonly accepted practices for retail sales, shall be exempt from the requirements of 4-2.1 and 4-2.3.

During development of the 1984 edition of the *Code*, the Technical Committee considered placing the word "similar" before the words "common consumer products." The intent was to help clarify what types of products might fall into the common consumer product category. On further consideration and after receipt of a comment objecting to the change, the addition was reconsidered and the proposed action was reversed. Addition of the word "similar" would, in effect, limit requirements from common consumer items to only medicines, beverages, foodstuffs, and cosmetics. Numerous other consumer products are marketed in containers that are not in strict compliance with packaging requirements in the *Code*, and there is no indication that such products are creating a firesafety problem. As the submitter of the comment argued, inclusion of the word "similar," with its limiting implication, would cause undue interference with public convenience without any increase in public safety.

Formal Interpretation 81-2 is pertinent here.

Question: Is it the intent of NFPA 30, Paragraph 4-2.3.1 to exempt kerosene fuel with a flash point of 150°F stored in 2- to 2½-gallon nonlisted plastic containers for retail sale from the requirements of Paragraphs 4-2.1 and 4-2.3?

Answer: No.

The reader is referred to 4-2.3.2 for additional information.

4-2.3.2 DOT Type III polyethylene nonreusable containers, constructed and tested in accordance with DOT specification 2U, treated if necessary to prevent permeation, may be used for storage of Class II and Class III liquids, in all capacities not to exceed 2½ gal.

This paragraph came about as a result of proposals received from container manufacturers who wanted to produce DOT 2U specification containers for marketing kerosene. Several comments were received in opposition to the paragraph and a good deal of Technical Committee discussion took place before the action was finalized. In the opinion of the Technical Committee, some guidance is necessary to address and deal with the increased use of plastic containers in this type of service. This paragraph will provide a recognized specification that both marketers and enforcing authorities can use.

4-2.3.3 Class IA and Class IB liquids may be stored in glass containers of not more than one gallon capacity if the required liquid purity (such as ACS analytical reagent grade or higher) would be affected by storage in metal containers or if the liquid would cause excessive corrosion of the metal container.

This exception is included to avoid unnecessarily restricting laboratory use of flammable and combustible liquids, while still providing an acceptable degree of firesafety.

4-3 Design, Construction, and Capacity of Storage Cabinets.

4-3.1 Not more than 120 gal (454 L) of Class I, Class II, and Class IIIA liquids may be stored in a storage cabinet. Of this total, not more than 60 gal (227 L) may be of Class I and Class II liquids and not more than three (3) such cabinets may be located in a single fire area, except that, in an industrial occupancy, additional cabinets may be located in the same fire area if the additional cabinet, or group of not more than three (3) cabinets, is separated from other cabinets or group of cabinets by at least 100 ft (30 m).

Depending on the particular occupancy of a building, certain lesser quantities of flammable or combustible liquids are permitted to be stored in a safe place, outside of a specific storage cabinet or room. (See Section 4-5 and Chapter 5 for additional details as to when storage cabinets are required.) Large quantities will often require storage in a separate storage room or area, or possibly may require storage in a flammable liquids warehouse.

Most commercially available and approved storage cabinets are built to hold 60 gal (227 L) or less of flammable and combustible liquids. A fire area is an area of a building separated from the rest of the building by construction having a fire resistance rating of at least 1 hr and having all communicating openings properly protected by an assembly having a fire protection rating of at least 1 hr. Note that in industrial occupancies, separation may be achieved by distance [100 ft (30 m)] as well as by construction. These are not to be considered equal concepts. Fire area has a clear and precise definition.

Industrial occupancies are intended to include factories making products of all kinds and properties devoted to operations such as processing, assembling, mixing, packaging, finishing or decorating, and repairing. (Also see Chapter 5.)

The reader should note that, although the cabinets are usually referred to as "flammable liquid" storage cabinets, combustible liquids are allowed to be stored in them as well. Keep in mind that the liquids stored in a cabinet should be mutually compatible.

Finally, it must be remembered that these cabinets are designed and constructed for flammable and combustible liquid storage *only*. They are not intended for the storage of small cylinders of compressed or liquefied gases, especially those that are flammable. Likewise, incompatible materials, whether liquid or solid, should not be stored in these cabinets.

4-3.2* Storage cabinets shall be designed and constructed to limit the internal temperature at the center, 1 in. (2.5 cm) from the top to not more than 325°F (162.8°C) when subjected to a 10-minute fire test with burners simulating a room fire exposure using the standard time-temperature curve as given in ASTM E 152-81a. All joints and seams shall remain tight and the door shall remain securely closed during the fire test.

The cabinet is not required to be vented for fire protection purposes; however, the following shall apply:

(a) If the cabinet is vented for other reasons, the cabinet shall be vented outdoors in such a manner that will not compromise the specified performance of the cabinet, as acceptable to the authority having jurisdiction.

(b) If the cabinet is not vented, the vent openings shall be sealed with a properly fitted metal bung.

A-4-3.2 Venting of storage cabinets has not been demonstrated to be necessary for fire protection purposes. Additionally, venting a cabinet could compromise the ability of the cabinet to adequately protect its contents from involvement in a fire since cabinets are not generally tested with any venting. Therefore, venting of storage cabinets is not recommended.

However, it is recognized that some jurisdictions may require storage cabinets to be vented and that venting may also be desirable for other reasons, such as health and safety. In such cases, the venting system should be installed so as to not affect substantially the desired performance of the cabinet during a fire. Means of accomplishing this may include thermally actuated dampers on the vent openings or sufficiently insulating the vent piping system to prevent the internal temperature of the cabinet from rising above that specified. Any make-up air to the cabinet should also be arranged in a similar manner.

If vented, the cabinet should be vented from the bottom with makeup air supplied to the top. Also, mechanical exhaust ventilation is preferred and should comply with NFPA 91, *Standard for the Installation of Blower and Exhaust Systems for Dust, Stock, and Vapor Removal or Conveying*. Manifolding the vents of multiple storage cabinets should be avoided.

> An approved storage cabinet is designed and constructed to protect the contents from external fires. The 10-minute fire test criterion is based on the estimated time for a room or portion of a building to become seriously involved in fire. The standard time-

temperature curve from which this information is taken is given in ASTM E152 and in NFPA 252, *Standard Methods of Fire Tests of Door Assemblies*, and appears below:

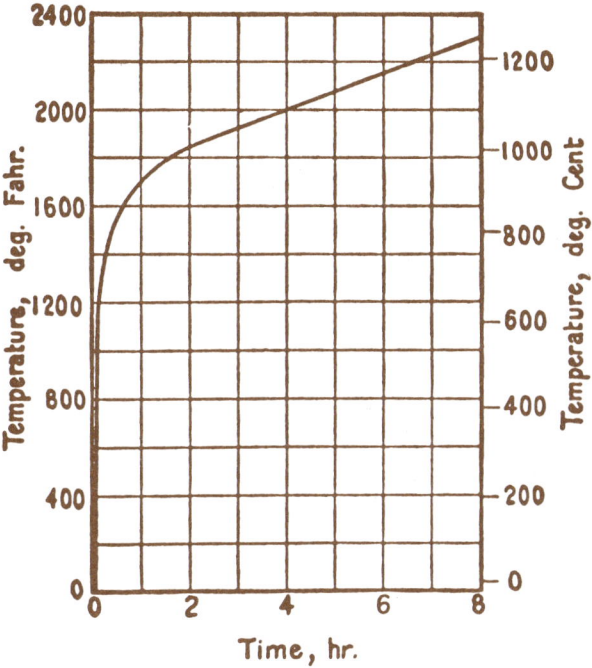

1000° F (538° C)....at 5 minutes
1300° F (704° C)....at 10 minutes
1550° F (843° C)....at 30 minutes
1638° F (892° C)....at 45 minutes
1700° F (927° C)....at 1 hour
1792° F (978° C)....at 1½ hours
1925° F (1052° C)....at 3 hours

Figure 4-1   Time-Temperature Curve.

As now more clearly stated in this edition of the *Code*, the cabinet is not required to be vented for fire protection purposes. However, vent openings are often provided by manufacturers because some jurisdictions mandate that the cabinet be vented to prevent vapor accumulation in the cabinet and because some users desire this feature if the cabinet will be used for toxic or noxious materials. It should be recognized that venting the cabinet may defeat its purpose. If it is not necessary or required that the cabinet be vented, then the vent openings should be kept tightly capped with the metal bungs provided for that purpose.

If the cabinet must be vented, then these procedures should be followed:

- Remove both metal bungs and replace with flash arrestor screens (normally provided with cabinets). The top opening will serve as the fresh air inlet.
- Connect the bottom opening to an exhaust fan by a substantial metal tubing having an inside diameter no smaller than the vent. The tubing should be rigid steel.
- The fan should have a nonsparking fan blade and nonsparking shroud. It should exhaust directly to outside.
- The total run of exhaust duct should not exceed 25 feet.

A recent question about the proper ventilation of a storage cabinet asked if it was acceptable to vent the cabinet directly to the interior of a standard laboratory hood via flexible plastic duct. This is totally improper and dangerous. Not only is the cabinet's integrity violated, but safety of the hood and anyone using it is seriously compromised.

It is important to remember that glass containers exposed to heat will fail at about 212°F (100°C) due to thermally induced stress. Storage cabinets do offer protection, but for a limited period of intense fire exposure. Their limitations must be recognized. Specially designed cabinets that provide extra protection for glass containers are available.

4-3.2.1 Metal cabinets constructed in the following manner are acceptable. The bottom, top, door, and sides of cabinet shall be at least No. 18 gage sheet steel and double walled with 1½ in. (3.8 cm) air space. Joints shall be riveted, welded, or made tight by some equally effective means. The door shall be provided with a three-point latch arrangement and the door sill shall be raised at least 2 in. (5 cm) above the bottom of the cabinet to retain spilled liquid within the cabinet.

See Figure 4-2.

The three-point latch arrangement on the doors is intended to help maintain the integrity of the cabinet under fire exposure. Without a three-point latch arrangement, the metal will warp when exposed to a fire and expose the cabinet's contents to the fire. Note that the *Code* does not specify a test for cabinets built in accordance with this paragraph.

NFPA 30—CONTAINER AND PORTABLE TANK STORAGE 127

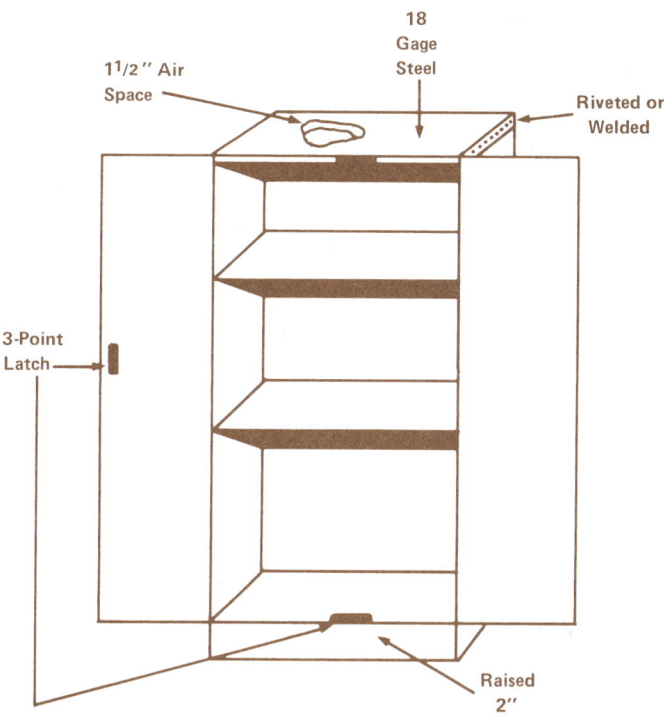

SI Units: 1 in. = 2.5 cm.

Figure 4-2 Metal cabinets constructed in this manner are acceptable.

4-3.2.2 Wooden cabinets constructed in the following manner are acceptable. The bottom, sides, and top shall be constructed of exterior grade plywood at least 1 in. (2.5 cm) in thickness, which shall not break down or delaminate under fire conditions. All joints shall be rabbetted and shall be fastened in two directions with wood screws. When more than one door is used, there shall be a rabbetted overlap of not less than 1 in. (2.5 cm). Doors shall be equipped with a means of latching and hinges shall be constructed and mounted in such a manner as to not lose their holding capacity when subjected to fire exposure. A raised sill or pan capable of containing a 2-in. (5-cm) depth of liquid shall be provided at the bottom of the cabinet to retain spilled liquid within the cabinet.

See Figure 4-3.

Although not required to do so, a cabinet built to these requirements will meet the test specifications of 4-3.2.

4-3.2.3 Listed cabinets that have been constructed and tested in accordance with 4-3.2 shall be acceptable.

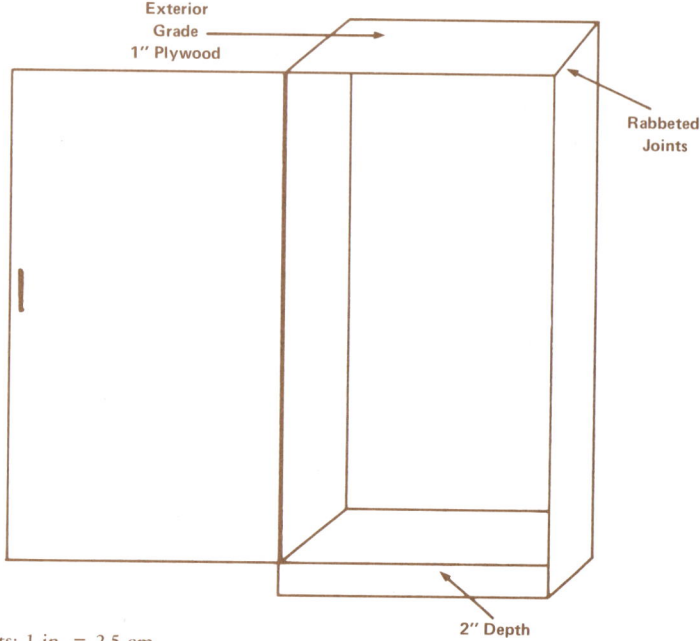

Figure 4-3 Wooden cabinets constructed in this manner are acceptable. Note that the *Code* does not require a three-point latch on the doors because wood does not tend to warp or distort when exposed to fire, as metal does.

4-4 Design, Construction, and Operation of Separate Inside Storage Areas. *(See Section 1-2, Definitions.)* (For additional information, see Appendix C.)

The reader is referred to the definitions in Section 1-2 of "inside room," "cutoff room," and "attached building," and also to Figure 1-5. Generally, inside rooms provide relatively large storage capacity for flammable and combustible liquids. In many occupancies, it is common for inside rooms to serve as intermediate storage locations. For example, many hospitals, large university science departments, and private research and development facilities have an outside building that is used for storing their bulk quantities of flammable and combustible liquids. These outside storage buildings then supply several inside storage rooms that may be located in different buildings or on different floors of a single building. In turn, these inside storage rooms supply the storage cabinets in the individual laboratories where the liquids are finally used. Because of the potential fire hazard from inside storage areas to the rest of the building, the *Code* sets rigid requirements for the design, construction, and operation of these rooms. Note that explosion relief is not required for inside rooms, even though Class I liquids may be dispensed within them, because an inside room has no exterior walls and only rarely will its ceiling coincide with the roof of the building.

4-4.1 Inside Rooms.

4-4.1.1 Inside rooms shall be constructed to meet the selected fire-resistance rating as specified in 4-4.1.4. Such construction shall comply with the test specifications given in NFPA 251, *Standard Methods of Fire Tests of Building Construction and Materials*. Except for drains, floors shall be liquidtight and the room shall be liquidtight where the walls join the floor. Where an automatic fire protection system is provided, as indicated in 4-4.1.4, the system shall be designed and installed in accordance with the appropriate NFPA standard for the type of system selected.

4-4.1.2 Openings in interior walls to adjacent rooms or buildings shall be provided with:

(a) Normally closed, listed 1½ hr (B) fire doors for interior walls with fire-resistance rating of 2 hr or less. Where interior walls are required to have greater than 2 hr fire-resistance rating, the listed fire doors shall be compatible with the wall rating. Doors may be arranged to stay open during material handling operations if doors are designed to close automatically in a fire emergency by provision of listed closure devices. Fire doors shall be installed in accordance with NFPA 80, *Standard for Fire Doors and Windows*.

(b) Noncombustible liquidtight raised sills or ramps at least 4 in. (10 cm) in height or otherwise designed to prevent the flow of liquids to the adjoining areas. A permissible alternative to the sill or ramp is an open-grated trench, which drains to a safe location, across the width of the opening inside of room.

> Ramping is the most common method. If an open-grated trench is used, it must extend across the entire opening (door) into the room and must be located on the inside of the room. The trench must also be designed to drain the collected spilled liquid to a safe location. This method may be preferred if there is an extensive need to transfer flammable liquids into and out of the room by means of hand trucks. (*See Figure 4-4.*)

4-4.1.3 Wood at least 1 in. (2.5 cm) nominal thickness may be used for shelving, racks, dunnage, scuffboards, floor overlay, and similar installations.

> Note that no mention is made of metal shelving, nor is there any control over its use. In fact, drum racks used in inside rooms are almost always metal. Although wood will add to the fire load in the room, it is preferred because it minimizes the chances of damage to or breakage of containers.

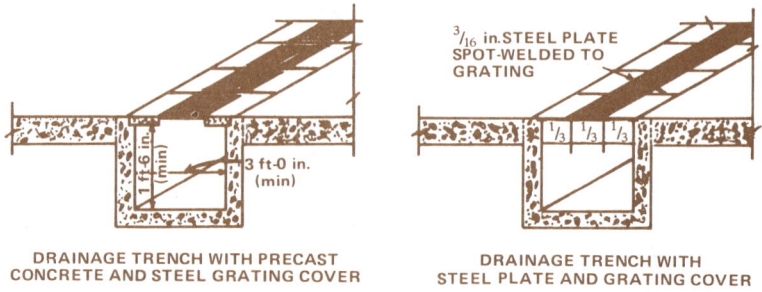

Figure 4-4 Drainage trench details.

4-4.1.4 Storage in inside rooms shall comply with the following:

Automatic Fire Protection* Provided	Fire Resistance	Maximum Floor Area	Total Allowable Quantities—Gallons/ Sq Ft/Floor Area
YES	2 hr	500 sq ft	10
NO	2 hr	500 sq ft	4**
YES	1 hr	150 sq ft	5
NO	1 hr	150 sq ft	2

SI Units: 1 sq ft = 0.09 m^2; 1 gal = 3.8 L.
*Fire protection system shall be sprinkler, water spray, carbon dioxide, dry chemical, halon, or other approved system.
**Total allowable quantities of Class IA and IB Liquids shall not exceed that permitted in Table 4-4.2.7 and the provisions of 4-4.2.10.

The second footnote (**) was added to the 1981 edition of the *Code*. An inside room without automatic fire protection could have had as much as 2,000 gal (7570 L) of a Class IA or Class IB liquid, while the maximum quantity is limited to 660 gal (2498 L) and 1,375 gal (5204 L), respectively, in a cutoff room or attached building. This change reconciles the discrepancy.

Note that decreasing the fire resistance rating of the construction by 50% is penalized by a 70% reduction in floor area. If automatic fire protection is not provided, the penalty is 60%.

4-4.1.5 Electrical wiring and equipment located in inside rooms used for Class I liquids shall be suitable for Class I, Division 2 classified locations; for Class II and Class III liquids, shall be suitable for general use. NFPA 70, *National Electrical Code*®, provides information on the design and installation of electrical equipment.

Caution: All "vaporproof" types of lighting fixtures are not suitable for use in atmospheres containing flammable vapors. This designation often refers only to the fixture's capability to prevent moisture from entering the fixture. Approved fixtures will be

NFPA 30—CONTAINER AND PORTABLE TANK STORAGE 131

properly labeled for their use and will normally be indicated as being "vaportight" or "explosionproof."

4-4.1.6 Every inside room shall be provided with either a gravity or a continuous mechanical exhaust ventilation system. Mechanical ventilation shall be used if Class I liquids are dispensed within the room.

(a) Exhaust air shall be taken from a point near a wall on one side of the room and within 12 in. (30 cm) of the floor with one or more make-up inlets located on the opposite side of the room within 12 in. (30 cm) from the floor. The location of both the exhaust and inlet air openings shall be arranged to provide, as far as practicable, air movements across all portions of the floor to prevent accumulation of flammable vapors. Exhaust from the room shall be directly to the exterior of the building without recirculation.

Exception: Recirculation is permitted where it is monitored continuously using a fail-safe system that is designed to automatically sound an alarm, stop recirculation, and provide full exhaust to the outside in the event that vapor-air mixtures in concentration over one-fourth of the lower flammable limit are detected.

If ducts are used, they shall not be used for any other purpose and shall comply with NFPA 91, *Standard for the Installation of Blower and Exhaust Systems for Dust, Stock, and Vapor Removal or Conveying*. If make-up air to a mechanical system is taken from within the building, the opening shall be equipped with a fire door or damper, as required in NFPA 91, *Standard for the Installation of Blower and Exhaust Systems for Dust, Stock, and Vapor Removal or Conveying*. For gravity systems, the make-up air shall be supplied from outside the building.

> The exception is a significant change made with the 1984 edition of the *Code*. Previously, recirculation of exhaust air was prohibited, regardless of measures taken to ensure safety. This resulted in high energy costs, especially in colder climates. With the availability of reliable vapor detection technology, the Technical Committee felt that recirculation could be allowed if the proper precautions were taken.
>
> Ventilation is vital to the prevention of flammable liquid fires and explosions. In a room where the potential accumulation of flammable vapors can fall within the flammable range of the stored material, every effort must be made to confine, remove, or dilute these vapors, thereby reducing the probability of ignition. Remember that the vapors from most flammable and combustible liquids are heavier than air, thus the requirement for exhaust ventilation to be initiated at or near the floor level.

(b) Mechanical ventilation systems shall provide at least one cubic foot per minute of exhaust per square foot of floor area (1 m^3 per 3 m^2), but not less than 150 cfm (4 m^3). The mechanical ventilation system for dispensing areas shall be equipped with an airflow switch or other equally reliable method that is interlocked to sound an audible alarm upon failure of the ventilation system.

> When relying on a mechanical ventilation system, it is important to know that the system is functioning at all times. This explains the requirement for the airflow (or other) interlocking switch, since air movement less than intended design might allow the accumulation of a hazardous level of flammable vapors in the room. Also see comments following 5-3.3.1.

4-4.1.7 In every inside room, an aisle at least 3 ft (0.90 m) wide shall be maintained so that no container is more than 12 ft (3.6 m) from the aisle. Containers over 30 gal (113.5 L) capacity storing Class I or Class II liquids shall not be stored more than one container high.

> Easy movement within the room is necessary in order to reduce the potential for spilling or damaging the containers and to provide both access for fire fighting and ready escape paths for occupants of the room, should a fire occur. To further reduce the possibility of damage to containers, Class I and II flammable liquid containers over 30 gallons (113.5 L) in capacity should not be stored more than one container high. Such containers are built to DOT specifications and are not required to withstand a drop test greater than 3 ft (0.90 m) when full.

4-4.1.8 Where dispensing is being done in inside rooms, operations shall comply with the provisions of Chapter 5.

4-4.1.9 **Basement Storage Areas.** Class I liquids shall not be permitted in inside storage rooms in basement areas.

4-4.2 **Cutoff Rooms and Attached Buildings.**

4-4.2.1 Construction design of exterior walls shall provide ready accessibility for fire fighting operations through provision of access openings, windows, or lightweight noncombustible wall panels. Where Class IA or IB liquids are dispensed, or where Class IA liquids are stored in containers larger than one gallon, the exterior wall or roof construction shall be designed to include explosion-venting features, such as lightweight wall assemblies, lightweight roof assemblies, roof hatches, or windows of the explosion-venting type. NFPA 68, *Guide for Explosion Venting*, provides information on this subject.

> Because some operations require storage of a greater quantity of flammable and combustible liquids than would be allowed in an inside storage room, a cutoff room or attached building may be used. These are allowed to store a greater quantity of liquids

because they have at least one exterior wall. The exterior wall provides ready access for fire fighting operations and the necessary vent area, should explosion vents be required.

Although explosion venting (more properly, deflagration venting) may be required by this paragraph, its use must be carefully considered. The user is referred to NFPA 68, *Guide for Explosion Venting*, for the proper calculation procedure for sizing the vent area and for pertinent details of vent construction and installation. In many cases, the exterior wall(s) cannot provide the required vent area. In such situations, the interior walls may have to be strengthened to accommodate the resulting overpressure. Careful consideration must also be given to the direction in which combustion gases will be vented to prevent injury to personnel. Although window units are allowed, the sash should not be made of any material that will break into sharp pieces, such as glass or rigid plastic. Doors in interior walls must have positive latches strong enough to prevent the door from opening due to the overpressure of an explosion in the room.

4-4.2.2 Where other portions of buildings or other properties are exposed, each opening in the exposing wall shall be protected with a listed 1½ hr (D) fire door installed in accordance with NFPA 80, *Standard for Fire Doors and Windows*, and the walls shall have a fire-resistance rating of not less than 2 hrs.

The (D) rating on the door indicates that the door is designed for installation in an exterior wall that is subject to severe fire exposure. Explosion vents should not be located in the same wall that requires the rated door.

4-4.2.3 Except as noted in 4-4.2.6, interior walls, ceiling, and floors shall have a fire-resistance rating of not less than 2 hrs where floor area of the room or building exceeds 300 sq ft (27 m^2) or a fire-resistance rating of not less than one hour for a floor area of 300 sq ft (27 m^2) or less. Such construction shall comply with the test specifications given in NFPA 251, *Standard Methods of Fire Tests of Building Construction and Materials*. Walls shall be liquidtight at the floor level.

4-4.2.4 Openings in interior walls to adjacent rooms or buildings shall be in accordance with 4-4.1.2(a).

Any opening in the interior wall of cutoff rooms or attached buildings to adjacent rooms or buildings must have fire doors and either a drainage trench or raised sills or ramps that meet the same requirements as those for inside rooms. (*See comments under 4-4.1.2.*)

4-4.2.5 Curbs, scuppers, special drains, or other suitable means shall be provided to prevent the flow of liquids under emergency conditions into adjacent building areas except where the individual container capacity is 5 gal (18.9 L) or less or if the liquids stored are only Class III liquids. The drainage system, if used, shall have sufficient capacity to carry off expected discharge of water from fire protection systems and hose streams.

> The exceptions reflect the reduced hazard involved with smaller quantities of flammable and combustible liquids and higher flash point liquids. The reader is cautioned to make sure that the most restrictive case is considered in the initial construction of these rooms, since remodeling to upgrade the facility for use with more hazardous liquids can be expensive. Users of cutoff rooms and attached buildings that lack curbs, scuppers, etc., must be advised so they understand that 5 gal (19 L) is the maximum allowable size of the individual container for any Class I or Class II flammable liquid. Because most flammable liquids that are immiscible with water are also lighter than water, it is important that the capacity of the drainage system be sufficient to drain the water from the fire protection system and hose streams, as well as the flammable liquid itself.

4-4.2.6 Roofs of attached buildings, one story in height, may be lightweight noncombustible construction if the separating interior wall as specified in 4-4.2.3 has a minimum 3-ft (0.90-m) parapet.

4-4.2.7 Unprotected storage in cutoff rooms and attached buildings shall comply with Table 4-4.2.7. (*See 4-4.2.10 for mixed storage of liquids.*)

> Table 4-4.2.7 specifies the maximum pile height, maximum quantity per pile, and maximum total quantity allowed for each class of liquid and is to be used for any cutoff room or attached building that is not provided with an automatic fire protection system. When applying the provisions of this table to actual situations, it is important to consider each restriction in succession to avoid overlooking individual limitations. Therefore, the first item to consider would be the maximum allowable pile height in accordance with the class of the liquid, then the maximum quantity per pile, and lastly, the maximum total quantity within the cutoff room or attached building. Note that there are different requirements for container storage than there are for portable tank storage. Larger quantities are permitted in portable tanks because they are vented for fire exposure conditions and are less likely to explode from internal overpressure. Containers and portable tanks cannot be in the same pile because of this fact.

Table 4-4.2.7 Indoor Unprotected Storage of Liquids in Containers and Portable Tanks

Class	Container Storage			Portable Tank Storage		
	Max. Pile Height (ft)	Max. Quant. per Pile (gal)	Max. Total Quant. (gal)	Max. Pile Height (ft)	Max. Quant. per Pile (gal)	Max. Total Quant. (gal)
IA	5	660	660	—	Not Permitted	—
IB	5	1,375	1,375	7	2,000	2,000
IC	5	2,750	2,750	7	4,000	4,000
II	10	4,125	8,250	7	5,500	11,000
IIIA	15	13,750	27,500	7	22,000	44,000
IIIB	15	13,750	55,000	7	22,000	88,000

SI Units: 1 ft = 0.30 m; 1 gal = 3.8 L.

In order to put Table 4-4.2.7 to practical use, three examples follow.

1. You are in charge of the chemical supply room of a large state university. You have just received 900 gal (3406.5 L) of isopropyl alcohol (Class IB) and 900 gal (3406.5 L) of 95 percent ethyl alcohol (Class IB), all in containers. To conserve space, you arrange each liquid in two piles of 450 gal (1703.2 L) each.

Solution: Both alcohols are Class IB liquids, so the 450 gal (1703.2 L) per pile is permitted by Table 4-4.2.7. Table 4-4.2.7 also allows a maximum total quantity of 1,375 gal (5204 L). The received quantity of flammable liquids is 1,800 gal (6813 L), however, and this is beyond the maximum quantity permitted.

2. On an inspection of a wire coating and insulation factory, you note that, among the many liquids in an attached building, there are four piles of portable tanks of a Class II liquid. Each pile is 6 ft (1.8 m) high and contains three 500 gal (1892) portable tanks.

Solution: Both the quantity per pile {1,500 gal (5700 L)} and the total quantity {6,000 gal (22 710 L)} are under the maximum quantities permitted by Table 4-4.2.7 for Class II liquids.

3. You have been hired by an insurance company to inspect the liquid storage room of a large manufacturing plant. In the storage room are eight small piles {under 5 ft (1.5 m) high} of containers storing degreasers with flash points above 140°F (60°C). Each pile contains 1,100 gal (4163 L) of the liquid.

Solution: The total amount of degreaser stored is substantially less than the maximum of 13,750 gal (52 040 L) specified for pile storage of a Class IIIA liquid in Table 4-4.2.7.

4-4.2.8 Protected storage in cutoff rooms and attached buildings shall comply with Section 4-6 as applicable. (*See 4-4.2.10 for mixed storage of liquids*.)

This paragraph directs the reader to Section 4-6, "Protection Requirements for Protected Storage of Liquids." If a cutoff room or attached building meets the protection requirements and storage and handling provisions of Section 4-6, it is allowed to store greater quantities of liquid, as indicated in Tables 4-6.1(a) and 4-6.1(b).

4-4.2.9 Wood at least 1-in. (2.5-cm) nominal thickness may be used for shelving, racks, dunnage, scuffboards, floor overlay, and similar installations.

4-4.2.10 Where two or more classes of liquids are stored in a single pile or rack section, the maximum quantities and height of storage permitted in that

NFPA 30—CONTAINER AND PORTABLE TANK STORAGE   137

pile or rack section shall be the smallest of the two or more separate quantities and heights. The maximum total quantities permitted shall be limited to a sum of proportional amounts that each class of liquid present bears to the maximum total permitted for its respective class; sum of proportional amounts not to exceed 100 percent.

Since containers of volatile liquids are more likely to rupture under fire conditions, this paragraph limits the maximum quantity and height of mixed storage in a pile or rack section to that of the most hazardous class of liquid present. For example, if both Class IB and II liquids are stored in a single pile inside an unprotected cutoff room, the maximum pile height is 5 ft (1.5 m), as shown in Table 4-4.2.7 for Class I liquids. The maximum quantity for the pile will be limited to 1,375 gallons (5225 L). If any Class IA liquid is added to the pile, the maximum quantity of liquid, per pile, is restricted to 660 gallons (2508 L).

To calculate the maximum total quantity allowed for each individual class of liquid present, proceed as follows, beginning with the lowest class of liquid present and proceeding in order of decreasing hazard:

- Compute the ratio of the amount of each class present to the maximum total quantity allowed for that class, and express the ratio as a percentage.
- Add the percentages as each is computed to maintain a running total.
- The total must not exceed 100%.

To illustrate, 1,000 gallons (3785 L) of a Class IB liquid in containers represents 73% of the maximum total quantity allowed by Table 4-4.2.7. Since the total of the percentages may not exceed 100%, storage of any other class of liquid is limited to 27% (i.e., 100 − 73) of the maximum total quantity allowed for that class. So, Class IA would be limited to 178 gallons (27% of 660) and Class II would be limited to 2,227.5 gallons (27% of 8,250). Similarly, the ratio of the Class IB liquid could be decreased to 70% (962.5 gallons) and the Class IA liquid increased to 30% (198 gallons).

The following examples further illustrate application of 4-4.2.10:

1. Given the following amounts of liquid in the containers indicated, what are the percentages of the maximum quantities for each, based on Table 4-4.2.7?

	Containers	Portable Tanks
Class IB	275 gal	0 gal
IC	275 gal	500 gal
II	4,125 gal	1,110 gal
IIIA	10,000 gal	11,000 gal

Class IB, Containers: 275/1,375 = 20%
Class IC, Containers: 275/2,750 = 10%
    Portable Tanks: 500/4,000 = 12.5%
Class II, Containers: 4,125/8,250 = 50%
    Portable Tanks: 1,110/11,100 = 10%
Class IIIA, Containers: 10,000/27,500 = 36.5%
    Portable Tanks: 11,000/22,000 = 50%
    TOTAL = 189%

2. Given the above percentages, what are two possible combinations of storage that will meet the requirement of 4-4.2.10? (Neglect the obvious choice of Class II containers and Class IIIA portable tanks.)

(a)   Class IB, Containers: 20%
        Class IC, Containers: 10%
            Portable Tanks: 12.5%
        Class II, Containers: 50 %
            TOTAL   92.5%

(b)   Class II, Portable Tanks: 10%
        Class IIIA, Containers: 36.5%
            Portable Tanks: 50%
            TOTAL   96.5%

3. What is the maximum quantity of a Class IIIA liquid that can be stored in portable tanks in an unprotected building that also contains 2,000 gal (7570 L) of a Class IC liquid in portable tanks?

Solution: According to Table 4-4.2.7, 2,000 gal (7570 L) of a Class IC liquid is 50 percent of the total of Class IC permitted 4,000 gal (15 140 L) in portable tank storage. Since the sum of proportional amounts cannot exceed 100 percent, one can store 50 percent of the allowable amount of Class IIIA. This maximum amount is 44,000 gal (166 540 L), so 22,000 gal (83 270 L) of Class IIIA can be stored in the same unprotected building as 2,000 gal (7570 L) of a Class IC liquid.

4. What is the maximum amount of Class IA liquid that can be stored in an unprotected building containing 1,650 gal (6245 L) of a Class II liquid, assuming container storage?

Solution: 1,650 gal (6245 L) = 20 percent of 8,250 gal (31 226 L). This means that 80 percent of the allowable amount of Class IA can be stored. Eighty percent of 660 gal (2498 L) = 528 gal (1998 L) of Class IA liquid.

4-4.2.11 Dispensing operations of Class I or Class II liquids are not permitted in cutoff rooms or attached buildings exceeding 1000 sq ft (93 m^2) floor area. In rooms where dispensing of Class I liquids is permitted, electrical systems shall comply with 4-4.1.5, except that within 3 ft (0.90 m) of a dispensing nozzle area, the electrical system shall be suitable for Class I, Division I; ventilation shall be provided per 4-4.1.6; and operations shall comply with the provisions of Chapter 5.

The rationale here is that dispensing introduces an additional hazard to the storage area. Therefore, the size of the room where dispensing is allowed is restricted. Where dispensing takes place, other restrictions are imposed in addition to the limitation on room size.

4-4.2.12 **Basement Storage Areas.** Class I liquids shall not be permitted in the basement areas of cutoff rooms and attached buildings. Class II and Class IIIA liquids may be stored in basements provided that automatic sprinkler protection and other fire protection facilities are provided in accordance with Section 4-6.

Basement storage of any kind presents a fire fighting problem. Access to most basements is restricted and ventilation of the area is usually more difficult to achieve. The storage itself adds to the fire loading and further restricts movement. If storage of Class I liquids were allowed, any vapors present would impose additional major difficulties. For all of these reasons, storage of Class I liquids is *not* allowed, and storage of combustible liquids (Class II and III) requires that the basement be protected.

4-5 Indoor Storage.

4-5.1 Basic Conditions.

4-5.1.1 The storage of any liquids shall not physically obstruct a means of egress. Class I liquids in other than separate inside storage areas or warehouses shall be so placed that a fire in the liquid storage would not preclude egress from the area.

4-5.1.2 The storage of liquids in containers or portable tanks shall comply with 4-5.2 through 4-5.7, as applicable. Where separate inside storage areas are required, they shall conform to Section 4-4. Where other factors substantially increase or decrease the hazard, the authority having jurisdiction may modify the quantities specified.

4-5.1.3 Liquids used for building maintenance painting or other similar infrequent maintenance purposes may be stored temporarily in closed containers outside of storage cabinets or separate inside storage areas, if limited in amount, not to exceed a 10-day supply at anticipated rates of consumption.

> These three paragraphs contain wording that is sometimes referred to as "code language," and it is worthy of comment. The words "so placed," "substantially," "infrequent," "temporarily," and "limited in amount" all imply that judgment is needed. Where such judgment is called for, the often-mentioned "authority having jurisdiction" enters the picture.
>
> Note the latitude given such an authority in 4-5.1.2, where modifications may be made based on factors that increase or decrease the hazard. This suggests that the modification may be *more or less* rigid than *Code* specifications, based on assessment of the particular situation.

4-5.1.4 Class I liquids shall not be stored in a basement, except as provided in 4-5.5.

> In contrast to the preceding three paragraphs, this "code language" is quite specific in that it prohibits basement storage of Class I liquids with the exception of mercantile occupancies to be discussed below. This paragraph is new to the *Code* and was added to eliminate any confusion about basement storage.

4-5.2 Dwellings and Residential Buildings Containing Not More Than Three Dwelling Units and Accompanying Attached and Detached Garages. Storage in excess of 25 gal (94.6 L) of Class I and Class II liquids combined shall be prohibited. In addition, storage in excess of 60 gal (227 L) of Class IIIA liquid shall be prohibited.

> A proposal to reduce the allowable amount to 10 gal (37.8 L) of Class I and II liquids was considered by the Technical Committee. The conclusion was reached that 25 gal (94.6 L) is a reasonable amount for three dwelling units.

4-5.3 Assembly Occupancies, Buildings Containing More Than Three Dwelling Units, and Hotels. Storage in excess of 10 gal (37.8 L) of Class I and Class II liquids combined or 60 gal (227 L) of Class IIIA liquids shall be in containers stored in storage cabinets, in safety cans, or in a separate inside storage area not having an opening communicating with that portion of the building used by the public.

> Because of the size of these buildings, there may be a need for larger quantities of flammable and combustible liquids. Given that increase, additional precautions are prescribed. The quantity re-

NFPA 30—CONTAINER AND PORTABLE TANK STORAGE   141

strictions are *total* quantities and not individual quantities for each dwelling unit or room to be occupied.

4-5.4 Office, Educational, and Institutional Occupancies. Storage shall be limited to that required for operation of office equipment, maintenance, demonstration, and laboratory work. This storage shall comply with the provisions of 4-5.4.1 through 4-5.4.4 except that the storage for industrial and educational laboratory work shall comply with NFPA 45, *Standard on Fire Protection for Laboratories Using Chemicals.*

This is a general requirement for total storage, requiring a judgmental assessment by the authority having jurisdiction. The next three paragraphs deal with specific storage requirements outside of storage cabinets or storage rooms.

Regarding laboratories, it should be noted that a laboratory stock room is governed by NFPA 30, *Flammable and Combustible Liquids Code*, specifically, the requirements for inside or cutoff rooms. Quantities of liquids in the laboratory work area are governed by NFPA 45, *Standard on Fire Protection for Laboratories Using Chemicals.*

4-5.4.1 Containers for Class I liquids outside of a separate inside storage area shall not exceed a capacity of 1 gal (3.8 L) except that safety cans can be of 2 gal (7.6 L) capacity.

Implicit in this requirement is the assessment that the safety can is the preferred type of storage container for these occupancies.

4-5.4.2 Not more than 10 gal (37.8 L) of Class I and Class II liquids combined shall be stored in a single fire area outside of a storage cabinet or a separate inside storage area unless in safety cans.

This means, simply, that a maximum of ten 1-gal (3.8-L) containers is permitted outside of a storage cabinet or storage room, per fire area. If the containers are safety cans, more than 10 gal (37.8 L) is allowed.

4-5.4.3 Not more than 25 gal (94.6 L) of Class I and Class II liquids combined shall be stored in a single fire area in safety cans outside of a separate inside storage area or storage cabinet.

Even if the storage is in safety cans, 25 gal (94.6 L) is the maximum allowed per fire area outside of storage cabinets or a storage room.

4-5.4.4 Not more than 60 gal (227 L) of Class IIIA liquids shall be stored outside of a separate inside storage area or storage cabinet.

4-5.5 Mercantile Occupancies, Retail Stores, and Other Related Areas Accessible to the Public.

4-5.5.1* In display areas that are accessible to the public, the storage of Class I, Class II, and Class IIIA liquids shall be limited to quantities needed for display and normal merchandising purposes but shall not exceed the limits as given by the following (*also see Table A-4-5.5.1*):

(a) In protected display areas, the total aggregate quantity of Class I, II, and IIIA liquids shall not exceed 2 gal per sq ft (81 L per m^2) of gross floor area, but, except for basement display areas, the quantity of Class IA liquids shall not exceed 1 gal per sq ft (40 L per m^2) of gross floor area. In basement display areas, the storage of Class IA liquids shall be prohibited.

(b) In unprotected display areas on other than the ground floor, the total aggregate quantity of Class IB, IC, II, and IIIA liquids shall not exceed 1 gal per sq ft (40 L per m^2) of gross floor area, and the storage of Class IA liquids shall be prohibited. In unprotected ground floor display areas, the total aggregate quantity of Class I, II, and IIIA liquids shall not exceed 2 gal per sq ft (81 L per m^2) of gross floor area, but the quantity of Class IA liquids shall not exceed 1 gal per sq ft (40 L per m^2) of gross floor area.

"Protected" shall mean protected with automatic sprinklers installed at least in accordance with NFPA 13, *Standard for the Installation of Sprinkler Systems*, requirements for Ordinary Hazard Group 2 Occupancies. The gross floor area used for computing the maximum quantity permitted shall be considered as that portion of the floor actually being used for merchandising liquids and immediately adjacent aisles.

A-4-5.5.1 The following table can be consulted for guidance in determining amounts of storage permitted in mercantile establishments.

	Allowable Storage Amounts, Gallons Per Sq Ft				
	IA	IB	IC	II	IIIA
Protected					
Basement	0	2	2	2	2
Ground Floor	1	2	2	2	2
Other Floors	1	2	2	2	2
Unprotected					
Basement	0	1	1	1	1
Ground Floor	1	2	2	2	2
Other Floors	0	1	1	1	1

Maximum total quantities permitted shall be limited to the sum of proportional amounts that each class of liquid present bears to the maximum total permitted for its respective class. The sum of proportional amounts shall not exceed 100 percent.

> This paragraph has traditionally been the source of many questions from users of the *Code*. It has been rewritten to more clearly state its requirements and an appendix item was added to further aid the user.
>
> The *Code* separates the requirements relating to the amount of flammable liquids needed for normal merchandising from the

NFPA 30—CONTAINER AND PORTABLE TANK STORAGE 143

quantity needed for inventory because the inventory area is not normally accessible to the public. Note that the *Code* specifically defines what is meant by the terms "protected" and "gross floor area." In computing the gross floor area used for merchandising flammable and combustible liquids, only that portion of the floor occupied by shelving that is actually used for the merchandising of flammable liquids, plus the aisle space adjacent to it, is to be considered. For example, in a department store that has 50 ft (15 m) of shelving on which all types of products are displayed, and only 5 ft (1.5 m) of that shelving is used to display flammable and combustible liquids, only the 5 ft (1.5 m) length is used to compute the gross floor area. If the shelving is 2 ft (0.6 m) deep and the aisle in front of the display is 4 ft (1.2 m) wide, the total width would be 6 ft (1.8 m). This would result in 30 sq ft (2.7 m^2) of gross floor area. If 2 gal per sq ft (81 L per m^2) is permitted, the *Code* would allow 60 gal (227 L) of liquid to be stored in this area of shelving. In those areas where only 1 gal per sq ft (40 L per m^2) of gross floor area is allowed, the area would be limited to displaying a total of 30 gal (113.5 L). (*See Figure 4-5.*)

Also, note that the protection required is more in line with what would normally be expected in a mercantile occupancy and not what the *Code* would require in a protected warehouse.

4-5.5.2 The aggregate quantity of additional stock in areas not accessible to the public shall not exceed the greater of that which would be permitted if the area were accessible to the public, or 60 gal (227 L) of Class IA, 120 gal (454 L) of Class IB, 180 gal (681 L) of Class IC, 240 gal (908 L) of Class II, or 660 gal (2498 L) of Class IIIA liquids, or 240 gal (908 L) in any combination of Class I and Class II liquids subject to the limitations of the individual class. These quantities may be doubled for areas protected as defined in 4-5.5.1. Storage of Class IA liquids shall be prohibited in basement storage areas.

This paragraph refers to the aggregate quantity of additional stock of flammable and combustible liquids used to replenish normal merchandising displays that are stored in areas not accessible to the public. This paragraph still applies the 2 gal per sq ft (81 L per m^2) of gross floor area for protected buildings, and 1 gal per sq ft (40 L per m^2) of floor area for unprotected buildings, as stated in 4-5.5.1. In addition, the maximum quantity stored is limited by this paragraph. Note that these maximum quantities can be doubled if the area is protected with an automatic sprinkler system installed in accordance with NFPA 13 requirements for ordinary hazard Group 2 occupancies [i.e., 120 gal (454 L) of Class IA; 240 gal (908 L) of Class IB; 360 gal (1362 L) of Class IC; 480 gal

144   FLAMMABLE AND COMBUSTIBLE LIQUIDS CODE HANDBOOK

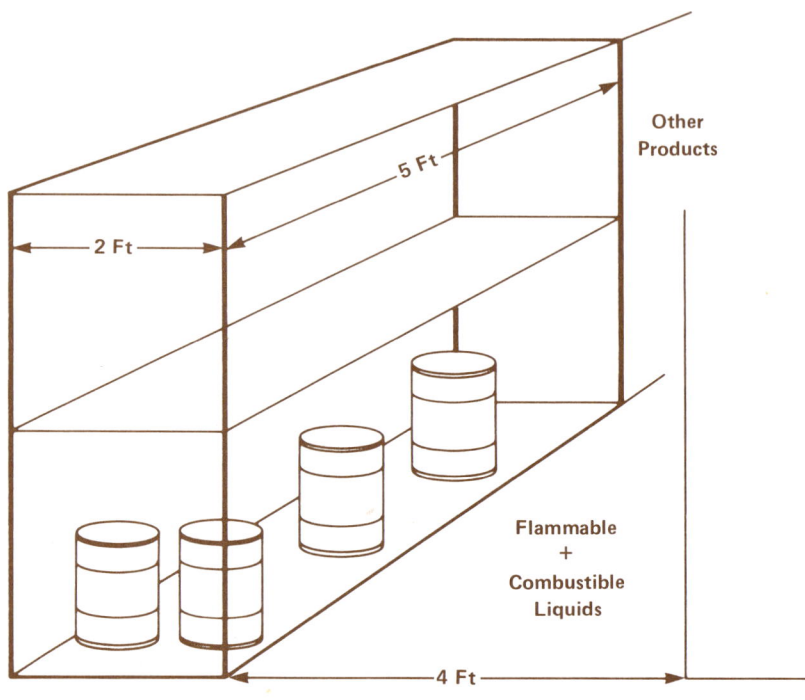

30 Ft² = GROSS FLOOR AREA

SI Units: 1 ft = 0.30 m; 1 sq ft = 0.09 m².

Figure 4-5   In computing the gross floor area used for merchandising flammable and combustible liquids, only that portion of the shelving that is actually used for the merchandising of flammable liquids plus adjacent aisle space is to be considered.

(1817 L) of Class II; 1320 gal (4996 L) of Class IIIA; or 480 gal (1817 L) in any combination of Class I and Class II liquids.}

4-5.5.3 Quantities in excess of those permitted in 4-5.5.2 shall be stored in accordance with other appropriate sections of this code.

Such storage would be in inside storage rooms, cutoff rooms, or attached buildings.

4-5.5.4 Containers shall not be stacked more than 3 ft (0.90 m) or 2 containers high, whichever is the greater, unless on fixed shelving or otherwise satisfactorily secured.

The intent of this paragraph is to minimize the likelihood of containers falling or being knocked over. It is *not* the intent of this paragraph to allow unlimited height or stacking of containers on top of each other when on fixed shelving. Rather, it is intended that each shelf be restricted to a 3 ft (or two-high) stack. The number

NFPA 30—CONTAINER AND PORTABLE TANK STORAGE 145

of such shelves is not limited. Containers 6 in. (15 cm) high can be stacked six high. Containers 15 in. (38 cm) high can only be stacked two high.

4-5.5.5 Shelving shall be of stable construction, of sufficient depth and arrangement such that containers displayed thereon shall not easily be displaced.

4-5.5.6 Leaking containers shall be removed immediately to an adequately ventilated area, and the contents transferred to an undamaged container.

4-5.6 General-Purpose Warehouses. *(See 1-2, Definitions.)*

4-5.6.1 General-purpose warehouses shall be separate, detached buildings or shall be separated from other type occupancies by a standard 4-hr fire wall, or, if approved, a fire partition having a fire-resistance rating of not less than 2 hr. Each opening in a fire wall shall be protected with an automatic-closing, listed 3-hr (A) fire door with the fusible link or other automatic actuating mechanism located in the opening or on both sides of the opening. Each opening in a fire partition shall be protected with an automatic-closing, listed 1½-hr (B) fire door. The doors shall be installed in accordance with NFPA 80, *Standard for Fire Doors and Windows.*

> The reader should not infer from this paragraph that the *Code* considers a fire wall and a fire partition to be equivalent. This is definitely not the case. The key word is "separation." If 4-hr separation is deemed necessary, then a 4-hr fire wall must be used. If the authority having jurisdiction determines that only a 2-hr separation is needed, either because of added protective features or other considerations, then a 2-hr fire partition may be used instead. The use of a fire partition is an exception to the basic requirement and is subject to approval of the authority having jursidiction.
>
> Fire partitions do not necessarily extend from the basement through the roof. They may be used to divide a floor or area into smaller segments and extend only from the floor to the underside of the floor above. In contrast, a fire wall is required to extend from the basement through all floors and the roof and thus *completely* separate two building areas, or two buildings.
>
> The (A) rated fire doors are intended for use in openings in walls separating buildings or dividing a single building into fire areas. The 3-hr rating indicates a 3-hr test exposure. The (B) rated door is intended for use in a 2-hr fire rated partition providing horizontal fire separation. *(See 4-4.1.2.)*

4-5.6.2 Warehousing operations that involve storage of liquids shall be restricted to separate inside storage areas or to liquid warehouses in accordance with Section 4-4 or 4-5.7, as applicable, except as provided in 4-5.6.3.

4-5.6.3 Class IB and IC liquids in containers of 1 gal (3.8 L) or less capacity, Class II liquids in containers of 5 gal (18.9 L) or less capacity, and Class III liquids in containers of 60 gal (227 L) or less capacity may be stored in warehouses handling combustible commodities, as defined in the scope of NFPA 231, *Standard for General Storage*, provided that the storage area is protected with automatic sprinklers in accordance with the provisions of this standard for 20 ft (6 m) storage of Class IV commodities and the quantities and height of liquid storage are limited to:

(a) Class IA liquids—not permitted
(b) Class IB & IC 660 gal (2498 L)—5 ft (1.5 m) high
(c) Class II 1375 gal (5204 L)—5 ft (1.5 m) high
(d) Class IIIA 2750 gal (10409 L)—10 ft (3.0 m) high
(e) Class IIIB 13,750 gal (52044 L)—15 ft (4.6 m) high

The liquid storage shall also conform to 4-5.6.4, 4-5.6.5, 4-5.6.6, 4-5.6.7, and 4-5.6.8.

> Recall that, for the purposes of this *Code*, a general-purpose warehouse is one that is not specifically designed to store flammable and combustible liquids. Usually, such warehouses are designed and constructed according to NFPA 231, *Standard for General Storage*, with the fire protection requirements based on the combustibility of the commodities to be stored. Where it is intended that a general-purpose warehouse store quantities of flammable and combustible liquids, the warehouse must also meet the design and construction requirements of 4-5.6.1 and 4-5.6.2. As an alternative to providing a separate inside storage area, as stated in 4-5.6.2, a general-purpose warehouse is allowed to store *limited* quantities of flammable and combustible liquids, provided that the warehouse is protected in accordance with NFPA 231, *Standard for General Storage*, for Class IV commodities and the quantities stored do not exceed the amounts specified in 4-5.6.3. Note also that Class IA liquids, including any aerosol products considered to be "flammable aerosols" by the U.S. Hazardous Substances Labeling Act, are not permitted to be stored in a general-purpose warehouse. Class IV commodities are products that contain appreciable amounts of combustible plastics, packaged in ordinary corrugated cartons, and products packaged using plastic packing materials. Most small appliances meet this definition. Audio and video equipment packed in foam plastic cocoons in corrugated cartons are another example of this commodity class.
>
> Storage of Class IB, IC, and II liquids well beyond the amounts allowed in 4-5.6.3, coupled with storage of flammable aerosols in direct violation of 4-5.6.3, resulted in the disastrous fire at the

K Mart Distribution Center in Falls Township, PA, in 1982. This fire is discussed in detail in the Supplement of this *Handbook*.

4-5.6.4 Liquids in Plastic Containers. Effective September 1, 1990, Class I and Class II liquids in plastic containers shall not be stored in general-purpose warehouses, but shall be stored in separate inside rooms or liquid warehouses in accordance with Section 4-4 or 4-5.7, as applicable.

Exception No. 1: Liquids in plastic containers may be stored in general-purpose warehouses in accordance with protection and storage limitations specified in 4-5.6.3 as follows:

(a) products containing not more than 50 percent by volume of water-miscible liquids and with the remainder of the solution being not flammable when packaged in individual containers,

(b) water-miscible liquids containing more than 50 percent by volume in individual containers not exceeding 16 oz. capacity.

Exception No. 2: Class I and Class II liquids in plastic containers may be stored in a general-purpose warehouse if in containers approved and fire-tested for use with these materials.

This paragraph represents the most controversial change between the 1984 and 1987 editions of this *Code*. During the revision process for this edition of the *Code*, a proposal was submitted that would have required Class I and II liquids in plastic containers to be stored in a separate area devoted *exclusively* to such storage and constructed according to the requirements of Separate Inside Storage Areas (Section 4-4) or Liquid Warehouses (4-5.7), whichever was applicable. The proposal was based on fire tests described in the commentary that follows E-4-6(c)(5).

The Committee accepted the basic intent of this proposal, but did add Exception No. 1 to cover certain water-miscible commodities that do not appear to present an unusual fire hazard. Also, the Committee did not feel that the special storage area needed to be devoted *exclusively* to storage of liquids in plastic containers and the wording was changed accordingly.

A substantial number of comments opposing the new requirement were received during the public review period. Many were submitted by manufacturers of products shipped in plastic containers and all pointed out that plastic containers offered certain advantages to the end user: ease of use, minimal spillage, no risk of corrosion to the container, and very few instances of "leakers."

After listening to both proponents and opponents, and after lengthy debate, the Committee decided to retain the proposed new requirements for the following reasons:

- The fire tests did indicate the potential for serious fires and previous fire incidents show that Class I and II liquids in plastic containers have had a major influence on fire development.
- The impact of the new requirements is not universal, given the maximum quantity restrictions of 4-5.6.3. Amounts greater than these maximums are already required by NFPA 30, *Flammable and Combustible Liquids Code*, to be stored in an inside storage room or in a liquid warehouse.

The Committee further decided to establish an "effective date" of September 1, 1990. Thus, although the new requirements are published in this edition of the *Code*, they are not effective, hence are not enforceable, until the effective date. The Committee did this because they felt that affected industries needed the additional time to enhance fire protection at existing facilities and to develop safer packaging systems. The industries involved have already begun preliminary work in developing more heat-resistant plastics and more ignition-resistant packaging systems.

When the 1987 edition of this *Code* was proposed for adoption, a floor amendment was successfully moved and adopted by the NFPA membership which essentially replaced the Committee's version of this proposal with the original wording, as submitted by the original proponent. As a result of further balloting required of the Committee by NFPA's standards writing regulations, the entire subject of special requirements for Class I and Class II liquids in plastic containers was referred to NFPA's Standards Council for adjudication. Normally, such a situation would result in the subject matter being returned to Committee. In this case, however, the Standards Council overturned the floor amendment and let stand the Committee actions. This one paragraph presents a microcosm of NFPA's standards writing system.

Undoubtedly, future editions of NFPA 30, *Flammable and Combustible Liquids Code*, will include further amendments to these requirements as the magnitude of the problem is more clearly defined and as steps are taken to reduce the risk.

4-5.6.5 Basement Storage Areas. Class I liquids shall not be permitted in the basement areas of buildings. Class II and Class IIIA liquids may be stored in basements provided that automatic sprinkler protection and other fire protection facilities are provided in accordance with Section 4-6.

4-5.6.6 Palletized, Solid Pile, or Rack Storage. Liquids in containers may be stored on pallets, in solid piles or on racks subject to the quantities and

NFPA 30—CONTAINER AND PORTABLE TANK STORAGE 149

heights limits of 4-5.6.3 provided the protection is in accordance with Section 4-6, as applicable.

In order to reduce the potential for fire spread from one pile to another, it is necessary to provide adequate separation between individual piles. Generally, adequate separation is automatically provided because of the space needed to operate a lift truck. However, the more important criteria are the fire characteristics of the liquids stored. Aisles must be wide enough and at frequent enough intervals to provide access for inventory control, detection of leaking containers, and use of portable extinguishers or hose streams, should the need arise.

4-5.6.7 Separation and Aisles. Palletized or solid pile storage shall be arranged so that piles permitted in 4-5.6.3 are separated from each other by at least 4-ft (1.2-m) aisles. Aisles shall be provided so that no container is more than 12 ft (3.6 m) from an aisle. Where liquids are stored on racks, a minimum 4-ft (1.2-m) wide aisle shall be provided between adjacent rows of racks and adjacent storage of liquids. Main aisles shall be a minimum of 8 ft (2.4 m) wide. Where ordinary combustible commodities are stored in the same area as liquids in containers, the minimum distance between the two types of storage shall be 8 ft (2.4 m).

4-5.6.8 Mixed Storage. Liquids shall not be stored in the same pile or in the same rack sections as ordinary combustible commodities. Where liquids are packaged together with ordinary combustibles, as in kits, the storage shall be considered on the basis of whichever commodity predominates. When two or more classes of liquids are stored in a single pile or single rack section, the maximum quantities permitted in the pile or rack section shall be the smallest of the two or more separate maximum quantities, and the height of storage permitted in that pile or rack section shall be the least of the two or more separate heights. The maximum total quantities permitted shall be limited to the sum of proportional amounts that each class of liquid present bears to the maximum total permitted for its respective class. The sum of proportional amounts shall not exceed 100 percent.

The requirements for storing two or more classes of flammable liquids in a single pile or rack are the same as the requirements for mixed storage in cutoff rooms and attached buildings. (See 4-4.2.8 and comments.)

4-5.7 Liquid Warehouses. *(See 1-2 Definitions.)*

4-5.7.1 Liquid warehouses shall be separate, detached buildings or shall be separated from other type occupancies by standard 4-hr fire walls, with communicating openings protected on each side of the wall with automatic-closing, listed 3-hr (A) fire doors. Fire doors shall be installed in accordance with NFPA 80, *Standard for Fire Doors and Windows.*

> Liquid warehouses must meet more restrictive construction standards than general-purpose warehouses. For example, they are not allowed to take advantage of the provision that allows the authority having jurisdiction to accept a 2-hr fire partition in lieu of the 4-hr fire wall. Because of the greater risk associated with a liquid warehouse, two fire doors, one on each side of the wall, are required for each opening in a fire wall.

4-5.7.2 If the warehouse building is located more than 10 ft (3 m) but less than 50 ft (15 m) from an important building or line of adjoining property that can be built upon, the exposing wall shall have a fire-resistance rating of at least 2 hrs with each opening protected with a listed 1½-hr (D) fire door.

> A (D) fire door is designed for installation in exterior walls that are subject to severe fire exposure from outside the building. (*See comment under 4-4.2.2.*)

4-5.7.3 If the warehouse is located 10 ft (3 m) or less from an important building or line of adjoining property that can be built upon, the exposing wall shall have a fire-resistance rating of 4 hrs with each opening protected with a listed 3-hr (A) fire door.

> The (A) rated door is designed for use in walls that separate buildings or that divide a building into fire areas. (*See comment under 4-5.6.1.*) Note that the *Code* contains no requirements for warehouses located beyond 50 ft (15 m) from an important building or the adjoining property that can be built upon. This implies that there are no construction requirements.

4-5.7.4 An attached warehouse, having communicating openings in the required 4-hr fire wall separation from the adjacent building area, shall have these openings protected by:

(a) Normally closed, listed 3-hr (A) fire doors on each side of the wall. These doors may be arranged to stay open during material handling operations, only if the doors are designed to close automatically in a fire emergency by provision of listed closure devices.

(b) Noncombustible, liquidtight raised sills or ramps, at least 4 in. (10 cm) in height, or other design features to prevent flow of liquids to the adjoining area.

4-5.7.5 Fire doors shall be installed in accordance with NFPA 80, *Standard for Fire Doors and Windows.*

4-5.7.6 The total quantity of liquids within a liquid warehouse shall not be restricted. The maximum pile heights and maximum quantity per pile,

NFPA 30—CONTAINER AND PORTABLE TANK STORAGE

arranged as palletized and/or solid pile storage, shall comply with Table 4-4.2.7, if unprotected, or Table 4-6.1(a) if protected, in accordance with Section 4-6. The storage heights of containers on protected racks shall comply with Table 4-6.1(b), as applicable.

Exception: An unprotected liquid warehouse located a minimum of 100 ft (30 m) from exposed buildings or adjoining property that can be built upon is not required to conform to Table 4-4.2.7, if there is protection for exposures. Where protection for exposures is not provided, a minimum 200 ft (61 m) distance is required.

It is important to understand that the operator of a properly constructed liquid warehouse is allowed to store as much liquid as practicable in the warehouse, so long as the maximum storage heights and maximum quantity per pile are not exceeded, according to the specified tables. This provision of 4-5.7 sometimes causes confusion, because Tables 4-4.2.7, 4-6.1(a), and 4-6.1(b) each contain a column for maximum total quantity. These maximum total quantities apply to both unprotected and protected storage in cutoff rooms and attached buildings. For storage in liquid warehouses, only the columns for maximum storage height, maximum quantity per pile, and maximum quantity (per rack) are used.

The Exception to 4-5.7.6 was added with the 1981 edition of the *Code* and reflects the Technical Committee's opinion that a detached, unprotected storage facility located an adequate distance from exposed structures would present a minimal risk. For example, bulk supplies of inexpensive, readily replaced flammable and combustible liquids could be stored in an isolated, unprotected liquid warehouse with supplies transferred to a properly protected facility on an as-needed basis. In this example, the benefits of full protection would be minimal.

4-5.7.7 Class I liquids shall not be permitted in the basement areas of liquid warehouses. Class II and Class IIIA liquids may be stored in basements provided that automatic sprinkler protection and other fire protection facilities are provided in accordance with Section 4-6.

See commentary following 4-4.2.12.

4-5.7.8 Limited amounts of combustible commodities, as defined in the scope of NFPA 231, *Standard for General Storage*, and NFPA 231C, *Standard for Rack Storage of Materials*, may be stored in liquid warehouses if protection is provided in accordance with Section 4-6, and the ordinary combustibles, other than those used for packaging the liquids, are separated a minimum of 8 ft (2.4 m) horizontally, by aisles or open racks, from the liquids in storage.

"Limited" is purposely left undefined. Its meaning must be determined by the authority having jurisdiction.

4-5.7.9 Empty or idle combustible pallet storage shall be limited to a maximum pile size of 2500 sq ft (232 m²) and to a maximum storage height of 6 ft (1.8 m). Idle pallet storage shall be separated from liquids by at least 8-ft (2.4-m) wide aisles. However, pallet storage in accordance with NFPA 231, *Standard for General Storage*, shall be acceptable.

> The intent of this requirement is to place a reasonable limit on the fire load presented by materials that might be considered of minor consequence when compared to the storage of flammable and combustible liquids.

4-5.7.10 Containers in piles shall be separated by pallets or dunnage to provide stability and to prevent excessive stress on container walls. Portable tanks stored over one tier high shall be designed to nest securely, without dunnage. (*See NFPA 386, Standard for Portable Shipping Tanks for Flammable and Combustible Liquids, for information on portable tank design.*) Materials handling equipment shall be suitable to handle containers and tanks safely at the upper tier level.

4-5.7.11 No container or portable tank shall be stored closer than 36 in. (0.90 m) to the nearest beam, chord, girder, or other roof member in an unprotected warehouse.

4-5.7.12 Solid pile and palletized storage shall be arranged so that piles are separated from each other by at least 4 ft (1.2 m). Aisles shall be provided so that no container or tank is more than 12 ft (3.6 m) from an aisle. Where storage on racks exists as permitted in this Code, a minimum 4-ft (1.2-m) wide aisle shall be provided between adjacent rows of racks and any adjacent storage of liquids. Main aisles shall be a minimum of 8 ft (2.4 m) wide, and access shall be maintained to all doors required for egress.

4-5.7.13 Mixed Storage. When two or more classes of liquids are stored in a single pile, the maximum quantity permitted in that pile shall be the smallest of the two or more separate maximum quantities and the heights of storage permitted in that pile shall be the least of the two or more separate heights as given in Tables 4-4.2.7 or 4-6.1(a), as applicable. When two or more classes of liquids are stored in the same racks as permitted in this Code, the maximum height of storage permitted shall be the least of the two or more separate heights given in Table 4-6.1(b).

> There is no upper limit on the total amount of liquid that can be stored. Therefore, one need not be concerned with proportional amounts of different classes totaling 100 percent, as is the case with other types of indoor storage.
>
> For individual piles, however, a restriction is placed on both total pile quantity and pile height. In essence, the pile takes on the

NFPA 30—CONTAINER AND PORTABLE TANK STORAGE

identity of the most hazardous class stored therein and the total amount in the pile cannot exceed the amount specified for that class. The same principle applies to the pile height.

4-6 Protection Requirements for Protected Storage of Liquids.

4-6.1 Containers and portable tanks storing flammable and combustible liquids may be stored in the quantities and arrangements specified in Tables 4-6.1(a) and 4-6.1(b), provided the storage is protected in accordance with 4-6.2 and 4-6.5, as applicable.

> The referenced tables are to be used for flammable and combustible liquid storage in *protected* areas. For *unprotected* storage arrangements, see Table 4-4.2.7.

4-6.1.1 Other quantities and arrangements may be used where suitably protected and approved by the authority having jurisdiction.

4-6.2 Where automatic sprinklers are used, they shall be installed in accordance with **NFPA 13**, *Standard for the Installation of Sprinkler Systems*, and approved by the authority having jurisdiction. (*For additional information, see Appendix D.*)

> Note that Table D-4-6.2(a) in Appendix D gives no advice on protection for 55-gal (208-L) containers of Class IB, IC, and II liquids stored more than one high, although such storage is permitted by Table 4-6.1(a).

4-6.2.1 Other systems such as automatic foam-water systems, automatic water-spray systems, or other combinations of systems may be considered acceptable if approved by the authority having jurisdiction. (*For additional information, see Appendix D.*)

4-6.3 Racks storing Class I or Class II liquids shall be either single-row or double-row as described in NFPA 231C, *Standard for Rack Storage of Materials*.

4-6.4 Ordinary combustibles other than those used for packaging the liquids shall not be stored in the same rack section as liquids, and shall be separated a minimum of 8 ft (2.4 m) horizontally, by aisles or open racks, from liquids stored in racks.

> When applying the provisions of Tables 4-6.1(a) and 4-6.1(b), it is important to consider each limitation in succession so that none will be overlooked. It is also necessary to make sure that the differing limits for container or portable tanks are recognized.

> A recent Formal Interpretation, FI 84-3, addressed an anomaly of Table 4-6.1(b).

Table 4-6.1(a) Storage Arrangements for Protected Palletized or Solid Pile Storage of Liquids in Containers and Portable Tanks

Class	Storage Level	Max. Stge. Height (ft.)		Max. Quantity per Pile (gal.)		Max. Quantity (gal.)	
		Containers	Port. Tanks	Containers	Port. Tanks	Containers	Port. Tanks
IA	Ground Floor	5	—	3,000	—	12,000	—
	Upper Floors	5	—	2,000	—	8,000	—
	Basements	—Not Permitted—		—	—	—	—
IB	Ground Floor	6½	7	5,000	20,000	15,000	40,000
	Upper Floors	6½	7	3,000	10,000	12,000	20,000
	Basements	—Not Permitted—		—	—	—	—
IC	Ground Floor	*6½	7	5,000	20,000	15,000	40,000
	Upper Floors	*6½	7	3,000	10,000	12,000	20,000
	Basements	—Not Permitted—		—	—	—	—
II	Ground Floor	10	14	10,000	40,000	25,000	80,000
	Upper Floors	10	14	10,000	40,000	25,000	80,000
	Basements	5	7	7,500	20,000	7,500	20,000
III	Ground Floor	20	14	15,000	60,000	50,000	100,000
	Upper Floors	20	14	15,000	60,000	50,000	100,000
	Basements	10	7	10,000	20,000	25,000	40,000

SI Units: 1 ft = 0.30 m; 1 gal = 3.8 L.
*These height limitations may be increased to 10 ft for containers of 5 gal or less in capacity.
NOTE: See Section 4-6 for protection requirements as applicable to this type of storage.

NFPA 30—CONTAINER AND PORTABLE TANK STORAGE

Table 4-6.1(b) Storage Arrangements for Protected Rack Storage of Liquids in Containers

Class	Type Rack	Storage Level	Max. Stge. Height (ft) Containers	Max. Quantity (gal) Containers
IA	Double Row or Single Row	Ground Floor Upper Floor Basements	25 15 Not Permitted	7,500 4,500 —
IB IC	Double Row or Single Row	Ground Floor Upper Floor Basements	25 15 Not Permitted	15,000 9,000 —
II	Double Row or Single Row	Ground Floor Upper Floor Basements	25 25 15	24,000 24,000 9,000
III	Multi-Row Double Row or Single Row	Ground Floor Upper Floor Basements	40 20 20	48,000 48,000 24,000

SI Units: 1 ft = 0.30 m; 1 gal = 3.8 L.
NOTE: See Section 4-6 for protection requirements as applicable to this type of storage.

Background: A paint storage room is located in an attached building at a manufacturing facility. Containers of Class I and Class II liquids are stored on racks. No dispensing is done in the room, but closed, partially full containers are stored as well as full containers. Protection is provided per NFPA 30, and each rack holds no more than the maximum quantity shown in the last column of Table 4-6.1(b).

Question #1: Does the column in Table 4-6.1(b), headed "Max. Quantity (gal)" apply to the total quantity allowed in a single rack?

Answer: Yes.

Question #2: Does the column in Table 4-6.1(b), headed "Max. Quantity (gal)" also apply to the total quantity allowed in the entire fire area?

Answer: Yes.

Some explanation is in order here. As can be seen, Table 4-6.1(b) has a column headed "Maximum Quantity," in contrast to Tables 4-4.2.7 and 4-6.1(a), which have *two* quantity columns: "Maximum Quantity per Pile" and "Maximum Total Quantity." Table 4-6.1(b) is several editions old and, in fact, predates the separate requirements for cutoff rooms and attached buildings. Prior to these latter requirements, Table 4-6.1(b) applied only to liquid warehouses.

156 FLAMMABLE AND COMBUSTIBLE LIQUIDS CODE HANDBOOK

Since no upper limit is placed on the quantities of liquid in a liquid warehouse, no "maximum total quantity" column was necessary.

With the adoption of separate, specific requirements for cutoff rooms and attached buildings, a cross-reference or footnote should have been added to the table to clearly explain its use in relation to 4-4.2, "Cutoff Rooms and Attached Buildings." As it now stands, the maximum quantity given by Table 4-6.1(b) is the upper limit for an individual rack section in a liquid warehouse (which can contain as many rack sections as is practical, given the separation constraints imposed by 4-5.7.12). This same maximum quantity is the upper limit for both an individual rack and for the entire storage area for cutoff rooms and attached buildings.

4-6.5 In-rack sprinklers shall be installed in accordance with the provisions of NFPA 231C, *Standard for Rack Storage of Materials*, except as modified by 4-6.2. Alternate lines of in-rack sprinklers shall be staggered. Multiple levels of in-rack sprinkler heads shall be provided with water shields unless otherwise separated by horizontal barriers, or unless the sprinkler heads are listed for such installations.

4-7 Fire Control.

4-7.1 Suitable fire extinguishers or preconnected hose lines, either 1½-in. (3.8-cm) lined or 1-in. (2.5-cm) hard rubber, shall be provided where liquids are stored. Where 1½-in. (3.8-cm) fire hose is used, it shall be installed in accordance with NFPA 14, *Standard for the Installation of Standpipe and Hose Systems*.

Portable fire extinguishers and preconnected hose lines are provided for first aid fire fighting and fire control. Combination (adjustable) nozzles capable of both spray (fog) and straight stream operation are preferred for this type of service. Although not covered in NFPA 14, *Standard for the Installation of Standpipe and Hose Systems*, 1-in. (2.5-cm) hard rubber hose line installations should follow the requirements of that standard.

4-7.1.1 At least one portable fire extinguisher having a rating of not less than 20-B shall be located outside of, but not more than 10 ft (3 m) from, the door opening into any separate inside storage area.

The 1981 edition of the *Code* changed the extinguisher requirement from 10-B to 20-B, based on a public proposal. NFPA 10, *Standard for Portable Fire Extinguishers*, requires 20-B and 40-B rated extinguishers for extra hazardous locations, depending on travel distance.

4-7.1.2 At least one portable fire extinguisher having a rating of not less than 20-B shall be located not less than 10 ft (3 m), nor more than 50 ft (15 m), from any Class I or Class II liquid storage area located outside of a separate inside storage area.

> The reason for requiring that portable fire extinguishers be located a distance away from the storage room is that fires involving Class I and Class II flammable liquids are likely to escalate rapidly. If the fire extinguisher is too close to the storage area, it may be impossible to get to it once the fire has started.

4-7.1.3 In protected general purpose and liquid warehouses, hand hose lines shall be provided in sufficient number to reach all liquid storage areas.

> It is the intent of this paragraph that the hose stream (not the hose itself) be able to reach all areas and sides of the flammable liquid storage area.

4-7.1.4 The water supply shall be sufficient to meet the fixed fire protection demand, plus a total of at least 500 gal (1892 L) per minute for inside and outside hose lines. (*See C-4-6.2.*)

> It is the intent of this paragraph to establish the minimim *total* water supply required by the entire storage area or facility, rather than a water supply requirement for each individual hose line.

4-7.2 Control of Ignition Sources. Precautions shall be taken to prevent the ignition of flammable vapors. Sources of ignition include but are not limited to: open flames; lightning; smoking; cutting and welding; hot surfaces; frictional heat; static, electrical, and mechanical sparks; spontaneous ignition, including heat-producing chemical reactions; and radiant heat.

> These are some examples of common ignition sources, although the list is neither all-inclusive nor applicable in all cases. Again, it is emphasized that control of ignition sources is the second line of defense; minimizing the possibility of a spill or leak is the primary objective of this *Code*.

4-7.3 Dispensing of Class I and Class II liquids in general-purpose or liquid warehouses shall not be permitted unless the dispensing area is suitably cut off from other ordinary combustible or liquid storage areas, as specified in Section 4-4, and otherwise conforms with the applicable provisions of Section 4-4.

> Because of the greater likelihood of a fire occurring during the dispensing or transferring of flammable liquids, the *Code* prohibits such activity from being conducted in the same areas where large quantities of flammable liquids are stored.

4-7.4 Materials with a water reactivity degree of 2 or higher as outlined in NFPA 704, *Standard System for the Identification of the Fire Hazards of Materials*, shall not be stored in the same area with other liquids.

Many flammable and combustible liquid storage areas are protected by automatic sprinkler or water spray systems and hose lines. Consequently, any storage of water-reactive material in the storage area creates an unreasonable risk. The identification system in NFPA 704, *Standard System for the Identification of the Fire Hazards of Materials*, is of particular value to responding fire service personnel in that it provides immediate information about the fire hazards involved.

4-8 Outdoor Storage.

Requirements for outdoor storage of flammable and combustible liquids are often very similar to the requirements for inside storage. The major difference is that, while outdoor storage provides natural ventilation, the fire exposure problem is more critical from and to buildings, flammable liquid tanks, or ordinary combustible materials. The *Code* recognizes that there is a significantly reduced potential for fire with smaller quantities of flammable and combustible liquids than there would be with larger quantities.

Outdoor storage also presents security problems. On the other hand, storing flammable and combustible liquids outdoors reduces the structural fire hazard. Generally, a fire in an outdoor storage facility is more readily controlled than one within a structure.

For the purposes of this section, outdoor storage is considered to also include any storage area that is covered by a roof to provide weather protection for the containers. This same area may have one or two (but no more) walls, without materially affecting natural ventilation.

4-8.1 Outdoor storage of liquids in containers and portable tanks shall be in accordance with Table 4-8, as qualified by 4-8.1.1 through 4-8.1.4 and 4-8.2, 4-8.3, and 4-8.4.

4-8.1.1 When two or more classes of materials are stored in a single pile, the maximum gallonage in that pile shall be the smallest of the two or more separate gallonages.

This means that the pile takes on the identity of the more hazardous class and the total amount in the pile cannot exceed that allowed for that class.

Table 4-8 Outdoor Liquid Storage in Containers and Portable Tanks

	1		2		3	4	5
	Container Storage-Max. per Pile		Portable Tank Storage Max. per Pile Gallons (1)		Distance Between Piles or Racks (ft)	Distance to Property Line That Can Be Built Upon (ft)(2)(3)	Distance to Street, Alley, or a Public Way (ft)(3)
Class	Gallons (1) (4)	Height (ft)	Gallons (1) (4)	Height (ft)			
IA	1,100	10	2,200	7	5	50	10
IB	2,200	12	4,400	14	5	50	10
IC	4,400	12	8,800	14	5	50	10
II	8,800	12	17,600	14	5	25	5
III	22,000	18	44,000	14	5	10	5

SI Units: 1 ft = 0.30 m; 1 gal = 3.8 L.
NOTES: (1) See 4-8.1.1 regarding mixed class storage.
(2) See 4-8.1.3 regarding protection for exposures.
(3) See 4-8.1.4 for smaller pile sizes.
(4) For storage in racks, the quantity limits per pile do not apply, but the rack arrangement shall be limited to a maximum of 50 feet in length and two rows or 9 feet in depth.

4-8.1.2   No container or portable tank in a pile shall be more than 200 ft (60 m) from a 12-ft (3.6-m) wide access way to permit approach of fire control apparatus under all weather conditions.

The phrase "under all weather conditions" was added to the 1981 edition of the *Code* as a result of a public proposal. The proponent contended that dirt access roads might be impassable in wet weather and the Committee agreed. This addition addresses the problem.

4-8.1.3   The distances listed in Table 4-8 apply to properties that have protection for exposures as defined. If there are exposures, and such protection for exposures does not exist, the distances in column 4 shall be doubled.

4-8.1.4   When total quantity stored does not exceed 50 percent of maximum per pile, the distances in columns 4 and 5 may be reduced 50 percent, but to not less than 3 ft (0.90 m).

The following three problems illustrate how Table 4-8 is applied:

1. There are 1,700 gal (6434.5 L) of a Class II liquid in drums stored outside a warehouse. How many gallons of a Class IB liquid can the plant store in the same pile?

Solution: The Class IB storage is the more hazardous, so provisions governing IB pile storage are applicable. The maximum allowed per pile is 2,200 gal (8327 L). Since the plant already has 1,700 gal (6434.5 L) of Class II, only 500 gal (1892.5 L) of Class IB can be stored in the same pile.

2. A manufacturing plant has no protection for exposures. Several piles of drums containing a Class IB liquid are located 125 ft (38 m) from the nearest property line that can be built upon. An industrial plant on the adjacent property is in the process of forming its own fire brigade. What will be the new distance requirement for the containers?

Solution: When there is no protection for exposures, the distance specified in column 4 must be doubled. Thus, 100 ft (30 m) is needed. The plant in question has its storage 125 ft (38 m) away, so there is no *Code* violation. When the protection for exposures is in effect, the plant can move its storage to within 50 ft (15 m) of its neighbor.

3. How close to adjacent property which can be built upon, and how close to a nearby street, is the manufacturing plant allowed to place 2,300 gal (8706 L) of kerosene (Class II) in drums? Assume there is no protection for exposures.

NFPA 30—CONTAINER AND PORTABLE TANK STORAGE

Solution: With no protection for exposures, the distance given in column 4 must be doubled to 50 ft (15 m). The plant is allowed to store 8,800 gal (33 308 L), but has only stored 2,300 gal (8706 L). This is substantially less than 50 percent of the allowable amount, so the plant can reduce the distance specified in column 4 by 50 percent. Therefore, storage can be placed 25 ft (7.6 m) from the property line that can be built upon.

Because there is less than 50 percent of the allowable amount, the plant may reduce the distance in column 5 by 50 percent, but to no less than 3 ft (0.90 m). Therefore, the plant's storage must be at least 3 ft (0.90 m) from the nearest street.

4-8.2 A maximum of 1,100 gal (4163 L) of liquids in closed containers and portable tanks may be stored adjacent to a building located on the same premises and under the same management provided that:

(a) The building is limited to a one-story building of fire-resistive or noncombustible construction and is devoted principally to the storage and handling of liquids, or

(b) The building has an exterior wall with a fire-resistance rating of not less than 2 hr and having no opening to above grade areas within 10 ft (3 m) horizontally of such storage and no openings to below grade areas within 50 ft (15 m) horizontally of such storage.

4-8.2.1 The quantity of liquids stored adjacent to a building protected in accordance with 4-8.2(b) may exceed that permitted in 4-8.2, provided the maximum quantity per pile does not exceed 1,100 gal (4163 L) and each pile is separated by a 10-ft (3-m) minimum clear space along the common wall.

4-8.2.2 Where the quantity stored exceeds the 1,100 gal (4163 L) permitted adjacent to the building given in 4-8.2(a), or the provisions of 4-8.2(b) cannot be met, a minimum distance in accordance with column 4 of Table 4-8 shall be maintained between buildings and the nearest container or portable tank.

4-8.3 The storage area shall be graded in a manner to divert possible spills away from buildings or other exposures or shall be surrounded by a curb at least 6 in. (15 cm) high. When curbs are used, provisions shall be made for draining of accumulations of ground or rain water or spills of liquids. Drains shall terminate at a safe location and shall be accessible to operation under fire conditions.

4-8.4 The storage area shall be protected against tampering or trespassers where necessary and shall be kept free of weeds, debris, and other combustible materials not necessary to the storage.

In addition to the requirements of this *Code* relative to outdoor storage, one must be aware of environmental requirements, particularly relating to the pollution of waterways. Additional dikes, curbing, or drainage systems may have to be provided in order to control any spill that may occur. Drainage or collection systems must be assessed from a fire protection standpoint to eliminate a fire hazard in areas where the drained flammable liquids are collected, no matter how remote from the storage.

References Cited in Commentary

NFPA 10, *Standard for Portable Fire Extinguishers*, NFPA, Quincy, MA, 1984.

NFPA 13, *Standard for the Installation of Sprinkler Systems*, NFPA, Quincy, MA, 1987.

NFPA 14, *Standard for the Installation of Standpipe and Hose Systems*, NFPA, Quincy, MA, 1986.

NFPA 251, *Standard Methods of Fire Tests of Building Construction and Materials*, NFPA, Quincy, MA, 1985.

NFPA 252, *Standard Methods of Fire Tests of Door Assemblies*, NFPA, Quincy, MA, 1984.

NFPA 325M, *Fire Hazard Properties of Flammable Liquids, Gases, and Volatile Solids*, NFPA, Quincy, MA, 1984.

NFPA 704, *Standard System for the Identification of the Fire Hazards of Materials*, NFPA, Quincy, MA, 1985.

ASTM E119, *Fire Tests of Building Construction and Materials*, American Society for Testing and Materials, Philadelphia, 1979.

ASTM E152, *Fire Tests of Door Assemblies*, American Society for Testing and Materials, Philadelphia, 1978.

ANSI/ASTM D 3435, *Specifications for Plastic Containers for Petroleum Products*, American Society for Testing and Materials, Philadelphia, 1983.

5 Operations
(See Appendix F for Cross-Reference Tables)

This new chapter on operations represents the most significant change between this edition of the *Code* and the 1984 edition. This chapter replaces the following four occupancy-specific chapters:

Chapter 5 Industrial Plants

Chapter 6 Bulk Plants and Terminals

Chapter 7 Processing Plants

Chapter 8 Refineries, Chemical Plants, and Distilleries

The rationale for combining the four distinct chapters was that the occupancies covered presented different hazards requiring different approaches to the fire problem. In many cases, however, it was not clear which chapter applied to a given situation. (The exception being Chapter 6 and, even here, a bulk plant might be a part of an integrated refining or processing operation.) For example, the hazards presented by a processing plant are generally the same as those presented by a chemical plant, although the scale might differ markedly. Or, an industrial plant (i.e., a facility whose use of flammable and combustible liquids is incidental to its principal business) may include a sizeable processing operation as one of the steps in its manufacturing process. To further confuse the user, many requirements were common to all four chapters, particularly those governing installation of electrical equipment.

The Technical Committee recognized several years ago that it would be beneficial to combine the four chapters into a single chapter on operations and established a Task Force to realize this goal. Several versions of this chapter were drafted, and each was reviewed by the full Committee and by several broad-based industry groups. Chapter 5 is the culmination of these efforts.

To aid the user, Appendix F is a cross-reference index to identify the source paragraph of the 1984 edition of the *Code* for each numbered paragraph of this chapter.

164 FLAMMABLE AND COMBUSTIBLE LIQUIDS CODE HANDBOOK

5-1 Scope.

5-1.1 This chapter applies to operations involving the use or handling of liquids either as a principal or incidental activity, except as covered elsewhere in this Code or in other NFPA Standards.

> This scope statement broadly states that the provisions of this Chapter apply wherever flammable and combustible liquids are used, regardless of quantity. The exceptions are tank and container storage, as covered in Chapters 2, 3, and 4, and operations covered by other NFPA standards, such as laboratories (NFPA 45, *Standard on Fire Protection for Laboratories Using Chemicals*), spray coating processes (NFPA 33, *Standard for Spray Application Using Flammable and Combustible Materials*), dipping processes (NFPA 34, *Standard for Dipping and Coating Processes Using Flammable and Combustible Liquids*), etc.
>
> "Incidental" is defined as an activity that is subordinate to the activity that establishes the basic occupancy or classification of the facility or production area.

5-1.2 The provisions of this chapter relate to the control of hazards of fire involving liquids. These provisions may not provide adequate protection for operations involving hazardous materials or chemical reactions nor do they consider health hazards resulting from exposure to such materials.

> The intent here is to warn the user that this chapter addresses *only* the hazards of fire. The hazards presented by "runaway" chemical reactions, exothermic decomposition of reactants, or exposure to or release of toxic materials are beyond the scope of NFPA 30, *Flammable and Combustible Liquids Code*, and require special consideration. In some cases, the control of these and other hazards may conflict with or take precedence over the provisions of this chapter.

5-2 General. Liquid processing operations shall be located and operated so that they do not constitute a significant fire or explosion hazard to life, to property of others, or to important buildings or facilities within the same plant. Specific requirements are dependent on the inherent risk in the operations themselves, including the liquids being processed, operating temperatures and pressures, and the capability to control any liquid or vapor releases or fire incidents that might occur. The interrelationship of the many factors involved must be based on good engineering and management practices to establish suitable physical and operating requirements. *(See 5-5.1.3.)*

> This section can be viewed as a general statement of the objectives of this chapter. It can also be viewed as providing for flexibility in applying the specific requirements that follow.

5-3 Facility Design.

5-3.1 Location.

5-3.1.1 The minimum distance of a processing vessel to adjoining property or to the nearest important building on the same property shall be based on the stability of the liquid and vessel capacity and shall be in accordance with Table 5-3.1.1, except as modified in 5-3.1.2.

> Table 5-3.1.1 is based on Table 2-6 and Table 7-2.1 from the 1984 edition. Most of the terms used have already been discussed elsewhere in this Handbook, primarily in Chapter 2. The "maximum operating liquid capacity" of a process vessel is analogous to the maximum capacity of a storage tank. However, some process vessels are designed to operate only partially filled with liquid, the remainder of the vessel containing a gas or vapor. It is the liquid capacity that is of importance here. There is one major difference from the 1984 edition in that the "nearest important building on the same property" has been qualified as being one that is *not* directly related to the process. The vessel may or may not be housed in a building, so the distances are to be measured from the vessel itself.
>
> The greater spacing required for unstable liquids recognizes the possibility that a runaway chemical reaction may produce pressures and flow rates that exceed the capacity of the vent system. Note that the distances specified in the table are doubled if protection for exposures is not provided.

5-3.1.2 Where process vessels are located in a building and the exterior wall facing the exposure (line of adjoining property that can be built upon or nearest important building on the same property) is greater than 25 ft (7.6 m) from the exposure and is a blank wall having a fire-resistance rating of not less than 2 hrs, any greater distances required in Table 5-3.1.1 may be waived. Where a blank wall having a fire-resistance rating of not less than 4 hrs is provided, distance requirements may be waived. In addition, when Class IA or unstable liquids are handled, the wall shall have explosion resistance in accordance with good engineering practice. (*See 5-3.2.7 relative to explosion relief of other walls of this building*).

> The original wording of the source paragraph (7-2.1.1 in the 1984 edition) only allowed the waiver for the blank 4-hour firewall. The new wording provides some flexibility by allowing a partial waiver for a blank 2-hour fire partition. It should be noted, however, that provisions for drainage or explosion relief may impair the integrity of a firewall or fire partition. In some cases, providing explosion relief will be incompatible with a blank wall.

Table 5-3.1.1 Location of Processing Vessels from Property Lines and Nearest Important Building on the Same Property Where Protection for Exposures is Provided

Vessel Maximum Operating Liquid Capacity (gal)	Minimum Distance from Property Line that Is or Can Be Built Upon, Including Opposite Side of Public Way (ft)				Minimum Distance from Nearest Side of Any Public Way or from Nearest Important Building on Same Property that Is Not an Integral Part of the Process (ft)			
	Stable Liquid Emergency Relief		Unstable Liquid Emergency Relief		Stable Liquid Emergency Relief		Unstable Liquid Emergency Relief	
	Not Over 2.5 psig	Over 2.5 psig	Not Over 2.5 psig	Over 2.5 psig	Not Over 2.5 psig	Over 2.5 psig	Not Over 2.5 psig	Over 2.5 psig
275 or less	5	10	15	20	5	10	15	20
276 to 750	10	15	25	40	5	10	15	20
751 to 12,000	15	25	40	60	5	10	15	20
12,001 to 30,000	20	30	50	80	5	10	15	20
30,001 to 50,000	30	45	75	120	10	15	25	40
50,001 to 100,000	50	75	125	200	15	25	40	60
Over 100,000	80	120	200	300	25	40	65	100

NOTE: Double all of above distances where protection for exposures is not provided.

5-3.1.3 Other liquid processing equipment, such as pumps, heaters, filters, exchangers, etc., shall not be located closer than 25 feet (7.6 m) to property lines where the adjoining property is or can be built upon, or to the nearest important building on the same property that is not an integral part of the process. This spacing requirement may be waived where exposures are protected as outlined in 5-3.1.2.

NOTE: Equipment operated at pressures over 1000 psig (7000 kPa) may require greater spacing.

This is a new paragraph. The 25-ft minimum separation distance reflects the philosophy that such equipment is inherently more prone to leakage and necessary repairs than are process vessels. The note is an important reminder that process equipment operating at high pressures requires special consideration. Leaks in equipment operating at high pressures may result in sizeable releases of vapor or atomized liquid, sometimes culminating in explosions.

5-3.1.4 Processing equipment in which unstable liquids are handled shall be separated from unrelated plant facilities that use or handle liquids by either 25-ft (7.6-m) clear spacing or a wall having a fire-resistance rating of not less than 2 hrs. The wall shall also have explosion resistance in accordance with good engineering practice.

The purpose of this blank wall is primarily to intercept any shrapnel from an explosion.

5-3.1.5 Each process unit or building containing liquid-processing equipment shall be accessible from at least one side for fire fighting and fire control.

5-3.2 Construction.

5-3.2.1 Processing buildings or structures shall be of fire-resistive or noncombustible construction, except that combustible construction may be used when automatic sprinklers or equivalent protection is provided, subject to approval of the authority having jurisdiction. (*See NFPA 220, Standard on Types of Building Construction.*)

5-3.2.2 Where walls are required for separation of processing operations from other occupancies or property lines, they shall have a fire-resistance rating of at least 2 hrs. In addition, when Class IA or unstable liquids are being stored or processed, the separating wall shall have explosion resistance in accordance with good engineering practice. (*See 5-3.2.7 relative to explosion relief of other walls of this building or area.*)

5-3.2.3 Class I liquids shall not be handled or used in basements. Where Class I liquids are handled or used above grade within buildings with basements or closed pits into which flammable vapors may travel, such below grade areas shall be provided with mechanical ventilation designed to prevent the accumulation of flammable vapors. Means shall be provided to prevent liquid spills from running into basements.

> This requirement is based on several incidents in which spilled liquid or vapors from a spill migrated to below grade levels and were ignited.

5-3.2.4 Provision for smoke and heat venting may be desirable to assist access for fire fighting. NFPA 204M, *Guide for Smoke and Heat Venting*, provides information on this subject.

5-3.2.5 Areas shall have exit facilities arranged to prevent occupants from being trapped in the event of fire. NFPA *101, Code for Safety to Life from Fire in Buildings and Structures*, provides information on the design of exit facilities. Exits shall not be exposed by the drainage facilities described in 5-3.4.

> When applying the provisions of NFPA *101, Life Safety Code*, the requirements for high-hazard industrial occupancies should be followed.

5-3.2.6 Adequate aisles shall be maintained for unobstructed movement of personnel and fire protection equipment.

5-3.2.7 Areas where Class IA or unstable liquids are processed shall have explosion venting through one or more of the following methods: (a) open air construction; (b) lightweight walls and/or roof; (c) lightweight wall panels and roof hatches; (d) windows of explosion-venting type. NFPA 68, *Guide for Explosion Venting*, provides information on this subject.

> This is a minimum requirement. Explosion venting may also be desirable where stable liquids or other classes of liquids are heated and their vapors released. As discussed earlier, hot vapors will cool and condense and may form an ignitible cloud of mist.

5-3.3 Ventilation.

5-3.3.1 Enclosed processing areas handling or using Class I liquids, or Class II or Class III liquids above their flash points, shall be ventilated at a rate of not less than 1 cu ft per minute per sq ft (0.3 m^3 per min per m^2) of solid floor area. This shall be accomplished by natural or mechanical ventilation with discharge or exhaust to a safe location outside the building without recirculation.

Exception: Recirculation is permitted where it is monitored continuously using a fail-safe system that is designed to automatically sound an alarm, stop recirculation, and provide full exhaust to the outside in the event that vapor-air mixtures in concentration over one-fourth of the lower flammable limit are detected.

Provision shall be made for introduction of make-up air in such a manner as to avoid short-circuiting the ventilation. Ventilation shall be arranged to include all floor areas or pits where flammable vapors may collect. Where natural ventilation is inadequate, mechanical ventilation shall be provided and shall be kept in operation while flammable liquids are being handled. Local or spot ventilation may be needed for the control of special fire or health hazards. Such ventilation, if provided, can be utilized for up to 75 percent of the required ventilation. NFPA 91, *Standard for the Installation of Blower and Exhaust Systems for Dust, Stock, and Vapor Removal or Conveying*, and NFPA 90A, *Standard for the Installation of Air Conditioning and Ventilating Systems*, provide information on this subject.

> The minimum ventilation rate of 1 cfm per sq ft (0.3 m^3/min per m^2) of floor area is based on an old rule of thumb: areas where flammable liquids are used should be ventilated at a rate of six air changes per hour. However, most industrial facilities are high-ceilinged; six air changes per hour involve exhausting a prodigious volume of air, with a correspondingly large energy loss in winter. Since most vapors are generated and tend to remain at or near floor level, it is reasonable to assume an arbitrary ceiling height of 10 ft (3 m). With each square foot of floor area translating to 10 cu ft (3 m^3), six air changes per hour equals 60 ft^3 (19 m^3) per hour, or 1 cfm for that one square foot of floor area.

See Figure 5-1 for an example of local exhaust ventilation.

5-3.3.2 Equipment used in a building and the ventilation of the building shall be designed to limit flammable vapor-air mixtures under normal operating conditions to the interior of equipment, and to not more than 5 ft (1.5 m) from equipment that exposes Class I liquids to the air. Examples of such equipment are dispensing stations, open centrifuges, plate and frame filters, open vacuum filters, and surfaces of open equipment.

> This requirement is usually superfluous, since industrial hygiene standards for employee health and safety would require airborne concentrations to be kept well below the lower flammable limit.

5-3.4 Drainage.

5-3.4.1 Emergency drainage systems shall be provided to direct flammable or combustible liquid leakage and fire protection water to a safe location. This may require curbs, scuppers, or special drainage systems to control the spread

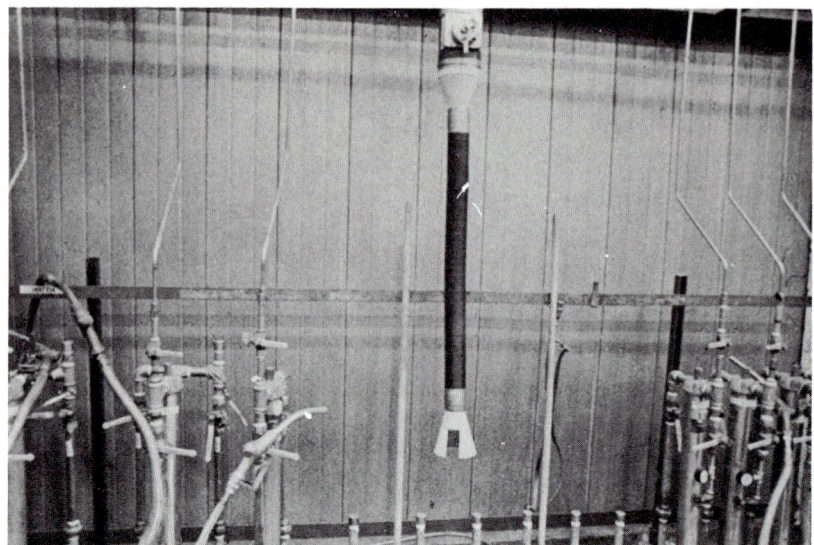

Figure 5-1 Some operations may require local or spot ventilation for control of special fire or health hazards. If provided, local or spot ventilation may be used for up to 75 percent of the required ventilation.

of fire (*see 2-2.3*). Appendix A of NFPA 15, *Standard for Water Spray Fixed Systems for Fire Protection*, provides information on this subject.

If scuppers are used, they must not be located in a wall that serves as a dike. The reference to Appendix A of NFPA 15, *Standard for Water Spray Fixed Systems for Fire Protection*, is to a description of a vented ditch designed so that any flame propagation through it is "lazy" due to lack of air and so that it will not be damaged due to ignition of vapors. In all cases, the system must discharge to a location acceptable to local, state, and federal environmental authorities.

5-3.4.2 Emergency drainage systems, if connected to public sewers or discharged into public waterways, shall be equipped with traps or separators.

The trap ensures that a liquid seal is maintained as material flows through it, thus preventing flame propagation beyond the trap. Separators are most useful where a two-phase system—oil and water, for example—is discharged and only one phase requires control. See Figure 5-2 for details.

5-3.4.3 A facility shall be designed and operated to prevent the normal discharge of flammable or combustible liquids to public waterways, public sewers, or adjoining property.

NFPA 30—OPERATIONS

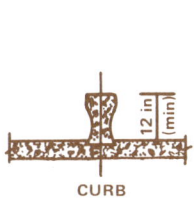
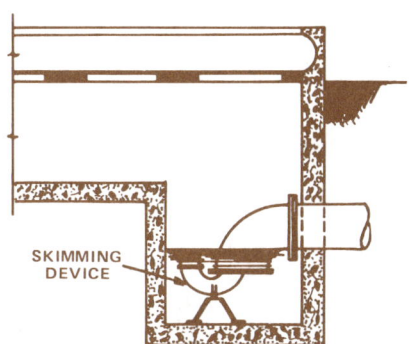

Figure 5-2 Details of a drainage system for areas containing flammable liquids.

It is sometimes possible to obtain permission to discharge combustible liquids to public sewer systems, but only if the treatment plant is capable of handling the effluent.

5-3.5 Electrical Equipment.

5-3.5.1 This section shall apply to areas where Class I liquids are stored or handled and to areas where Class II or Class III liquids are stored or handled at a temperature above their flash points (*see 1-1.3*).

Where Class II or Class III liquids are handled at temperatures sufficiently below their flash points, ordinary or general-purpose electrical equipment and wiring methods are adequate. However, some consideration should be given to locating electrical equipment so that any sparks or incendiary particles from an electrical failure cannot fall into open process equipment.

5-3.5.2 All electrical equipment and wiring shall be of a type specified by, and installed in accordance with, NFPA 70, *National Electrical Code*.

NFPA 70, *National Electrical Code*, specifies the types of equipment, equipment enclosures, and wiring methods for various locations. The interest of this *Code* is in those locations that may be hazardous due to ignitible atmospheres caused by generation of vapors from flammable and combustible liquids. These are designated as "Class I Hazardous Locations" by NFPA 70, *National Electrical Code*.

5-3.5.3 So far as it applies, Table 5-3.5.3 shall be used to delineate and classify areas for the purpose of installation of electrical equipment under normal conditions. In the application of classified areas, a classified area shall not extend beyond an unpierced floor, wall, roof, or other solid partition. The

172 FLAMMABLE AND COMBUSTIBLE LIQUIDS CODE HANDBOOK

designation of classes and divisions is defined in Chapter 5, Article 500, of NFPA 70, *National Electrical Code*. [*See NFPA 497A, Recommended Practice for Classification of Class I Hazardous (Classified) Locations for Electrical Installations in Chemical Process Areas, and NFPA 497M, Manual for Classification of Gases, Vapors, and Dusts for Electrical Equipment in Hazardous (Classified) Locations, for guidance*].

Chapter 5, Article 500, of NFPA 70, *National Electrical Code*, recognizes two degrees of hazard with regard to Class I hazardous locations: Division 1 and Division 2. In a Division 1 location, an ignitible atmosphere is assumed to be present all or most of the time, either because of open handling of liquids or because of frequent leaks or repairs. Therefore, any breakdown or malfunction of the electrical system that results in an arc or spark will likely lead to an ignition. In a Division 2 location, an ignitible atmosphere is not normally present, but may be produced because of an abnormal operating condition involving the equipment handling the liquid. Therefore, ignition is considered possible only if there are simultaneous breakdowns of both the process equipment and the electrical system—an unlikely event.

The basic design criteria for electrical equipment suitable for hazardous locations are:

(a) arcing and sparking parts are enclosed;

(b) equipment enclosures are capable of withstanding an internal explosion, should vapor find its way inside and be ignited; and

(c) the hot gases resulting from an internal explosion are cooled by the time they are forced to the outside of the enclosure, so that they cannot ignite the surrounding atmosphere. A simple diagram of an explosionproof electrical enclosure is shown in Figure 5-3. Electrical equipment must be approved for the division in which it is located.

5-3.5.4 The area classifications listed in Table 5-3.5.3 are based on the premise that the installation meets the applicable requirements of this code in all respects. Should this not be the case, the authority having jurisdiction shall have the authority to classify the extent of the area.

Particular attention must be paid to adequacy of ventilation. Inadequate ventilation means larger volumes may contain an ignitible atmosphere. Consequently, the area classified as hazardous may have to be enlarged beyond the limits described in Table 5-3.5.3.

Table 5-3.5.3 Electrical Area Classifications

Location	NEC Class I Division	Extent of Classified Area
Indoor equipment installed in accordance with 5-3.3.2 where flammable vapor-air mixtures may exist under normal operation	1	Area within 5 feet of any edge of such equipment, extending in all directions.
	2	Area between 5 feet and 8 feet of any edge of such equipment, extending in all directions. Also, area up to 3 feet above floor or grade level within 5 feet to 25 feet horizontally from any edge of such equipment.*
Outdoor equipment of the type covered in 5-3.3.2 where flammable vapor-air mixtures may exist under normal operation	1	Area within 3 feet of any edge of such equipment, extending in all directions.
	2	Area between 3 feet and 8 feet of any edge of such equipment, extending in all directions. Also area up to 3 feet above floor or grade level within 3 feet to 10 feet horizontally from any edge of such equipment.
Tank—Aboveground	1	Area inside dike where dike height is greater than the distance from the tank to the dike for more than 50 percent of the tank circumference.
Shell, Ends, or Roof and Dike Area	2	Within 10 feet from shell, ends, or roof of tank. Area inside dikes to level of top of dike.
Vent	1	Within 5 feet of open end of vent, extending in all directions.
	2	Area between 5 feet and 10 feet from open end of vent, extending in all directions.
Floating Roof	1	Area above the roof and within the shell.

*The release of Class I liquids may generate vapors to the extent that the entire building, and possible a zone surrounding it, should be considered a Class I, Division 2 location.

Table 5-3.5.3 Electrical Area Classifications, (continued)

Location	NEC Class I Division	Extent of Classified Area
Underground Tank Fill Opening	1	Any pit, box, or space below grade level, if any part is within a Division 1 or 2 classified area.
	2	Up to 18 inches above grade level, within a horizontal radius of 10 feet from a loose fill connection, and within a horizontal radius of 5 feet from a tight fill connection.
Vent—Discharging Upward	1	Within 3 feet of open end of vent, extending in all directions.
	2	Area between 3 feet and 5 feet of open end of vent, extending in all directions.
Drum and Container Filling Outdoors, or Indoors with Adequate Ventilation	1	Within 3 feet of vent and fill openings, extending in all directions.
	2	Area between 3 feet and 5 feet from vent or fill opening, extending in all directions. Also, up to 18 inches above floor or grade level within a horizontal radius of 10 feet from vent or fill openings.
Pumps, Bleeders, Withdrawal Fittings, Meters and Similar Devices		
Indoors	2	Within 5 feet of any edge of such devices, extending in all directions. Also up to 3 feet above floor or grade level within 25 feet horizontally from any edge of such devices.
Outdoors	2	Within 3 feet of any edge of such devices, extending in all directions. Also up to 18 inches above grade level within 10 feet horizontally from any edge of such devices.
Pits		
Without Mechanical Ventilation	1	Entire area within pit if any part is within a Division 1 or 2 classified area.
With Adequate Mechanical Ventilation	2	Entire area within pit if any part is within a Division 1 or 2 classified area.
Containing Valves, Fittings, or Piping, and not within a Division 1 or 2 Classified Area	2	Entire pit.

Table 5-3.5.3 Electrical Area Classifications, (continued)

Location	NEC Class I Division	Extent of Classified Area
Drainage Ditches, Separators, Impounding Basins		
Outdoor	2	Area up to 18 inches above ditch, separator, or basin. Also up to 18 inches above grade within 15 feet horizontally from any edge.
Indoor		Same as pits.
Tank Vehicle and Tank Car* Loading Through Open Dome	1	Within 3 feet of edge of dome, extending in all directions.
	2	Area between 3 feet and 15 feet from edge of dome, extending in all directions.
Loading Through Bottom Connections With Atmospheric Venting	1	Within 3 feet of point of venting to atmosphere, extending in all directions.
	2	Area between 3 feet and 15 feet from point of venting to atmosphere, extending in all directions. Also up to 18 inches above grade within a horizontal radius of 10 feet from point of loading connection.
Office and Rest Rooms	Ordinary	If there is any opening to these rooms within the extent of an indoor classified area, the room shall be classified the same as if the wall, curb, or partition did not exist.
Loading Through Closed Dome With Atmospheric Venting	1	Within 3 feet of open end of vent, extending in all directions.
	2	Area between 3 feet and 15 feet from open end of vent, extending in all directions. Also within 3 feet of edge of dome, extending in all directions.
Loading Through Closed Dome With Vapor Control	2	Within 3 feet of point of connection of both fill and vapor lines, extending in all directions.
Bottom Loading With Vapor Control Any Bottom Unloading	2	Within 3 feet of point of connections, extending in all directions. Also up to 18 inches above grade within a horizontal radius of 10 feet from point of connections.

*When classifying extent of area, consideration shall be given to fact that tank cars or tank vehicles may be spotted at varying points. Therefore, the extremities of the loading or unloading positions shall be used.

Table 5-3.5.3 Electrical Area Classifications, (continued)

Location	NEC Class I Division	Extent of Classified Area
Storage and Repair Garage for Tank Vehicles	1	All pits or spaces below floor level.
	2	Area up to 18 inches above floor or grade level for entire storage or repair garage.
Garages for Other Than Tank Vehicles	Ordinary	If there is any opening to these rooms within the extent of an outdoor classified area, the entire room shall be classified the same as the area classification at the point of the opening.
Outdoor Drum Storage	Ordinary	
Indoor Warehousing Where There is No Flammable Liquid Transfer	Ordinary	If there is any opening to these rooms within the extent of an indoor classified area, the room shall be classified the same as if the wall, curb, or partition did not exist.
Piers and Wharves		See Figure 5-3.5.6.

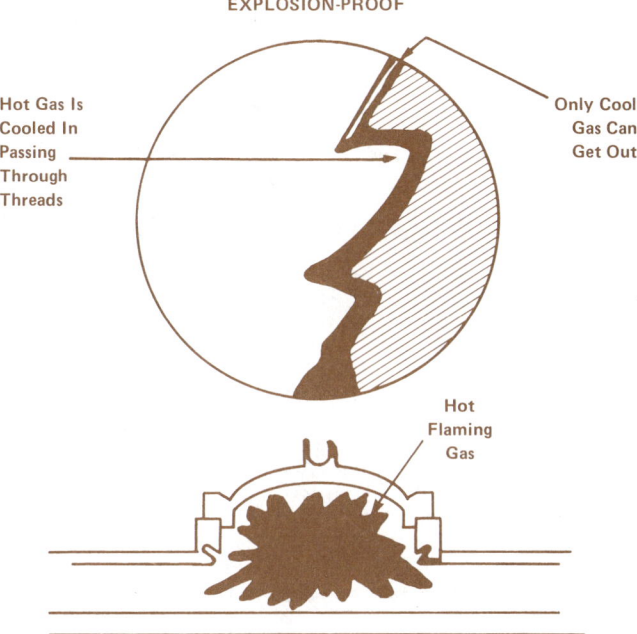

Figure 5-3 Explosionproof enclosure. Note how the hot gases are cooled as they are forced past the threads of the cover.

5-3.5.5 Where the provisions of 5-3.5.1, 5-3.5.2, 5-3.5.3, and 5-3.5.4 require the installation of electrical equipment suitable for Class I, Division 1 or Division 2 locations, ordinary electrical equipment including switchgear may be used if installed in a room or enclosure that is maintained under positive pressure with respect to the classified area. Ventilation make-up air shall not be contaminated. NFPA 496, *Standard for Purged and Pressurized Enclosures for Electrical Equipment*, provides details for these types of installations.

5-3.5.6 For marine terminals handling flammable liquids, Figure 5-3.5.6 shall be used as a minimum basis to delineate and classify areas for the purpose of installation of electrical equipment.

5-4 Liquid Handling, Transfer, and Use.

5-4.1 General.

5-4.1.1 Class I liquids shall be kept in closed tanks or containers when not actually in use. Class II and Class III liquids shall be kept in closed tanks or containers when ambient or process temperature is at or above their flash point.

178 FLAMMABLE AND COMBUSTIBLE LIQUIDS CODE HANDBOOK

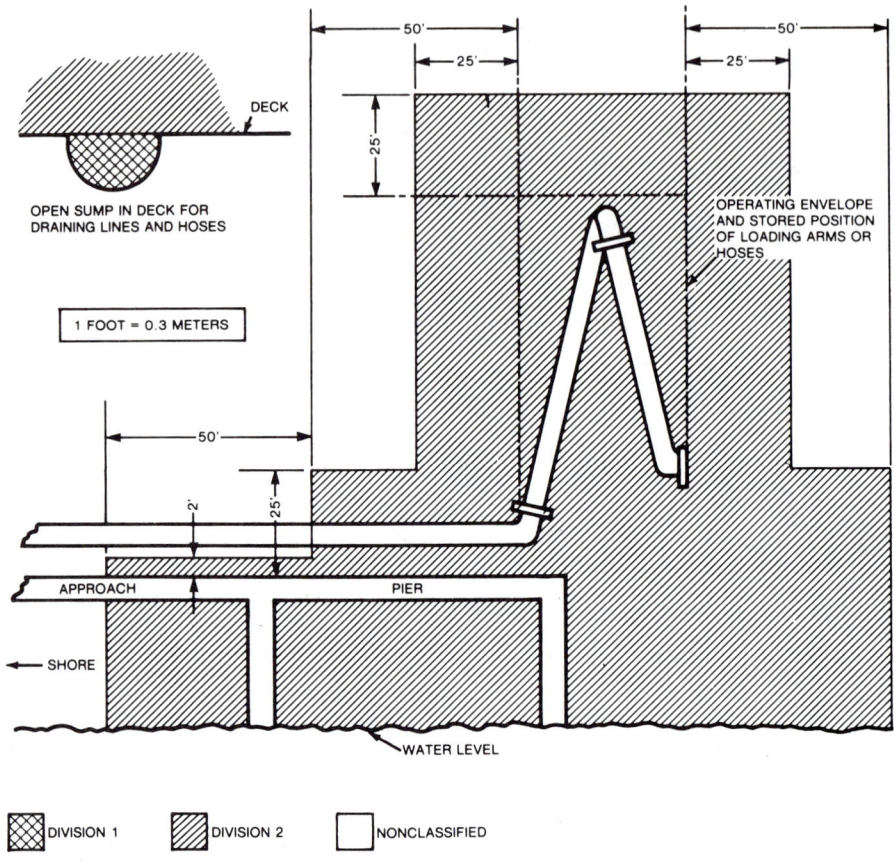

NOTES:
1. The "source of vapor" shall be the operating envelope and stored position of the outboard flange connection of the loading arm (or hose).
2. The berth area adjacent to tanker and barge cargo tanks is to be Division 2 to the following extent:
    (a) 25 ft (7.6 m) horizontally in all directions on the pier side from that portion of the hull containing cargo tanks.
    (b) From the water level to 25 ft (7.6 m) above the cargo tanks at their highest position.
3. Additional locations may have to be classified as required by the presence of other sources of flammable liquids on the berth, or by Coast Guard or other regulations.

Figure 5-3.5.6 Marine Terminal Handling Flammable Liquids.

Note that Class II and Class III liquids must be kept in closed containers only if exposed to ambient temperatures or process temperatures that exceed their flash points. Containers should always be kept covered when not actually in use.

5-4.1.2 Where liquids are used or handled, provisions shall be made to promptly and safely dispose of leakage or spills.

5-4.1.3 Class I liquids shall not be used outside closed systems where there are open flames or other ignition sources within the classified areas as set forth in Table 5-3.5.3.

5-4.1.4 Transferring liquids by means of pressurizing the container with air is prohibited. Transferring liquids by pressure of inert gas is permitted only if controls, including pressure-relief devices, are provided to limit the pressure so it cannot exceed the design pressure of the vessel, tank, container, and piping system.

> Since the drums ordinarily used for shipping liquids do not qualify as pressure containers, the use of gas pressure to transfer liquid is limited to containers built to the ASME *Boiler and Pressure Vessel Code* or to containers qualified as pressure vessels by U.S. Department of Transportation regulations.
>
> Air is prohibited as a pressurizing medium at all times because a flammable atmosphere might be created within the container. If an ignition were to occur within the container, the resulting overpressure would likely exceed what the container could withstand. Keep in mind that pressures above ambient will decrease both the lower flammable limit and the minimum ignition energy.

5-4.1.5 Positive displacement pumps shall be provided with pressure relief discharging back to the tank, pump suction, or other suitable location, or shall be provided with interlocks to prevent overpressure.

> The intent of this requirement is to prevent a failure of the pumping system due to overpressure caused by a line blockage, shut valve, etc.

5-4.1.6 Piping, valves, and fittings shall be in accordance with Chapter 3, "Piping, Valves, and Fittings."

5-4.1.7 Listed flexible connectors may be used where vibration exists. Approved hose may be used at transfer stations.

> Flexible connectors are often needed between process equipment and connected piping systems to accommodate vibration or to absorb piping stresses developed by temperature and pressure changes in the process system. Note that flexible connectors must be listed, while hose need only be acceptable to the authority having jurisdiction. [*See 5-4.3.2(f).*]

5-4.2* Equipment. Equipment shall be designed and arranged to prevent the unintentional escape of liquids and vapors and to minimize the quantity escaping in the event of accidental release.

A-5-4.2 Where the vapor space of equipment is usually within the flammable range, the probability of explosion damage to the equipment can be limited by inerting, by providing an explosion suppression system, or by designing the equipment to contain the peak explosion pressure that can be modified by explosion relief. Where the special hazards of operation, sources of ignition, or exposures indicate a need, consideration should be given to providing protection by one or more of the above means.

See NFPA 68, *Guide for Explosion Venting*, and NFPA 69, *Standard on Explosion Prevention Systems*, for additional information on various methods of mitigating losses from explosions.

5-4.3 Incidental Use of Liquids.

5-4.3.1 This section shall be applicable where the use and handling of liquids is only incidental to the principal business, such as automobile assembly, construction of electronic equipment, furniture manufacturing, or other similar activities.

> The intent of this section is to provide for the safe use of flammable and combustible liquids such as paint thinners, cleaning solvents, degreasers, etc.

5-4.3.2 Class I and Class II liquids shall be drawn from or transferred into vessels, containers, or portable tanks in the following manner only:

(a) from original shipping containers with a capacity of 5 gal (19 L) or less,

(b) from safety cans,

(c) through a closed piping system,

(d) from portable tanks or containers by means of a device drawing through an opening in the top of the tank or container, or,

(e) by gravity through a listed self-closing valve or self-closing faucet, or,

(f) if hose is used in the transfer operation, it shall be equipped with a self-closing valve without a hold-open latch in addition to the outlet valve. Only listed or approved hose shall be used.

5-4.3.3 Except as provided in 5-4.3.4 and 5-4.3.5, all storage shall comply with Chapter 4, "Container Storage."

5-4.3.4 The quantity of liquid that may be located outside of storage cabinets, inside storage rooms, cut-off rooms and attached buildings, general purpose warehouses, liquid warehouses, or other specific processing areas that are cut off by at least a 2-hr fire-rated separation from the general plant area shall not exceed the greater of the quantity in either (a) or the sum of (b), (c), (d), and (e) below:

(a) A supply for one day, or

(b) 25 gal (95 L) of Class IA liquids in containers,

(c) 120 gal (454 L) of Class IB, IC, II, or III, liquids in containers,

(d) Two portable tanks each not exceeding 660 gal (2498 L) of Class IB, IC, Class II, or Class IIIA liquids, and

(e) 20 portable tanks each not exceeding 660 gal (2498 L) of Class IIIB liquids.

Note that the quantity of liquid allowed is *either* a one-day supply, whatever that quantity might be, *or* the sum of the quantities allowed by (b), (c), (d), and (e). Note that in (d), two portable tanks are allowed, to eliminate the need for shutdown while switching from one tank to another. The number of portable tanks allowed in (e) recognizes the greater degree of safety in handling of portable tanks.

5-4.3.5 Where quantities of liquids in excess of the limits in 5-4.3.4 are necessary, storage shall be in tanks, which shall comply with the applicable requirements of Chapter 2, "Tank Storage," and Sections 5-3, 5-4.1, and 5-4.2.

The use of tanks, pumps, and piping systems eliminates the need for frequent opening and handling of small containers, greatly reducing the likelihood of spills.

5-4.3.6 Areas in which liquids are transferred from one tank or container to another container shall be separated from other operations that might represent an ignition source by distance or by fire-resistant construction. Drainage or other means shall be provided to control spills. Natural or mechanical ventilation shall be provided in accordance with 5-3.3, "Ventilation." NFPA 91, *Standard for the Installation of Blower and Exhaust Systems for Dust, Stock, and Vapor Removal or Conveying*, provides information on the design and installation of mechanical ventilation.

Note that this paragraph makes no mention of required distance or fire resistance. This will require considerable judgement on the part of the *Code* user. For example, a 1 gpm (0.06 L/sec) leak will feed an 8-sq-ft (0.75-m^2) pool of burning liquid. While no one would want to stand close to such a fire, a simple metal partition would effectively stop the radiant heat.

5-4.4 Loading and Unloading Operations.

5-4.4.1 Tank Vehicles and Tank Cars.

5-4.4.1.1 Tank vehicle and tank car loading or unloading facilities shall be separated from aboveground tanks, warehouses, other plant buildings, or the nearest line of adjoining property that can be built upon by a distance of at least 25 ft (7.6 m) for Class I liquids and at least 15 ft (4.6 m) for Class II and Class III liquids, measured from the nearest fill spout or (liquid or vapor) transfer connection. These distances may be reduced by utilizing fixed fire protection systems, dikes, fire-rated barriers, or combinations of any of these. Buildings for pumps or shelters for personnel may be a part of the facility.

> The separation distances specified here take precedence over those specified elsewhere in this *Code*, especially those in Table 2-6 that relate to separation between a tank and the nearest important building. The reason for the separation is to increase the chance of controlling a fire originating at a tank vehicle before it spreads to nearby tanks or buildings. As noted, the authority having jurisdiction may allow reduced separation where fixed fire protection is provided.

5-4.4.1.2 Static Protection. Bonding facilities for protection against static sparks during the loading of tank vehicles through open domes shall be provided (a) where Class I liquids are loaded, or (b) where Class II or Class III liquids are loaded into vehicles that may contain vapors from previous cargoes of Class I liquids.

> Filling tank vehicles at high flow rates through open domes has always presented a risk of ignition by static discharge, and this paragraph is an attempt to minimize the problem. Bonding the vehicle to the filling line ensures that the fill stem and the dome opening are at equal potential. This minimizes the chance for static discharge between the two. Normally, either the vehicle or the fill line (or both) is grounded so that static charge can be bled off to earth. In practice, bonding should be required during all top loading and unloading operations, since the operator usually has no knowledge about previous cargoes. For additional information, see NFPA 77, *Recommended Practice on Static Electricity*, and API 2003, *Protection Against Ignitions Arising Out of Static, Lightning, and Stray Currents*.

5-4.4.1.3 Protection as required in 5-4.4.1.2 shall consist of a metallic bond wire permanently electrically connected to the fill stem or to some part of the rack structure in electrical contact with the fill stem. The free end of such wire shall be provided with a clamp or equivalent device for convenient attachment to some metallic part in electrical contact with the cargo tank of the tank vehicle.

5-4.4.1.4 Such bonding connection shall be made to the vehicle or tank before dome covers are raised and shall remain in place until filling is completed and all dome covers have been closed and secured.

5-4.4.1.5 Bonding, as specified in 5-4.4.1.2, 5-4.4.1.3, and 5-4.4.1.4, is not required:

(a) where vehicles are loaded exclusively with products not having a static accumulating tendency, such as asphalts, including cutback asphalts, most crude oils, residual oils, and water-soluble liquids;

(b) where no Class I liquids are handled at the loading facility and the tank vehicles loaded are used exclusively for Class II and Class III liquids;

(c) where vehicles are loaded or unloaded through closed-bottom or -top connections whether the hose or pipe is conductive or nonconductive.

5-4.4.1.6 Filling through open domes into the tanks of tank vehicles or tank cars that contain vapor-air mixtures within the flammable range, or where the liquid being filled can form such a mixture, shall be by means of a downspout that extends near the bottom of the tank. This precaution is not required when loading liquids that are nonaccumulators of static charges. NFPA 77, *Recommended Practice on Static Electricity*, provides additional information on static electricity protection.

> The bonding methods specified will usually be effective in preventing the buildup of a static charge. As noted, liquids that inherently do not accumulate a charge do not require bonding. Understand, however, that bonding will not *totally* eliminate the problem *inside* the tank because the charge residing on the surface of the liquid will not be bled off to the tank shell. (On rare occasions, nonconductive liquids may accumulate enough charge to lead to nonincendive corona discharge.) When loading liquids having low conductivity, charge generation is reduced by discharging the liquid close to the bottom of the tank.

5-4.4.1.7 Stray Currents. To protect against stray currents, tank car facilities where flammable and combustible liquids are loaded or unloaded through open domes shall be protected by permanently bonding the fill pipe to at least one rail and to the rack structure, if of metal. Multiple pipes entering the rack area shall be permanently bonded together. In addition, in areas where excessive stray currents are known to exist, all pipes entering the rack area shall be provided with insulating sections to electrically isolate the rack piping from the pipelines. These precautions are not necessary where Class II or Class III liquids are handled exclusively and there is no probability that tank cars will contain vapors from previous cargoes of Class I liquids.

> Stray currents may result where there is a major defect in an electrical installation in the area of a loading or unloading facility. If the defect can be identified, it should be corrected. Permanent rail-to-pipe rack bonding should always be provided. If stray currents cannot be controlled, the best practice is to electrically

isolate the piping at the loading rack from its supply lines and bond this piping to the rail adjacent to the rack. Temporary bonding during loading and unloading operations is likely to be inadequate and should not be used.

Note that stray currents are not a problem with tank vehicles, since the rubber tires afford adequate insulation.

5-4.4.1.8 Equipment such as piping, pumps, and meters used for the transfer of Class I liquids between storage tanks and the fill stem of the loading rack shall not be used for the transfer of Class II or Class III liquids.

Exception No. 1: This provision shall not apply to water-miscible liquids when the class is determined by the concentration of liquid in water.

Exception No. 2: This provision shall not apply where the equipment is cleaned between transfers.

The intent of this requirement is to reduce the possibility of contamination of a combustible liquid with a flammable liquid, which could conceivably expose the consumer to an unrecognized risk.

5-4.4.1.9 Remote pumps located in underground tanks shall have a listed leak-detection device installed on the pump discharge side that will indicate if the piping system is not essentially liquid-tight. This device shall be checked and tested at least annually according to the manufacturer's specifications to insure proper installation and operation.

This paragraph was added to the 1984 edition of the *Code* because of the requirement in NFPA 30A, *Automotive and Marine Service Station Code*, for leak detection for remote pumps at service stations. The Technical Committee concluded the same protective feature is appropriate for a bulk loading facility, when loading with remote pumps in underground storage tanks.

5-4.4.1.10 When top loading a tank vehicle with Class I or Class II liquids without a vapor control system, valves used for the final control of flow shall be of the self-closing type and shall be manually held open except where automatic means are provided for shutting off the flow when the vehicle is full. Automatic shutoff systems shall be provided with a manual shutoff valve located at a safe distance from the loading nozzle to stop the flow if the automatic system fails. When top loading a tank vehicle with vapor control, flow control shall be in accordance with 5-4.4.1.11 and 5-4.4.1.12.

These requirements are intended to provide safeguards against overfilling of tank vehicles. When the practice of top loading prevailed and an operator was required to be on the top of the tank to observe the fill mark, a manually operated valve was an acceptable safeguard. With the advent of bottom-loading practices, it became unnecessary for the operator to be on the top of the tank, but other safeguards were required. The usual solution has been to employ a preset delivery meter that automatically stops the flow of liquid when a preset quantity has been delivered to the tank. This has not been considered completely adequate, and the additional requirement of an automatic shutoff device (electrical or otherwise) that will stop the flow of liquid when the tank is full has been deemed necessary. Such dual shutoff systems are considered adequate where vapor recovery is employed, so that it is unnecessary to open the top openings of the tank during filling.

5-4.4.1.11 When bottom loading a tank vehicle with or without vapor control, a positive means shall be provided for loading a predetermined quantity of liquid, together with a secondary automatic shutoff control to prevent overfill. The connecting components between the loading rack and the tank vehicle required to operate the secondary control shall be functionally compatible. The connection between the liquid loading hose or pipe and the truck piping shall be by means of a dry disconnect coupling.

The requirement for the dry disconnect coupling is to eliminate spills when disconnecting the fill hose from the vehicle.

5-4.4.1.12 When bottom loading a tank vehicle that is equipped for vapor control, but when vapor control is not used, the tank shall be vented to the atmosphere, at a height not lower than the top of the cargo tank of the vehicle, to prevent pressurization of the tank. Connections to the plant vapor control system shall be designed to prevent the escape of vapor to the atmosphere when not connected to a tank vehicle.

Vapor may be released only where there is a reasonable chance for dissipation. Vapor return connections are frequently at about the same level as liquid connections. If vapor return is not being used, means must be provided to limit vapor release near ground level and to release the vapor at least as high as the top of the tank or to pipe the vapor to a safe remote location.

5-4.4.2 Wharves.

5-4.4.2.1 This section shall apply to all wharves, except marine service stations as covered in NFPA 30A, *Automotive and Marine Service Station Code*. If liquids are handled in bulk quantities across general purpose piers or wharves, NFPA 307, *Standard for the Construction and Fire Protection of Marine Terminals, Piers, and Wharves*, shall be followed.

5-4.4.2.2 Handling packaged cargo of liquids, including full and empty drums, bulk fuel, and stores over a wharf during cargo transfer shall be subject to the approval of the wharf supervisor and the senior deck officer on duty.

> The handling of package cargo and stores during cargo transfer does not constitute an unreasonable risk if the activity is confined to areas remote from the cargo loading connection. It is the joint responsibility of the ships' officers and the wharf representatives to prescribe times and places where such transfer can be safely carried out.

5-4.4.2.3 Wharves at which liquid cargoes are to be transferred in bulk quantities to or from tank vessels shall be at least 100 ft (30 m) from any bridge over a navigable waterway, or from an entrance to or superstructure of any vehicular or railroad tunnel under a waterway. The termination of the wharf loading or unloading fixed piping shall be at least 200 ft (60 m) from a bridge or from an entrance to or superstructure of a tunnel.

5-4.4.2.4 Substructure and deck shall be substantially designed for the use intended. Deck may employ any material that will afford the desired combination of flexibility, resistance to shock, durability, strength, and fire resistance. Heavy timber construction is acceptable.

> Because of the wide variety in size and use of wharves, it is impossible to prescribe details of construction. It becomes an engineering problem to determine which type of material or manner of construction will best meet the requirements for the particular operation intended.

5-4.4.2.5 Tanks used exclusively for ballast water or Class II or Class III liquids may be installed on suitably designed wharves.

> The installation of tanks for Class II and Class III liquids is permitted on structurally adequate wharves because of the reduced fire risk with these liquids. Ballast water tanks can be installed on the wharves for the same reason, although it is obvious that the problem of supporting large tanks will usually dictate that they be installed on shore.

5-4.4.2.6 Loading pumps capable of building up pressures in excess of the safe working pressure of cargo hose or loading arms shall be provided with bypasses, relief valves, or other arrangements to protect the loading facilities against excessive pressure. Relief devices shall be tested at least annually to determine that they function satisfactorily at their set pressure.

5-4.4.2.7 All pressure hoses and couplings shall be inspected at intervals appropriate to the service. With the hose extended, the hose and couplings

NFPA 30—OPERATIONS 187

shall be tested using the in-service maximum operating pressure. Any hose showing material deterioration, signs of leakage, or weakness in its carcass or at the couplings shall be withdrawn from service and repaired or discarded.

5-4.4.2.8 Piping, valves, and fittings shall be in accordance with Chapter 3, with the following exceptions and additions.

(a) Flexibility of piping shall be assured by appropriate layout and arrangement of piping supports so that motion of the wharf structure resulting from wave action, currents, tides, or the mooring of vessels will not subject the pipe to excessive strain.

> Assuring adequate flexibility of piping on wharves is important because a wharf structure is usually flexible and subject to movement from the action of wind, waves, and possible impact of vessels during mooring. Failure of piping under these circumstances can release liquid that, if ignited, can result in a serious fire. The spread of burning liquid on water is likely to endanger all of the wharf piping, since much of the piping is frequently installed beneath the wharf surface to provide clear space for handling of dry cargo. In addition, the wharf structure will not be able to withstand the effects of a prolonged fire in most instances.

(b) Pipe joints that depend on the friction characteristics of combustible materials or on the grooving of pipe ends for mechanical continuity of piping shall not be permitted.

> These types of pipe joints have been found to be particularly susceptible to damage from even short-duration exposure to fire.

(c) Swivel joints may be used in piping to which hoses are connected, and for articulated swivel-joint transfer systems, provided the design is such that the mechanical strength of the joint will not be impaired if the packing materials should fail, as by exposure to fire.

> This requirement ensures that swivel-joint connections do not completely disengage because of exposure to fire.

(d) In addition to the requirements of 3-6.1, each line conveying Class I or Class II liquids leading to a wharf shall be provided with a readily accessible block valve located on shore near the approach to the wharf and outside of any diked area. Where more than one line is involved, the valves shall be grouped in one location.

> The intent here is that pipelines that lead to a wharf be equipped with block valves located on shore, so they are accessible for operation even if a liquid fire floating on the water makes it impossible to reach valves located on the wharf itself. In some

places, it may be desirable to install additional block valves on wharf lines at points where a group of loading spots branch off from the main lines, as on a "T"-headed wharf.

(e) Means shall be provided for easy access to cargo line valves located below the wharf deck.

> The intent is to make it easy to operate valves located below the wharf deck by means of trap doors or similar arrangements, even though it is necessary to keep the wharf surface unobstructed for the passage of motor vehicles. Such trap doors are usually conspicuously painted, and the parking of vehicles or storage of dry cargo over them is forbidden.

5-4.4.2.9 Pipelines on wharves shall be adequately bonded and grounded if Class I or Class II liquids are handled. If excessive stray currents are encountered, insulating joints shall be installed. Bonding and grounding connections on all pipelines shall be located on the wharf side of hose riser insulating flanges, if used, and shall be accessible for inspection.

> Wharf pipelines usually have screwed or welded flange connections and are thus electrically continuous, eliminating the need for any special bonding. However, if for any reason nonconductive connections are installed, a survey should be made to determine the desirability of placing electrical bonds around them. Insulating connections provided at connections for cargo hose are a deliberate attempt to isolate the vessel from possible stray currents originating in shoreside installations, and bonds around them are obviously undesirable. If the presence of continuous or intermittent stray currents in shore piping is revealed by test, all wharf piping should be electrically isolated from the shore piping with insulating connections.

5-4.4.2.10 Hose or articulated swivel-joint pipe connections used for cargo transfer shall be capable of accommodating the combined effects of change in draft and maximum tidal range, and mooring lines shall be kept adjusted to prevent surge of the vessel from placing stress on the cargo transfer system. Hose shall be supported to avoid kinking and damage from chafing.

> This is an important operating requirement and is the responsibility of both vessel and wharf personnel.

5-4.4.2.11 Material shall not be placed on wharves in such a manner as to obstruct access to fire fighting equipment or important pipeline control valves. Where the wharf is accessible to vehicle traffic, an unobstructed roadway to the shore end of the wharf shall be maintained for access of fire fighting apparatus.

5-4.4.2.12 Loading or unloading shall not commence until the wharf supervisor and the person in charge of the tank vessel agree that the tank vessel is properly moored and all connections are properly made.

5-4.4.2.13 Mechanical work shall not be performed on the wharf during cargo transfer, except under special authorization based on a review of the area involved, methods to be employed, and precautions necessary.

5-5 Fire Prevention and Control.

5-5.1 General.

As pointed out in 5-5.1.2, it is not possible to present detailed information on fire protection and prevention systems that will be applicable to all of the types of facilities covered by Chapter 5, "Operations." Each facility will be unique in some respects and will require judgement on the part of both the facility operator and the authority having jurisdiction regarding proper application of the *Code* and adequate design of fire protection systems. Often, the assistance of outside consultants and design engineers will be necessary.

5-5.1.1 This section covers the commonly recognized management control systems and methods used to prevent or minimize the loss from fire or explosion in liquid processing facilities.

NOTE: Other recognized factors of fire prevention and control, involving construction, location, separation, etc., are covered elsewhere in this chapter.

5-5.1.2 The wide range in size, design, and location of liquid processing facilities precludes the inclusion of detailed fire prevention and control systems and methods applicable to all such facilities. The authority having jurisdiction may be consulted on specific cases, where applicable; otherwise, qualified engineering judgment shall be exercised per 5-5.1.3.

5-5.1.3 The extent of fire prevention and control provided for the liquid-processing facility shall be determined by an engineering evaluation of the operation, followed by the application of sound fire protection and process engineering principles. The evaluation shall include, but not be limited to:

(a) analysis of fire and explosion hazards of the liquid operations,

(b) analysis of hazardous materials, hazardous chemicals, or hazardous reactions in the operations and the safeguards taken to control such materials, chemicals, or reactions,

(c) analysis of facility design requirements in Section 5-3 of this chapter,

(d) analysis of the liquid handling, transfer, and use requirements in Section 5-4 of this chapter,

(e) analysis of local conditions, such as exposure to and from adjacent properties, flood potential, or earthquake potential,

(f) consideration of fire department or mutual aid response.

Other factors to be considered are environmental exposure, possible need for evacuation of neighboring areas, safe shutdown procedures, and isolation of each operation from the rest of the facility.

5-5.2 Control of Ignition Sources.

5-5.2.1 Precautions shall be taken to prevent the ignition of flammable vapors. Sources of ignition include, but are not limited to:

(a) open flames
(b) lightning
(c) hot surfaces
(d) radiant heat
(e) smoking
(f) cutting and welding
(g) spontaneous ignition
(h) frictional heat or sparks
(i) static electricity
(j) electrical sparks
(k) stray currents
(l) ovens, furnaces, and heating equipment.

As explained in an earlier chapter, control of potential ignition sources is very important, but primary emphasis should always be on prevention of the release of ignitible concentrations of vapors.

Note that there is no mention here of nonsparking tools. Over the years, it has become more accepted that ordinary steel hand tools cannot generate ignition-capable sparks, except under unusual circumstances. (*See API PSD 2214, Spark Ignition Properties of Hand Tools.*)

5-5.2.2 Smoking shall be permitted only in designated and properly identified areas.

5-5.2.3 Welding, cutting, and similar spark-producing operations shall not be permitted in areas containing flammable liquids until a written permit authorizing such work has been issued. The permit shall be issued by a person in authority following his/her inspection of the area to assure that proper precautions have been taken and will be followed until the job is completed. (*See NFPA 51B, Standard for Fire Prevention in Use of Cutting and Welding Processes.*)

It is important that no "blanket" permits be allowed. Each permit should cover a specific job and a new permit should be required for the same job after each shift change or other interruption in work.

5-5.2.4 Static Electricity. All equipment such as tanks, machinery, and piping where an ignitable mixture may be present shall be bonded or connected to a ground. The bond or ground or both shall be physically applied or shall be inherently present by the nature of the installation. Electrically isolated sections of metallic piping or equipment shall be bonded to the other portions of the system or individually grounded to prevent hazardous accumulations of static electricity. NFPA 77, *Recommended Practice on Static Electricity*, provides information on this subject.

5-5.3 Inspection and Maintenance.

5-5.3.1 All fire protection equipment shall be properly maintained and periodic inspections and tests shall be done in accordance with both standard practice and equipment manufacturer's recommendations.

5-5.3.2 Maintenance and operating practices shall control leakage and prevent spillage of flammable liquids.

Clean up operations should be conducted in a manner that minimizes vapor loss. Many commercially available absorbents and adsorbents have been developed, primarily to mitigate environmental damage, but are still of great benefit. Also, some fire-suppression foams and recently developed vapor-suppression foams are helpful in controlling vapors from large-scale spills.

5-5.3.3 Combustible waste material and residues in operating areas shall be kept to a minimum, stored in covered metal containers, and disposed of daily.

5-5.3.4 Ground areas around facilities where liquids are stored, handled, or used shall be kept free of weeds, trash, or other unnecessary combustible materials.

5-5.3.5 Aisles established for movement of personnel shall be maintained clear of obstructions to permit orderly evacuation and ready access for manual firefighting activities.

5-5.4 Emergency Planning and Training.

This entire subsection on emergency planning and training was only briefly addressed in previous editions of the *Code*. Considerably more detail is now provided, but it must still be recognized that each facility will require an individual approach that may necessitate considerable judgement and consultation between the operator, the authority having jurisdiction, and local emergency services.

5-5.4.1 An emergency action plan, consistent with the available equipment and personnel, shall be established to respond to fire or other emergencies. This plan shall include the following:

(a) Procedures to be used in case of fire, such as sounding the alarm, notifying the fire department, evacuating personnel, and controlling and extinguishing the fire.

(b) Appointment and training of persons to carry out firesafety duties.

(c) Maintenance of fire protection equipment.

(d) Holding fire drills.

(e) Shutdown or isolation of equipment to reduce the escape of liquid.

(f) Alternate measures for the safety of occupants while any fire protection equipment is shut down.

5-5.4.2 Personnel responsible for the use and operation of fire protection equipment shall be trained in the use of that equipment. Refresher training shall be conducted at least annually.

5-5.4.3 Planning of effective fire control measures shall be coordinated with local emergency response agencies.

5-5.4.4 Procedures shall be established to provide for safe shutdown of operations under emergency conditions. Provisions shall be made for periodic training, inspection, and testing of associated alarms, interlocks, and controls.

5-5.4.5 The emergency procedure shall be kept readily available in an operating area and updated regularly.

5-5.4.6 Where premises are likely to be unattended for considerable periods of time, a summary of the emergency plan shall be posted or located in a strategic and accessible location.

5-5.5 Detection and Alarm.

5-5.5.1 An approved means for prompt notification of fire or emergency to those within the plant and to the available public or mutual aid fire department shall be provided.

5-5.5.2 Those areas, including buildings, where a potential exists for a flammable liquid spill, shall be monitored as appropriate. Some methods may include:

(a) Personnel observation or patrol;

(b) Process monitoring equipment that would indicate a spill or leak may have occurred;

(c) Provision of gas detectors to continuously monitor the area where facilities are unattended.

> This is an entirely new requirement and is somewhat analogous to tank overfill prevention requirements addressed in Chapter 2, "Tank Storage."

5-5.6 Portable Fire-Control Equipment.

5-5.6.1 Listed portable fire extinguishers shall be provided for facilities in such quantities, sizes, and types as may be needed for the special hazards of operation and storage as determined per 5-5.1.3. NFPA 10, *Standard for Portable Extinguishers*, provides information on the suitability of various types of extinguishers.

5-5.6.2 When the need is indicated per 5-5.1.3, water may be utilized through standpipe and hose systems (*see NFPA 14, Standard for the Installation of Standpipe and Hose Systems*), or through hose connections from sprinkler systems using combination spray and straight stream nozzles to permit effective fire control (*see NFPA 13, Standard for the Installation of Sprinkler Systems*).

5-5.6.3 When the need is indicated per 5-5.1.3, mobile foam apparatus shall be provided. NFPA 11C, *Standard for Mobile Foam Apparatus*, provides information on the subject.

5-5.6.4 Automotive and trailer-mounted fire apparatus, where determined necessary, shall not be used for any purpose other than fire fighting.

5-5.7 Fixed Fire Control Equipment.

5-5.7.1 A reliable water supply or other suitable fire control agent shall be available in pressure and quantity to meet the fire demands indicated by the special hazards of operation, storage, or exposure as may be determined by 5-5.1.3.

5-5.7.2 Hydrants, with or without fixed monitor nozzles, shall be provided in accordance with accepted practice. The number and placement will depend on the hazard of the liquid-processing facility, storage, or exposure as may be determined by 5-5.1.3 See NFPA 24, *Standard for the Installation of Private Fire Service Mains and Their Appurtenances*, for information on this subject.

5-5.7.3 Where the need is indicated by the hazards of liquid processing, storage, or exposure as determined by 5-5.1.3, fixed protection may be required utilizing approved sprinkler systems, water spray systems, deluge systems, fire resistive materials, or a combination of these. See NFPA 13, *Standard for the Installation of Sprinkler Systems*, and NFPA 15, *Standard for Water Spray Fixed Systems for Fire Protection*, for information on these subjects.

5-5.7.4 The following fire control systems may be appropriate for the protection of specific hazards as determined per 5-5.1.3 If provided, such systems shall be designed, installed, and maintained in accordance with the following NFPA standards:

(a) NFPA 11, *Standard for Low Expansion Foam and Combined Agent Systems*,

(b) NFPA 11A, *Standard for Medium and High Expansion Foam Systems*,

(c) NFPA 12, *Standard on Carbon Dioxide Extinguishing Systems*,

(d) NFPA 12A, *Standard on Halon 1301 Fire Extinguishing Systems*,

(e) NFPA 12B, *Standard on Halon 1211 Fire Extinguishing Systems*,

(f) NFPA 16, *Standard on Deluge Foam-Water Sprinkler and Foam-Water Spray Systems*,

(g) NFPA 17, *Standard for Dry Chemical Extinguishing Systems*.

References Cited in Commentary

NFPA 15, *Standard for Water Spray Fixed Systems for Fire Protection*, NFPA, Quincy, MA, 1985.

NFPA 30A, *Automotive and Marine Service Station Code*, NFPA, Quincy, MA 1987.

NFPA 33, *Standard for Spray Application Using Flammable and Combustible Materials*, NFPA, Quincy, MA, 1985.

NFPA 34, *Standard for Dipping and Coating Processes Using Flammable or Combustible Liquids*, NFPA, Quincy, MA, 1987.

NFPA 45, *Standard on Fire Protection for Laboratories Using Chemicals*, NFPA, Quincy, MA, 1986.

NFPA 70, *National Electrical Code*, NFPA, Quincy, MA, 1987.

NFPA 77, *Recommended Practice on Static Electricity*, NFPA, Quincy, MA, 1983.

NFPA 101, *Life Safety Code*, NFPA, Quincy, MA, 1985.

API Recommended Practice 2003, *Protection Against Ignitions Arising Out of Static, Lightning, and Stray Currents*, American Petroleum Institute, Washington, DC, 1982.

API Petroleum Safety Data Sheet 2214, *Spark Ignition Properties of Hand Tools*, American Petroleum Institute, Washington, DC, 1980.

ASME *Boiler and Pressure Vessel Code*, American Society of Mechanical Engineers, New York, NY, 1983, as amended.

6 Referenced Publications

6-1 The following documents or portions thereof are referenced within this document and shall be considered part of the requirements of this document. The edition indicated for each reference is the current edition as of the date of the NFPA issuance of this document. These references are listed separately to facilitate updating to the latest edition by the user.

6-1.1 NFPA Publications. The following publications are available from the National Fire Protection Association, Batterymarch Park, Quincy, MA 02269.

NFPA 10-1984, *Standard for Portable Fire Extinguishers*
NFPA 11-1983, *Standard for Low Expansion Foam and Combined Agent Systems*
NFPA 11A-1983, *Standard for Medium and High Expansion Foam Systems*
NFPA 11C-1986, *Standard for Mobile Foam Apparatus*
NFPA 12-1985, *Standard on Carbon Dioxide Extinguishing Systems*
NFPA 12A-1985, *Standard on Halon 1301 Fire Extinguishing Systems*
NFPA 12B-1985, *Standard on Halon 1211 Fire Extinguishing Systems*
NFPA 13-1987, *Standard for the Installation of Sprinkler Systems*
NFPA 15-1985, *Standard for Water Spray Fixed Systems for Fire Protection*
NFPA 16-1986, *Standard on Deluge Foam-Water Sprinkler and Foam-Water Spray Systems*
NFPA 17-1985, *Standard for Dry Chemical Extinguishing Systems*
NFPA 24-1984, *Standard for the Installation of Private Fire Service Mains and Their Appurtenances*
NFPA 30A-1987, *Automotive and Marine Service Station Code*
NFPA 45-1986, *Standard on Fire Protection for Laboratories Using Chemicals*
NFPA 51B-1984, *Standard for Fire Prevention in Use of Cutting and Welding Process*
NFPA 69-1986, *Standard on Explosion Prevention Systems*
NFPA 70-1987, *National Electrical Code*
NFPA 77-1983, *Recommended Practice on Static Electricity*
NFPA 80-1986, *Standard for Fire Doors and Windows*
NFPA 90A-1985, *Standard for the Installation of Air Conditioning and Ventilating Systems*

196   FLAMMABLE AND COMBUSTIBLE LIQUIDS CODE HANDBOOK

NFPA 91-1983, *Standard for the Installation of Blower and Exhaust Systems for Dust, Stock, and Vapor Removal or Conveying*

NFPA 99-1987, *Standard for Health Care Facilities*

NFPA *101-1985, Life Safety Code*

NFPA 220-1985, *Standard on Types of Building Construction*

NFPA 231-1987, *Standard for General Storage*

NFPA 231C-1986, *Standard for Rack Storage of Materials*

NFPA 251-1985, *Standard Methods of Fire Tests of Building Construction and Materials*

NFPA 302-1984, *Fire Protection Standard for Pleasure and Commercial Motor Craft*

NFPA 303-1984, *Fire Protection Standard for Marinas and Boatyards*

NFPA 307-1985, *Standard for the Construction and Fire Protection of Marine Terminals, Piers, and Wharves*

NFPA 321-1987, *Standard on Basic Classification of Flammable and Combustible Liquids*

NFPA 329-1987, *Recommended Practice for Handling Underground Leakage of Flammable and Combustible Liquids*

NFPA 385-1985, *Standard for Tank Vehicles for Flammable and Combustible Liquids*

NFPA 386-1985, *Standard for Portable Shipping Tanks for Flammable and Combustible Liquids*

NFPA 496-1986, *Standard for Purged and Pressurized Enclosures for Electrical Equipment*

NFPA 497A-1986, *Recommended Practice for Classification of Class I Hazardous (Classified) Locations for Electrical Installations in Chemical Process Areas*

NFPA 497M-1986, *Manual for Classification of Gases, Vapors, and Dusts for Electrical Equipment in Hazardous (Classified) Locations*

NFPA 704-1985, *Standard System for the Identification of the Fire Hazards of Materials.*

6-1.2 Other Publications.

ASTM Publications are available from the American Society for Testing and Materials, 1916 Race Street, Philadelphia, PA 19103.

ASTM A 395-82, *Ferritic Ductile Iron Pressure Retaining Castings for Use at Elevated Temperatures*

ASTM D 86-82, *Standard Method of Test for Distillation of Petroleum Products*

ASTM D 56-79, *Standard Method of Test for Flash Point by the Tag Closed Cup Tester*

ASTM D 93-80, *Standard Method of Test for Flash Point by the Pensky-Martens Closed Tester*

ASTM D 3828-81, *Standard Methods of Tests for Flash Point of Petroleum and Petroleum Products by Setaflash Closed Tester*

NFPA 30—REFERENCED PUBLICATIONS

ASTM D 3278-82, *Standard Method of Tests for Flash Point of Liquids by Setaflash Closed Tester*
ASTM D 5-73(1978), *Test for Penetration for Bituminous Materials*
ASTM D 323-82, *Standard Method of Test for Vapor Pressure of Petroleum Products (Reid Method)*
ASTM D 92-78, *Cleveland Open Cup Test Method*
ASTM/ANSI D 3435-80, *Plastic Containers (Jerry Cans) for Petroleum Products*

ANSI B31, *American National Standard Code for Pressure Piping*, American Society of Mechanical Engineers, United Engineering Center, 345 East 47 Street, NY 10017.

ASME, *Boiler and Pressure Vessel Code*, American Society of Mechanical Engineers, United Engineering Center, 345 East 47th St., New York, NY 10017.

API Publications are available from the American Petroleum Institute, 1220 L Street, N.W., Washington, DC 20005.
API 650, *Welded Steel Tanks for Oil Storage*, Sixth Edition, 1980
API Specifications 12B, *Bolted Tanks for Storage of Production Liquids*, Twelfth Edition, January, 1977
API 12D, *Field Welded Tanks for Storage of Production Liquids, Eighth Edition*, January, 1982
API 12F, *Shop Welded Tanks for Storage of Production Liquids*, Seventh Edition, January, 1982
API 620, *Recommended Rules for the Design and Construction of Large, Welded, Low-Pressure Storage Tanks*, Fifth Edition, 1982
API 2000, *Venting Atmospheric and Low Pressure Storage Tanks*, 1982
API 1615, *Installation of Underground Petroleum Storage Systems*, 1979
API 1621, *Recommended Practice for Bulk Liquid Stock at Retail Outlets*, 1977

UL Publications are available from Underwriters Laboratories Inc., 333 Pfingsten Road, Northbrook, IL 60062.

UL 142-1981, *Standard for Steel Aboveground Tanks for Flammable and Combustible Liquids*
UL 80-1980, *Standard for Steel Inside Tanks for Oil Burner Fuel*
UL 842-1980, *Standard for Valves for Flammable Fluids*

sti-P_3-1983, *Specifications for sti-P_3 System for External Corrosion Protection of Underground Steel Storage Tanks*, available from Steel Tank Institute, 666 Dundee Road, Suite 705, Northbrook, IL 60062.

Appendix A

Additional Explanatory Material

The material contained in Appendix A is included in the text within this *Handbook* and therefore is not repeated here.

Appendix B

Emergency Relief Venting for Fire Exposure for Aboveground Tanks

This Appendix is not a part of the requirements of this NFPA document but is included for information purposes only.

The requirements for emergency venting given in Table 2-8 and the modification factors in 2-2.5.7 are derived from a consideration of:

1. Probable maximum rate of heat transfer per unit area;

2. Size of tank and the percentage of total area likely to be exposed;

3. Time required to bring tank contents to boil;

4. Time required to heat unwet portions of the tank shell or roof to a temperature where the metal will lose strength;

5. Effect of drainage, insulation, and the application of water in reducing fire exposure and heat transfer.

Table 2-8 is based on a composite curve that is considered to be composed of three straight lines when plotted on log-log paper. The curve may be defined in the following manner:

The first straight line is drawn on log-log paper between the point 400,000 Btu/hr, at 20 sq ft (1.858 m^2) exposed surface area and the point 4,000,000 Btu/hr, at 200 sq ft (18.58 m^2) exposed surface area. The equation for this portion of the curve is $Q = 20,000A$.

The second straight line is drawn on log-log graph paper between the points 4,000,000 Btu/hr, at 200 sq ft (18.58 m^2) exposed surface area and 9,950,000 Btu/hr, at 1,000 sq ft (92.9 m^2) exposed surface area. The equation for this portion of the curve is $Q = 199,300A^{0.566}$.

The third straight line is plotted on log-log graph paper between the points 9,950,000 Btu/hr, at 1,000 sq ft (92.9 m^2) exposed surface area and 14,090,000 Btu/hr, at 2,800 sq ft (260.12 m^2) exposed surface area. The equation for this portion of the curve is $Q = 963,400A^{0.338}$.

Q = 20,000 A		Q = 199,300 A^0.566		Q = 963,400 A^0.338	
A	Q	A	Q	A	Q
20	400,000	200	4,000,000	1,000	10,000,000
30	600,000	250	4,539,000	1,200	10,593,000
40	800,000	300	5,032,000	1,400	11,122,000
50	1,000,000	350	5,491,000	1,600	11,601,000
60	1,200,000	400	5,922,000	1,800	12,040,000
70	1,400,000	500	6,719,000	2,000	12,449,000
80	1,600,000	600	7,450,000	2,400	13,188,000
90	1,800,000	700	8,129,000	2,800	14,000,000
100	2,000,000	800	8,768,000	and over	
120	2,400,000	900	9,372,000		
140	2,800,000	1,000	10,000,000		
160	3,200,000				
180	3,600,000				
200	4,000,000				

For areas exceeding 2,800 sq ft (260.12 m^2) it has been concluded that complete fire involvement is unlikely, and loss of metal strength from overheating will cause failure in the vapor space before development of maximum possible vapor evolution rate. Therefore, additional venting capacity beyond the vapor equivalent of 14,090,000 Btu/hr will not be effective or required.

For tanks and storage vessels designed for pressures over 1 psig, additional venting for exposed surfaces beyond 2,800 sq ft (260.12 m^2) is believed to be desirable because, under these storage conditions, liquids are stored close to their boiling points. Therefore, the time to bring the container contents to boiling conditions may not be significant. For these situations a heat input value should be determined on the basis of

$$Q = 21,000 \, A^{0.82}$$

The flow capacities are based on the assumption that the stored liquid will have the characteristics of hexane, and the vapor liberated has been transposed to equivalent free air at 60°F (15.6°C) and 14.7 psia (101.3 kPa) by using appropriate factors in:

$$\text{CFH} = \frac{70.5Q}{L\sqrt{M}}$$

where 70.5 is the factor for converting pounds of gas to cubic feet of air; Q = the total heat input per hour expressed in Btu; L = latent heat of vaporization; and M = molecular weight.

No consideration has been given to possible expansion from the heating of the vapor above the boiling point of the liquid, its specific heat, or the difference in density between the discharge temperature and 60°F (15.6°C), since some of these changes are compensating.

Since tank vent valves are ordinarily rated in CFH standard air, the figures derived from Table 2-8 may be used with the appropriate tank pressure as a basis for valve selection.

Table B-2 gives for a variety of chemicals the constants which can be used to compute the vapor generated and equivalent free air for liquids other than hexane, where greater exactness is desired. Inspections of the table will show that the use of hexane in deriving Table 2-8 provides results which are within an acceptable degree of accuracy for the listed liquids.

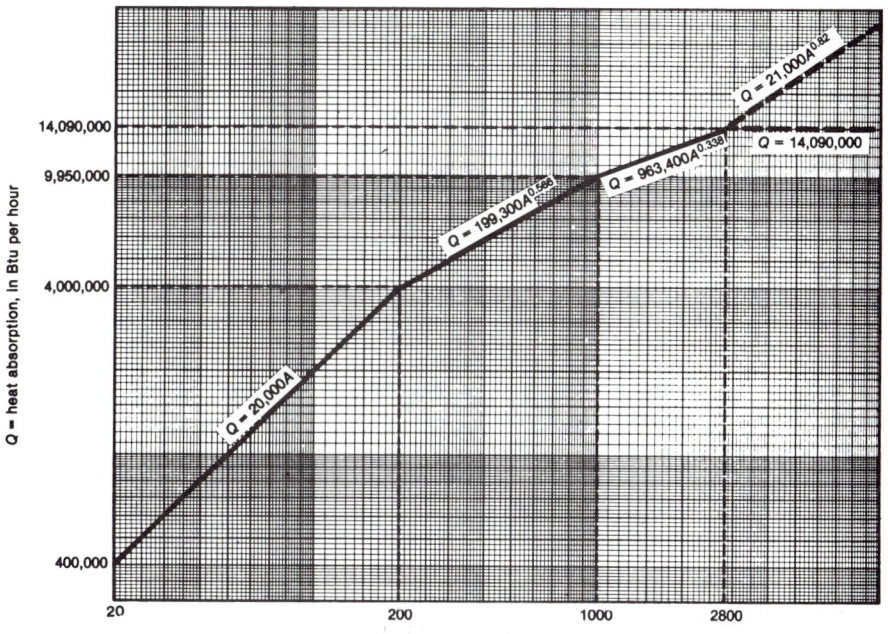

NOTE: See Table B-1 for approximate wetted area for horizontal tanks.
Figure B-1 Curve for Determining Requirements for Emergency Venting During Fire Exposure.

The equations used to develop the above table and graph were derived by combining three separate equations as shown in Figure B-1 on page 208.

Each of the equations is represented by a straight line. All three are intended to yield a sufficiently accurate estimate of the heat absorbed by a tank exposed to fire so that any calculation of the required flow capacity of emergency vents is adequately conservative.

The first equation, $Q = 20,000A$, is based on work reported in the NFPA *Quarterly* of October, 1943, by Duggan, Gilmour, and

Table B-1 Approximate Wetted Areas For Horizontal Tanks
(Wetted Area Equals 75 Percent Total Area)

Tank Diameter, Feet											
Tank Length, Feet	3	4	5	6	7	8	9	10	11	12
	APPROXIMATE WETTED AREA OF TANKS WITH FLAT HEADS									
3	32									
4	39	55								
5	46	65	88							
6	53	74	100	128						
7	60	84	112	142	173					
8	67	93	124	156	190	226				
9	74	102	136	170	206	245	286			
10	81	112	147	184	223	264	308	353		
11	88	121	159	198	239	283	329	377	428	
12	95	131	171	213	256	301	350	400	454	509
13	102	140	183	227	272	320	371	424	480	537
14	109	150	194	241	289	339	393	447	506	565
15	116	159	206	255	305	358	414	471	532	594
16	123	169	218	269	322	377	435	495	558	622
17	130	178	230	283	338	395	456	518	584	650
18	137	188	242	298	355	414	477	542	610	678
19		197	253	312	371	433	499	565	636	707

Tank Diameter, Feet											
Tank Length, Feet	3	4	5	6	7	8	9	10	11	12
	APPROXIMATE WETTED AREA OF TANKS WITH FLAT HEADS									
38					685	791	902	1013	1129	1244
39					701	810	923	1036	1155	1272
40					718	828	944	1060	1181	1301
41					734	847	966	1083	1207	1329
42					751	866	987	1107	1233	1357
43					767	885	1008	1130	1259	1385
44						904	1029	1154	1284	1414
45						923	1051	1178	1310	1442
46						941	1072	1201	1336	1470
47						960	1093	1225	1362	1498
48						979	1114	1248	1388	1527
49						998	1135	1272	1414	1555
50							1157	1295	1440	1583
51							1178	1319	1466	1612
52							1199	1342	1492	1640
53							1220	1366	1518	1668
54							1246	1389	1544	1696

Table B-1 Approximate Wetted Areas For Horizontal Tanks, (continued)
(Wetted Area Equals 75 Percent Total Area)

Tank Diameter, Feet	3	4	5	6	7	8	9	10	11	12
Tank Length, Feet	APPROXIMATE WETTED AREA OF TANKS WITH FLAT HEADS									
20	206	265	326	388	452	520	589	662	735
21	216	277	340	404	471	541	612	688	763
22	225	289	354	421	490	562	636	714	792
23	235	300	368	437	508	584	659	740	820
24	244	312	383	454	527	605	683	765	848
25		324	397	470	546	626	706	791	876
26		336	411	487	565	647	730	817	905
27		347	425	503	584	668	754	843	933
28		359	440	520	603	690	777	869	961
29		371	454	536	621	711	801	895	989
30		383	468	553	640	732	824	921	1018
31		395	482	569	659	753	848	947	1046
32			496	586	678	775	871	973	1074
33			510	602	697	796	895	999	1103
34			524	619	715	817	918	1025	1131
35			539	635	734	838	942	1051	1159
36			553	652	753	860	966	1077	1187
37			567	668	772	881	989	1103	1216

Tank Diameter, Feet	3	4	5	6	7	8	9	10	11	12
Tank Length, Feet	APPROXIMATE WETTED AREA OF TANKS WITH FLAT HEADS									
55							1263	1413	1570	1725
56								1437	1593	1753
57								1460	1622	1781
58								1484	1648	1809
59								1507	1674	1839
60								1531	1700	1866
61									1726	1894
62									1752	1923
63									1778	1951
64									1803	1979
65									1829	2007
66									1855	2036
67										2064
68										2092
69										2120
70										2149
71										2177
72										2205

SI Units: 1 ft = 0.30 m; 1 sq ft = 0.09 m^2.

FLAMMABLE AND COMBUSTIBLE LIQUIDS CODE HANDBOOK

Table B-2 Values of $L\sqrt{M}$ for Various Flammable Liquids

Chemical	$L\sqrt{M}$	Molecular Weight	Heat of Vaporization Btu per lb at Boiling Point
Acetaldehyde	1673	44.05	252
Acetic acid	1350	60.05	174
Acetic anhydride	1792	102.09	177
Acetone	1708	58.08	224
Acetonitrile	2000	41.05	312
Acrylonitrile	1930	53.05	265
n-Amyl alcohol	2025	88.15	216
iso-Amyl alcohol	1990	88.15	212
Aniline	1795	93.12	186
Benzene	1493	78.11	169
n-Butyl acetate	1432	116.16	133
n-Butyl alcohol	2185	74.12	254
iso-Butyl alcohol	2135	74.12	248
Carbon disulfide	1310	76.13	150
Chlorobenzene	1422	112.56	134
Cyclohexane	1414	84.16	154
Cyclohexanol	1953	100.16	195
Cyclohexanone	1625	98.14	164
o-Dichlorobenzene	1455	147.01	120
cis-Dichloroethylene	1350	96.95	137
Diethyl amine	1403	73.14	164
Dimethyl acetamide	1997	87.12	214
Dimethyl amine	1676	45.08	250
Dimethyl formamide	2120	73.09	248
Dioxane (diethylene ether)	1665	88.10	177
Ethyl acetate	1477	88.10	157
Ethyl alcohol	2500	46.07	368
Ethyl chloride	1340	64.52	167
Ethylene dichloride	1363	98.97	137
Ethyl ether	1310	74.12	152
Furan	1362	68.07	165
Furfural	1962	96.08	200
Gasoline	1370-1470	96.0	140-150
n-Heptane	1383	100.20	138
n-Hexane	1337	86.17	144
Hydrogen cyanide	2290	27.03	430
Methyl alcohol	2680	32.04	474
Methyl ethyl ketone	1623	72.10	191
Methyl methacrylate	1432	100.14	143
n-Octane	1412	114.22	132
n-Pentane	1300	72.15	153
n-Propyl acetate	1468	102.13	145
n-Propyl alcohol	2295	60.09	296
iso-Propyl alcohol	2225	60.09	287
Tetrahydro furan	1428	72.10	168
Toluene	1500	92.13	156
Vinyl acetate	1532	86.09	165
o-Xylene	1538	106.16	149

NOTE: For data on other chemicals, see chemistry handbook.

Fisher. The second equation, $Q = 34{,}500 A^{0.82}$, is the basis for the emergency venting requirements of NFPA 58, *Standard for the Handling and Storage of Liquefied Petroleum Gases*, and assumes that the total surface area of the tank is exposed to flame. The third equation, $Q = 21{,}000 A^{0.82}$, has been in use since before 1966 and is based on test programs conducted in 1944 by the Reserve Rubber Corporation, and in 1947 by the American Petroleum Institute. In these tests, tanks of water were exposed to gasoline and kerosene fires and the amount of heat absorbed by the tanks was determined. From this information, the quantity of vapor evolved and, consequently, the required venting capacity were determined.

A summary of the test results and an extensive bibliography are given in *Pressure-Relieving Systems for Marine Bulk Liquid Containers*, published in 1973 by the National Academy of Sciences.

Work done for Union Carbide Corporation at West Virginia University showed that a sustained external temperature of 1600°F (871°C) would bring most flammable liquids to their boiling points within 15 minutes. However, also at that temperature, unwet portions of the tank shell would soften and fail in less than 10 minutes. Thus, the tank would have self-vented and emergency vents would not be necessary. Accordingly, the first equation, $Q = 20{,}000 A$, was used for tanks whose wetted area did not exceed 200 sq ft (18.5 m²). This is about equal to a 2500-gal (9463-L) tank. Thus, the first equation is considered applicable only up to the point $A = 200$.

The second equation, $Q = 34{,}500 A^{0.82}$, is considered valid from $A = 200$ up to $A = 1000$. For a totally engulfed tank, $A = 1000$ is equivalent to a 25,000- to 30,000-gallon horizontal tank. As stated, this equation comes from NFPA 58, *Standard for the Storage and Handling of Liquefied Petroleum Gases*, and liquefied petroleum gases are seldom stored in tanks larger than this.

The third equation, $Q = 21{,}000 A^{0.82}$, was considered valid up to $A = 2800$. This corresponds to a value of Q equal to about 14,090,000 Btu/hr. This value of Q leads to a required vent flow capacity of 743,000 cu ft/hr (21,042 m³/hr), using the formula $CFH = 70.5 Q / L\sqrt{M}$ and assuming $L\sqrt{M}$ to be 144, the value for hexane, which is a reasonable assumption.

The value of 743,000 happens to be the amount of vapor that would be released through an 18-in. emergency vent. The Technical Committee felt that the time required to boil a liquid requiring a larger vent would lead to softening of the unwetted portion of the

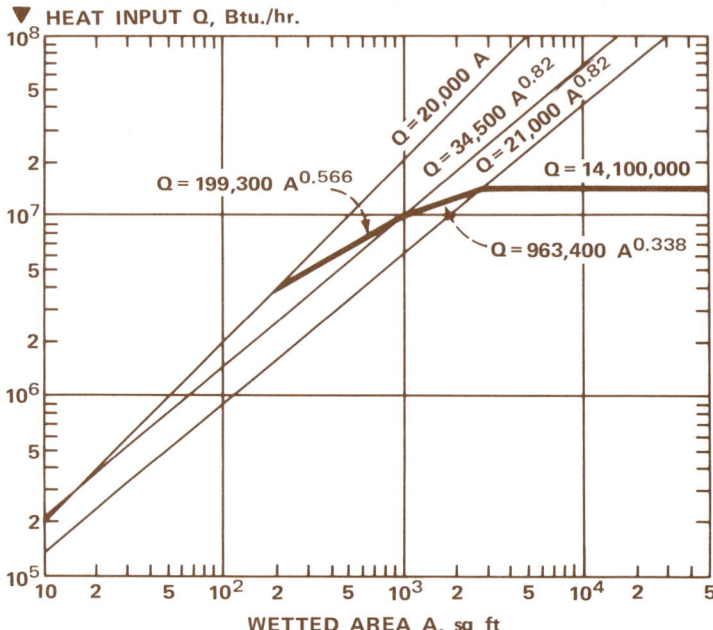

Figure B-1 Curve for Determining Requirements for Emergency Venting During Fire Exposure (Without Graph Background).

metal shell, so that the tank would self-vent before the emergency vent functioned. However, when large, low-pressure tanks are used, it is probable that the contents would be a low-boiling material, so it is reasonable to extend the line $Q = 21{,}000 A^{0.82}$ from $A = 2800$.

The formula, $CFH = 70.5 Q/L\sqrt{M}$ {at 60°F (15.6°)}, is derived by noting that Q/L represents the pounds of material vaporized by a heat input of Q, L being the latent heat of vaporization. One molecular weight of any material, expressed in lb, will produce 359 cu ft (10 m³) of vapor at 32°F (0°C) and normal atmospheric pressure of 14.7 psia. Assuming air to have an average molecular weight of 29, $359/\sqrt{29} = 66.7$. Multiplying this figure by 288.72/273.16, the ratio of the absolute temperatures, in °K, of 0°C and 15.6°C, renders the 70.5 in the formula.

Appendix C

Abandonment or Removal of Underground Tanks

This Appendix is not a part of the requirements of this NFPA document but is included for information purposes only.

C-1 Introduction.

C-1-1 Care is required not only in the handling and use of flammable or combustible liquids, but also in abandoning tanks that have held flammable or combustible liquids. This is particularly true of underground service station tanks that are most frequently used for the storage of motor fuel and occasionally for the storage of other flammable or combustible liquids, such as crankcase drainings (which may contain some gasoline). Through carelessness, explosions have occurred because flammable or combustible liquid tanks had not been properly conditioned before being abandoned.

> Although accidents from these causes may be infrequent, their results can be tragic. One such incident caused the death of three fire fighters and two service station employees when vapors from an abandoned gasoline tank exploded. The vapors had accumulated in the crawl space under the service station building. Therefore, it is certainly important enough to recommend practices to control the hazards associated with abandoned underground tanks.

C-1-2 In order to prevent accidents caused by improper conditioning, it is recommended that the procedures outlined below be followed when underground tanks are removed, abandoned, or temporarily taken out of service.

C-1-3 Underground tanks taken out of service may be safeguarded or disposed of by any one of the three following means:

(a) Placed in a "temporarily out of service" condition. Tanks should be rendered "temporarily out of service" only when it is planned that they will be returned to active service within a reasonable period or pending removal or abandonment within 90 days.

(b) Abandoned in place, with proper safeguarding.

(c) Removed.

The method used will depend on agreement between the property owner and the authority having jurisdiction based on previous use of the tank, its current condition, and future use of the property. Keep in mind, however, that environmental regulations may require removal of the tank at some point in time.

C-1-4 In cases where tanks are either rendered "temporarily out of service" or permanently abandoned, records should be kept of tank size, location, date of abandonment, and method used for placing the abandoned tank in a safe condition.

C-1-5 Procedures for carrying out each of the above methods of disposing of underground tanks are described in the following sections. No cutting torch or other flame or spark-producing equipment shall be used until the tank has been completely purged or otherwise rendered safe. In each case, the numbered steps given shall be carried out successively.

C-2 Rendering Tanks "Temporarily Out of Service."

C-2-1 Cap or plug all lines such as fill line, gage opening, pump suction, and vapor return. Secure against tampering.

C-2-2 Disconnect piping at all tank openings.

C-3 Abandoning Underground Tanks in Place.

C-3-1 Remove all flammable or combustible liquid from the tank and from all connecting lines.

C-3-2 Disconnect the suction, inlet, gage, and vent lines.

C-3-3 Fill the tank completely with an inert solid material. Cap remaining underground piping.

C-4 Removal of Underground Tanks.

C-4-1 Remove all flammable or combustible liquids from tank and from connecting lines.

C-4-2 Disconnect piping at all tank openings. Remove sections of connecting lines that are not to be used further and cap or plug all tank openings. After removal, the tank may be gas freed on the premises if it can be done safely at that location, or may be transported to an area not accessible to the public and the gas freeing completed at that location.

C-5 Disposal of Tanks.

C-5-1 If a tank is to be disposed of as junk, it should be retested for flammable vapors and, if necessary, rendered gas-free. After junking and before releasing to junk dealer, a sufficient number of holes or openings should be made in it to render it unfit for further use. NFPA 327, *Standard Procedures for Cleaning or Safeguarding Small Tanks and Containers*, provides information on safe procedures for such operations.

Holes are made in the tank to discourage its possible future use as a container for edible products that could be contaminated by residual deposits.

Appendix D

This Appendix is not a part of the requirements of this NFPA document but is included for information purposes only.

The following contains additional information and recommendations relating to the requirements in Chapter 4. The individual items bear the same number as the text of Chapter 4 to which they apply.

D-4-4 The preferred method of storage of liquids in buildings is in cutoff rooms or in attached buildings rather than in inside rooms because of fire department accessibility and the advantages of providing explosion venting where needed.

D-4-6.2

(a) Sprinkler system densities and areas of application presented in this appendix are based upon limited test data and fire experience. Design criteria in this appendix do not apply to storage in plastic drums. *(See Appendix E for additional information on this subject.)*

(b) For design criteria for specific installations, insurance engineers, fire protection consultants, and other knowledgeable persons should be consulted.

(c) **Palletized and Solid Pile Storage.** For protected storage of liquids, as specified in Table 4-6.1(a), automatic sprinkler protection should be provided in accordance with Table D-4-6.2(a).

(d) **Rack Storage.** In protected storage of liquids arranged, as specified in Table 4-6.1(b), automatic sprinkler protection should be provided in accordance with Tables D-4-6.2(b) and D-4-6.2(c), as applicable, except that racks with solid shelves should be provided with in-rack sprinklers at every tier or level.

D-4-6.2.1

(a) Automatic aqueous film-forming foam (AFFF)-water sprinkler systems for container storage of liquids has been shown to be an acceptable method for providing fixed protection. *(See Appendix E for additional information on this subject.)*

(b) For design criteria for specific installations, insurance engineers, fire protection consultants, and other knowledgeable persons should be consulted.

(c) Rack storage of liquids in containers [drums of 55 gal (208 L) capacity] stored on-end on wood pallets on conventional double-row racks to a maximum height of storage of 25 ft (7.6 m) should be provided protection in accordance with Table D-4-6.2.1.

As seen in all three tables under the heading for "Area," a distinction is made between the sprinkler design area for high-temperature and ordinary-temperature sprinkler heads. Ordinary heads are rated at 135 to 170°F (57.8 to 76.7°C). For purposes of this *Code*, a high-temperature head is any head rated above 170°F. The inherent delay in operation of the high-temperature head tends to limit sprinkler operation to immediately above and adjacent to the fire area, so that fewer heads operate and the chances of overtaxing the system are diminished.

Overtaxing a sprinkler system occurs when a fire grows so rapidly that too many heads open and the discharge pattern is adversely affected due to decreased discharge pressure. For example, using 285°F (140.9°C) sprinkler heads in lieu of 160°F (71.1°C) heads will cause fewer total heads to operate in a fire situation and thus keep the individual sprinkler head nozzle pressure higher. As more heads operate, the total water flow is divided between the heads and the reduced flow per head causes a lower nozzle pressure. Note that if higher temperature sprinkler heads are used, the maximum area over which sprinklers may be expected to operate is reduced. However, decreasing the area of operation for a hydraulically calculated sprinkler system may eliminate any factors of safety inherent in the recommended design bases.

The effect of the storage arrangement is also considered. Higher storage piles may have a tendency to shield the fire from effective application of the sprinkler discharge. Pile storage also allows for the possibility of container rupture due to collapsing piles and falling containers. Portable tanks can be stored in greater quantities per pile because of emergency relief vents on portable tanks. However, the potential impingement of flames from emergency relief vents on other storage must be considered.

Table D-4-6.2(a) Automatic Sprinkler Protection for Solid Pile and Palletized Storage of Liquids in Containers and Portable Tanks (Flammable Aerosols Not Included)

Storage Conditions		Ceiling Sprinkler Design and Demand				Minimum Hose Stream Demand (gpm)	Minimum Duration Sprinklers & Hose Streams
Class Liquid	Container Size and Arrangement	Density gpm/sq ft	Area (sq ft) High Temp.	Area (sq ft) Ord. Temp.	Maximum Spacing		
IA	5 gal. or less, with/without cartons, palletized or solid pile	0.30	3000	5000	100 sq ft	750	2 hrs
IA	containers greater than 5 gal., on end or side, palletized or solid pile	0.60	5000	8000	80 sq ft	750	2 hrs
IB,* IC,* & II*	5 gal. or less, with/without cartons, palletized or solid pile	0.30	3000	5000	100 sq ft	500	2 hrs
IB,* IC,* & II*	containers greater than 5 gal., on pallets or solid pile, one high	0.25	5000	8000	100 sq ft	500	2 hrs
II	containers greater than 5 gal., on pallets or solid pile, more than one high on end or side	0.60	5000	8000	80 sq ft	750	2 hrs
IB,* IC,* II*	portable tanks, one high	0.30	3000	5000	100 sq ft	500	2 hrs

* See Appendix E, introductory paragraphs.

Table D-4-6.2(a) Automatic Sprinkler Protection for Solid Pile and Palletized Storage of Liquids in Containers and Portable Tanks, (continued)
(Flammable Aerosols Not Included)

Class Liquid	Storage Conditions Container Size and Arrangement	Ceiling Sprinkler Design and Demand				Minimum Hose Stream Demand (gpm)	Minimum Duration Sprinklers & Hose Streams
		Density gpm/sq ft	Area (sq ft)		Maximum Spacing		
			High Temp.	Ord. Temp.			
II	portable tanks, two high	0.60	5000	8000	80 sq ft	750	2 hrs
	5 gal. or less, with/without cartons, palletized or solid pile	0.25	3000	5000	120 sq ft	500	1 hr
	container greater than 5 gal, on pallets or solid pile, on end or sides, up to three high	0.25	3000	5000	120 sq ft	500	1 hr
III	container greater than 5 gal, on pallets or solid pile, on end or sides, up to 18 feet high	0.35	3000	5000	100 sq ft	750	2 hrs
	portable tanks, one high	0.25	3000	5000	120 sq ft	500	1 hr
	portable tanks, two high	0.50	3000	5000	80 sq ft	750	2 hrs

NOTES:
(1) See Table 4-6.1(a) and Section 4-6 for additional information pertaining to protected palletized or solid piling of liquids.
(2) Minimum hose stream demand includes small hand hose (1½ inches) required in 4-7.1.3.
(3) The design area contemplates the use of wet pipe systems. Where dry pipe systems are required, it introduces a possible delay which needs to be compensated for by increased areas of application (plus 30 percent).

SI Units: 1 gal = 3.8 L; 1 sq ft = 0.09 m^2; 1 ft = 0.30 m.

Table D-4-6.2(b) Automatic Sprinkler Protection Requirements for Rack Storage of Liquids in Containers of Five Gallon Capacity or Less,* in Cartons on Conventional Wood Pallets or Without Cartons but Strapped to Pallets
(*Flammable Aerosols Not Included)

Class Liquid	Ceiling Sprinkler Design & Demand				In-Rack Sprinkler Arrangement and Demand				Minim. Hose Stream Demand (gpm)	Minim. Duration Sprinkler & Hose Stream
	Density gpm/ sq ft	Area (sq ft)		Max. Spacing	Racks up to 9 ft (2.7 m) deep	Racks over 9 ft (2.7 m) to 12 ft (3.7 m) deep	Minim Nozzle Pressure	Number of Sprinklers Operating		
		High Temp.	Ord. Temp.							
I (Max. 25' height)	0.40	3000	5000	80 sq ft/hd.	a) ord. temp. sprinklers 8 feet apart horizontally b) one line sprinklers above each level of storage c) locate in longitudinal flue space, staggered vertically d) shields req'd. where multilevel	a) ord. temp. sprinklers 8 feet apart horizontally b) two lines sprinklers above each level of storage c) locate in transverse flue spaces, staggered vertically and within 20 in. of aisle d) shields required where multilevel	30 psi.	a) 8 sprinklers if only one level b) 6 sprinklers ea. on two levels, if only two levels c) 6 sprinklers ea. on top 3 levels, if 3 or more levels d) hydraulically most remote	750	2 hrs

Table D-4-6.2(b) Automatic Sprinkler Protection Requirements for Rack Storage of Liquids in Containers of Five Gallon Capacity or Less,* in Cartons on Conventional Wood Pallets or Without Cartons but Strapped to Pallets, (continued)
(*Flammable Aerosols Not Included)

Class Liquid	Ceiling Sprinkler Design & Demand				In-Rack Sprinkler Arrangement and Demand				Minim. Hose Stream Demand (gpm)	Minim. Duration Sprinkler & Hose Stream
	Density gpm/sq ft	Area (sq ft) High Temp.	Area (sq ft) Ord. Temp.	Max. Spacing	Racks up to 9 ft (2.7 m) deep	Racks over 9 ft (2.7 m) to 12 ft (3.7 m) deep	Minim Nozzle Pressure	Number of Sprinklers Operating		
II (max. 25' height)	0.30	3000	5000	100 sq ft/hd.	a) ord. temp. sprinklers 8 feet apart horizontally b) one line sprinklers betw. levels at nearest 10 foot vertical intervals c) locate in longitudinal flue space, staggered vertically d) shields required where multilevel	a) ord. temp. sprinklers 8 feet apart horizontally b) two lines betw. levels at nearest 10 foot vertical intervals c) locate in transverse flue spaces, staggered vertically and within 20 in. of aisle d) shields required where multilevel	30 psi.	a) hydraulically most remote—6 sprinklers at each level, up to max. of three levels	750	2 hrs
III max.	0.25	3000	5000	120 sq ft/hd.	Same as Class II	Same as Class II	30 psi.	Same as Class II	500	2 hrs

NOTES:
(1) See Table 4-6.1(b) and Section 4-6 for additional information pertaining to protected rack storage.
(2) Additional in-rack protection required for solid shelves, as indicated in D-4-6.2(d).
(3) See 4-6.3 for types of racks permitted.
(4) See 4-6.5 for additional information pertaining to in-rack sprinklers.
(5) Minimum hose stream demand includes small hand hose (1½ inches) required in 4-7.1.3.
(6) The design area contemplates the use of wet pipe systems. Where dry pipe systems are required, it introduces a possible delay which needs to be compensated for by increased areas of application (plus 30 percent).

SI Units: 1 gal = 3.8 L; 1 sq ft = 0.09 m²; 1 ft = 0.30 m; 1 in. = 2.5 cm.

Table D-4-6.2(c) Automatic Sprinkler Protection for Rack Storage of Liquids in Containers Greater Than Five Gallon Capacity

Class Liquid	Ceiling Sprinkler Design & Demand				In-Rack Sprinkler Arrangement and Demand				Minim. Hose Stream Demand (gpm)	Minim. Duration Sprinkler & Hose Stream
	Density gpm/ sq ft	Area (sq ft) High Temp.	Area (sq ft) Ord. Temp.	Max. Spacing	On-Side Storage Racks up to 9 ft	On-End Storage (on pallets) up to 9 ft deep racks	Minim. Nozzle Pressure	Number of Sprinklers Operating		
IA (max. 25' height)	0.60	3000	5000	80 sq ft/hd.	a) ord. temp. sprinklers 8 feet apart horizontally	a) ord. temp. sprinklers 8 feet apart horizontally	30 psi.	a) hydraulically most remote—6 sprinklers at each level	1000	2 hrs
					b) one line sprinklers above each tier of storage	b) one line sprinklers above each tier of storage				
					c) locate in longitudinal flue space, staggered vertically	c) locate in longitudinal flue space, staggered vertically				
					d) shields required where multilevel	d) shields required where multilevel				
IB, IC & II (max. 25' height)	0.60	3000	5000	100 sq ft/hd.	a) see a) above	a) see a) above	30 psi.	a) see a) above	750	2 hrs
					b) one line sprinklers every three tiers of storage	b) see b) above				
					c) see c) above	c) see c) above				
					d) see d) above	d) see d) above				

Table D-4-6.2(c) Automatic Sprinkler Protection for Rack Storage of Liquids in Containers Greater Than Five Gallon Capacity, (continued)

Class Liquid	Ceiling Sprinkler Design & Demand					In-Rack Sprinkler Arrangement and Demand				Minim. Hose Stream Demand (gpm)	Minim. Duration Sprinkler & Hose Stream
	Density gpm/ sq ft	Area (sq ft)		Max. Spacing		On-Side Storage Racks up to 9 ft	On-End Storage (on pallets) up to 9 ft deep racks	Minim. Nozzle Pressure	Number of Sprinklers Operating		
		High Temp.	Ord. Temp.								
III (max. 40' height)	0.25	3000	5000	120 sq ft/hd.		a) see a) above	a) see a) above	15 psi.	a) see a) above	500	1 hr
						b) one line sprinklers every sixth level (maximum)	b) one line sprinklers every third level (maximum)				
						c) see c) above	c) see c) above				
						d) see d) above	d) see d) above				

NOTES:
(1) See Table 4-6.1(b) and D-4-6.2(b) for additional information pertaining to protected rack storage.
(2) Additional in-rack protection required for solid shelves, as indicated in D-4-6.2(d).
(3) See 4-6.3 for types of racks permitted.
(4) See 4-6.5 for additional information pertaining to in-rack sprinklers.
(5) Minimum hose stream demand includes small hand hose (1½ inches) required in 4-7.1.3.
(6) The design area contemplates the use of wet pipe systems. Where dry pipe systems are required, it introduces a possible delay which needs to be compensated for by increased areas of application (plus 30 percent).
(7) Where there is only one tier of drums above the highest line of in-rack sprinklers, the ceiling water demand density may be reduced to 0.25 gpm/sq ft over 5000 sq ft.

SI Units: 1 gal = 3.8 L; 1 sq ft = 0.09 m^2; 1 ft = 0.30 m; 1 in. = 2.5 cm.

Table D-4-6.2.1 Automatic AFFF-Water Protection (1) Requirements for Rack Storage of Liquids* in Containers (*Flammable Aerosols Not Included)

Class Liquid	Ceiling Sprinklers Design & Demand			In-Rack Sprinkler Arrangement and Demand (4)				Hose Stream Demand (3)	Duration AFFF Supply	Duration Water Supply
	Density gpm/sq ft	Area (sq ft)		On-End Storage, of drums (on pallets) up to 25 ft		Minimum Nozzle Pressure	Number of Sprinklers Operating			
		High Temp.	Ord. Temp.							
IA, IB IC, II	0.30	1500	2550	a) ord. temp. sprinkler up to 10 feet apart horizontally b) one line sprinklers above each level of storage c) locate in longitudinal flue space, staggered vertically d) shields required for multilevel		30 psi.	3 sprinklers per level	500	15 min	2 hrs

NOTES:
(1) System shall be a closed head wet system with approved devices for proportioning AFFF.
(2) Except as modified herein, in-rack sprinklers shall be installed in accordance with NFPA 231C, *Standard for Rack Storage of Materials*.
(3) Hose stream demand includes inside hand hose (1½ inches) required in 4-7.1.3.
(4) Maximum height of storage should be limited to 25 feet.

SI Units: 1 gal = 3.8 L; 1 sq ft = 0.09 m²; 1 ft = 0.30 m; 1 in. = 2.5 cm

Appendix E

This Appendix is not a part of the requirements of this NFPA document but is included for information purposes only.

SI Units: 1 gal = 3.8 L; 1 ft = 0.30 m; 1 sq ft = 0.09 m^2

Appendix D explains fire test data and loss experience that were used to help promulgate protection tables that are presented in Appendix C. While these data are limited, they do illustrate the seriousness of a potential drum rupture in a fire and the primary failure mode of built-up internal pressure in combination with the weakening of the rim joint, due to localized overheating. The possibility of a BLEVE-type explosion (Boiling Liquid Expanding Vapor Explosion) is also demonstrated. Due to the many unknowns, conservative practice would be to limit all Class I liquids stored in drums to not over one drum high, since protection tables were developed with this philosophy.

Very limited fire tests and fire experience, relative to flammable aerosols, indicate the serious problem they present to the fire protection engineer. Exploding pressurized aerosol cans are to be expected, together with the flaming fireball and rocketing action, spreading fire to a potentially larger area. The protection philosophy expressed is primarily to limit storage heights and to contemplate a larger area of application. Use of pressure-relieving can designs would be expected to affect favorably the design considerations for fixed protection.

> The following tests substantiate that, even with sprinkler protection, drums containing a Class I flammable liquid, can rupture under severe fire exposure conditions within 2 minutes after their exposure to fire. Burning of petroleum liquid from one 55-gal drum can release well over 7,000,000 Btu. This intense heat can easily overtax a sprinkler system unless high-temperature heads are used. It is therefore important to design sprinkler systems and arrange storage so that cooling water can be applied to all exposed parts of a drum. This requires early application of a moderate volume of water or later application of larger volumes of water to effect sufficient cooling. The standard sprinkler discharges much of its water as a fine spray that can be carried away by fire gases, with little cooling effect on containers or portable tanks. Specially designed sprinkler heads, such as those used in water spray systems, may be needed.

Recent fire incidents have further verified the need to tightly control storage in aisles and to adhere to storage requirements relative to quantities per pile, maximum pile height, and pile separation by aisles. Modifications of storage arrangements and changes in stored commodities without a re-evaluation and/or modification of the fire protection design may lead to failure of the protection system, with disastrous fire loss.

E-4-6(a) Fire Tests—Drum Storage:

(1) **1949 Fire Tests.** A series of fire tests were made in 1949 at the Factory Mutual test center in Norwood, Massachusetts. The tests were conducted in the 15-ft-high section of the fire test building used at that time. The tests used ICC Specification 5 drums, which were 14 gage compared with the 16 gage Specification 17C drums and 18 gage Specification 17E drums used more commonly today.

The tests involved storage horizontally on metal racks up to four drums high, and palletized upright, three drums high. Test drums contained either water, gasoline, or benzene, located in the first or second tier and equipped with pressure- and temperature-sensing connections. The gasoline and benzene drums were piped to manual vents so that pressure could be relieved before the drums ruptured. Other drums in the array contained water or were empty.

Sprinkler protection consisted of open, old-type sprinklers, which could be manually turned on, either at the start of the fire (short preburn) or at a time simulating the first sprinkler operation (long preburn). Sprinklers were spaced either at 100 sq ft/head with a flow rate of 0.22 or 0.28 gpm/sq ft or spaced at 50 sq ft/head with a flow rate of 0.44 or 0.56 gpm/sq ft.

Gasoline was pumped through piping to designated discharge points in or near the pile at flow rates from 1 to 15 gpm. In some tests, 5 or 10 gal of fuel were poured on the floor below the drums and ignited. Duration of flows were the length of time required to empty a single drum at the rate of flow used.

When sprinkler discharge was turned on immediately, the pressure that developed in the test drums was due almost entirely to the vapor pressure as the body of liquid increased in temperature. When sprinkler discharge was started, simulating normal sprinkler operation, there was a rapid pressure increase due to heating of the vapor space. This usually dropped when cooling by sprinkler discharge started.

Early tests showed that 100 sq ft spacing of sprinklers and densities of 0.22 and 0.28 gpm/sq ft would not prevent excessive temperature and pressure increases in drums. Spacing of 50 sq ft per sprinkler was used in subsequent tests. Test measurement and visual observation indicated that 0.56 gpm/sq ft provided considerably better cooling and flushing away of fuel than the 0.44 gpm/sq ft sprinkler density.

When fuel was discharged on the floor, only the bottom tier of storage was severely exposed. When fuel was discharged at a higher level, simulating a leaking drum, those drums in the immediate vicinity in upper tiers were severely exposed.

The rate of fuel flow had very little effect on the heating of any particular drum. The lower rates, 1 to 2 gpm, had a much longer duration and resulting exposure was greater before the 55-gal duration supply was used up.

With on-side drum storage in racks, the rate of temperature rise in the test drum on the lowest tier was 3 to 5 times as high with storage more than one drum high than it was with one-high storage. Tests with on-end palletized storage were only conducted three-high.

When 5 or 10 gal of gasoline were spilled on the floor and then ignited, the 5-gal spill gave a more severe exposure to drums because of the longer time before sprinklers would have operated. The 10-gal spill exposed more drums, but the exposure to any one drum was no more severe.

A very small leak from a drum filled with gasoline gave a very severe exposure, because of the localized exposure to the leaking drum and insufficient heat at the ceiling to operate the sprinklers.

Drums containing benzene heated much more rapidly than drums containing water because of the lower specific heat of benzene. Early pressure build-up in the vapor space is more pronounced with water, possibly because of more film vaporization on the early stages of the fire.

(2) 1967 Fire Tests. A series of fire tests were made to compare the effects of severe fire exposure to water- and heptane-filled drums. The tests were carried out in the Factory Mutual explosion tunnel, using new ICC-17E (18 gage) 55-gal drums.

A single drum was encircled with a ring of oil burners. Temperatures were measured at various points in the drum. The fuel rate to the oil burners was about 1 gpm. There was no cooling applied to the drum.

Using heptane, the drum ruptured at about 17 psig, at a drum rim temperature of 1190°F (643.4°C). The cover seam unrolled and a BLEVE-type explosion resulted, after a fire exposure of 3 to 4 minutes.

On similar tests using water, failure occurred at 40 psig after 10 minutes.

The tests indicated that the heptane-filled drum will rupture much sooner and at a much lower internal pressure than a water-filled drum. This is attributed to the fact that drums were found to leak around the joint of the rim before the rupture. The small leakage of heptane vapor through the rim joint causes a localized flame at this already weakened location on the rim, whereas steam issuing from a similar leak in a water-filled drum tends to cool the metal at this point.

(3) 1974 Fire Tests. A series of fire tests were made to evaluate protection of on-end drum storage with AFFF foam discharging from a standard sprinkler system. The tests were conducted in the 30-foot high area of the Factory Mutual test center in Rhode Island.

Based on the 1967 tests, a standard for success was that no drum should exceed 15 psig pressure.

Tests were made with water-filled drums, palletized, 2, 3, and 4 pallets high, and on racks, 5 tiers high.

Fuel was heptane, piped to the base of the top tier of storage, with a 10-gal floor spill in each case. Sprinklers were automatic, 286°F (141.1°C) heads.

Test 1: In this test, storage was 4 pallet-loads high. Fuel discharge rate was 2 gpm. Sprinkler discharge density was 0.30 gpm/sq ft. The first sprinkler opened at 34 sec. Only 4 sprinklers operated, but the three-dimensional fire in the pile continued strong. Several drums bulged, 2 ruptured, and 6 exceeded 15 psig pressure.

Test 2: In this test, storage was 3 tiers high, sprinkler density was 0.60 gpm/sq ft. Other conditions were the same as Test 1.

Two sprinklers opened at about 1 minute 20 sec. A considerable number of drums were deformed. Four of the 8 monitored drums exceeded 15 psig pressure.

Test 3: This test was rack storage with 160°F (71.1°C) automatic sprinklers in each tier except the bottom. Fuel rate was 2 gpm. Ceiling protection was 0.30 gpm/sq ft.

Five in-rack sprinklers and one ceiling sprinkler opened. One drum in the first tier, which had no in-rack sprinklers, reached a pressure of 16 psig. Two drums fell from the fifth tier, due to burning away of a pallet.

Test 4: Test 4 was a repeat of Test 3, except the fuel flow rate was 15 gpm.

Eight ceiling sprinklers and 5 in-rack sprinklers operated. Ceiling temperatures reached 1665°F (909.5°C). One monitored drum in the first tier reached 20 psig. Several drums were bulged.

Test 5: Test 5 was a repeat of Test 2, except storage was 2 tiers high.

The fuel was a greater distance from the ceiling so sprinklers did not operate until 3½ to 4 minutes after ignition. Damage to drums was severe, with many rupturing and all eight monitored drums going over 15 psig.

Generally, results were good in rack storage, where in-rack sprinklers were provided at each tier. For palletized storage, the AFFF protection controlled the floor fire, although pallets hindered spread of foam. Ceiling sprinklers only did not adequately protect palletized storage where an elevated spill resulted in a three-dimensional fire within the pile.

Most of the ruptured drums failed at the top chime, but one drum developed a slow leak at a bottom chime. In Test 5, several drums were heated by a localized fire which did not open sprinklers at the roof. This slow overpressurization can lead to superheated liquid release and a resulting severe BLEVE when the drum eventually ruptures.

E-4-6(b) Fire Tests—Small Containers.

(1) **1957 Fire Test (Nonpressurized Smaller Containers).** A fire test was made on 10½-ft high storage of paint in 1-gal cans in cartons. The storage was palletized, but the pallets were fire-stopped, so it was equivalent to solid piled storage. The paint varied in flash point from 105 to 170°F (40.5 to

76.7°C) (Class II and IIIA). Sprinkler protection was 160°F (71.1°C) heads, 10 × 10 ft, with a density of 0.23 gpm/sq ft. Ceiling height was 15 ft.

Six sprinklers operated and controlled the fire. Temperatures over the fire reached a maximum of 1100°F (593.3°C) and dropped below 500°F (260°C) after 10 minutes. Five hundred and three cans had their covers blown off and 20 cans had burst seams. The paint released from the cans was slight, but it would be much more significant if a pile had toppled over or if cans had not all been stored cover-side up.

(2) **1970 Fire Test (Pressurized Containers).** A fire test was made in the 30-ft high section of the Factory Mutual Rhode Island test facility. The storage was 13 and 16-oz cans of lacquer in shipping cartons stored 2 pallet by 2 pallet by 2 pallet high on racks. Storage height was 9 ft 9 in. Protection was by twelve 160°F (71.1°C) sprinklers spaced 10 × 10 ft providing a discharge density of 0.30 gpm/sq ft.

Fifty seconds after ignition, containers began to burst. At 62 sec, 3 sprinklers operated. The fire became more and more intense and with all 12 sprinklers operating, there was no suppressing effect. The discharge was increased to 0.50 gpm/sq ft without effect. After about 5 minutes, the fuel was nearly exhausted. Containers were thrown to every corner of the test building.

Temperatures over the fire were over 1000°F (537.8°C) for 3½ minutes and over 1700°F (926.6°C) for 2 minutes.

E-4-6(c) Fire experience examples involving flammable and combustible liquids in containers stored in buildings.

(1) **1951 Fire.** Drums of petroleum naphtha were stored temporarily in a general purpose warehouse used mainly for storing can ends in wood boxes. Storage was 1 drum high on pallets.

Two drums had small punctures and leaks near the bottom, caused either maliciously or by moving equipment. The leak was ignited, and one drum ruptured at the bottom seam. A drum rupture resulted which opened 272 sprinklers. The fire department was called promptly and they and sprinklers were able to contain the fire, helped by the low combustible concentration in the warehouse and by failure of any other drums to rupture.

Forty-two million can ends were wet down, but fire damage was limited. No explosion damage was reported. (The intensity of the BLEVE may have been limited by much of the liquid leaking from the drum before it ruptured.) Total damage was about $200,000.

(2) **1965 Fire.** Pressurized containers of paint were stored 15 ft high on racks. A fire started in the top tier from a gas-fired radiant heater. Bursting containers spread burning paint over a large area, opening one hundred eighty-eight 165°F (73.9°C) sprinklers. The fire spread 25 ft along a rack but was slowed by aisles and inert material. A portion of the roof over the fire area collapsed.

(3) 1966 Fire. Pressurized containers of alcohol-base hair spray and deodorant were stored palletized, 17 ft high. The fire was contained within a 1,200 sq ft pile by 107 operating sprinklers. Damage exceeded $400,000.

(4) 1971 Distribution Warehouse Fire. A sprinklered 67,000 sq ft, one-story, noncombustible warehouse for automotive equipment and supplies was destroyed by fire from undetermined cause. Storage consisted of various metal, plastic and rubber parts in cardboard cartons, plus flammable and combustible liquids in containers ranging from 1 pt aerosol cans up to, and including, 55-gal metal drums. Method of storage was mostly on wooden pallets on open metal racks, double row, with 3 and 4 tiers to a total storage height of 15 to 17 ft. A considerable portion of the racks were used for storage of flammable and combustible liquids in 5-gal and 55-gal metal containers on wooden pallets, 4 tiers high. Both flammable and nonflammable aerosols in pint cans in cartons were palletized and stored in portions of the racks. Ceiling sprinkler design was wet pipe, extra-hazardous schedule, using 17/32 orifice, 165°F (73.9°C) heads, supplied from a fairly strong city water supply (52 psi static, 38 psi residual, with 1,580 gpm flowing). A review of the hydraulics indicates system was capable of supplying a density of 0.20 gpm/sq ft for the most remote 2,000 sq ft area.

Despite immediate fire department response to a central station water flow alarm and use of a fire department siamese connection, the fire spread beyond the capability of the sprinkler system and the system was soon overtaxed, resulting in early roof collapse and breaking of sprinkler piping, and thus requiring closing of the main control valve. Numerous "fireball" explosions of aerosol cans and ruptures of 55-gal drums were reported, several affecting manual fire fighting operations, requiring about 5 hrs for control.

(5) 1975 Fire. About one hundred 55-gal drums of Class IB and IC liquids were stored palletized, 3 drums high, in a corner of a general-purpose warehouse, together with ordinary combustible commodities up to 11 ft high in racks. The roof was Class II steel deck, 15 ft high.

Sprinklers were on an ordinary hazard system, 160°F (71.1°C) heads.

Employees discovered a large fire in progress in the drum storage area. Shortly after the public fire department arrived, drums started to rupture, creating large fireballs. One drum failed at the bottom and rocketed through the roof, landing 750 ft from the building. The roof partially collapsed and one system was then shut off. Most of the building and contents were severely damaged.

The fire probably started in an open waste pail near the drum storage. Total loss was about $3,300,000.

In the commentary to 4-5.6, General-Purpose Warehouses, the amendment regarding special treatment of Class I and Class II liquids in plastic containers was discussed. The following commentary describes tests conducted by Factory Mutual Research Corporation to substantiate their proposal.

(a) *1981 Fire Tests.* The first test simulated palletized storage of a Class II liquid in plastic containers. The test involved a single pallet load of 60 cartons, each containing three 1-gal (3.8-L) plastic containers, for a total of 180 gallons of liquid. The liquid involved was a paint thinner having a flash point of 104°F (40°C). The ceiling height in the test bay was 30 ft (9 m). Ceiling sprinklers were spaced on a 100-sq-ft-per-head spacing; the sprinklers were rated at 286°F (141°C); the sprinkler density was 0.30 gpm/ft^2.

This test fire opened 40 sprinkler heads and developed ceiling temperatures exceeding 2200°F (1204°C). The burning commodity produced copious amounts of heavy smoke and a 10-ft (3-m) diameter pool fire. The sprinkler system could neither extinguish nor control the fire, and all the combustible commodity was consumed.

The second test involved two pallet loads of an alcohol-based hair spray packaged in 8-oz. polyethylene bottles, twelve bottles per carton. Each pallet held 96 cartons, for a total of 144 gal. Sprinkler protection was the same as it was in the first test.

This test fire opened only two heads, and the fire was controlled. The results seemed to indicate that the smaller container size and lower heat of combustion of the liquid itself resulted in a greatly reduced fire hazard.

(b) *1985 Fire Tests.* A series of three tests were conducted using paint thinner, isopropyl alcohol, and corn oil. Each test used two pallet-loads of material, side by side, each pallet load consisting of 36 cartons of six 1-gal (3.8-L) containers each.

The first test involved the paint thinner. The test array was protected by 160°F/0.64 in. orifice large-drop sprinklers on a 10 ft × 10 ft spacing. The sprinkler discharge pressure was 75 psig, yielding about 94 gpm per sprinkler. The resulting fire opened four sprinkler heads within four minutes. Thirty-eight more heads opened in the next three minutes. Sprinkler discharge pressure could not be maintained and fell to 45 psig (83 gpm). Again, the test fire could not be controlled.

The second test involved the isopropyl alcohol. This test array was protected by 280°F, ½-in. orifice sprinklers on a 10 ft × 10 ft spacing. Discharge density was 0.30 gpm/sq ft. The resulting fire opened four sprinkler heads in three minutes and an additional 29 heads in the next two minutes.

Although the 0.30 density was maintained throughout the test, the fire could not be controlled.

The third test involved the corn oil and used the same sprinkler protection as the isopropyl alcohol test just described. One minute after ignition, oil began to leak down the side of one of the plastic containers, but did not ignite. After 30 minutes, the oil had still not ignited and no sprinkler heads had operated. At this point, the fire test zone was ventilated and the resulting draft caused the oil to ignite. Two sprinkler heads eventually opened 42 minutes into the test and reduced the fire intensity.

Appendix F
Chapter 5 Source Tables

The following tables may be used as a cross-reference between individual paragraphs in Chapter 5, *Operations*, and the source paragraphs in the 1984 Edition of NFPA 30.

Paragraph in Chapter 5	Source Paragraph in 1984 Edition
5-1 Scope	5-1, 7-1,
5-1.1	5-1.1 (Revised)
5-1.2 (New)	
5-2 General	5-3.2 (In General)
5-3 Facility Design (New)	
5-3.1 Location	7-2, 8-3
5-3.1.1	7-2.1
5-3.1.1 Table	Tables 7-2.1 & 2-6
5-3.1.2 (Revised)	7-2.1.1
5-3.1.3 (New)	
5-3.1.4	5-3.3
5-3.1.5	7-8.2 (In Concept)/ 8-3.1 (In Part)
5-3.2 Construction	7-3.1
5-3.2.1 (Revised)	7-3.1.1 (In Part)
5-3.2.2 (New)	
5-3.2.3	6-2.3.2
5-3.2.4 (New)	
5-3.2.5	6-2.1, 7-3.1.2
5-3.2.6 (Also see 5-5.3.5)	7-3.4.1, (Also see 5-9.2)
5-3.2.7	7-3.4.1
5-3.3 Ventilation	5-3.5, 6-2.3, 7-3.3
5-3.3.1	5-3.5.1, 6-2.3.1, 6-2.3.3 (In General), 7-3.3.1
5-3.3.2	5-3.5.2, 7-3.3.2
5-3.4 Drainage	5-3.4, 6-7, 7-3.2
5-3.4.1	5-3.4.1, 6-7.1, 7-3.2.1
5-3.4.2	5-3.4.2, 7-3.2.2
5-3.4.3	5-3.4.3, 7-3.2.3, 8-3.1 In General
5-3.5 Electrical Equipment	5-7, 6-5, 7-7.3
5-3.5.1 (Revised)	5-7.1, 6-5.1, 7-7.3.1
5-3.5.2	5-7.2, 6-5.2, 7-7.3.2
5-3.5.3	5-7.3, 6-5.3, 7.-7.3.3
5-3.5.4	5-7.4, 6-5.4, 7-7.3.4
5-3.5.5	5-7.6, 7-7.3.6
5-3.5.6 Table	Tables 5-7.3, 6-5.3, & 7-7.3
5-3.5.6 Figure	Figure 6-5.3
5-4 Liquid Handling Transfer and Use	5-2, 5-4.2

Paragraph in Chapter 5	Source Paragraph in 1984 Edition
5-4.1 General	
5-4.1.1	5-2.2, 5-2.4.1, 6-1.1, 6-1.2
5-4.1.2	5-2.4.2
5-4.1.3	5-2.4.3
5-4.1.4	5-2.4.5
5-4.1.5	7-4.3.2
5-4.2 Equipment	7-4.4, 7-4.4.1
5-4.3 Incidental Use of Liquids	5-2,
5-4.3.1	5-2.1
5-4.3.2(a)-(e)	5-2.4.4
5-4.3.3	5-2.2.1, 7-4.1.4
5-4.3.4(a)-(e)	5-2.2.2
5-4.3.5	5-2.2.3, 7-4.1.1, 8-1.1, 8-1.2 (Intent of)
5-4.3.6	5-2.3
5-4.4 Loading and Unloading Operations	5-4, 6-3
5-4.4.1 Tank Vehicles and Tank Cars	5-4, 7-5
5-4.4.1.1	5-4.1, 6-3.1, 7-5.1
5-4.4.1.2	6-3.7
5-4.4.1.3	6-3.7.1
5-4.4.1.4	6-3.7.2
5-4.4.1.5(a)-(c)	6-3.7.3
5-4.4.1.6	6-3.7.4
5-4.4.1.7	6-3.8
5-4.4.1.8 (Exceptions H-2 New)	6-3.2
5-4.4.1.9	6-3.3
5-4.4.1.10	6-3.4.1, 6-3.4.2
5-4.4.1.11	6-3.5.1, 6-3.5.3
5-4.4.1.12	6-3.5.2, 6-3.6.1
5-4.4.2 Wharves	6-4, 8-2, 8-2.1
5-4.4.2.1 (New)	
5-4.4.2.2	6-4.1.1
5-4.4.2.3	6-4.1.2
5-4.4.2.4	6-4.2
5-4.4.2.5	6-4.3
5-4.4.2.6	6-4.4
5-4.4.2.7	6-4.4.1
5-4.4.2.8	6-1.4, 6-4.5, 7-4.2, 8-1.3
(a)	6-4.5.1
(b)	6-4.5.2
(c)	6-4.5.3
(d)	6-4.5.4
(e)	6-4.5.5
5-4.4.2.9	6-4.5.6
5-4.4.2.10	6-4.5.7, 6-4.5.8
5-4.4.2.11	6-4.6.2, 6-4.6.3
5-4.4.2.12	6-4.7
5-4.4.2.13	6-4.7.1
5-5 Fire Prevention and Control	5-5, 6-8, 7-6, 8-4
5-5.1 General	
5-5.1.1	
5-5.1.2	7-6.2 (Intent of)
5-5.1.3(a)-(f)	
5-5.2 Control of Ignition Sources	5-6, 6-6, 7-7
5-5.2.1(a)-(l)	5-6.1, 6-2.2 (In General)

Paragraph in Chapter 5	Source Paragraph in 1984 Edition
5-5.2.2	7-7.1.1, 8-4.1
5-5.2.3	5-8.1 (In General), 7-7.2.2 (In General), 8-4.2 (In General)
5-5.2.4 Static Electricity	5-6.2, 7-7.1.2, 6-3.9 (In General)
5-5.3 Inspection and Maintenance	
5-5.3.1	5-5.6, 6-8.2, 7-6.4
5-5.3.2	5-9.1
5-5.3.3	5-9.3, 7-8.3
5-5.3.4	5-9.4, 7-8.4
5-5.3.5 (Also see 5-3.2.6)	5-9.2 (Also see 7-8.2)
5-5.4 Emergency Planning and Training	
5-5.4.1(a)-(f)	6-8.3, 8-4.8
5-5.4.2	_____
5-5.4.3	_____
5-5.4.4	_____
5-5.4.5	_____
5-5.4.6	_____
5-5.5 Detection and Alarm	
5-5.5.1	5-5.5, 7-6.3, 8-4.7, 8-4.9
5-5.5.2	_____
5-5.5.3(a)-(c)	_____
5-5.6 Portable Fire Control Equipment	
5-5.6.1	5-5.1 (Intent of), 6-4.6, 6-8.1, 7-6.1, 8-4.4
5-5.6.2	6-4.6.1 (Intent of), 7-6.2.3
5-5.6.3	_____
5-5.6.4	_____
5-5.7 Fixed Fire Control Equipment	
5-5.7.1	5-5.2, 7-6.2.1, 8-4.5
5-5.7.2	7-6.2.2
5-5.7.3	5-5.4
5-5.7.4(a)-(f)	5-5.3, 7-6.2.4, 8-4.6

Source Paragraph in 1984 Edition	Paragraph in 1987 Edition
Chapter 5	Chapter 5
5-1	5-1
5-1.1	5-1.1
5-1.2	_____
5-2	5-4, 5-4.3
5-2.1	5-4.3.1
5-2.2	5-4.1.1
5-2.2.1	5-4.3.3
5-2.2.2	5-4.3.4(a)-(e)
5-2.2.3	5-4.3.5
5-2.3	5-4.3.6
5-2.4	5-4
5-2.4.1	5-4.1.1
5-2.4.2	5-4.1.2
5-2.4.3	5-4.3.2(a)-(e)
5-3.4.5	5-4.1.4
5-3	_____

Source Paragraph in 1984 Edition	Paragraph in 1987 Edition
5-3.1	
5-3.2	5-2
5-3.3	5-3.1.4
5-3.4	5-3.4
5-3.4.1	5-3.4.1
5-3.4.2	5-3.4.2
5-3.4.3	5-3.4.3
5-3.5	5-3.3
5-3.5.1	5-3.3.1
5-3.5.2	5-3.3.2
5-3.6	
5-4	5-4.4, 5-4.4.1
5-4.1	5-4.1.1.1
5-5	5-5
5-5.1	5-5.6.1
5-5.2	5-5.7.1
5-5.3	5-5.7.4(a)-(f)
5-5.4	5-5.7.3
5-5.5	5-5.5.1
5-5.6	5-5.3.1
5-6	5-5.2
5-6.1	5-5.2.1(a)-(l)
5-6.2	5-2.4 (In General)
5-7	5-3.5
5-7.1	5-3.5.1 (Revised)
5-7.3	5-3.5.3
Table 5-7.3	Table 5-3.5.6
5-7.4	5-3.5.4
5-7.5	
5-7.6	5-3.5.5
5-8	
5-8.1	5-5.2.3
5-9	
5-9.1	5-5.3.2
5-9.2	5-3.2.6, 5-5.3.5
5-9.3	5-5.3.3
5-9.4	5-5.3.4
Chapter 6	
6-1	
6-1.1	5-4.1.1
6-1.2	5-4.1.1
6-1.3	
6-1.4	5-4.4.2.8
6-2	
6-2.1	5-3.2.5
6-2.2	5-5.2.1(a)-(l)
6-2.3	5-3.3
6-2.3.1	5-3.3.1
6-2.3.2	5-3.2.3
6-2.3.3	5-3.3.1
6-3	5-4.4
6-3.1	5-4.4.1.1
6-3.2	5-4.4.1.8 (Exception H-2 New)
6-3.3	5-4.4.1.9

Source Paragraph in 1984 Edition	Paragraph in 1987 Edition
6-3.4	
6-3.4.1	5-4.4.1.10
6-3.4.2	5-4.4.1.10
6-3.5	
6-3.5.1	5-4.4.1.11
6-3.5.2	5-4.4.1.12
6-3.5.3	5-4.4.1.11
6-3.6	
6-3.6.1	5-4.4.1.12
6-3.7	5-4.4.1.2
6-3.7.1	5-4.4.1.3
6-3.7.2	5-4.4.1.4
6-3.7.3	5-4.4.1.5(a)-(e)
6-3.7.4	5-4.4.1.6
6-3.8	5-4.4.1.7
6-3.9	5-4.4.2
6-4	
6-4.1	
6-4.1.1	5-4.4.2.2
6-4.1.2	5-4.4.2.3
6-4.2	5-4.4.2.4
6-4.3	5-4.4.2.5
6-4.4	5-4.4.2.6
6-4.4.1	5-4.4.2.7
6-4.5	5-4.4.2.8
6-4.5.1	5-4.4.2.8(a)
6-4.5.2	5-4.4.2.8(b)
6-4.5.3	5-4.4.2.8(c)
6-4.5.4	5-4.4.2.8(d)
6-4.5.5	5-4.4.2.8(e)
6-4.5.6	5-4.4.2.9
6-4.5.7	5-4.4.2.10
6-4.5.8	5-4.4.2.10
6-4.6 (Intent of)	5-5.6.1
6-4.6.1 (Intent of)	5-5.6.2
6-4.6.2	5-4.4.2.11
6-4.6.3	5-4.4.2.11
6-4.7	5-4.4.2.12
6-4.7.1	5-4.4.2.13
6-5	5-3.5
6-5.1	5-3.5.1 (Revised)
6-5.2	5-3.5.2
6-5.3	5-3.5.3
6-5.3.1	New 3/12/86
Table 6-5.3	Table 5-3.5.3
Figure 6-5.3	Figure 5-3.5.6
6-5.4	5-3.5.4
6-6	5-5.2
6-6.1	
6-7	5-3.4
6-7.1	5-3.4.1
6-8	5-5
6-8.1	5-5.6.1
6-8.2	5-5.3.1
6-8.3	5-5.4.1(a)-(f)

236 FLAMMABLE AND COMBUSTIBLE LIQUIDS CODE HANDBOOK

Source Paragraph in 1984 Edition	Paragraph in 1987 Edition
Chapter 7	
7-1	5-1
7-1.1	
7-2	5-3.1
7-2.1	5-3.1.1
Table 7-2.1	Table 5-3.1.1
7-2.1.1	5-3.1.2 (Revised)
7-3	
7-3.1	5-3.2
7-3.1.1 (In Part)	5-3.2.1 (Revised)
7-3.1.2	5-3.2.5
7-3.2	5-3.4
7-3.2.1	5-3.4.1
7-3.2.2	5-3.4.2
7-3.2.3	5-3.4.3
7-3.3	5-3.3
7-3.3.1	5-3.3.1
7-3.3.2	5-3.3.2
7-3.4	
7-3.4.1 (Also see 5-9.2)	5-3.2.6 (Also see 5-5.3.4), 5-3.2.7
7-4	
7-4.1	
7-4.1.1	5-4.3.5
7-4.1.2	
7-4.1.3	
7-4.1.4	5-4.3.3
7-4.2	
7-4.2.1	5-4.4.2.8
7-4.2.2	
7-4.2.3	
7-4.3	
7-4.3.1	
7-4.3.2	5-4.1.5
7-4.4	5-4.2
7-4.4.1	5-4.2
7-4.4.2	
7-5	5-4.4.1
7-5.1	5-4.4.1.1
7-6	5-5
7-6.1	5-5.6.1
7-6.2 (Intent of)	5-5.1.2
7-6.2.1	5-5.7.1
7-6.2.2	5-5.7.2
7-6.2.3	5-5.6.2
7-6.2.4	5-5.7.4(a)-(f)
7-6.3	5-5.3.1
7-6.4	5-5.3.1
7-7	
7-7.1	
7-7.1.1	5-5.2.1(a)-(l)
7-7.1.2	5-5.2.4 (In General)
7-7.2	
7-7.2.1	
7-7.2.2 (In General)	5-5.2.3
7-7.3	5-3.5

Source Paragraph in 1984 Edition	Paragraph in 1987 Edition
7-7.3.1	5-3.5.1 (Revised)
7-7.3.2	5-3.5.2
7-7.3.3	5-3.5.3
7-7.3.4	5-3.5.4
7-7.3.5	
7-7.3.6	5-3.5.5
Table 7-7.3	5-3.5.6
7-8	
7-8.1	
7-8.2 (In Concept)	5-3.1.5
7-8.3	5-5.3.3
7-8.4	5-5.3.4
Chapter 8	
8-1	
8-1.1	5-4.3.5
8-1.2 (Intent of)	5-4.3.5
8-1.3	5-4.4.2.8
8-2	5-4.4.2
8-2.1	5-4.4.2
8-3	5-3.1
8-3.1 (In Part)	5-3.1.5, 5-3.4.3
8-4	5-5
8-4.1	5-5.2.2
8-4.2	5-5.2.3
8-4.3	
8-4.4	5-5.6.1
8-4.5	5-5.7.1
8-4.6	5-5.7.4(a)-(f)
8-4.7	5-5.5.1
8-4.8	5-5.4.1(a)-(f)
8-4.9	5-5.5.1

Appendix G

Referenced Publications

This Appendix lists publications which are referenced within this NFPA document for information purposes only and thus is not considered part of the requirements of the document.

G-1 The following documents or portions thereof are referenced within this standard for informational purposes only and thus should not be considered part of the requirements of this document. The edition indicated for each reference is current as of the date of the NFPA issuance of this document. These references are listed separately to facilitate updating to the latest edition by the user.

G-1.1 NFPA Publications. The following publications are available from the National Fire Protection Association, Batterymarch Park, Quincy, MA 02269.

NFPA 10-1984, *Standard for Portable Fire Extinguishers*
NFPA 14-1986, *Standard for the Installation of Standpipe and Hose Systems*
NFPA 24-1987, *Standard for the Installation of Private Fire Service Mains and Their Appurtenances*
NFPA 31-1987, *Standard for the Installation of Oil Burning Equipment*
NFPA 32-1985, *Standard for Drycleaning Plants*
NFPA 33-1985, *Standard for Spray Application Using Flammable and Combustible Materials*
NFPA 34-1987, *Standard for Dipping and Coating Processes Using Flammable or Combustible Liquids*
NFPA 35-1987, *Standard for the Manufacture of Organic Coatings*
NFPA 36-1985, *Standard for Solvent Extraction Plants*
NFPA 37-1984, *Standard for Installation and Use of Stationary Combustion Engines and Gas Turbines*
NFPA 51-1987, *Standard for the Design and Installation of Oxygen-Fuel Gas Systems for Welding, Cutting, and Allied Processes*
NFPA 68-1987, *Guide for Explosion Venting*
NFPA 71-1987, *Standard for the Installation, Maintenance, and Use of Signaling Systems for Central Station Service*

NFPA 72A-1987, *Standard for the Installation, Maintenance, and Use of Local Protective Signaling Systems for Guard's Tour, Fire Alarm, and Supervisory Service*

NFPA 72B-1986, *Standard for the Installation, Maintenance, and Use of Auxiliary Protective Signaling Systems for Fire Alarm Service*

NFPA 72C-1986, *Standard for the Installation, Maintenance, and Use of Remote Station Protective Signaling Systems*

NFPA 72D-1986, *Standard for the Installation, Maintenance, and Use of Proprietary Protective Signaling Systems*

NFPA 77-1983, *Recommended Practice on Static Electricity*

NFPA 78-1986, *Lightning Protection Code*

NFPA 204M-1985, *Guide for Smoke and Heat Venting*

NFPA 327-1987, *Standard Procedures for Cleaning or Safeguarding Small Tanks and Containers*

NFPA 395-1984, *Standard for the Storage of Flammable and Combustible Liquids on Farms and Isolated Construction Projects*

NFPA 1221-1987, *Standard for the Installation, Maintenance, and Use of Public Fire Service Communications*

NFPA 30 — Index

© 1987 National Fire Protection Association, All Rights Reserved.

The copyright in this index is separate and distinct from the copyright in the document which it indexes. The licensing provisions set forth for the document are not applicable to this index. This index may not be reproduced in whole or in part by any means without the express written permission of the National Fire Protection Association, Inc.

-A-

Aerosol
 Definition 1-2
 Flammable 4-1.3
  Definition 1-2
Alarm systems 5-5.5
Apartment house
 Definition 1-2
Application of code 1-1

-B-

Barrel
 Definition 1-2
Basements .4-4.1.9, 4-4.2.12, 4-5.6.4, 5-3.2.3
 Definition 1-2
Boil-over
 Definition 1-2
Boil-over liquids, tank location .... 2-2.1.4, Table 2-3
Boiling point
 Definition 1-2
Buildings
 Attached 4-4.2, D-4-4
  Definition 1-2
 Over three dwelling units 4-5.3
 Processing 5-3
 Three or less dwelling units 4-5.3

-C-

Cabinets, storage .... see Storage cabinets
Cars, tank .... see Tank vehicles and cars
Classification of liquids 1-2
 Contamination, changed by 1-1.2
Combustible liquids
 Definition 1-2
 Class IIIB, tank location .... Table 2-5
Containers .... Chap. 4, D-4
 Closed
  Definition 1-2
 Definition 1-2
 Design, construction, and capacity ... 4-2
 Filling facilities, bulk plants 5-4
 Small, fire tests .... E-4-6(b)
Contamination of liquids 1-1.2
Corrosion
 Aboveground tanks, internal 2-1.6
 Piping, external 3-5
 Underground tanks 2-3.3
Currents, stray 5-4.4.1.7

-D-

Detection systems 5-5.5
Dikes around tanks 2-2.3.3
Distilleries
 Definition 1-2
Drainage
 Cutoff rooms and attached buildings .4-4.2.5
 Inside rooms .... 4-4.1.2(b)
 Processing buildings 5-3.4
Drums
 Design, capacity .... 4-2.1, Table 4-2.3
 Fire tests .... E-4-6(a)
Dwelling units 4-5.3
 Definition 1-2
Dwellings 4-5.2
 Definition 1-2

-E-

Electrical area, Classification systems ......
  5-3.5.4, Table 5-3.5.3
Electrical equipment
 Cutoff rooms and attached buildings ....
  4-4.2.11
 Inside rooms 4-4.1.5
 Processing plants 5-3.5
Emergency planning and training 5-5.4
Exits 1-5
 Processing buildings 5-3.2.5
Explosion venting
 Cutoff rooms and attached buildings .4-4.2.1
 Processing plants 5-3.2.7
Exposures, protection for ... Tables 2-1, 2-2, 2-3, and 2-4
 Definition 1-2
Extinguishers, portable fire
 Containers and portable tanks 4-7.1.1, 4-7.1.2
 Processing plants 5-5.6.1

-F-

Fire apparatus 5-5.6.3, 5-5.6.4
Fire area
 Definition 1-2
Fire control 4-7, 5-5
 Processing plants 7-6
Fire prevention 5-5
Fire protection and identification 2-8
Fire tests .... see Tests, fire

Fittings
  Materials for 3-2
  Processing plants 5-4.4.2.8
Flame arrestors 2-2.4.7
Flammable liquids
  Definition 1-2
Flash point 1-1.2
  Definition 1-2
Flooding areas, tanks in 2-5.6

-G-

Garages, attached and detached 4-5.2

-H-

Hazardous materials or chemicals
  Definition 1-2
Hazardous reaction or chemical reaction
  Definition 1-2
Hotels 4-5.3
  Definition 1-2
Housekeeping .... See Maintenance
Hydrants 5-5.7.2

-I-

Ignition sources, control of 4-7.2, 5-5.2
Impounding
  Around tanks by diking 2-2.3.3
  Remote 2-2.3.2
Incidental liquid use or storage
  Definition 1-2
Inspection 5-5.3

-J-

Joints, pipe 3-3, 5-4.4.2.8, 5-4.4.2.10

-L-

Leakage
  Detection and inventory, underground
    tanks 2-10, 5-4.4.1.9
  Drainage system for 5-3.4.1
Liquids .... see also specific types such as
                      Combustible liquids
  Boilover .... Table 2-3
    Definition 1-2
  Handling, transfer, and use 5-4
  Incidental use 5-4.3
  Stable .... Tables 2-1, 2-2
    Definition 1-2

Unstable .... 4-1.3, Table 2-4
  Definition 1-2
Loading operations 5-4.4
  Wharves 5-4.4.2.1.2

-M-

Maintenance 5-5.3
Marine terminals 5-3.5.6
Metrication 1-1.9

-O-

Occupancies
  Assembly 4-5.3
    Definition 1-2
  Classification of
    Definition 1-2
  Educational 4-5.4
    Definition 1-2
  Institutional 4-5.4
    Definition 1-2
  Mercantile 4-5.5, A-4-5.5.1
    Definition 1-2
  Office 4-5.4
    Definition 1-2
  Outdoor
    Definition 1-2
Openings, tank (non-vent)
  Aboveground 2-2.7
  Inside buildings 2-4.4
  Underground 2-3.6
Operating unit (vessel)
  Definition 1-2
Operations .... Chap. 5
  Definition 1-2
  Facility design 5-3
  Fire prevention 5-5
  General 5-2
  Liquid handling, transfer and use 5-4

-P-

Petroleum, crude
  Definition 1-2
Piers .... see Wharves
Piping systems .... Chap. 3
  Identification 3-8, A-3-8
  Materials 3-2
  Pipe joints 3-3
  Protection from corrosion 3-5
  Supports 3-4
  Testing 3-7
  Valves 3-6
  Wharves 5-4.4.2.8
Piping, vent
  Aboveground tanks 2-2.6
  Tanks inside buildings 2-4.3
  Underground tanks 2-3.5

INDEX

Plants
  Bulk
    Definition 1-2
  Chemical .... Chap. 8
    Definition 1-2
  Operations .... Chap. 5
Process or processing
  Definition 1-2
Process unit (vessel)
  Definition 1-2

-R-

Reactive liquids .... see Unstable liquids
Refineries
  Definition 1-2
Rooms
  Cut-off 4-4.2, D-4-4
    Definition 1-2
  Inside 4-4.1, D-4-4
    Definition 1-2

-S-

Safety cans
  Definition 1-2
Scope of code 1-1
Service stations
  Automatic
    Definition 1-2
  Definition 1-2
  Inside buildings
    Definition 1-2
  Marine
    Definition 1-2
Spillage, aboveground tanks 2-2.3
Sprinkler systems
  Containers and portable tanks 4-6.2, D-4-6.2
  Processing plants 5-5.6.2
Stable liquids
  Definition 1-2
  Tank location .... Tables 2-1, 2-2
Standpipe and hose systems 5-5.6.2
Static protection ... 5-4.4.1.2 thru 5-4.4.1.7, 5-5.2.4
Storage 1-3
  Indoor 4-5
  Mixed 4-5.6.7, 4-5.7.13
  Outdoor 4-8
  Palletized, solid pile, or rack ...... 4-5.6.6, 4-5.7.6, 4-5.7.8 thru 4-5.7.13, 4-6.1 thru 4-6.6, D-4-6
  Protected 4-6, D-4-6
Storage area, separate inside 4-4
  Definition 1-2
Storage cabinets, design, construction, and capacity of 4-3, A-4-3.2
Stores, retail 4-5.5

-T-

Tank vehicles and cars, loading and unloading 5-4.4.1

Tanks, storage .... Chap. 2
  Aboveground
    Flooding areas, in 2-5.6
    Impounding 2-2.3.2, 2-2.3.3
    Installation 2-2
    Location .... 2-2.1, Tables 2-1 thru 2-6
    Openings (non-vent) 2-2.7
    Spacing between adjacent .... 2-2.2, Table 2-7
    Spillage control 2-2.3
    Venting .... 2-2.4 thru 2-2.6, App. B
  Atmospheric 2-1.3
    Definition 1-2
  Design and construction 2-1
  Fire protection and identification 2-8
  Floating roof 2-2.1.1
  Inside buildings 2-4
  Low pressure 2-1.4
    Definition 1-2
    Use as atmospheric tank 2-1.3.2
  Overfilling, prevention of 2-9
  Portable
    Definition 1-2
    Design, construction, and capacity 4-2
    Over 660 gallons .... Chap. 2
    Under 660 gallons .... Chap. 4
  Sources of ignition 2-6
  Supports, foundations, and anchorage ... 2-5
  Testing 2-7
  Underground
    Abandonment, removal, or reuse ... 2-3.4, App. C
    Burial depth and cover 2-3.2
    Corrosion protection, external 2-3.3
    Flooding areas, in 2-5.6.3
    Installation 2-3
    Leakage detection and inventory records . 2-10, 5-4.4.1.9
    Location 2-3.1
    Openings (non-vent) 2-3.6
    Vents 2-3.5
    Vertical 2-2.1.2, 2-2.5.3
Terminals, bulk
  Definition 1-2
Tests, fire .... App. E

-U-

Unit operation or process
  Definition 1-2
Unloading operation 5-4.4
  Wharves 5-4.4.2.12
Unstable liquids
  Definition 1-2
  Handling 5-3.1.4
  Tank location .... Table 2-4

-V-

Valves 3-6
  Materials for 3-2
Vapor control .... see Ventilation

Vapor pressure
  Definition 1-2
Vapor processing equipment
  Definition 1-2
Vapor processing system
  Definition 1-2
Vapor recovery system
  Definition 1-2
Vehicles, tank .... see Tank vehicles and cars
Ventilation
  Definition 1-2
  Processing buildings 5-3.3
Venting .... see also Piping, vent
  Aboveground tanks
    Emergency relief .... 2-2.5, App. B
    Normal 2-2.4
  Explosion .... see Explosion venting
  Processing buildings 5-3.2.4
  Tanks inside buildings ..... 2-4.2 thru 2-4.3
  Underground 2-3.5

Vessels, pressure 1-4, 2-1.5
  Definition 1-2
  Use as atmospheric tank 2-1.3.2
  Use as low-pressure tank 2-1.4.4
Volatility of liquids 1-1.3

-W-

Warehouses
  General purpose 4-5.6
    Definition 1-2
  Liquid 4-5.7
    Definition 1-2
Waste disposal .... see Maintenance
Wharves 5-4.4.2
  Definition 1-2

Supplement

Case Investigations of Recent Incidents

This supplement is not part of the requirements of this NFPA *Code*, but is included for information purposes only. It is printed in black for ease of reading.

Fuel Oil Storage Tank Fire Boil-Over
Tacoa, Venezuela
December 19, 1982

Introduction

What is believed to be the most serious loss-of-life tank fire in history occurred in Venezuela on December 19, 1982. The storage tank, located a few miles northwest of Caracas in the small seaside village of Tacoa, supplied fuel to an electric generating plant that provided power to Caracas' population of three million. Two workers died when the tank's contents first ignited. After six hours of intense burning, the contents of the tank erupted in an extremely violent boil-over (*see "What Is a Boil-Over?"*). The final toll: more than 150 people dead, scores more injured, others still unaccounted for, and damage estimated at $50 million. Forty of those who died were fire fighters, which also makes the Tacoa incident the gravest of its kind in terms of loss of life of fire personnel.

Background

The Tacoa plant and an immediately adjacent sister plant, Arrecifes, supply 1700 megawatts of power to Caracas and the surrounding metropolitan area—96 percent of the power consumed by the region. Although this incident caused complete evacuation of the Tacoa plant, some of its capacity was maintained throughout the tank fire. Following the boil-over of the tank, burning fuel flowed toward the plant's three steam-driven turbines, but a security wall prevented it from endangering the main plant.

Fuel storage tank 8, which measured approximately 180 ft in diameter by 56 ft in height, was built in the late 1970s for the purpose of storing heavy residual fuel oil (Fuel Oil #6). The tank could hold more than 10 million gallons. The roof of the tank was of weak roof-to-shell seam design to provide for emergency relief venting.

Topography played a key role in the events that followed the boil-over of tank 8. The two electric generating plants were at sea level, while the fuel and water storage tanks sat above them on a steep hillside. The site of tank 8 was approximately 180 ft above sea level, at a distance of a little more than 1000 ft from the sea.

Tank 9, which was of the same design and size and stored a similar product, was 220 ft away from tank 8, measured from tank shell to tank shell. Situated lower on the hillside, tank 9's base was 105 ft above sea level. Both tanks complied with NFPA 30, *Flammable and Combustible Liquids Code*, in the three most important characteristics relating to safe tank storage: proper spacing, adequate containment, and adequate emergency relief venting. The tank design, the shell-to-shell spacing, and the shell-to-adjacent property spacing met the requirements for non-boil-over liquids. Each tank was enclosed by a dike of sufficient capacity to contain the entire tank contents. It should be noted that a dike is not intended to contain a boil-over.

The weak roof-to-shell seam design requirement is intended to prevent catastrophic failure of a tank due to overpressure caused by a ground or spill fire.

Each tank was equipped with an automatic, fixed-foam fire extinguishing system that had three foam chambers spaced symmetrically around the top rim. Tanks 8 and 9 also had pneumatic heat detection systems with detectors located just above the vents inside the tanks. Automatic or manual activation of a tank's pneumatic system started the fire pumps and foam system for that tank and also started the water cooling system for the other tank.

The water cooling system was supplied by a 4-in. pipe that terminated at the top center of the cone roof. The pipe discharged onto a deflector plate designed to distribute water evenly over the roof and down the side of the tank. Along the top of the dike surrounding the tank there were three fixed, 500-gpm fog nozzles.

Three elevated water storage tanks, each with a capacity of 317,000 gal (1200 m^3), held the water supply for the fire protection system. The tanks fed an 8-in. fire-water loop around tanks 8 and 9. Three pumps, two electric and one diesel, were available to boost pressure in the water system. The water supply in the storage tanks was reserved primarily for fire protection needs and was supplemented by two seawater pumps that could be used to draft from the ocean. The fixed-foam system was designed for automatic actuation and, during this incident, it appears to have operated in accordance with its design. The system is believed to have met the requirements of NFPA 11, *Standard for Low Expansion Foam and Combined Agent Systems*. However, it is possible that the foam system for tank 8 may have been damaged, at least partially, upon ignition.

What Is a Boil-Over?

The NFPA Technical Committee on Flammable and Combustible Liquids, which is responsible for NFPA 30, *Flammable and Combustible Liquids Code*, has developed the following definition of the term boil-over:

> **Boil-Over.** An event in the burning of certain oils in an open-top tank when, after a long period of quiescent burning, there is a sudden increase in fire intensity associated with expulsion of burning oil from the tank. Boil-over occurs when the residues from surface burning become more dense than the unburned oil and sink below the surface to form a hot layer that progresses downward much faster than the regression of the liquid surface. When this hot layer, called a "heat wave," reaches water or water-in-oil emulsion at the bottom of the tank, the water is superheated, then boils almost explosively, overflowing the tank. Oils subject to boil-over must have components having a wide range of boiling points, including both light ends and a viscous residue. These characteristics are present in most crude oils and can be produced in synthetic mixtures.

As this definition indicates, three elements must be present for a boil-over to occur:

- fire in an open-top tank;
- a water layer in the tank;
- development in the tank of a "heat wave," which is determined by the nature of the stored product.

When an open-top tank containing a product with a wide range of boiling points, such as crude oil, begins to burn, the components with higher boiling points sink below the surface and form a heavy heated layer. This heated layer transmits heat to the cooler oil below, where light end components having lower boiling points continue their movement toward the surface. These light end components keep feeding the fire, and the fire continues to radiate heat back toward the tank contents. As it moves toward the bottom, the hot layer of heavier components grows in both size and density and may reach temperatures in the range of 300 to 600°F. The descending layer or "heat wave" continues to distill components with lower boiling points from the oil below. When the heat wave reaches a water or water-in-oil emulsion layer, it superheats the water, causing the water to flash to steam immediately at temperatures well above 212°F, expanding at a ratio of about 1600 to 1.

It is estimated that this steam explosion can propel burning oil and vapor to a height ten times the diameter of the tank. In one extraordinary crude oil tank fire in 1926, photographs show a mass of flame estimated to be 1100 ft in diameter at its base and 6000 ft high.

The Incident

At about 11:30 p.m. on December 18, 1982, a high-temperature indicator signaled personnel in the plant control room that the oil temperature near the boiler end of a feedline to the power plant was above normal. The signal was set to activate at 176°F and the chart recorder indicated a temperature of 190°F. Only two of the six steam heating units in tank 8 had been operating at that time. Personnel were sent to the tank to shut down one of these two heaters and the temperature returned to 176°F, according to the recorder.

At about 6:00 a.m. on December 19, a three-man crew went to tank 8 to perform a routine gaging operation. One man remained in a vehicle within the dike, while the other two went to the tank roof. Less than two minutes later, as estimated by the man in the car, a violent explosion took place. The roof of the tank blew off and landed in the dike. The tank burst into flame and a fire ignited within the dike. Fuel return lines from the generating plant, installed through the tank roof, were severed when the roof blew off; oil from these lines fed the dike fire. When the roof landed, it also damaged the water loop at the base of the tank. The man in the dike area escaped and ran back to the plant. His two co-workers died in the explosion.

It is estimated that the depth of the product in the tank was about 20 ft (6.1 m) (3.5 million gallons) when ignition occurred. This would mean that the vapor space above the product surface measured approximately 36 ft (11 m) in depth.

The generating plant had no fire brigade. The nearest fire station was about 20 minutes away, and the only access to Tacoa was by means of a winding and narrow road cut into the hillside.

During the next few hours, whatever fire apparatus could be summoned into service responded to the tank fire. The fire chief from the Caracas Airport came to the scene, as did the district fire chief and a fire protection expert from one of the country's nationalized petroleum companies. The road to the plant was crowded with the vehicles of spectators. Fire fighting efforts were severely hindered by the remoteness of the site, inadequate access, hilly terrain, and the damage to the fixed-foam fire protection systems.

It was reported that television and radio reports kept calling for additional civil defense personnel to respond to Tacoa. During the early hours of the tank fire, a message was transmitted that the fire was considered contained and under control. Apparently, those in charge had decided that there was little possibility of extinguishing the fire and that the fire would safely burn itself out within the tank and dike. Therefore, the incident became a spectator fire. Media people were on-site to record the event. Fire fighters, civil defense personnel, and plant workers stood within 100 to 200 ft of the burning tank, while a handful of fire fighters operated a fixed-monitor nozzle from the top of the dike.

At about 12:15 p.m., a devastatingly violent boil-over blew tank contents hundreds of feet into the air, forming a giant fireball. Below, burning oil overflowed the dike. Those who were not killed instantly by the intense radiant heat were caught in a downhill flow of burning oil. More than 1000 ft away from the tank, some people jumped into the sea to escape the heat; it was reported that a few people drowned. The burning oil followed the roadway and the contour of the land, flowing up to 1300 ft away from the tank. Nearby buildings, including about 70 occupied dwellings, ignited and burned. More than 60 vehicles were destroyed, including most of the fire apparatus on the scene. Several persons representing various media were among the fatalities, as were 17 plant employees. The boil-over also claimed the lives of dozens of civil defense personnel and more than 40 uniformed fire fighters.

Following the boil-over of tank 8, fire ignited in the dike enclosure around tank 9. Heat from this fire apparently damaged gaskets and distorted joints in the piping of tank 9, resulting in a continuous supply of oil to the fire in the dike. Several hours later, tank 9's roof opened at the seam and its contents ignited; this tank continued to burn for about two days. It did not experience a boil-over, however, because its roof was never completely open. As the contents burned, the tank roof settled inside and eventually sunk to the bottom, causing the tank shell to fold in on itself. In the end, tank 9 stood only a few feet high. This behavior is typical in a fire where the roof of the tank is only partially opened.

Reportedly, during the boil-over phenomenon in tank 8, air rushing in at the base of the fireball lifted roof panels on the water side of the generating plant, some 1100 feet away. Shortly after the boil-over, the fire in the tank 8 dike area and in tank 8 itself was extinguished, even though a few feet of product remained. It is theorized that the steam explosion and the inrush of air caused by the boil-over may have achieved extinguishment by separating the fire from the fuel and, in effect, blowing out the fire.

Analysis

It is a grim fact that none of those actively engaged in fire suppression operations at the Tacoa incident survived the sudden, almost volcanic

Figure S-1 A new electric generating facility was built at Tacoa, Venezuela in the late 1970s. Two large storage tanks that contained the plant's fuel supply were built into the top of the hillside overlooking the plant. The base of tank 8, on the right, was about 180 ft above sea level. The old generating facility is located at the lower left.

NFPA 30—SUPPLEMENT 251

Figure S-2 The aerial photo shows tank 8 (nearer bottom) and tank 9 prior to the incident.

Figure S-3 This aerial photo was taken several days after the incident. Tank 8 is standing to its full height. The roof of tank 9 settled into the tank, causing the tank to crumple and fold to just a few feet in height. The old power plant (top right) was completely destroyed.

Figure S-4 Note the emergency personnel at the site. Fire fighters can be seen at the top of the dike, while other personnel are along the roadway fence. At this point, the fire in tank 8 had been declared under control. Just minutes after this photo was taken, the boil-over occurred. All of the people shown above were reportedly killed by the boil-over.

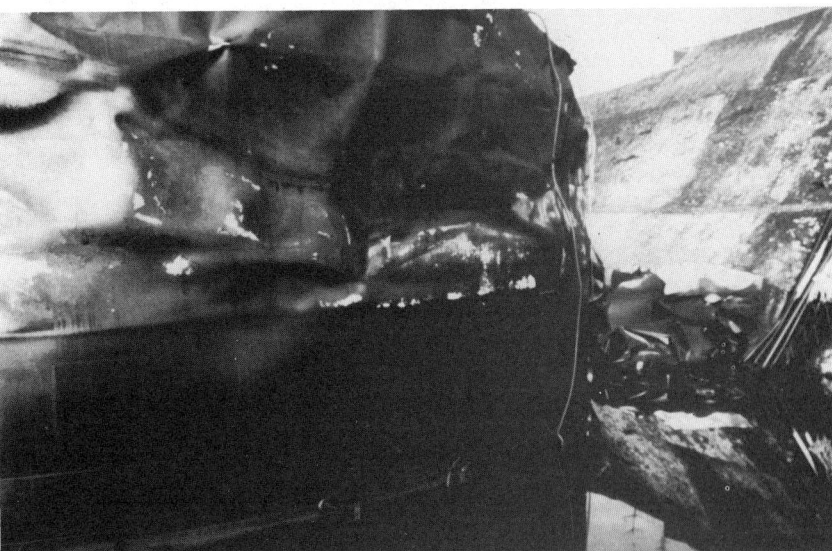

Figure S-5 The crumpled roof of tank 8 can be seen off to the right. The line on the tank indicates the liquid level in the tank at the time of the boil-over. Above that level, heat from the fires in the dike and tank caused the steel shell to disfigure.

254 FLAMMABLE AND COMBUSTIBLE LIQUIDS CODE HANDBOOK

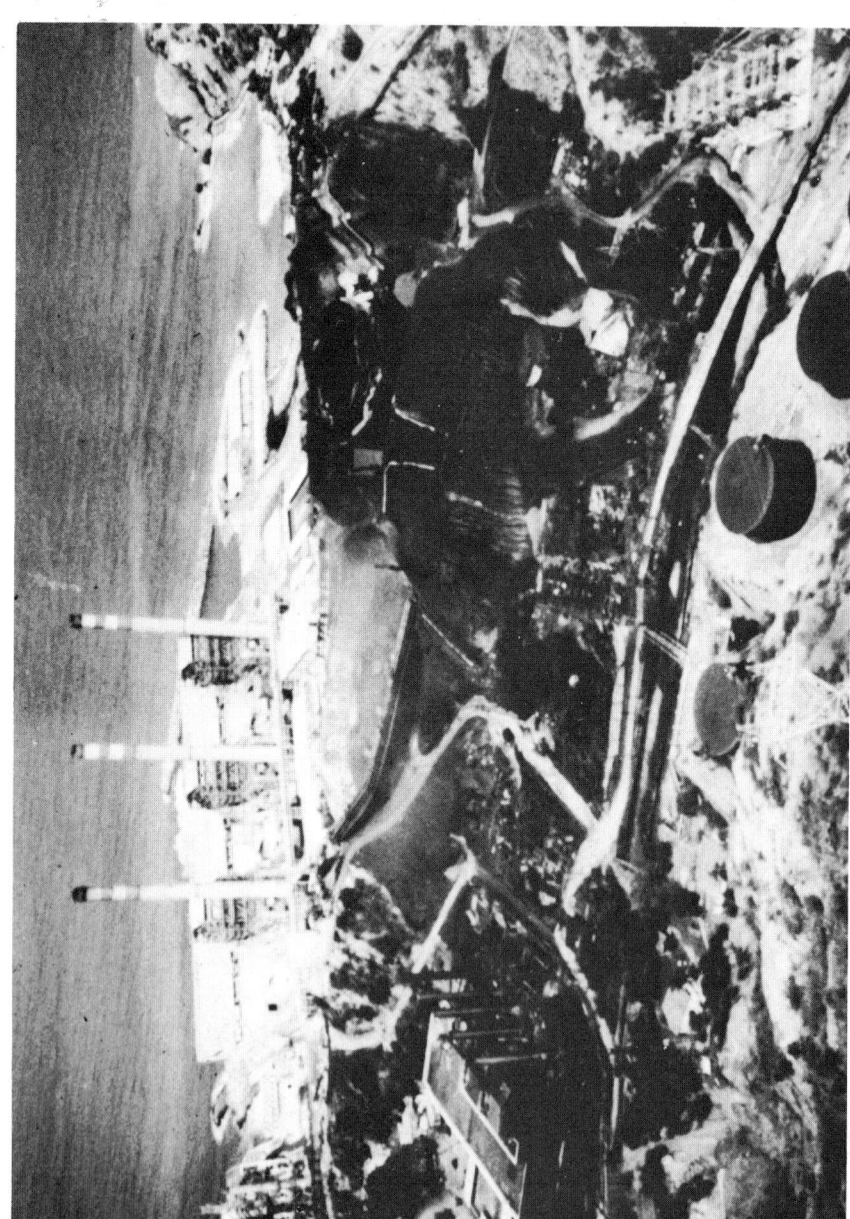

Figure S-6 The blackened earth offers vivid evidence of the extent of the destruction caused by the exceedingly violent boil-over. Burning oil cascaded downhill to the sea, up to a distance of 1300 ft in some areas.

boil-over. Consequently, few details could be pieced together about the fire attack plan or strategy. Regardless of strategy used, it appears that fire fighters did not anticipate a boil-over.

In early investigations of the incident, it was suggested that the product in tank 8 may not have been Fuel Oil #6, or that it may have been contaminated.

Based on information available to NFPA, there is no recorded instance of a boil-over involving Fuel Oil #6. In the past, experimental efforts to induce such an occurrence have failed. Thelong-held belief is that Fuel Oil #6 lacks the wide range of boiling points necessary to produce the descending hot oil layer characteristic of a boil-over. Furthermore, Fuel Oil #6 cannot be ignited easily. Despite appearances to the contrary, it is entirely possible that the fuel in tank 8 may have met the criteria specified by the American Society for Testing and Materials for Fuel Oil #6. Available records indicated that the last delivery of product to tank 8 met each of the various ASTM specifications for Fuel Oil #6. Ignition of the tank contents may have been caused by tank heating procedures, which raised the temperature of the product higher than was necessary or safe, without taking additional precautions. In addition, current practices for producing Fuel Oil #6 may, in fact, result in a product with a boil-over ingredient: a wide range of boiling points.

Had there been advance knowledge that a boil-over liquid was to be stored, the tanks at Tacoa, as installed, would not have been in compliance with NFPA 30, *Flammable and Combustible Liquids Code*. Paragraph 2-2.1.4 of the *Code* reads:

Liquids with boil-over characteristics shall not be stored in fixed roof tanks larger than 150 ft (45.7 m) in diameter, unless an approved inerting system is provided on the tank.

Fire fighters should be alerted to the extremely violent nature of a boil-over. It is also important to note that the NFPA film, *Fighting Petroleum Storage Fires*, emphasizes that fire fighting efforts should not begin until an adequate supply of foam, sufficient to achieve final extinguishment, is on hand and in place. Even in the best of circumstances, achieving extinguishment of fires in open-top tanks more than 150 ft in diameter is exceedingly difficult.

Detecting the stages of a potential boil-over can prevent a boil-over disaster. There is a fire fighting technique that can be used to detect the development of a heat wave in a burning petroleum storage tank. First, the liquid level of the tank must be determined by visual inspection. This is easy to do since the tank wall above the liquid level will be somewhat distorted by the heat and fire. A water stream should be directed on the tank shell *below* the liquid level. If the water vaporizes immediately, it indicates that a heat wave is descending toward the bottom of the tank. The extent of the heat wave also can be assessed by finding the point at which the water stream no longer vaporizes. That point delineates the bottom of the heat wave.

Hindsight provides us with two additional valuable lessons:

- There is no justification for having large numbers of fire fighting personnel in the vicinity of a fire incident when they are not actively engaged in fire operations; and
- Where it is known that a boil-over liquid is being stored, tanks should not be situated at high elevations.

This supplement report was based on an article in *Fire Service Today*.

Gasoline Storage Tank Overfill and Fire
Newark, New Jersey
January 7, 1983

Introduction

The National Fire Protection Association (NFPA) investigated the Newark gasoline storage tank fire in order to document and analyze significant factors that resulted in the loss. This study was conducted under a Major Fires Investigation Agreement with the Federal Emergency Management Agency/United States Fire Administration (FEMA/USFA) and the National Bureau of Standards/Center for Fire Research (NBS/CFR).

Background

In a predominantly industrial area just southeast of the Newark Airport on Newark Bay in Newark, New Jersey, the Texaco Oil Company maintained a flammable liquid storage tank farm off Doremus Avenue. The complex consisted of 36 storage tanks for various petroleum products, including gasoline. In addition, there were many pressure tanks containing liquefied flammable gas in the immediate area, and other oil companies maintained storage facilities in the area (*see Figure S-7*). Also within the complex were various structures in support of the fuel-handling depot, such as truck stations and buildings housing supervisory personnel, gage equipment, and pump controls.

Located apart from the concentrated storage area were three large, covered floating-roof storage tanks constructed in the early 1960s, numbered in the diagram as Nos. 67, 65, and 64. The dimensions and capacity of these tanks are shown in the table below.

Tank No.	Diameter (ft)	Height (ft)	Capacity (Million gallons)
67	80	50	1.76
65	120	56	4.5
64	187	56	10.89

Tank Nos. 67 and 65 were spaced 50 ft apart, and tank Nos. 64 and 65 were 80 ft apart. This complies with the minimum spacing required for these tanks of 34 and 77 ft, respectively, as established in NFPA 30, Flammable and Combustible Liquids Code.

These three tanks were contained in a single diked area in the western corner of the storage yard, adjacent to several railroad track spurs. The earthen and crushed-rock dike was irregular in shape, but the long side was approximately 900 ft and it was approximately 6 ft high. The impoundment area could hold approximately 12 million gallons and could contain the largest possible spill from the largest tank (No. 64), also as required by NFPA 30, *Flammable and Combustible Liquids Code*.

Each tank was equipped with a vertical riser intended for use with a portable foam pump/generator reportedly stored on the premises of the storage facility. In addition, private hydrants were provided on the perimeter of the diked area. Underground pipelines served to load and unload these tanks from a pipeline company at a remote location in Woodbridge Township, New Jersey.

At the time of the incident, it is believed that tank No. 67 was full (1.76 million gallons), tank No. 65 contained 140,000 gallons, and tank No. 64 held about 1.38 million gallons. The total of 3.28 million gallons of gasoline held by the three tanks combined was involved in the fire.

The Incident

Tank Transfer Operations and Explosion

At 6:50 p.m., on Thursday, January 6, 1983, the filling of tank No. 67 with high-octane unleaded gasoline began via the underground supply line from the pipeline company. The scheduled delivery totaled approximately 1.6 million gallons (38,000 bbls.), to be completed at approximately 12:10 a.m. on Friday morning, January 7. This would require a flow rate of approximately 5000 gpm.

At 7:20 p.m. that same evening, simultaneous off-loading of tank No. 67 to a remote tank, No. 5 in Figure S-7, began. The scheduled transfer amount was 1.09 million gallons (26,000 bbls.) and would provide the required storage capacity for the incoming shipment, according to oil company calculations.

Shortly before midnight on Thursday, January 6, two terminal operators visited the diked area in a pickup truck as the expected fill time approached. Presumably, the purpose of this visit was to secure the operation, including closing of the valves at the pipeline company valve station, which was adjacent to the dike area.

On arrival, the operators discovered tank No. 67 overflowing from the vent pipes at the top of the tank. The operators returned to the terminal control building by driving north from the diked area to Delancey Street, then east to the control building, a distance of approximately four-tenths of a mile. Upon reaching their destination, emergency shutdown procedures were implemented, and employees were advised to vacate the premises. It should be noted that the route taken by the evacuating employees passed by the truck terminal building where some controls reportedly existed.

Initially, the emergency procedures called for shutting down the terminal area, which would halt the off-loading to tank No. 5. At the same time, the pipeline company was notified to shut down the supply operation.

At approximately 12:02 a.m., January 7, Conrail employees on duty in the nearby railroad yards discovered the overflow and radioed that they were shutting down their diesel engines because of the strong smell of fuel. Conrail then dispatched a security officer to the scene.

Approximately 1000 ft north-northwest of the overflow incident, there was a metal drum refinishing plant. Part of the drum refinishing operation utilized an incinerator to burn off residues in used barrels. This incinerator was not being used at the time, but the unit was fired continuously for efficiency purposes. At approximately 12:10 a.m., two barrel refinishing employees on a loading platform were forced back inside as the smell of gasoline vapors was "too strong to breathe." One of the workers telephoned their supervisor to report the situation. Immediately thereafter, several small explosions occurred, followed by a violent blast.

The weather did not appear to have had a great impact on the ignition scenario, inasmuch as winds were very light and nearly still at the time of the incident. The drum refinishing operation was slightly below the grade level of the tank area; what winds existed were from the southeast at about 3 knots (3.5 mph), which placed the incinerator of the refinishing operation in the path of any wind-driven vapors.

Fire Department Response and Operations

At 12:16 a.m., Newark Fire Alarm Headquarters received a telephone call from the police relaying a radio communication that there had been a large explosion in the vicinity of the Doremus Avenue industrial area. At about the same time, the fire alarm operators began to receive numerous reports—ranging from a supposed airplane crash to an exploding vehicle on the highway—and decided to strike Box Alarm 5782. This first alarm response included four engine companies, two ladder companies, a battalion chief, a deputy chief, and a rescue unit. Before the incident was over, four alarms had been sounded with a total response of 15 engines, four ladders, several rescue units, and about 90 fire fighters.

At approximately 12:18 a.m., the first arriving companies reported numerous spot fires and burning automobiles. They then discovered the body of the single fatality. They made their approach down the access road to the diked area, where two of the three involved tanks were found collapsed, buckled inward, and burning. The third tank (No. 67 in the diagram) was still relatively intact and full of gasoline. The contents of all three tanks was burning furiously.

The incident was declared under control at 4:28 p.m. on Saturday, January 8. However, the gasoline in the tank of origin continued to burn for more than 24 hours, finally burning itself out late Sunday night, January 9, 1983.

Explosion Damage and Casualties

The blasts, especially the last (and largest) one, appeared to have exerted a great deal of force. A remote, empty, storage tank (No. 9), almost 1,200 ft away, was flattened by the impact, and tank No. 4, nearly 1,500 ft away, was also damaged.

Other reported consequences of the blasts included flattened railroad freight cars and heavy damage to the drum refinishing plant. At the truck terminal building, large tank trucks were tossed about, several automobiles were incinerated, and numerous fires burned in the general area. In addition, the impact of the blasts damaged several structures of surrounding industrial concerns. Losses were estimated in the millions.

Apparently leaving the premises because of the emergency, one employee was caught in the open at the moment of the blast and killed. The burned body was found near the charred automobiles at the truck terminal area. In total, 24 persons were treated for various injuries resulting from the incident. Those injured included railroad, tank storage facility, and drum refinishing company employees. There were no fire fighter or police injuries. It is speculated that the cause of the largest blast was the ignition by the drum refinishing incinerator of the vapor cloud from the large spill at the diked area of tanks Nos. 67, 65, and 64.

Analysis

A tank overfill precipitated this incident.

NFPA 30, *Flammable and Combustible Liquids Code*, 1981 edition, required that, in order to avert potential problems, tanks receiving transfer of Class I liquids (such as gasoline) be either (1) gaged at frequent intervals during the transfer, (2) equipped with high-level alarms to signal on-duty personnel, or (3) equipped with a high-level alarm system to automatically shut down or divert the flow.

The system for monitoring the level in tank No. 67 was completely manual, in compliance with option (1) above. Although the standard

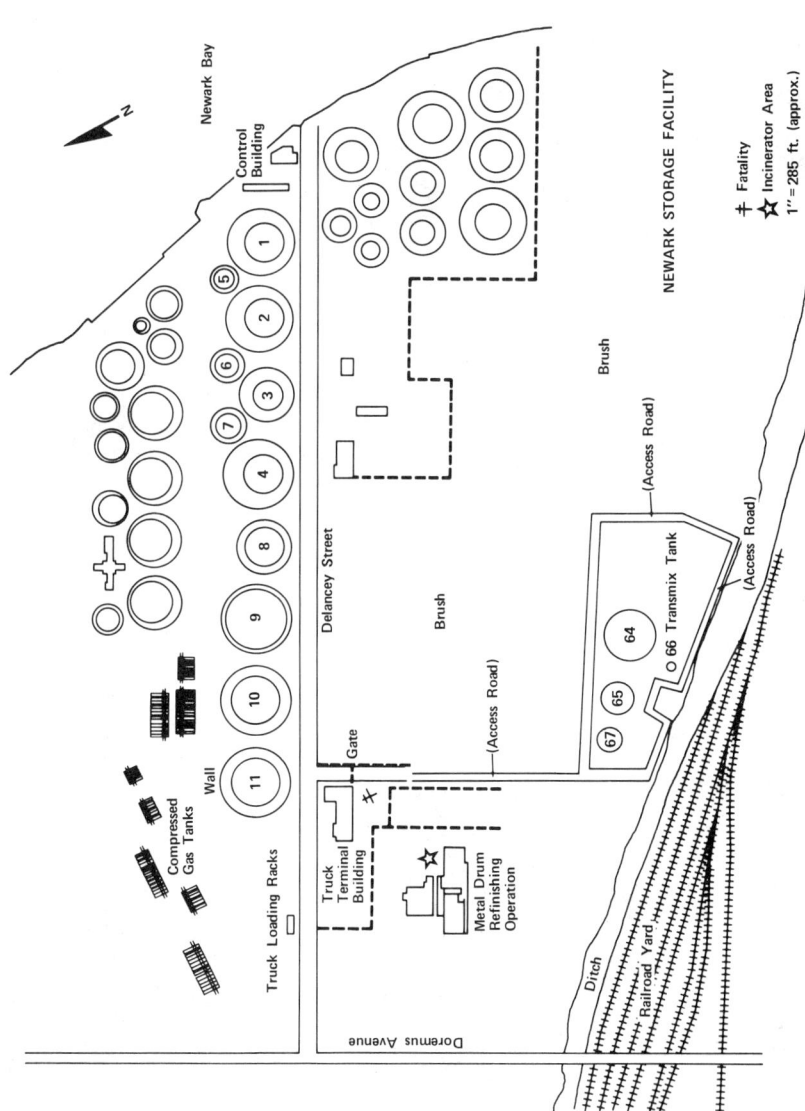

Figure S-7　Diagram of the Newark Storage Facility.

Figure S-8 Aerial view from the north of the facility prior to the incident. The three isolated tanks to the right were directly involved in the incident. *Courtesy of Newark, NJ Fire Department.*

Figure S-9 This view of the storage facility following the incident shows the proximity of the railroad yard, and remote damage to the large empty storage tank in the left center. *Courtesy of Newark, NJ Fire Department.*

264 FLAMMABLE AND COMBUSTIBLE LIQUIDS CODE HANDBOOK

Figure S-10 This view of the drum refinishing company shows the devastation from the explosions. The metal stack in the upper right is the incinerator location. *Courtesy of Newark, NJ Fire Department.*

operating procedures of the tank storage facility stipulated this kind of gaging, no data was available documenting gaging activities prior to the incident. A "check" of the transfer operation was to commence at approximately 12:00 a.m., Friday, January 7, as tank storage facility personnel prepared to secure the valves following completion of the transfer. It is unknown exactly when the tank began to overflow.

The configuration of the area and an apparent shift in the wind direction brought the vapors from the spill into contact with the suspected ignition source—the incinerator at the metal drum refinishing plant. However, ignition of the vapors by any number of other ignition sources, such as automobile or truck engines, smoking materials, or perhaps the railroad diesel engines operating adjacent to the tanks, would have occurred regardless of the wind direction.

Although notification of the Newark Fire Department was part of the tank storage facility's standard emergency operating procedures, it appears that during the initial emergency operations at the storage facility, the fire department was not notified. It is doubtful that immediate notification of the fire service would have prevented the eventual ignition and explosions. However, it is quite possible that, had the fire department arrived earlier, fire service personnel might have been caught by the blast, thus increasing loss of life from the incident.

A decision to let the fires in the tanks burn themselves out was made after early attempts to control the blaze with the Port Authority foam truck proved unsuccessful and an evaluation was made of the condition of the tanks and exposure factors. Furthermore, a considerable amount of transfer piping was damaged, and the burning tanks were adequately diked and located in a relatively remote area. Attempts to extinguish the blaze might have resulted in further injury. Salvaging the remaining contents was doubtful, and the loss of the fuel weighed against possible loss of life was insignificant. (*See commentary in this Handbook relating to Section 2-9 of NFPA 30*).

This supplement report was taken from an NFPA Summary Investigation Report by John Bouchard of the NFPA, in cooperation with FEMA/USFA and NBS/CFR.

General-Purpose Warehouse Fire
Falls Township, Pennsylvania
June 21, 1982

Introduction

One of the largest warehouse fires ever occurred on June 21, 1982. This fire involved palletized storage of petroleum-based aerosol products and resulted in the total destruction of K Mart Corporation's 1.2 million-square-foot distribution center in Falls Township, PA. The fire developed rapidly throughout the area in which it started, and rocketing aerosol containers spread the fire to adjacent areas. Although the facility was considered well-protected, the hydraulically designed sprinkler system was quickly overwhelmed, resulting in early collapse of the roof and impairment of the sprinkler system.

There was no loss of life. Property damage was estimated at more than $100 million.

Background

The K Mart Distribution Center was located in a Falls Township, PA industrial park, about 12 miles northeast of Philadelphia. The facility was one of ten regional distribution centers for K Mart's retail stores and served all K Mart stores in the northeastern United States.

The overall dimensions of the single-story warehouse were 1085 by 1180 ft. Fire walls divided the warehouse into four quadrants, as shown in Figure S-11. Also, a 115- × 445-ft receiving area was located along the east side of Quadrant D. A 100- × 490-ft shipping area was located along the south side of Quadrant A. There was a 120- × 160-ft office area at the southeast corner.

The warehouse was of unprotected noncombustible construction, with a concrete floor and Class I steel deck roof. Clear height inside the building was 24 ft. The roof framing was 48-foot-span steel joist, supported by 48-foot-span steel trusses. Roof framing was supported by steel columns. None of the structural steel was protected for fire exposure. Exterior walls were a combination of insulated metal panel and poured concrete and 12-in. hollow concrete block. The walls that subdivided the building were 12-in. hollow concrete block with 18-in. parapets. The interior walls were considered to be 3-hour rated. However, some of the openings in these walls were not provided with fire doors. Instead, 0.30 gpm per foot deluge curtains protected the openings. Heat and smoke vents were provided using 4- × 6-ft drop-type vents on a 1:96 ratio to floor area.

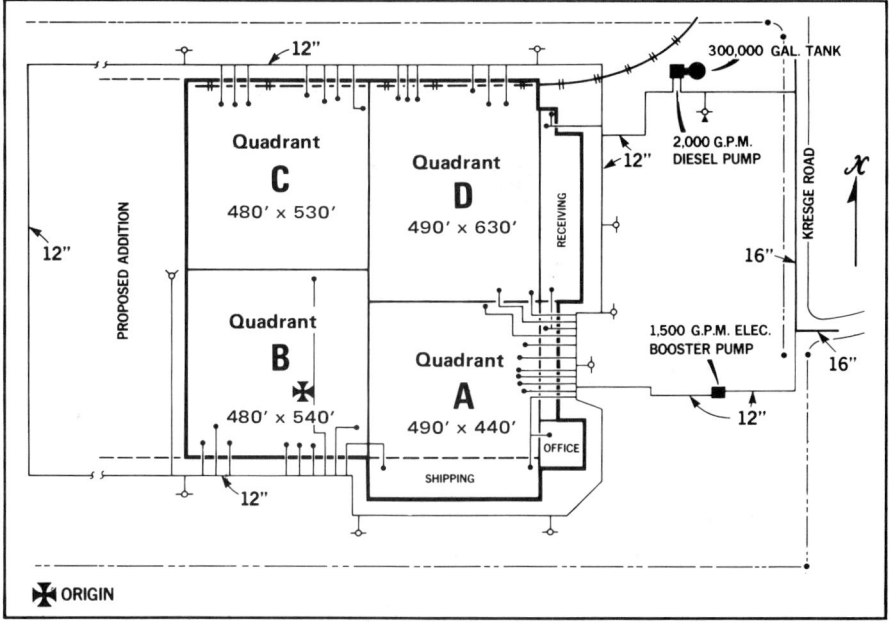

Figure S-11   Plan of K Mart Distribution Center.

Referring to Figure S-11, the area of origin, Quadrant B, was a product selection area. Storage in this area included many different paper and plastic commodities, as well as the aerosol products. Commodity classifications thus ranged from Class I to Class IV, as defined in NFPA 231C, *Standard for Rack Storage of Materials*. The storage arrangement consisted of four modules used for picking stock for shipment. Each module consisted of two double-row racks, 350 ft long, one on either side of a 10 ft "alley," through which ran a 3 ft-wide conveyor. On each side of each module there was a 12- to 15-ft aisle, then reserve stock storage consisting of a single-row rack of stored commodity and a row of palletized storage, five pallets deep and up to four pallets high. (*See Figure S-12*).

The facility was fully protected with hydraulically designed wet-pipe sprinkler systems. No in-rack sprinklers were provided. Design density was 0.40 gpm/sq ft over the most remote 3,000 sq ft. All systems used 286°F, 17/32-inch orifice standard upright sprinkler heads. Water was supplied from a 2000-gpm/128-psig diesel-driven fire pump taking suction from a 300,000-gallon tank, and from a 1500-gpm/80-psi electric motor-driven booster pump taking suction from the 12 in. lead-in from a 16-in. municipal main. The underground fire protection loop consisted of a 12-in. pipeline that completely encircled the building and that had been extended to accommodate a proposed addition.

268   FLAMMABLE AND COMBUSTIBLE LIQUIDS CODE HANDBOOK

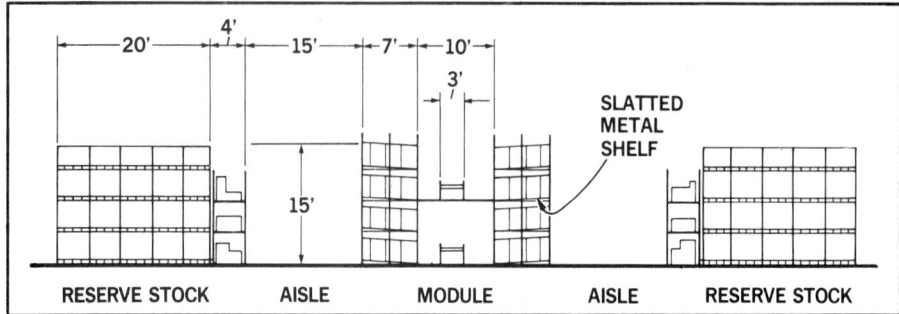

Figure S-12   Sectional View of the Storage Arrangement in Quadrant B.

The Incident

Some time around 12:30 p.m. on the day of the fire, a lift truck driver drove into Quadrant B to pick (select) an order. He had just positioned the forks under a load and was checking his order sheets when he heard something drop behind him, turned, and saw a ball of flame. He reported that there was little smoke, but the flame was a pale orange-red and it was burning intensely, as though being fed. The driver went to retrieve a fire extinguisher, but by the time he returned, flames were at ceiling height.

Other workers in the area described flames crawling up the sides of boxes and involving all tiers down to floor level. A lot of "popping" sounds were heard. The general manager of the facility returned from lunch at 12:30 p.m. and reported that fire had broken through the roof at that time. The fire alarm was sounded and employees began to evacuate the area.

At 12:35 p.m., sprinklers in two systems were operating, along with the electric fire pump. The county dispatch station was called at 12:36, with a second call at 12:38.

Within this time period, two more sprinkler systems were operating. In the meantime, maintenance personnel had checked both pumps and determined they were operating properly. The facility's fire brigade attempted to attack the fire with 1½-inch hose lines. When they entered Quadrant B, they saw thick, black smoke throughout the area. They also observed that sprinklers were operating normally and heard explosions that seemed to be located in the center of the building. Within minutes, the spreading smoke forced brigade members to leave Quadrant B. Deluge curtains were operating by this time.

Falls Township Fire Company No. 1 received the alarm at 12:38 p.m. Fire fighters reported seeing heavy black smoke as they approached the industrial park, and immediately requested a second alarm. Fire was

Figure S-13 An aerial view from southwest of the distribution center early in the fire. Quadrant B is fully involved.
(JAY CRAWFORD, *Bucks County Courier Times*)

venting through the roof's heat and smoke vents as the first fire department units arrived on the scene. Yard hydrants were used to supply a ladder pipe and 2½-inch handlines that were taken inside in an attempt to contain the fire to Quadrant B. Two fire fighters went inside but were unable to locate standpipe connections because of the fire conditions and were ordered out. Explosions could be heard and flashes of light were visible. Other fire fighters climbed to the roof on the west edge. Just as they started to vent the roof, it began to sag and they were ordered off the roof.

Second and third alarms were transmitted at 12:41 and 12:44 p.m. Three deluge sets were used inside at fire wall openings to contain the fire to Quadrant B. Other fire companies attempted to work handlines into the far corner of Quadrant B, but were driven out. Fire fighters were still trying to contain the fire at the north-south fire wall, but flames were leaping over the fire wall parapet. Fire fighters inside the building noted exploding aerosol cans going through the deluge curtain, trailing flaming contents behind them. About the same time, the ladder truck stationed along the west side of Quadrant B reported fire and aerosol cans coming through the roof and igniting the roof covering.

At approximately 12:47 p.m., power was disconnected, cutting all power to the plant, including the electric fire pump. At this time, the

Figure S-14 Aerial view from the same direction at the height of the fire.
(JAY CRAWFORD, *Bucks County Courier Times*)

Figure S-15 Aerial view from the northwest shows total destruction of the warehouse areas. This photo was taken three days after the fire.
(JAY CRAWFORD, *Bucks County Courier Times*)

diesel pump was still operating and parts of the six sprinkler systems in Quadrant B were operating.

At 12:59 p.m., a fourth alarm was dispatched. About this time, an engine that was positioned along the south wall of Quadrant B pulled back because water pressure was not sufficient for an attack from the exterior, due to broken sprinkler system piping. An effort was made to shut off sprinklers in the area, but the intense heat and explosions made access to the valves too hazardous to attempt.

An interior attack continued from Quadrant C. As the fire spread and structural steel continued to deform, breakage of sprinkler piping continued to reduce water pressure until 1:10 p.m., when hose lines were connected to public mains outside the property lines.

At 1:19 p.m., a fifth alarm was dispatched, and the fire department attempted another interior attack from the east side of the complex. By 1:22 p.m., fire had spread through most of the building, and by 1:37 p.m., the west end of the building was totally involved.

At 1:40 p.m., the west wall of the complex began to collapse, burying the hydrant located along this wall. By 1:46 p.m., this wall had completely collapsed. The fire officer in charge ordered all men out of the building at 1:50 p.m. An external attack was continued for about 20 minutes, until the fire achieved "firestorm" condition and was declared totally out of control.

When the fire died down, extinguishment efforts were resumed. Because the diesel pump had been turned off due to overheating, only public water flowing through the electric pump bypass was available for hose stream use. In addition, water for hose streams was still being drawn from public hydrants outside the complex. Hoses were played on the fire until 9:00 p.m., when the fire was declared under control. Because of the vast size of the location, isolated hot spots continued to flare up. The fire department, in conjunction with demolition crews, continued extinguishment until June 28, seven days after ignition, when the fire was declared finally extinguished.

Several fire fighters suffered from smoke inhalation and exhaustion during fire fighting operations, but there were no serious injuries or fatalities. The warehouse was totally destroyed. The office building and a maintenance room east of Quadrant D were only slightly damaged, however. Six railroad box cars and 33 truck trailers were also destroyed.

Analysis

All of the agencies that investigated this fire agreed that it was accidental. The Bucks County Fire Marshal reported the cause to be a fallen carton of carburetor and choke cleaner in aerosol cans; the fall caused one or more cans to rupture, spraying the liquid and propellant in the area where a lift truck was located. It is most likely that the source of ignition was the electrically-powered lift truck.

Development and spread of the fire was extremely rapid. It was estimated that 40 to 50 pallet loads of the carburetor and choke cleaner (1056 cans per pallet-load) had been in the immediate vicinity of the area of origin at the time. The pallet loads were stacked to a height of 15 ft.

The amount of Class I and Class II liquids, in both pressurized and nonpressurized containers, was substantial. Inventory records show that the total quantities of petroleum-based aerosols and alcohol-based aerosols were approximately 32,000 gallons and 14,800 gallons, respectively. In addition, over 100,000 gallons of high-flash point liquids in nonpressurized containers were present. Liquefied petroleum gas in the form of 18,693 cans of butane lighter fluid, over 109,000 disposable butane cigarette lighters, and more than 42,000 14-ounce propane cylinders were stored throughout the warehouse. Other storage that may have contributed to fire spread included more than 37,000 auto, trailer, and bicycle tires.

Tests and inspections of the sprinkler system and the underground piping uncovered no deficiencies that could have obstructed water flow to the sprinkler heads. All piping proved to be exceptionally clean. All sprinkler control valves were found to be fully open with seals intact. There was no evidence, either physical or eyewitness, to indicate any abnormal or deficient operation of any of the fire protection equipment.

The facility's Plant Emergency Organization consisted of individuals who were well trained and fully aware of their duties. The Emergency Action Plan was well developed. The fire department had recently preplanned their tactics for this facility. The plan called for an attack on a fire at its point of origin, if possible. The fall-back position was to confine the fire to one quadrant. The actual tactics used were consistent with the preplan and were well executed.

The two major factors in the loss of this facility were the storage throughout the building of large quantities of flammable and combustible liquid products in aerosol containers and failure of the protection at the firewall openings. The loss graphically illustrates the need for proper protection of flammable liquid storage, regardless of container type.

Tests conducted by Factory Mutual Research Corp. demonstrated that storage of aerosol containers of petroleum-based liquids presents a severe challenge to fire protection systems normally provided in general-purpose warehouses. Rocketing containers will greatly impede fire fighting operations and will spread fire over large areas of a building. This virtually guarantees that fire growth will outpace a sprinkler system's ability to gain control of the fire. In the specific case of firewall openings, deluge curtains are quite effective in stopping fire from passing through, but are powerless against rocketing containers.

Of particular interest here is that conditions in this facility did not comply with NFPA 30, *Flammable and Combustible Liquids Code*. Subsection 4-5.6 of NFPA 30 limits the combined capacity of containers of flammable and combustible liquids that may be stored in a general-purpose warehouse as follows:

Class of Liquid	Total Capacity
IA	None
IB & IC	660 gal
II	1,375 gal
IIIA	2,750 gal
IIIB	13,750 gal

Considering the quantities of such liquids actually stored, even neglecting the fact that aerosols were present, at least one quadrant of the warehouse should have been designed according to 4-5.7, i.e., as a "liquid warehouse," as defined by NFPA 30, *Flammable and Combustible Liquids Code*. All storage of flammable and combustible liquids could have then been isolated from the rest of the warehouse.

Regarding the firewall openings, it is evident that the deluge curtain systems should have been supplemented with some type of physical barrier arranged to block the openings in event of a fire. Had the nature of the threat posed by aerosol containers been fully appreciated, such a feature could have been a basic element in the fire protection system.

Finally, had the warehouse, or a portion of it, been protected according to the requirements for liquid warehouses, in-rack sprinkler protection would have been recommended according to Appendix D of NFPA 30, *Flammable and Combustible Liquids Code*. It is likely that in-rack sprinklers would have slowed the progress of the fire to an extent that an interior attack by the fire department would have been more successful.

This supplement report was taken from an NFPA Summary Investigation Report by Richard Best of the NFPA, in cooperation with FEMA/USFA and NBS/CFR.

Automotive and Marine Service Station Code

NFPA 30A-1987

Information on referenced publications can be found in Chapter 9.

Foreword

This standard, known as the *Automotive and Marine Service Station Code*, is recommended for use as the basis of legal regulations. Its provisions are intended to reduce the hazard to a degree consistent with reasonable public safety, without undue interference with public convenience and necessity, which requires the use of flammable and combustible liquids. Thus, compliance with this standard does not eliminate all hazard in the use of flammable and combustible liquids.

Development of NFPA 30A

Prior to 1984, the subject of service stations was covered in Chapter 7 of NFPA 30, *Flammable and Combustible Liquids Code*. With the 1984 edition of NFPA 30, Chapter 7, augmented by new text and updated information, became a self-standing document designated NFPA 30A, *Automotive and Marine Service Station Code*. Both NFPA 30 and NFPA 30A were, at the time, the responsibility of the same NFPA technical committee, the Committee on Flammable and Combustible Liquids.

There were several reasons for developing a separate code for service stations.

First, the Committee had decided to restructure NFPA 30 into a "horizontal" code, i.e, one that does not treat individual occupancies separately. It was soon realized that service stations could not be adequately addressed in such a restructured NFPA 30, so a task group was assigned to write a new code on service stations, using the original chapter from NFPA 30 as a starting point.

Second, an estimated million and a half vehicles are fueled by propane, and a sizable number by compressed natural gas. These and other gaseous fuels are frequently available at the same stations that dispense gasoline and diesel fuel. In order to address these new marketing practices, it was felt that a separate technical committee, composed of representatives of the gas industry as well as the liquid fuel dispensing field, would be needed. Extracting the service station chapter from NFPA 30 was an appropriate first step in response to the marketing issue. A separate Committee on Automotive and Marine Service Stations has now been established and will be responsible for amendments to this 1987 edition of NFPA 30A, *Automotive and Marine Service Station Code*.

Third, dispensing or transferring of fuels is an integral part of all service station operations. As is commonly known, the transferring of liquids is intrinsically more hazardous than storage of the same liquids. Public access to, and participation in, the dispensing operation is an inherent cause for concern regarding firesafety. A self-standing code better reflects the scope and significance of fire protection for these occupancies.

Last, environmental protection has become an increasingly important issue. For service stations, this has introduced new requirements and restrictions in an effort to reduce the potential fire and pollution hazards associated with the mishandling of fuels. As an individual code, NFPA 30A will be better able to address technological advancements pertinent to environmental safety.

1 General Provisions

1-1 Scope and Application.

1-1.1 This *Code* applies to automotive and marine service stations, and to service stations located inside buildings.

One normally thinks of service stations as public facilities. However, this *Code* also applies to private automotive service stations, such as those at garages, police and fire stations, industrial plants, automotive truck terminals, and private marine service stations.

1-1.2 This *Code* shall not apply to those service stations, or portions of service stations, where liquefied petroleum gases, liquefied natural gases, or compressed natural gases are dispensed as automotive fuels. [*See NFPA 58, Standard for Storage and Handling of Liquefied Petroleum Gases; and NFPA 52, Standard for Compressed Natural Gas (CNG) Vehicular Fuel Systems.*]

Until such time as NFPA 30A addresses the routine fueling of automobiles and marine craft with gaseous fuels, the references to NFPA 58, *Standard for the Storage and Handling of Liquefied Petroleum Gases*, and NFPA 52, *Standard for Compressed Natural Gas (CNG) Vehicular Fuel Systems*, will suffice.

1-1.3 Reference shall also be made to NFPA 302, *Standard on Fire Protection for Pleasure and Commercial Motor Craft*, for safety precautions while fueling at marine service stations; to NFPA 303, *Fire Protection Standard for Marinas and Boatyards*, for additional requirements applicable to marine service stations; and to NFPA 88B, *Standard on Repair Garages*, for additional requirements for automotive repair facilities.

1-2 Definitions.

Approved. Acceptable to the "authority having jurisdiction."

NOTE: The National Fire Protection Association does not approve, inspect or certify any installations, procedures, equipment, or materials nor does it approve or evaluate testing laboratories. In determining the acceptability of installations or procedures, equipment or materials, the authority having jurisdiction may base acceptance on compliance with NFPA or other appropriate standards. In the absence of such standards, said authority may require evidence of proper installation, procedure or use. The authority having jurisdiction may also refer to the listings or labeling practices of an organization concerned with product evaluations which is in a position to determine compliance with appropriate standards for the current production of listed items.

Authority Having Jurisdiction. The "authority having jurisdiction" is the organization, office or individual responsible for "approving" equipment, an installation or a procedure.

NOTE: The phrase "authority having jurisdiction" is used in NFPA documents in a broad manner since jurisdictions and "approval" agencies vary as do their responsibilities. Where public safety is primary, the "authority having jurisdiction" may be a federal, state, local or other regional department or individual such as a fire chief, fire marshal, chief of a fire prevention bureau, labor department, health department, building official, electrical inspector, or others having statutory authority. For insurance purposes, an insurance inspection department, rating bureau, or other insurance company representative may be the "authority having jurisdiction." In many circumstances the property owner or his designated agent assumes the role of the "authority having jurisdiction"; at government installations, the commanding officer or departmental official may be the "authority having jurisdiction."

Basement. A story of a building or structure having ½ or more of its height below ground level and to which access for fire fighting purposes is unduly restricted.

In any particular case, an interpretation of this definition is best left to the authority having jurisdiction, who should know to what extent access for fire fighting will be required. Openings for the injection of gaseous extinguishing agents, water spray, or high-expansion foam may, in some cases, be considered sufficient.

Bulk Plant or Terminal. That portion of a property where liquids are received by tank vessel, pipelines, tank car, or tank vehicle, and are stored or blended in bulk for the purpose of distributing such liquids by tank vessel, pipeline, tank car, tank vehicle, portable tank, or container.

Combustible Liquid. A liquid having a flash point at or above 100°F (37.8°C).

Combustible Liquids shall be subdivided as follows:

(a) Class II liquids shall include those having flash points at or above 100°F (37.8°C) and below 140°F (60°C).

(b) Class IIIA liquids shall include those having flash points at or above 140°F (60°C) and below 200°F (93°C).

(c) Class IIIB liquids shall include those having flash points at or above 200°F (93°C).

Closed Container. A container as herein defined, so sealed by means of a lid or other device that neither liquid nor vapor will escape from it at ordinary temperatures.

Container. Any vessel of 60 U.S. gal (227 L) or less capacity used for transporting or storing liquids.

Flammable Liquid. A liquid having a flash point below 100°F (37.8°C) and having a vapor pressure not exceeding 40 lb psi absolute (2,068 mmHg) at 100°F (37.8°C) shall be known as a Class I liquid.

Class I Liquids shall be subdivided as follows:

(a) Class IA shall include those having flash points below 73°F (22.8°C) and having a boiling point below 100°F (37.8°C).

(b) Class IB shall include those having flash points below 73°F (22.8°C) and having a boiling point at or above 100°F (37.8°C).

(c) Class IC shall include those having flash points at or above 73°F (22.8°C) and below 100°F (37.8°C).

Labeled. Equipment or materials to which has been attached a label, symbol or other identifying mark of an organization acceptable to the "authority having jurisdiction" and concerned with product evaluation, that maintains periodic inspection of production of labeled equipment or materials and by whose labeling the manufacturer indicates compliance with appropriate standards or performance in a specified manner.

Listed. Equipment or materials included in a list published by an organization acceptable to the "authority having jurisdiction" and concerned with product evaluation, that maintains periodic inspection of production of listed equipment or materials and whose listing states either that the equipment or material meets appropriate standards or has been tested and found suitable for use in a specified manner.

NOTE: The means for identifying listed equipment may vary for each organization concerned with product evaluation, some of which do not recognize equipment as listed unless it is also labeled. The "authority having jurisdiction" should utilize the system employed by the listing organization to identify a listed product.

Portable Tank. Any closed vessel having a liquid capacity over 60 U.S. gal (227 L) and not intended for fixed installation.

Safety Can. An approved container, of not more than 5-gal (18.9 L) capacity, having a spring-closing lid and spout cover and so designed that it will safely relieve internal pressure when subjected to fire exposure.

The safety can is not designed or intended for use in areas where the periodic release of flammable vapors may create a hazardous atmosphere (such as in the trunk of an automobile). The main purpose of the safety can is preventing explosion of the overheated container, while still providing the utility of a closed container. To accomplish this, a spring-operated cap is provided on the pouring spout, eliminating the need for a flame arrestor in the spout. Even if the vapors coming past the spring-loaded cover are in the flammable range, their velocity would be at least an order of magnitude greater than the intrinsic velocity of a flame through the vapors, so a flashback into the safety can would be unlikely should the vapors be ignited by an external source. (*See Figure 1-4.*) In spite of this, it is customary to find safety cans fitted with flame arrestors that meet specific listing requirements.

Service Stations.

Automotive Service Station. That portion of a property where liquids used as motor fuels are stored and dispensed from fixed equipment into the fuel tanks of motor vehicles or approved containers and shall include any facilities available for the sale and service of tires, batteries and accessories, and for minor automotive maintenance work. Major automotive repairs, painting, body and fender work are excluded.

Marine Service Station. That portion of a property where liquids used as fuels are stored and dispensed from fixed equipment on shore, piers, wharves, or floating docks into the fuel tanks of self-propelled craft, and shall include all facilities used in connection therewith.

Service Station Located Inside Buildings. That portion of an automotive service station located within the perimeter of a building or building structure that also contains other occupancies. The service station may be enclosed or partially enclosed by the building walls, floors, ceilings, or partitions, or may be open to the outside. The service station dispensing area shall mean that area of the service station required for dispensing of fuels to motor vehicles. Dispensing of fuel at manufacturing, assembly, and testing operations is not included within this definition.

Vapor Processing Equipment. Those components of a vapor processing system that are designed to process vapors or liquids captured during filling operations at service stations, bulk plants, or terminals.

Vapor Processing System. A system designed to capture and process vapors displaced during filling operations at service stations, bulk plants, or terminals by use of mechanical and/or chemical means. Examples are systems using blower-assist for capturing vapors, and refrigeration, absorption and combustion systems for processing vapors.

Vapor Recovery System. A system designed to capture and retain, without processing, vapors displaced during filling operations at service stations, bulk plants, or terminals. Examples are balanced-pressure vapor displacement systems and vacuum-assist systems without vapor processing.

NFPA 30A—GENERAL PROVISIONS

Ventilation. As specified in this code, ventilation is for the prevention of fire and explosion. It is considered adequate if it is sufficient to prevent accumulation of significant quantities of vapor-air mixtures in concentration over one-fourth of the lower flammable limit.

Ventilation is vital to the prevention of flammable liquid fires and explosions. Ventilation is used to remove vapors to a safe location and to dilute vapor concentration. This can be accomplished through natural or forced air movement.

The lower flammable limit is the minimum concentration of vapor in air below which propagation of a flame will not occur in the presence of an ignition source. The upper flammable limit is the maximum concentration of vapor in air above which propagation of flame will not occur. If the vapor concentration is below the lower flammable limit, it is "too lean" to propagate flame; if it is above the upper flammable limit, it is "too rich."

When the vapor concentration is between the lower and upper flammable limits, ignition can occur and explosions may result.

When the *Code* describes ventilation as being adequate when vapor-air mixtures are not over one-fourth of the lower flammable limit, a safety factor of four-to-one is established.

2 Storage

2-1 General Provisions.

This *Code* sets forth several general storage provisions for service stations. Included are provisions for venting, stations adjoining bulk plants, storage and pits in basement areas, inventory records, tank storage, tanks inside buildings, and container storage on service station properties.

2-1.1 Liquids shall be stored in:

(a) approved closed containers not exceeding 60-gal (227 L) capacity, or

(b) tanks in special enclosures inside buildings as described in Section 2-2, or

(c) aboveground tanks supplying marine service stations as provided in 2-1.6, or

(d) an approved tank that is part of a fuel dispensing system as provided for in 8-3.6, or

(e) tanks located underground as in Section 2-3 of NFPA 30, *Flammable and Combustible Liquids Code*, or

(f) tanks or containers inside service station buildings as provided for in 2-3.3 and 2-3.4.

2-1.2 Vent pipes on tanks storing gasoline shall be in accordance with NFPA 30, *Flammable and Combustible Liquids Code*, Sections 2-3.5.1, 2-3.5.2 and 2-3.5.6, as applicable, and shall discharge only upward in order to disperse vapors. (*Also see 8-3.4, 8-3.5, and 8-3.6 of this Code.*)

Tanks at service stations are generally required to be installed underground. (*For exceptions, see 2-1.6, Section 2-2, and 8-3.5. Also see NFPA 30, Flammable and Combustible Liquids Code, 2-2.6.2 and 2-3.5.1, for venting requirements.*) However, due to current and proposed environmental regulations, there is increasing interest in aboveground installation of tanks at public service stations.

The requirement for service station tanks to discharge vapors in an upward direction only prohibits the use of a U-bend or weather-hood to keep out rain and foreign matter. Experience has shown that the risk of serious contamination of the tank contents, which may accompany upward discharge of vapor from an open vent, is small. Furthermore, several serious fire incidents have occurred when vapors were directed downward. Existing service station vent pipes that have weatherhoods, U-bends, or any other type of vent cap that forces the vapor downward or otherwise hinders the discharge of vapor, should be corrected immediately.

2-1.3 Aboveground tanks, located at a bulk plant, shall not be connected by piping to a service station. Apparatus dispensing Class I liquids into the fuel tanks of motor vehicles of the public shall not be located at a bulk plant unless separated by a fence or similar barrier from the area in which bulk operations are conducted.

This restriction forbidding the connection of bulk storage tanks to service station tanks or dispensers is deemed necessary to reduce the likelihood of overfilling underground tanks. The intent is that bulk storage tanks not be used as a source of supply to service station dispensers, either directly or indirectly via underground tanks.

2-1.4 Class I liquids shall not be stored or handled within a building having a basement or pit into which flammable vapors can travel, unless such area is provided with ventilation that will prevent the accumulation of flammable vapors therein.

Again, the reader is reminded that flammable liquid vapors are heavier than air and will normally seek low levels.

2-1.5 Accurate daily inventory records shall be maintained and reconciled on all Class I liquid and diesel fuel storage tanks for indication of possible leakage from tanks or piping. The records shall be kept at the premises or made available for inspection by the enforcing authority within 24 hrs of a written or verbal request. The records shall include, as a minimum, records showing by product, daily reconciliation between sales, use, receipts, and inventory on hand. If there is more than one system consisting of a tank(s) serving separate pump(s) or dispenser(s) for any product, the reconciliation shall be maintained separately for each tank system. API Publication 1621, *Recommended Practice for Bulk Liquid Stock Control at Retail Outlets*, provides information on this subject.

Numerous fires and explosions have resulted from leaking underground service station tanks. In some cases, nearby buildings have been evacuated, sometimes for several weeks, because of the presence of flammable vapors. Frequently, the source of the leak is difficult to locate. Gasoline from a leaking underground tank has been known to spread on the water table for distances up to three miles. Because of this problem, the *Code* specifies that accurate daily inventory records be kept. If such records are maintained and discrepancies reconciled, leaks can often be discovered and corrected before they constitute a major hazard.

> NFPA 329, *Recommended Practice for Underground Leakage of Flammable and Combustible Liquids,* provides guidance in determining the source of a leak, as well as procedures for testing tanks and removing liquids that are trapped underground. See also API Publication 1621, *Recommended Practice for Bulk Liquid Stock Control at Retail Outlets.*

2-1.6 Tanks supplying marine service stations and pumps not integral with the dispensing device shall be on shore or on a pier of the solid-fill type, except as provided in (a) and (b).

(a) Where shore location would require excessively long supply lines to dispensers, the authority having jurisdiction may authorize the installation of tanks on a pier provided that applicable portions of NFPA 30, *Flammable and Combustible Liquids Code*, Chapter 2, relative to spacing, diking and piping are complied with and the quantity so stored does not exceed 1,100 gal (4164 L) aggregate capacity.

(b) Shore tanks supplying marine service stations may be located aboveground where rock ledges or high water tables make underground tanks impractical.

> Marine service stations must be located where there is adequate water depth to accommodate the vessels served. Suitable locations are often near steep or rocky shores where excavation to completely bury a tank is difficult. A tank should be located above the high water level to avoid water in the excavation, possible corrosion, and leakage. This paragraph and the following, 2-1.7, recognize these risks and provide means for avoiding them.

2-1.7 Where tanks are at an elevation which produces a gravity head on the dispensing device, the tank outlet shall be equipped with a device, such as a solenoid valve, positioned adjacent to and downstream from the valve specified in Section 2-2.7.1 of NFPA 30, *Flammable and Combustible Liquids Code,* so installed and adjusted that liquid cannot flow by gravity from the tank in case of piping or hose failure when the dispenser is not in use.

2-2 Special Enclosures.

2-2.1 When installation of tanks in accordance with NFPA 30, *Flammable and Combustible Liquids Code,* Section 2-3 is impractical because of property or building limitations, tanks for liquids may be installed in buildings if enclosed as described in 2-2.2 and upon specific approval of the authority having jurisdiction.

2-2.2 Enclosure shall be substantially liquid- and vapor-tight without backfill. Sides, top, and bottom of the enclosure shall be of reinforced concrete at least 6 in. (15 cm) thick, with openings for inspection through the top only. Tank connections shall be so piped or closed that neither vapors nor liquid can escape into the enclosed space. Means shall be provided to use portable equipment to discharge to the outside any liquid or vapors that might accumulate should leakage occur.

> The intent is to ensure that overfilling of the tank cannot release liquid into adjacent spaces and to provide access to the space between the tank and the enclosure to facilitate ventilation and the removal of any spilled liquid.

2-2.3 At automotive service stations provided in connection with tenant or customer parking facilities in large buildings of commercial, mercantile or residential occupancy, tanks containing Class I liquids installed in accordance with 2-2.2 shall not exceed 6,000 gal (22 710 L) individual or 18,000 gal (68 130 L) aggregate capacity.

2-3 Inside Buildings.

2-3.1 Except where stored in tanks as provided in 2-2, no Class I liquids shall be stored within any service station building except in closed containers of aggregate capacity not exceeding 120 gal (454.2 L). One container not exceeding 60 gal (227 L) capacity equipped with a listed pump is permitted.

> The container equipped with a listed pump referred to in the last sentence should be included within the 120 gal (454.2 L) maximum capacity. The need for such a container and pump was much greater when alcohol was the predominant antifreeze and when white gasoline was dispensed for gasoline stoves and lanterns. The purpose of permitting just one container to be equipped with a pump is that the second such container should be a backup supply only.

2-3.2 Class I liquids may be transferred from one container to another in lubrication or service rooms of a service station building provided the electrical installation complies with Table 6 and provided that any heating equipment complies with Chapter 7. See also 8-6 for other possible sources of ignition.

2-3.3 Class II and Class IIIA liquids may be stored and dispensed inside service station buildings from approved tanks of not more than 120 gal (454 L) for each class, with an aggregate capacity not exceeding 240 gal (908 L).

2-3.4 Class IIIB liquids may be stored and dispensed inside service station buildings in tanks or containers, subject to approval of the authority having jurisdiction.

Prior to the 1984 edition of NFPA 30A, *Automotive and Marine Service Station Code*, no distinction was made in the two preceding sections between Class IIIA and Class IIIB liquids. In addition, the wording was vague and subject to misinterpretation. It was unclear, for example, whether or not there was any limit on the total quantity that might be stored. The change is intended to clarify the limit on Class IIIA liquids and to clearly establish that there is no limit on high flash point (Class IIIB) liquids such as motor oils. In addition, the change allows the authority having jurisdiction to exercise greater judgment in allowing storage of Class IIIB liquids inside service station buildings and in determining what kind of tank is acceptable.

References Cited in Commentary

NFPA 30, *Flammable and Combustible Liquids Code*, NFPA, Quincy, MA, 1987.

NFPA 52, *Standard for Compressed Natural Gas (CNG) Vehicular Fuel Systems*, 1984.

NFPA 58, *Standard for Storage and Handling of Liquefied Petroleum Gases*, 1986.

NFPA 329, *Recommended Practice for Handling Underground Leakage of Flammable and Combustible Liquids*, NFPA, Quincy, MA, 1987.

American Petroleum Institute, *Recommended Practice for Bulk Liquid Stock Control at Retail Outlets*, API Publication 1621, Washington, D.C., 1977.

3 Piping, Valves, and Fittings

3-1 The design, fabrication, assembly, test, and inspection of the piping system shall be in accordance with NFPA 30, *Flammable and Combustible Liquids Code*, Chapter 3, except that, where dispensing is from a floating structure, suitable lengths of oil-resistant flexible hose may be employed between the shore piping and the piping on the floating structure as made necessary by change in water level or shoreline.

Requirements for the design, fabrication, assembly, testing, and inspection of piping systems at service stations are basically the same as those in Chapter 3 of NFPA 30, *Flammable and Combustible Liquids Code*. Major differences are the exceptions to the requirements included for marine service stations, as specified in Sections 3-1 through 3-4, plus the additional testing required for piping systems at service stations, as specified in Section 3-5.

3-2 Where excessive stray currents are encountered, piping handling Class I and Class II liquids at marine service stations shall be electrically insulated from the shore piping.

This is because shore-based stray currents might be transmitted through a conductive hose to the tank fill opening, which is often grounded to the vessel hull, making sparks at the fill opening possible.

3-3 Piping shall be located so as to be protected from physical damage.

3-4 A readily accessible valve to shut off the supply from shore shall be provided in each pipeline at or near the approach to the pier and at the shore end of each marine pipeline adjacent to the point where a flexible hose is attached.

3-5 After completion of the installation, including any paving, that section of the pressure piping system between the pump discharge and the connection for the dispensing facility shall be tested for at least 30 min at the maximum operating pressure of the system.

3-6* Each fill pipe for liquid storage shall be identified by color code or other marking to identify the product for which the tank is used. The color code or marking shall be maintained in legible condition throughout the life of the tank installation.

A-3-6 Where fill pipes for Class II or Class IIIA liquids are located in the same immediate area with fill pipes for Class I liquids, consideration should be given to providing positive means such as different pipe sizes, connection devices, special locks, or other methods designed to prevent the erroneous transfer of Class I liquids into or from any container or tank used for Class II or Class IIIA liquids.

Color coding of the fill pipe or fill opening is customarily done as a convenience for delivery personnel so that the different grades of gasoline are delivered to their proper tanks. Mixing of different grades of gasoline does not constitutue a hazard. However, where diesel fuel or kerosene are also dispensed, there is a definite risk of inadvertent mixing of Class I and Class II liquids, with the attendant serious consequences. For this reason, the Committee decided to mandate color coding.

Reference Cited in Commentary

NFPA 30, *Flammable and Combustible Liquids Code*, NFPA, Quincy, MA, 1987.

4 Fuel Dispensing System

4-1 Location of Dispensing Devices and Emergency Power Cutoff.

4-1.1 Dispensing devices at an automotive service station shall be so located that all parts of the vehicle being served will be on the premises of the service station. Openings beneath enclosures shall be sealed to prevent the flow of leaking fuel to lower building spaces.

Dispensing devices at marine service stations may be located on open piers, wharves, floating docks, or on shore, or on piers of the solid-fill type, and shall be located apart from other structures so as to provide room for safe ingress and egress of craft to be fueled. Dispensing devices shall be in all cases at least 20 ft (6 m) from any activity involving fixed sources of ignition. Dispensing devices located inside buildings shall comply with Chapter 5.

This paragraph prohibits the installation of dispensing devices on the sidewalk in front of a garage, since all parts of the vehicle being served must be on the premises of the service station. The paragraph is intended to control sources of ignition and to decrease the possibility of accidents with the dispensing device or the vehicle being fueled.

Sealing the openings beneath the dispensing device enclosure is particularly important for dispensing devices located in parking garages or other buildings that have floors at lower levels than the dispensing devices themselves.

Usually, the piping that supplies the dispensing devices is buried and, thus, firmly supported. In a serious incident that occurred in 1974 in St. John's, New Brunswick, an emergency shutoff valve in the base of a dispensing device apparently failed to operate when the device was knocked over by a truck. Gasoline flowed into a basement area located beneath the dispensing island, was ignited, and the resulting explosion killed five persons. In this case, the piping leading to the dispensing devices passed through the basement area, with no support other than that provided by some beams that also supported the service station floor and the apron at the dispensing island.

4-1.2 A clearly identified and easily accessible switch(es) or circuit breaker(s) shall be provided at a location remote from dispensing devices, including remote pumping systems, to shut off the power to all dispensing devices in the event of an emergency.

Since a fire or gasoline spill at the dispensing island may make it impossible to operate the dispensing island switches that shut off the flow of gasoline, the *Code* requires a clearly identified emergency power cutoff to be provided at a location remote from the dispensing device. The term "clearly identified" means that a sign is to be posted indicating where the cutoff switch is located. This emergency power cutoff should be readily accessible and not blocked by storage of such things as tires or cases of lubricating oil. All service station operators, as well as responding fire fighters, should know the location of this emergency power cutoff.

A recent fire at a Florida self-serve service station dramatically emphasizes the importance of this requirement. The fire occurred when one of the station attendants attempted to change a fuel filter in the supply line of one of the dispensing devices without shutting off power to the remote pump. (In a remote pumping system, the pump pressurizes the lines to all dispensing devices simultaneously.) A patron at an adjacent island began pumping fuel into his vehicle just as the attendant removed the filter from the supply pipe at the dispensing device. The results were predictable and catastrophic: gasoline spewed out of the open supply pipe, causing a sizeable spill. Apparently, neither of the two attendants knew or remembered the location of the emergency disconnect. The spill was ignited, probably by an automobile electrical system, and the resulting fire killed a child in one of the vehicles and severely burned two patrons.

4-2 Fuel Dispensing Devices.

4-2.1 Class I liquids shall be transferred from tanks by means of fixed pumps designed and equipped to allow control of the flow and prevent leakage or accidental discharge.

4-2.2 Dispensing devices for Class I liquids shall be listed. Existing listed or labeled dispensing devices may be modified provided that the modifications made are "Listed by Report" by an approved testing laboratory or as otherwise approved by the authority having jurisdiction. Modification proposals shall contain a description of the component parts used in the modification and the recommended methods of installation on specific dispensing devices, and it shall be made available to the authority having jurisdiction upon request.

"Listed by Report," a special form of listing employed by Underwriters Laboratories Inc., covers products or construction for which there are no generally recognized installation requirements. Information concerning proper field installation is contained in a report identified by the reference and date shown by the listing, copies of which may be obtained from the listing company.

4-2.3 A control shall be provided that will permit the pump to operate only when a dispensing nozzle is removed from its bracket or normal position with respect to the dispensing device, and the switch on this dispensing device is manually actuated. This control shall also stop the pump when all nozzles have been returned, either to their brackets or to the normal nondispensing position.

The term "all nozzles" should be interpreted to mean all nozzles being fed from any one pump. A proposal was submitted to the Technical Committee to allow a single-action dispensing nozzle that activates the pump upon removal from its bracket. After due consideration, the proposal was rejected. The Committee felt that the second positive action by the user ensured greater attention to the dispensing operation. The single-action dispensing nozzle failed to provide a positive pump shutoff. The Committee felt that the proponent did not demonstrate that safety was enhanced by the single-action nozzle.

4-2.4 Liquids shall not be dispensed by applying pressure to drums, barrels and similar containers. Listed pumps taking suction through the top of the container or listed self-closing faucets shall be used.

Since the drums ordinarily used for liquids are not qualified as pressure containers, and no containers made to UL specifications are so qualified, this paragraph essentially limits the use of gas pressure to containers built to the ASME *Boiler and Pressure Vessel Code*, or to those qualified as pressure containers under DOT regulations. Note that, by definition, containers have a capacity of 60 gal (227 L) or less. The reason for banning the use of air, even though the vapor space above the liquid in the container may already contain air, is that the compressed air will raise the UFL (upper flammable limit) of a mixture of vapor with air.

4-2.5 The dispensing device, except those attached to containers, shall be mounted and bolted on a concrete island or protected against collision damage by suitable means. If located indoors, the dispensing device shall also be mounted and bolted either on a concrete island or protected against collision damage by suitable means and shall be located in a position where it cannot be struck by a vehicle that is out of control descending a ramp or other slope. The installation shall be in accordance with the manufacturer's instructions.

4-2.6 Hose length at service stations shall not exceed 18 ft (5.5 m) unless approved by the authority having jurisdiction. All hose shall be listed. When not in use, hose shall be so secured as to protect it from damage.

> The U.S. Bureau of Weights and Measures sets a limit of 18 ft (5.5 m), and NFPA 30, *Flammable and Combustible Liquids Code*, has set limits in the past. Most hoses used on dispensing devices are substantially less than 18 ft (5.5 m) in length. However, 8-3.4 allows hoses of up to 50 ft (15.3 m) in length at private service stations.

4-2.7 A listed emergency breakaway device designed to retain liquid on both sides of the breakaway point shall be installed on each hose dispensing Class I liquids. Such devices shall be installed and maintained in accordance with the manufacturer's instructions.

Where hoses are attached to a hose-retrieving mechanism, the listed emergency breakaway device shall be installed between the point of attachment of the hose-retrieving mechanism to the hose and the hose nozzle valve.

Exception: Such devices shall not be required at marine service stations.

> This new requirement has been added to NFPA 30A, *Automotive and Marine Service Station Code*, in response to a number of recent incidents in which dispensing devices were pulled over when patrons drove away from the island with the nozzle still in the automobile's filler tube—in some cases, while the pump was still delivering fuel to the vehicle. Almost all of the incidents occurred at self-serve islands. In several cases, the shear valve did not function properly, and serious fires occurred. In at least one case, an attendant was seriously burned.
>
> The breakaway device is intended to fail before any significant strain is put on the dispensing device. Where the hose is connected to a retrieving mechanism, the breakaway device must be installed downstream of the point where the retrieving cable is attached to the hose. Otherwise, any stress on the hose will be transmitted to the dispensing device via the retrieving cable and not via the breakaway device, as intended.

4-2.8 Dispensing devices used to fill portable containers with home heating fuels shall not be located on the same island where Class I liquids are dispensed. Class I dispensers shall not be located on the same island as LP-gas dispensing operations.

> This new requirement is intended to eliminate recent fire incidents involving portable kerosene heaters. In these cases, users had inadvertently filled kerosene containers with gasoline, then used

NFPA 30A—FUEL DISPENSING SYSTEM

the gasoline to refuel the heaters. The Technical Committee similarly felt that LP-gas dispensers should be separated from the refueling islands.

4-3 Remote Pumping Systems.

At many newer and larger service stations, remote pumping systems are used where the pump is located at the tank and supplies several dispensers with the same grade of gasoline. The supply lines of these systems operate under pressure. Most commercially available remote delivery pumps are installed within the tank (i.e., submersible) or in a separate enclosure at the tank.

4-3.1 This section shall apply to systems for dispensing Class I liquids where such liquids are transferred from storage to individual or multiple dispensing devices by pumps located other than at the dispensing devices.

4-3.2 Pumps shall be listed and designed or equipped so that no part of the system will be subjected to pressures above its allowable working pressure.

4-3.3 Each pump shall have installed on the discharge side a listed leak detection device that will provide an indication if the piping and dispensers are not essentially liquidtight. Each leak-detecting device shall be checked and tested at least annually according to the manufacturer's specifications to ensure proper installation and operation.

Without such a device, a leak in the piping between the pump and the dispenser might continue undetected. The remote pumping system leak detectors are mechanical devices that require periodic testing to determine that they are operating properly.

4-3.4 Pumps installed above grade, outside of buildings, shall be located not less than 10 ft (3 m) from lines of adjoining property that can be built upon, and not less than 5 ft (1.5 m) from any building opening. When an outside pump location is impractical, pumps may be installed inside buildings as provided for dispensers in 4-1, or in pits as provided in 4-3.5. Pumps shall be substantially anchored and protected against physical damage.

4-3.5 Pits for subsurface pumps or piping manifolds of submersible pumps shall withstand the external forces to which they can be subjected without damage to the pump, tank, or piping. The pit shall be no larger than necessary for inspection and maintenance, and shall be provided with a fitted cover.

4-3.6 A listed rigidly anchored emergency shutoff valve, incorporating a fusible link or other thermally actuated device, designed to close automatically in event of severe impact or fire exposure shall be installed in accordance with the manufacturer's instructions in the supply line at the base of each individual island-type dispenser or at the inlet of each overhead dispensing device. An emergency shutoff valve incorporating a slip-joint feature shall not be used. The automatic closing feature of this valve shall be checked at the time of initial installation and at least once a year thereafter by manually tripping the hold-open linkage.

The valve described in 4-3.6 must stop the flow of gasoline if the dispensing device is either physically damaged by a vehicle or pulled over by a vehicle driving away with the nozzle still in its tank. (Backup protection is provided by the breakaway coupling required by 4-2.7.) Such a stress should release a spring-loaded mechanism that, in turn, closes the valve. Further protection for this valve is provided by a shear section that will break upon impact or severe stress. The shear section of the valve should be installed within ½ in. of the pump island level, and the entire assembly should be rigidly anchored to the island. This is to ensure that the piping will break at the shear section and that the spring and thermally actuated device will function to close the valve. (*See Figure 4-1.*)

The wording that disallows slip-joint features came about because, in the Technical Committee's opinion, such devices are not proper for this particular application.

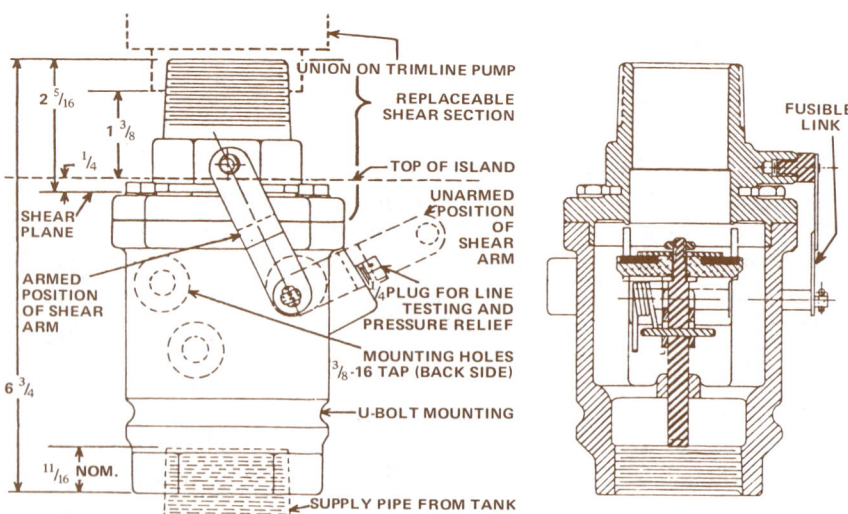

Figure 4-1 Drawings show where the fusible link and shear valve are located. To trip the valve manually for the annual inspection, disconnect the fusible link from its top connection. Resetting the fusible link rearms and opens the valve. (*Drawings courtesy of Gilbarco, Inc., Greensboro, NC.*)

NFPA 30A—FUEL DISPENSING SYSTEM

4-3.7 A vapor return pipe inside the dispenser housing shall have a shear section or flexible connector so that the liquid emergency shutoff valve will function as described in 4-3.6.

The requirement for a shear section or flexible connection in any vapor return pipe within the dispenser housing ensures that the vapor pipe does not add any strength to the system that might interfere with prompt action of the emergency shutoff valve required by 4-3.6.

4-4 Vapor Recovery Systems.

The U.S. Environmental Protection Agency, as well as state and local air pollution authorities, may soon require recovery of gasoline vapors at automotive service stations. At the present time, laws regarding the recovery of gasoline vapors are being enforced in two phases. Phase I requires vapor recovery when making a delivery to an underground tank. Phase II, which is currently being implemented in some sections of the United States, requires vapor recovery when an automobile is being fueled. Phase II involves the capture of vapors being expelled from the automobile fuel tank as the liquid fills the tank and displaces the vapors.

At present, two types of systems are being used for Phase II vapor capture at automotive service stations:

(a) the vapor recovery system, and

(b) the vapor processing system.

For each system, the *Code* specifies equipment requirements and regulates vapor discharge. (*See Figure 4-2.*)

The vapor recovery system captures and retains, without processing, flammable liquid vapors displaced during the filling of the tanks or containers, or during vehicle fueling. Most systems accomplish this through a balanced pressure-displacement system that returns gasoline vapors, via vapor return hoses and piping, to the underground tanks.

4-4.1 Dispensing devices incorporating provisions for vapor recovery shall be listed.

4-4.2 Hose nozzle valves used on vapor recovery systems shall be listed.

4-4.3 Means shall be provided in the vapor return path from each dispensing outlet to prevent the discharge of vapors when the hose nozzle valve is in its normal nondispensing position.

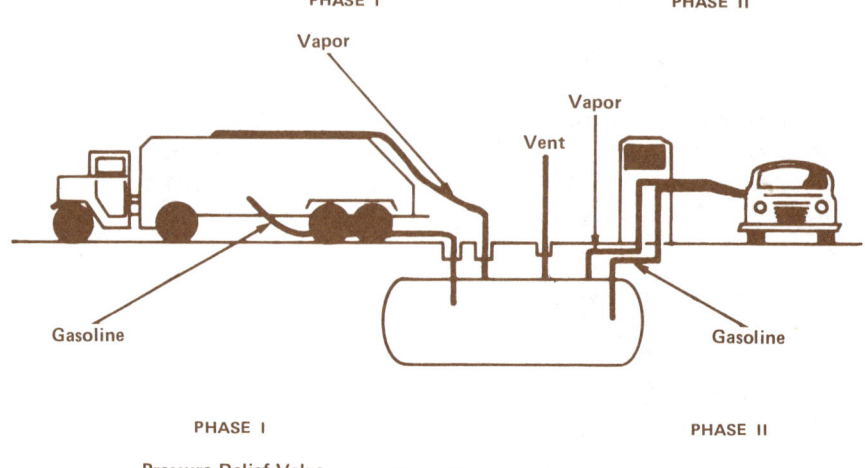

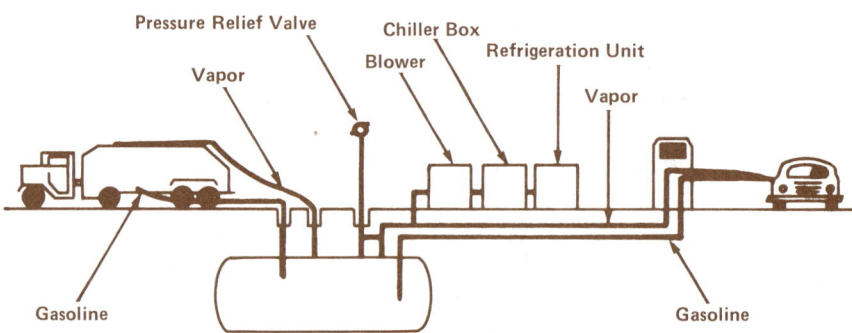

Figure 4-2 (Top) Vapor Recovery System. (Bottom) Vapor Processing System.

4-5 Vapor Processing Systems.

Vapor processing captures and processes the flammable liquid vapors displaced during the filling of tanks or containers or during vehicle fueling. The vapor is captured through the use of mechanical and/or chemical means by systems that use blower-assist for capturing vapors, and refrigeration, adsorption, or combustion for processing them. Generally, those systems using refrigeration, and in some cases adsorption, are found in large bulk plants. The systems require the use of listed dispensing devices. Restrictions relative to modifying the dispensing devices and the prevention of vapor discharge when the dispenser is not in use are the same for both the vapor processing system and the vapor recovery system. Operators are not permitted to modify listed vapor recovery and/or processing systems.

4-5.1 Vapor processing system components consisting of hose nozzle valves, blowers or vacuum pumps, flame arresters or systems for prevention of flame propagation, controls, and vapor processing equipment shall be individually listed for use in a specified manner.

4-5.2 Dispensing devices used with a vapor processing system shall be listed. Existing listed or labeled dispensing devices may be modified for use with vapor processing systems provided they are "Listed by Report" as specified in 4-2.2.

4-5.3 Means shall be provided in the vapor return path from each dispensing outlet to prevent the discharge of vapors when the hose nozzle valve is in its normal nondispensing position.

4-5.4 Vapor processing systems employing blower-assist shall not be used unless the system is designed to prevent flame propagation through system piping, processing equipment, and tanks.

> Systems employing blower-assist are to be designed to prevent flame propagation through the piping, processing equipment, and tanks. This additional design requirement is necessary because the introduction of air by the blower can dilute the vapors in the piping, bringing them into the flammable range.

4-5.5 If a component is likely to contain a flammable vapor-air mixture under operating conditions, and can fail in a manner to ignite the mixture, it shall be designed to withstand an internal explosion without failure to the outside.

> For example, a fan used in a blower-assist operation may overheat because of a worn bearing or may cause sparks by the fan blades rubbing against the housing. Since either of these situations could provide a source of ignition, the fan housing must be designed to withstand a possible explosion should there also be an abnormal air leak into the system. When a vapor processing system component is located in an area where the public can be exposed to the hazards of exploding fragments, such as on a pump island, this requirement assumes added significance.

4-5.6 Vapor processing equipment shall be located outside of buildings at least 10 ft (3 m) from adjacent property lines that can be built upon, except as provided for in 4-5.7. Vapor processing equipment shall be located a minimum of 20 ft (6 m) from dispensing devices. Processing equipment shall be protected against physical damage by the provision of guardrails, curbs, or fencing.

4-5.7 Where the required distance to adjacent property lines that can be built upon as specified in 4-5.6 cannot be obtained, means shall be provided to protect vapor processing equipment against fire exposure. Such means may include protective enclosures which extend at least 18 in. (45.7 cm) above the equipment, constructed of fire resistant or noncombustible materials, installation in below-grade spaces, or protection with an approved water spray system. If protective enclosures or below-grade spaces are used, positive means shall be provided to ventilate the volume within the enclosure to prevent pocketing of flammable vapors. In no case shall vapor processing equipment so protected be located within 5 ft (1.5 m) of adjacent property lines that can be built upon.

4-5.8 Electrical equipment shall be in accordance with Table 6.

4-5.9 Vents on vapor processing systems shall be not less than 12 ft (3.6 m) above adjacent ground level, with outlets so directed and located that flammable vapors will not accumulate or travel to an unsafe location or enter buildings.

4-5.10 Combustion or open flame-type devices shall not be installed in a classified area. (*See Table 6.*)

> On the other hand, where an open flame device is an inherent part of a process that cannot be safeguarded from vapor access, it is obviously unnecessary to place restrictions on the type of electrical equipment to be used in this area.

5 Service Stations Located Inside Buildings

5-1 General.

5-1.1 A service station is permitted inside a building subject to approval of the authority having jurisdiction.

5-1.2 The service station shall be separated from other portions of the building by wall, partition, floor, or floor-ceiling assemblies having a fire resistance rating of not less than 2 hr.

5-1.3 Interior finish of service stations shall be constructed of noncombustible or approved limited-combustible materials.

See NFPA 220, *Standard on Types of Building Construction*, for definitions of these terms.

5-1.4 Door and window openings in interior walls shall be provided with listed 1½-hr (B) fire doors. Doors shall be self-closing, or may remain open during normal operations if they are designed to close automatically in a fire emergency by provision of listed closure devices. Fire doors shall be installed in accordance with NFPA 80, *Standard for Fire Doors and Windows*.

5-1.5 Fire doors shall be kept unobstructed at all times. Appropriate signs and markings shall be used.

5-1.6 Openings in interior partitions and walls for ducts shall be protected by listed fire dampers. Openings in floor or floor-ceiling assemblies for ducts shall be protected with enclosed shafts. Enclosure of shafts shall be with wall or partition assemblies having a fire-resistance rating of not less than 2 hr. Openings in enclosed shafts, for ducts, shall be protected with listed fire dampers.

5-2 Dispensing Area.

5-2.1 The dispensing area shall be located at street level, with no dispenser located more than 50 ft (15 m) from the vehicle exit to, or entrance from, the outside of the building.

5-2.2 Dispensing shall be limited to the area required to serve not more than four vehicles at one time.

5-3 Ventilation.

5-3.1 Forced air heating, air conditioning, and ventilating systems serving the service station area shall not be interconnected with any such systems serving other parts of the building. Such systems shall be installed in accordance with the provisions of NFPA 90A, *Standard for the Installation of Air Conditioning and Ventilating Systems.*

5-3.2 A mechanical exhaust system shall be provided to serve only the dispensing area. This system shall be interlocked with the dispensing system such that air flow is established before any dispensing device can operate. Failure of air flow shall automatically shut down the dispensing system.

5-3.3 The exhaust system shall be designed to provide air movement across all portions of the dispensing area floor, and to prevent the flow of flammable vapors beyond the dispensing area. Exhaust inlet ducts shall not be less than 3 in. (7.6 cm) nor more than 12 in. (0.30 m) above the floor. Exhaust ducts shall not be located in floors, or penetrate the floor of the dispensing area, and shall discharge to a safe location outside the building.

5-3.4 The exhaust system shall provide ventilation at a rate of not less than 1 cu ft per minute per sq ft (1 m^3 per 3 m^2) of dispensing area.

5-3.5 The exhaust system shall be installed in accordance with the provisions of NFPA 91, *Standard for the Installation of Blower and Exhaust Systems for Dust, Stock and Vapor Removal or Conveying.*

5-3.6 The provisions of 5-3.2, 5-3.3, 5-3.4 and 5-3.5 do not apply to a service station located inside a building if 2 or more sides of the dispensing area are open to the building exterior such that natural ventilation can normally be expected to dissipate flammable vapors.

5-4 Piping.

5-4.1 Piping systems shall comply with the provisions of NFPA 30, *Flammable and Combustible Liquids Code,* Chapter 3.

5-4.2 All fuel and flammable vapor piping inside buildings but outside the service station area shall be enclosed within a horizontal chase or a vertical shaft used only for this piping. Vertical shafts and horizontal chases shall be constructed of materials having a fire-resistance rating of not less than 2 hr.

5-5 Drainage Systems.

5-5.1 Floors shall be liquidtight. Emergency drainage systems shall be provided to direct flammable or combustible liquid leakage and fire protection water to a safe location. This may require curbs, scuppers, or special drainage systems.

5-5.2 Emergency drainage systems, if connected to public sewers or discharged into public waterways, shall be equipped with traps or separators.

6 Electrical Equipment

6-1 Chapter 6 shall apply to areas where Class I liquids are stored, handled or dispensed. For areas where Class II or Class III liquids are stored, handled or dispensed, the electrical equipment may be installed in accordance with the provisions of NFPA 70, *National Electrical Code*®, for nonclassified locations.

6-2 All electrical equipment and wiring shall be of a type specified by and shall be installed in accordance with NFPA 70, *National Electrical Code*. All electrical equipment integral with the dispensing hose or nozzle shall be suitable for use in Division 1 locations.

6-3 Table 6 shall be used to delineate and classify areas for the purpose of installation of electrical equipment under normal circumstances. A classified area shall not extend beyond an unpierced wall, roof, or other solid partition. The designation of classes and divisions is defined in Chapter 5, Article 500, of NFPA 70, *National Electrical Code*.

Note that Table 6 limits the types of permanently installed electrical wiring and equipment that may be placed in the specified areas. It is not applicable to the electrical system of an automobile, nor is it applicable or intended to restrict the presence of other nonelectric equipment, such as the hot surfaces on an automobile.

6-4 The area classifications listed in Table 6 shall be based on the premise that the installation meets the applicable requirements of this *Code* in all respects. Should this not be the case, the authority having jurisdiction shall have the authority to determine the extent of the classified area.

Note that no electrical area classification is shown for the interior of the dispensing device. Area classification within the dispensing device enclosure is covered by ANSI/UL 87, *Power Operated Dispensing Devices for Petroleum Products*.

Reference Cited in Commentary

ANSI/UL87, *Power Operated Dispensing Devices for Petroleum Products*, Underwriters Laboratories Inc., Northbrook, IL, 1981.

Table 6 Electrical Equipment Classified Areas—Service Stations

Location	NEC Class I, Group D Division	Extent of Classified Area
Underground Tank Fill Opening	1	Any pit, box or space below grade level, any part of which is within the Division 1 or 2 classified area.
	2	Up to 18 in. above grade level within a horizontal radius of 10 ft from a loose fill connection and within a horizontal radius of 5 ft from a tight fill connection.
Vent—Discharging Upward	1	Within 3 ft of open end of vent, extending in all directions.
	2	Area between 3 ft and 5 ft of open end of vent, extending in all directions.
Dispensing Units (except overhead type)* Pits	1	Any pit, box or space below grade level, any part of which is within the Division 1 or 2 classified area.
Dispenser	1	The area within a dispenser enclosure up to 4 ft vertically above the base except that area defined as Division 2. Any area within a nozzle boot.
	2	Areas within a dispenser enclosure above the Division 1 area. Areas within a dispenser enclosure isolated from Division 1 by a solid partition or a solid nozzle boot but not completely surrounded by Division 1 area. Within 18 in. horizontally in all directions extending to grade from the Division 1 area within the dispenser enclosure. Within 18 in. horizontally in all directions extending to grade from the opening of a nozzle boot not isolated by a vapor-tight partition, except that the classified area need not be extended around a 90° or greater corner.

*Ceiling mounted hose reel.

For SI Units: 1 in. = 2.5 cm; 1 ft = 0.30 m.

Table 6 Electrical Equipment Classified Areas—Service Stations, (continued)

Location	NEC Class I, Group D Division	Extent of Classified Area
Outdoor	2	Up to 18 in. above grade level within 20 ft horizontally of any edge of enclosure.
Indoor		
with Mechanical Ventilation	2	Up to 18 in. above grade or floor level within 20 ft horizontally of any edge of enclosure.
with Gravity Ventilation	2	Up to 18 in. above grade or floor level within 25 ft horizontally of any edge of enclosure.
Dispensing Units, Overhead Type*	1	Within the dispenser enclosure and 18 in. in all directions from the enclosure where not suitably cut off by ceiling or wall. All electrical equipment integral with the dispensing hose or nozzle.
	2	An area extending 2 ft horizontally in all directions beyond the Division 1 area and extending to grade below this classified area.
	2	Up to 18 in. above grade level within 20 ft horizontally measured from a point vertically below the edge or any dispenser enclosure.
Remote Pump—Outdoor	1	Any pit, box or space below grade level if any part is within a horizontal distance of 10 ft from any edge of pump.
	2	Within 3 ft of any edge of pump, extending in all directions. Also up to 18 in. above grade level within 10 ft horizontally from any edge of pump.
Remote Pump—Indoor	1	Entire area within any pit.
	2	Within 5 ft of any edge of pump, extending in all directions. Also up to 3 ft above floor or grade level within 25 ft horizontally from any edge of pump.

*Ceiling mounted hose reel.
For SI Units: 1 in. = 2.5 cm; 1 ft = 0.30 m.

Table 6 Electrical Equipment Classified Areas—Service Stations, (continued)

Location	NEC Class I, Group D Division	Extend of Classified Area
Lubrication or Service Room —with Dispensing	1	Any pit within any unventilated area.
	2	Any pit with ventilation.
	2	Area up to 18 in. above floor or grade level and 3 ft horizontally from a lubrication pit.
Dispenser for Class I Liquids	2	Within 3 ft of any fill or dispensing point, extending in all directions.
Lubrication or Service Room —without Dispensing	2	Entire area within pit used for lubrication or similar services where Class I liquids may be released.
	2	Area up to 18 in. above any such pit, and extending a distance of 3 ft horizontally from any edge of the pit.
Special Enclosure Inside Building Per 2-2	1	Entire enclosure.
Sales, Storage and Rest Rooms	Nonclassified	If there is any opening to these rooms within the extent of a Division 1 area, the entire room shall be classified as Division 1.
Vapor Processing Systems Pits	1	Any pit, box or space below grade level, any part of which is within a Division 1 or 2 classified area or which houses any equipment used to transport or process vapors.
Vapor Processing Equipment Located within Protective Enclosures (see 4-5.7)	2	Within any protective enclosure housing vapor processing equipment.
Vapor Processing Equipment Not within Protective Enclosures (excluding piping and combustion devices)	2	The space within 18 in. in all directions of equipment containing flammable vapor or liquid extending to grade level. Up to 18 in. above grade level within 10 ft horizontally of the vapor processing equipment.
Equipment Enclosures	1	Any area within the enclosure where vapor or liquid is present under normal operating conditions.
	2	The entire area within the enclosure other than Division 1.
Vacuum-Assist Blowers	2	The space within 18 in. in all directions extending to grade level. Up to 18 in. above grade level within 10 ft horizontally.

For SI Units: 1 in. = 2.5 cm; 1 ft = 0.30 m.

NFPA 30A—ELECTRICAL EQUIPMENT 309

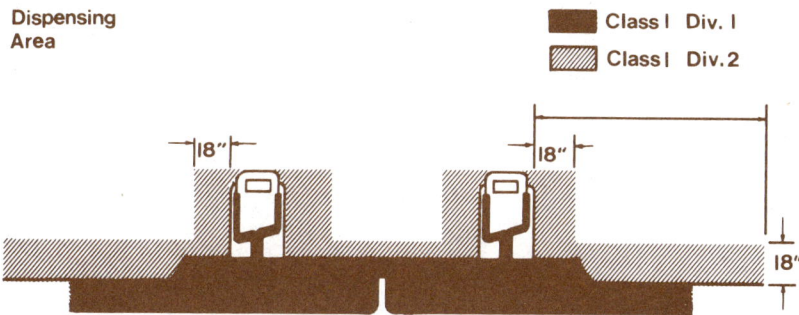

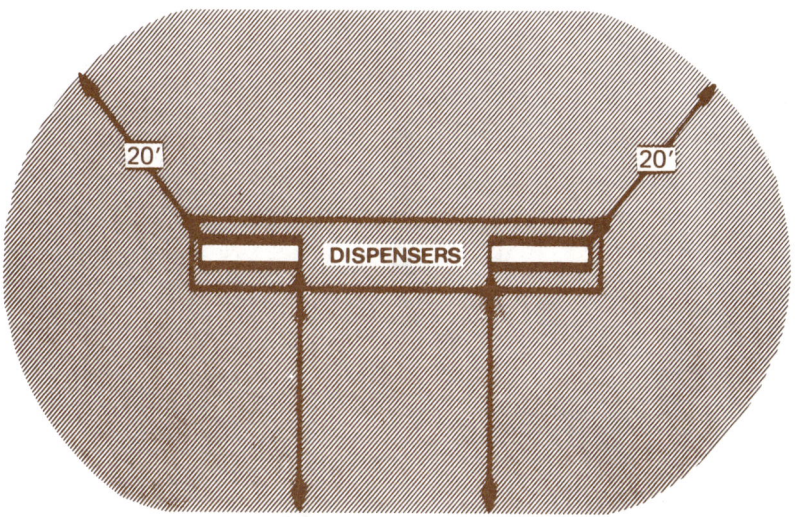

Figure 6-1 Classified areas adjacent to dispensing devices as detailed in Table 6.

7 Heating Equipment

7-1 Heating equipment shall be installed as provided in 7-2 through 7-6.

7-2 Heating equipment may be installed in the conventional manner except as provided in 7-3, 7-4, 7-5, or 7-6.

Heating equipment can be a source of ignition for flammable vapors in service stations if installed so that ignitible vapor-air mixtures can reach it under normal use conditions.

7-3 Heating equipment may be installed in a special room separated from an area classified as Division 1 or Division 2 in Table 6 by walls having a fire-resistance rating of at least 1 hr and without any openings in the walls within 8 ft (2.4 m) of the floor into an area classified as Division 1 or Division 2 in Table 6. This room shall not be used for combustible storage, and all air for combustion purposes shall come from outside the building.

The opening at the top of the wall allows heated air to enter the service area, but the 8-ft (2.4-m) wall height is enough to keep flammable vapors from passing into the special room. Air for combustion purposes is that required to supply the combustion chamber of the heating unit. This air inlet must be carefully located to avoid pulling flammable liquid vapors into the heating unit.

7-4 Heating equipment using gas or oil fuel may be installed in the lubrication or service room where there is no dispensing or transferring of Class I liquids, including the open draining of automotive gasoline tanks, provided the bottom of the combustion chamber is at least 18 in. (46 cm) above the floor and the heating equipment is protected from physical damage.

Generally, flammable vapors would not be present in a service station building. However, an 18-in. (46-cm) height requirement is stipulated as protection against inadvertent ignition of any flammable vapors that may be at floor level due to leakage or spillage during automobile repair or other activities within the building. The word "transferring" was clarified in the 1984 edition of the *Code* by the inclusion of the phrase "including the open draining of automotive gasoline tanks." Under no circumstances should service station or garage attendants use Class I flammable liquids as cleaning agents for either tools or floors. Using gasoline to remove grease deposits from garage floors has resulted in numerous flash fires and several explosions.

Note that gas- or oil-fired heating units are specified. Coal- or wood-burning devices are not allowed because of the problem of live ashes or embers. Even if the ash pit is 18 in. (46 cm) above the floor, live particles might constitute a source of ignition while they are being removed from the heating unit.

7-5 Heating equipment using gas or oil fuel listed for use in garages may be installed in the lubrication or service room where Class I liquids are dispensed or transferred, provided the equipment is installed at least 8 ft (2.4 m) above the floor.

Spilled Class I liquid releases vapor at floor level. The vapor will not rapidly diffuse upward, and the 8-ft (2.4-m) height limit guards against the chance that the heater will become an ignition source. See commentary on Section 7-4 regarding the intent or meaning of the word "transferred."

7-6 Electrical heating equipment shall conform to Chapter 6.

8 Operational Requirements

8-1 Fuel Delivery Nozzles.

8-1.1 A listed automatic-closing type hose nozzle valve, with or without latch-open device, shall be provided on island-type dispensers used for the dispensing of Class I liquids.

The words "with or without latch-open device" were added to the 1981 edition of NFPA 30, *Flammable and Combustible Liquids Code.* Prior to this change, latch-open devices were not permitted on nozzles unless the dispensing was performed by the service station attendant. At self-service stations, where the public had access to nozzles, latch-open devices were prohibited.

There were several reasons for this change. Enforcing authorities advised that many citizens chocked open the nozzles with whatever device was at hand, including the gas cap from the automobile. Some enterprising individuals even marketed a combination key holder and latch-open device for one's personal use. Enforcement of the ban on latch-open devices proved extremely difficult. In locations where latch-open devices were allowed, no unusual fire incidents were reported to NFPA. Finally, several consumers complained that the prohibition of the latch-open device inconvenienced the consumer, questioned his intelligence, and gave more credit for common sense and concern for safety to the service station attendant than to the public at large.

For all these reasons, the change was made. By using the wording "with or without," latch-open devices become optional and the final decision to allow them rests with the local authority having jurisdiction. The Technical Committee decided that there was insufficient justification for continuing the outright ban on the use of the latch-open device.

8-1.2 If a hose nozzle valve is provided with a latch-open device other than recommended by the valve manufacturer, the latch-open device shall be an integral part of the valve assembly, and such valve latch-open device combination shall conform to the applicable requirements of Section 19 of UL 842-1980, *Standard for Valves for Flammable Fluids.*

This requirement is intended to clarify the intent of the *Code*; namely, that makeshift or portable devices are not to be used to hold open the hose nozzle valve. Only installed devices are to be employed, and the installation must meet the applicable UL requirements.

8-1.2.1 At any installation where the normal flow of product may be stopped other than by the hose nozzle valve, such as at pre-pay stations, the system shall include listed equipment with a feature that causes or requires the closing of the hose nozzle valve before product flow can be resumed or before the hose nozzle valve can be replaced in its normal position in the dispenser; or the hose nozzle valve shall not be equipped with a latch-open device.

In the Committee's opinion, this wording is required to eliminate the possibility of product spillage that may occur at prepay-type service station facilities. This wording allows for different approaches to be used in remedying the problem, including simply removing the latch-open device.

8-1.3 Overhead-type dispensing devices shall be provided with a listed automatic-closing type hose nozzle valve without a latch-open device.

Exception: A listed automatic-closing type hose nozzle valve with latch-open device may be used if the design of the system is such that the hose nozzle valve will close automatically in the event the valve is released from a fill opening or upon impact with a driveway.

8-1.4 Dispensing nozzles used at marine service stations shall be of the automatic-closing type without a latch-open device.

The rationale for prohibiting latch-open devices at marine service stations is that overfilling a boat's fuel tank results in quite a serious condition. Gasoline spilled into the bilge or interior of a boat can be much more hazardous than a similar spill on the ground at a service station. Aboard a boat, the vapors will be more confined, and dispersal will take a longer period of time. Control of sources of ignition may also be more difficult. The absence of a latch-open device requires greater attention to the task at hand on the part of the individual performing the dispensing operation.

8-1.5 A hose nozzle valve used for dispensing Class I liquids into a container shall be manually held open during the dispensing operation.

8-2 Dispensing into Portable Containers. No delivery of any Class I or Class II liquid shall be made into portable containers unless the container is constructed of metal or is approved by the authority having jurisdiction, has a tight closure and is fitted with a spout or so designed that the contents can be poured without spilling. (*See NFPA 30, Flammable and Combustible Liquids Code, Section 4-2.1, for further information.*)

> Portable containers of flammable and combustible liquids may be subject to a great deal of physical abuse simply because they are portable. They also may be used or carried near a variety of ignition sources. Therefore, it is important that the container be constructed to withstand impact. The possibility of leakage and escaping vapors must also be controlled. Containers should also be designed to minimize spillage when the contents are being transferred.

8-2.1 No sale or purchase of any Class I, Class II, or Class III liquids shall be made in containers unless such containers are clearly marked with the name of the product contained therein.

> Because the entire contents of a portable container may not be used at the time of purchase, it is important that the container be clearly marked with the name of the contents to prevent a serious fire at a later date. The station operator is permitted to refuse to dispense fuel into an unsuitable container.

8-2.2 Portable containers shall not be filled while located inside the trunk or passenger compartment of a vehicle.

> This requirement is intended to eliminate a practice that was called to the Committee's attention as being commonplace. The practice of filling containers that are in the trunk or passenger compartment is, in the Committee's opinion, very dangerous due to the generation of fuel vapors that are allowed to accumulate in a confined space.

8-3 Attendance or Supervision of Dispensing.

> The provisions of 8-3.3, 8-3.4, and 8-3.5 are more easily understood if they are treated as exceptions to the basic provisions on the storage of liquids in service stations.

8-3.1 Each service station shall have an attendant or supervisor on duty whenever the station is open for business, who shall dispense liquids into fuel tanks or into containers, except as covered in Sections 8-4 and 8-5.

> Prior to this edition of the *Code*, this requirement read "Each service station *open to the public* shall have an attendant or supervisor on duty whenever the station is open for business." With the

growing use of card- and key-operated dispensing devices, the phrase "open to the public" has become less easily defined. In its broadest sense, a service station that is open to the public has an unlimited user or customer base. Anyone can make use of the facility, regardless of method of payment. By default, this defines any service station not open to the public as, essentially, a private fleet operation. With the advent of card- and key-operated dispensing devices at otherwise public service stations, "open to the public" has become nebulous because only a select group of customers can make use of these facilities.

Rather than continue to use an ambiguous definition, the Committee broadened the requirement to include all service stations. Exceptions to the general rule are covered in subsequent paragraphs.

8-3.2 Listed "self-service" dispensing devices are permitted at service stations provided that all dispensing of Class I liquids by a person other than the service station attendant is under the supervision and control of a qualified attendant.

Exception: See Section 8-5.

8-3.3 The provisions of 2-1.1 shall not prohibit the temporary use of movable tanks in conjunction with the dispensing of flammable or combustible liquids into the fuel tanks of motor vehicles or other motorized equipment on premises not normally accessible to the public. Such installations shall only be made with the approval of the enforcing authority. The approval shall include a definite time limit.

8-3.4 The provisions of 2-1.1 shall not prohibit the dispensing of Class I and Class II liquids in the open from a tank vehicle to a motor vehicle located at commercial, industrial, governmental, or manufacturing establishments, and intended for fueling vehicles used in connection with their businesses. Such dispensing may be permitted provided:

(a) An inspection of the premises and operations has been made and approval granted by the authority having jurisdiction.

(b) The tank vehicle complies with the requirements covered in NFPA 385, *Standard for Tank Vehicles for Flammable and Combustible Liquids.*

(c) The dispensing hose does not exceed 50 ft (15 m) in length.

(d) The dispensing nozzle is a listed automatic-closing type without a latch-open device.

(e) Nighttime deliveries shall only be made in adequately lighted areas.

(f) The tank vehicle flasher lights shall be in operation while dispensing.

(g) Fuel expansion space shall be left in each fuel tank to prevent overflow in the event of temperature increase.

Originally, this section was intended to allow the refueling of construction vehicles and equipment at isolated construction sites. Over the years, however, many new types of motorized construction equipment have been developed, and the refueling of these from a tank vehicle is common at any construction site—urban, suburban, or rural. Also, this section has been interpreted as allowing the refueling of motor vehicles from a tank vehicle in a parking lot, access to which is limited to employees of the user or owner of the lot.

Because of the previously discussed ambiguity involving the phrase "open to the public," the Committee added the words "located at commercial, industrial, governmental, or manufacturing establishments" to define the facilities covered by this section. The phrase "intended for fueling vehicles used in connection with their business" further clarifies the intent of this section to apply *only* to vehicles directly related to the function of the facility.

8-3.5 The provisions of 2-1.1 shall not prohibit the dispensing of Class I and Class II liquids in the open from a fuel dispensing system supplied by an aboveground tank, not to exceed 6000 gal (22 710 L), located at commercial, industrial, governmental or manufacturing establishments, and intended for fueling vehicles used in connection with their business. Such dispensing may be permitted provided:

(a) An inspection of the premises and operations has been made and approval granted by the authority having jurisdiction.

(b) The tank is safeguarded against collision, spillage, and overfill, to the satisfaction of the authority having jurisdiction.

(c) The tank system is listed or approved for such aboveground use.

(d) The tank complies with requirements for emergency relief venting, and the tank and dispensing system meet the electrical classification requirements of the *Code*.

(e) The tank storage shall comply with NFPA 30, *Flammable and Combustible Liquids Code*, Chapter 2.

This section, added to the 1984 edition of NFPA 30A, *Automotive and Marine Service Station Code*, introduces an unusual concept to service station dispensing. As a general rule, all tanks at service stations are required to be underground. In order to make allowances for new technology and to respond to a demonstrated need, the Technical Committee accepted and modified a public proposal to address an aboveground dispensing system that could offer a degree of safety equivalent to that of an underground tank installation. The wording will, in the Committee's opinion, provide adequate safeguards for such installations in cases where the authority having jurisdiction is willing to permit them.

8-4 Attended Self-Service Stations.

8-4.1 Self-service station shall mean that portion of property where liquids used as motor fuels are stored and subsequently dispensed from fixed approved dispensing equipment into the fuel tanks of motor vehicles by persons other than the service station attendant, and may include facilities available for sale of other retail products.

Over the past 25 years, the concept of self-service stations has steadily found increased acceptance by both the public and the fire service. For many years, the *Code* has permitted self-service dispensing without an attendant supervising the dispensing at "private" or "not open-to-the-public" stations, but *not* at stations "open to the public," where an attendant has been required. This is still the case for "attended self-service stations." With this edition of NFPA 30A, *Automotive and Marine Service Station Code*, the above requirements are qualified as applying to attended self-service stations, because of the recognition of unattended self-service operations in Section 8-5.

Based on the incidence data accumulated over the past several years, it is not possible to determine the relative safety between full-service stations and self-service stations. It cannot be stated that one is more hazardous than the other, because the nature of the fire problem is very much the same for both. As an example, a dispensing device can be knocked over by a vehicle just as easily in either facility.

8-4.2 Listed dispensing devices such as, but not limited to, coin-operated, card-operated, and remote controlled types are permitted at self-service stations.

8-4.3 All attended self-service stations shall have at least one attendant on duty while the station is open for business. The attendant's primary function shall be to supervise, observe, and control the dispensing of Class I liquids while said liquids are actually being dispensed.

8-4.4 It shall be the responsibility of the attendant to (1) prevent the dispensing of Class I liquids into portable containers not in compliance with Section 8-2; (2) prevent the use of hose nozzle valve latch-open devices that do not comply with 8-1.2; (3) control sources of ignition; and (4) immediately activate emergency controls and handle accidental spills and fire extinguishers if needed. The attendant or supervisor on duty shall be mentally and physically capable of performing the functions and assuming the responsibility prescribed in this section.

As with regulations governing other occupancies, NFPA 30A, *Automotive and Marine Service Station Code*, deals with the problems of sources of ignition and fire control. By eliminating or controlling the major sources of ignition, such as smoking or open flames in the areas used for fueling, receiving, or dispensing Class I liquids, and shutting off all motors being fueled, hazards are held to an acceptable level. The requirement regarding latch-open devices is intended to call attention to the fact that only installed devices that comply with this *Code* are to be used, and that portable do-it-yourself types of latch-open devices are both illegal and dangerous.

8-4.5 Emergency controls specified in 4-1.2 shall be installed at a location acceptable to the authority having jurisdiction, but controls shall not be more than 100 ft (30 m) from dispensers.

8-4.6 Operating instructions shall be conspicuously posted in the dispensing area.

8-4.7 The dispensing area shall at all times be in clear view of the attendant, and the placing or allowing of any obstacle to come between the dispensing area and the attendant control area shall be prohibited. The attendant shall at all times be able to communicate with persons in the dispensing area.

8-5 Unattended Self-Service Stations.

8-5.1 Unattended self-service shall be permitted, subject to the approval of the authority having jurisdiction.

This entire section on unattended self-service stations is new to the 1987 edition of the *Code*. As explained earlier, changes in the marketing of motor fuels have led to confusion about what is meant by "open to the public" versus "not open to the public." Enforcing authorities have had difficulty determining whether card- or key-operated dispensing devices constitute "public" or "private" facilities. In some cases, legal disputes have resulted.

Once the Committee decided to recognize and address unattended self-service stations, the ambiguity reached a critical stage. The Committee decided that, by eliminating the phrases "open to the public," "not open to the public," and "private," they could clarify the intended requirements for all types of service station operations. Thus, the addition of this new section on unattended self-service stations has resulted in small but important changes in the preceding two sections.

Section 8-5 clearly allows the local authority to permit the installation of unattended self-service stations in his/her jurisdiction if he/she deems them acceptable. The various requirements that follow are intended to provide a reasonable degree of safety in the absence of an attendant.

8-5.2 Listed dispensing devices shall be used. Coin- and currency-type devices shall only be permitted with the approval of the authority having jurisdiction.

This requirement assumes that the dispensing device is card- or key-operated. However, currency-operated devices may be used where the authority having jurisdiction approves their use.

8-5.3 Emergency controls specified in 4-1.2 shall be installed at a location acceptable to the authority having jurisdiction, but the controls shall be more than 20 ft (7 m) but less than 100 feet (30 m) from the dispensers. Additional emergency controls shall be installed on each group of dispensers or the outdoor equipment used to control the dispensers. Emergency controls shall shut off power to all dispensing devices at the station. Controls shall be manually reset only in a manner approved by the authority having jurisdiction.

This requirement places special significance on the location of emergency power disconnects. They must be close enough to the dispensing island to be quickly accessible to a patron, but not so close as to be directly involved in a fire at the island. The intent of the requirement for manual reset is to ensure that operation of the station is not resumed until the person responsible for the station has rectified whatever emergency condition may exist.

8-5.4 Operating instructions shall be conspicuously posted in the dispensing area, and shall include location of emergency controls, and a requirement that the user must stay outside of his/her vehicle, in view of the fueling nozzle during dispensing.

8-5.5 In addition to those warning signs specified in 8-9.1, emergency instructions shall be conspicuously posted in the dispenser area incorporating the following or equivalent wording:

Emergency Instructions
   In case of fire or spill:
 1. Use emergency stop button.
 2. Report accident by calling (specify local fire number) on the phone. Report location.

8-5.6 A listed, automatic-closing type hose nozzle valve with latch-open device shall be provided. The system shall include listed equipment with a feature that causes or requires the closing of the hose nozzle valve before the product flow can be resumed or before the hose nozzle valve can be replaced in its normal position in the dispenser.

> A nozzle valve with latch-open device is required to prevent the illegal use of a foreign object to hold the nozzle valve open.

8-5.7 A telephone or other approved, clearly identified means to notify the fire department shall be provided on the site in a location approved by the authority having jurisdiction.

8-5.8 Additional fire protection shall be provided where required by the authority having jurisdiction. Additional fire protection considerations may include such items as fixed suppression systems, automatic fire detection, manual fire alarm stations, transmission of alarms to off-site locations, and limiting gallonage delivered per transaction.

> This section allows the local authority having jurisdiction to require other fire protection systems or features as a condition of approval of an unattended self-service station. The additional provisions, if any, may vary greatly, depending on the specific installation.

8-6 Drainage and Waste Disposal.

8-6.1 Provision shall be made in the area where Class I liquids are dispensed to prevent spilled liquids from flowing into the interior of service station buildings. Such provision may be made by grading driveways, raising door sills, or other equally effective means.

8-6.2 Crankcase drainings and liquids shall not be dumped into sewers, streams or adjoining property, but shall be stored in tanks or drums outside any building until removed from the premises.

> Small tanks or drums are often used for the storage of crankcase drainings and similar liquids. One must be aware of the possibility that these waste oils may be contaminated with lower flash point flammable liquids. Thus, waste oils are not to be overlooked when applying regulations. For environmental and safety reasons, crankcase drainings must not be dumped into sewers.

8-7 Sources of Ignition.

8-7.1 In addition to the previous restrictions of this chapter, the following shall apply: There shall be no smoking or open flames in the areas used for fueling, servicing fuel systems for internal combustion engines, or receiving or dispensing of Class I liquids. Conspicuous and legible signs prohibiting smoking shall be posted within sight of the customer being served. The motors of all equipment being fueled shall be shut off during the fueling operation except for emergency generators, pumps, etc., where continuing operation is essential.

8-8 Fire Control.

8-8.1 Each service station shall be provided with at least one listed fire extinguisher having a minimum classification of 20B:C located so that an extinguisher will be within 100 ft (30 m) of each pump, dispenser, underground fill pipe opening, and lubrication or service room.

8-9 Signs.

8-9.1 Warning signs shall be conspicuously posted in the dispensing area incorporating the following or equivalent wording: (a) WARNING—It is unlawful and dangerous to dispense gasoline into unapproved containers; (b) No Smoking; and (c) Stop Motor.

This provision formerly applied to self-service stations only. The Technical Committee has recognized that it is applicable to all service stations.

9 Referenced Publications

9-1 The following documents or portions thereof are referenced within this document and shall be considered part of the requirements of this document. The edition indicated for each reference shall be the current edition as of the date of the NFPA issuance of this document. These references shall be listed separately to facilitate updating to the latest edition by the user.

9-1.1 NFPA Publications. National Fire Protection Association, Batterymarch Park, Quincy, MA 02269.

NFPA 30-1987, *Flammable and Combustible Liquids Code*
NFPA 70-1987, *National Electrical Code*
NFPA 80-1986, *Standard for Fire Doors and Windows*
NFPA 90A-1985, *Standard for the Installation of Air Conditioning and Ventilating Systems*
NFPA 91-1983, *Standard for the Installation of Blower and Exhaust Systems for Dust, Stock and Vapor Removal or Conveying*
NFPA 302-1984, *Standard on Fire Protection for Pleasure and Commercial Motor Craft*
NFPA 303-1986, *Fire Protection Standard for Marinas and Boatyards*
NFPA 385-1985, *Standard for Tank Vehicles for Flammable and Combustible Liquids*.

9-1.2 Other Publications.

API Publication 1621, *Recommended Practice for Bulk Liquid Stock Control at Retail Outlets*, American Petroleum Institute, 1220 L Street, NW, Washington, DC 20005.

UL 842-1980, *Standard for Valves for Flammable Fluids*, Underwriters Laboratories Incorporated, 333 Pfingsten Road, Northbrook, IL 60062.

Appendix A

The material contained in Appendix A is included in the text within this *Handbook* and therefore is not repeated here.

NFPA 30A — Index

© 1987 National Fire Protection Association, All Rights Reserved.

The copyright in this index is separate and distinct from the copyright in the document which it indexes. The licensing provisions set forth for the document are not applicable to this index. This index may not be reproduced in whole or in part by any means without the express written permission of the National Fire Protection Association, Inc.

-A-

Application of standard 1-1
Attendants, service station 8-3
   Self-service stations 8-4
Automotive service stations
   Definition 1-2
   Dispensing devices, location of 4-1.1
   Tanks 2-2.3

-B-

Basements
   Definition 1-2
Bulk plant .... see Plants, bulk

-C-

Class I liquids
   Definition 1-2
   Drainage 8-6
   Dispensing 4-3.1, 8-3
   Electrical equipment in area of ..... Chap. 6
   Inside buildings 2-1.4, 2-3.1, 2-3.2
   Inventory of 2-1.5
   Tanks at automatic service stations .. 2-2.3
Class II liquids
   Definition 1-2
   Dispensing 8-3.4, 8-3.5
   Electrical equipment in area of 6-1
   Storage 2-3.3
Class IIIA liquids
   Definition 1-2
   Electrical equipment in area of 6-1
   Storage 2-3.3, 2-3.4
Class IIIB liquids
   Definition 1-2
   Electrical equipment in area of 6-1
   Storage 2-3.4
Combustible liquids
   Definition 1-2
Containers
   Closed
      Definition 1-2
   Definition 1-2
   Portable, dispensing liquids into .. 4-2.8, 8-2

-D-

Dispensing area
   Drainage system 5-5

Service stations inside buildings 5-2
Supervision 8-3
Ventilation 5-3
Dispensing devices 4-2
   Fuel delivery nozzles 8-1
   Location 4-1
   Self-service 8-3.2
   Vapor processing system 4-5.2
   Vapor recovery 4-4.1
Drainage systems 8-6
   Service stations, inside buildings 5-5

-E-

Enclosures, special 2-2
Electrical equipment .... Chap. 6
   Classified areas .... Table 6

-F-

Fire control 8-8
Fire dampers
   Service stations, inside buildings 5-1.6
Fire doors
   Service stations, inside building .5-1.4, 5-1.5
Fire protection 8-5.8
Fittings .... Chap. 3
Flammable liquids
   Definition 1-2
Fuel dispensing system .... Chap. 4
   Emergency power cutoff 4-1.2
   Location 4-1
Fuel dispensing device 4-2,
              see Dispensing device

-H-

Heating equipment .... Chap. 7
Hose, length 4-2.6

-I-

Ignition, sources of 8-7
Inventory records 2-1.5

-L-

Liquids ...... see specific type such as Class I

-M-

Marine service stations
  Definition 1-2
  Dispensing devices, location 4-1.1
  Piping and valves .... Chap. 3
  Tanks 2-1.6

-N-

Nozzles, fuel delivery 8-1, 8-5.6

-P-

Piping .... Chap. 3
  Identification of 3-6, A-3-6
  Service stations, inside buildings 5-4
  Vent 2-1.2
Plants, bulk
  Aboveground tanks at 2-1.3
  Definition 1-2
Power cutoff, emergency 4-1.2
Pumping systems, remote 4-3
Pumps .... 4-3.2 thru 4-3.5

-S-

Safety can
  Definition 1-2
Scope of standard 1-1
Self-service stations 8-3.2, 8-4
  Attended 8-4
  Definition 8-4.1
  Emergency controls 8-4.5
  Supervision 8-3.2, 8-4.3, 8-4.4, 8-4.7
  Unattended 8-5
Service stations .... see also Automotive service stations; Marine service stations; Self-service stations
  Definition 1-2
  Inside buildings .... Chap. 5
    Definition 1-2
Signs, warning 8-5.5, 8-9

Storage .... Chap. 2
  General provisions 2-1
  Inside buildings 2-3
  Special enclosures 2-2
Supervision of dispensing ... see Attendants, Service station

-T-

Tanks .... Chap. 2
  Aboveground 2-1.3
  Elevation of, and gravity head 2-1.7
  Enclosures 2-2
  Inside buildings 2-2.1, 2-3
  Marine service stations 2-1.6
  Portable
    Definition 1-2
  Tank vehicles, dispensing from 8-3.4
  Terminal, bulk .... see also Plants, bulk
    Definition 1-2

-V-

Valves .... Chap. 3
  Emergency shutoff 4-3.6, 4-3.7
  Hose nozzle 4-4.2, 4-4.3, 8-1
Vapor processing equipment .... 4-5.6 thru 4-5.8
  Definition 1-2
Vapor processing system 4-5
  Definition 1-2
Vapor recovery system 4-4
  Definition 1-2
  Equipment location 4-5.6, 4-5.7, 4-5.9, 4-5.10
Ventilation
  Definition 1-2
  Service stations inside buildings 5-3

-W-

Warning signs .... see Signs, warning
Waste disposal 8-6